“This is a remarkable resource for understanding Pentecostali
ciological descriptions of the movement, Black serves up a p
all the right questions and giving clear answers documented from Scripture and from a dazzling survey of international Pentecostal primary texts. The resulting survey locates Pentecostalism securely within the vast common ground shared by all evangelical believers, while giving an appropriate amount of special attention to the unique ideas of Pentecostalism. I cannot imagine a better book to equip Christians for constructive conversations about these issues, under the guidance of the one Spirit (Eph 4:4).”

—Fred Sanders,
Professor, Torrey Honors College at Biola Univeristy, USA

“Jonathan Black’s *40 Questions About Pentecostalism* is an exceptionally good theological introduction to the modern Pentecostal movement. A faithful ‘insider,’ Black writes with knowledge, insight, and clarity. He emphasizes the evangelical nature of this dynamic, global movement and thus also the biblical foundations and core beliefs that provide for its cohesion amid considerable diversity. Black’s meticulous research, which draws upon sources from every continent, enables him to speak with conviction and represent mainstream classical Pentecostalism well. This book will benefit both interested observers in search of understanding and committed Pentecostals desiring to go deeper. I warmly recommend it to all.”

—Robert Menzies,
Director of the Asian Center for Pentecostal Theology,
Author of *Christ-Centered*, *Pentecost: This Story Is Our Story*,
and *Spirit and Power: Foundations of Pentecostal Experience*

“Once again Jonathan has given us a practical, entertaining, edifying, and inspiring book. His powers of synthesis and argumentation make this book a practical tool that I can’t wait to have at hand. This book is timely, and I am convinced that the Lord will use it to help Pentecostals of today and tomorrow rediscover their roots. Its presentation in the form of questions is wise and practical. I believe it will be a blessing to many. Thank you, Jonathan.”

—Eric Maréchal,
President of the Apostolic Church of Belgium

“Jonathan Black’s book not only answers key theological questions from a global perspective but also fleshes out important beliefs and practices which are central to, yet not usually associated with, Pentecostalism such as its worship of Word *and* Sacrament. This is a remarkable achievement. For anyone looking for an accurate and up-to-date understanding of this global phenomenon, I cannot recommend this book too highly.”

—Simon Chan,
Editor, *Asia Journal of Theology*,
Professor Emeritus of Systematic Theology, Trinity Theological College, Singapore

“Jonathan is (perhaps uniquely!) gifted in being able to successfully combine a depth and breadth of Pentecostal theological and historical research with an engaging, accessible writing style which means this book is eminently suitable for, and deserves, a wide readership. This latest work of his will certainly become a core text for our theology students and recommended reading for our ministers-in-training.”

—Jenny Kimble,
Dean of Undergraduate Studies, Regents Theological College, UK

"Pentecostalism bewilders scholars and laypersons alike. In this excellent volume, Jonathan Black provides an academically robust account of the movement's core characteristics with impressive clarity and conviction. Anyone curious about the historical and theological roots of Pentecostalism does not need to look any further!"

—Tommy H. Davidsson,
Associate Professor, The Norwegian School of Leadership and Theology

"'It seemed good to the Holy Spirit and to us.' These were the words proclaimed from the first council of the Church who found the mind of Christ and the grace to minister his life, as they came together as one body. So, too, in this excellent and comprehensive work, Jonathan powerfully illustrates how the Holy Spirit continues to transcend earthly boundaries of nationality, generation, and culture, to call the church up into one mind on fundamental truths of the faith. Asking questions remains foundational to our growth, not just in the knowledge of Christ, but in the humility and gentleness of he who always looked to his Father as the answer to every question. The answers Jonathan shares in this book ultimately point readers not to one part of the church, but to one Lord, one faith, one baptism—one God and Father of all, who is over all and through all and in all."

—Phelim Doherty,
Deputy National Leader of The Apostolic Church, UK

"Pentecostalism in all its diversity and global variety is an extraordinary phenomenon which has, in just over 100 years, encircled the globe and established itself in practically every country. This excellent introduction provides a careful and precise account of Pentecostal origins, variants, and beliefs. The text is anchored in primary sources and enhanced by reference to reputable scholars and academic sources. This is a first-class book from which to begin a study of one of the most vibrant religious movements in today's world."

—William K. Kay,
Fellow of the Institute for Pentecostal Theology, Regents Theological College, UK

"As a lifelong Pentecostal, I have read several books about the Pentecostal movement and its history. What is marvelous about Jonathan Black's book is that he has written a text that is profoundly theologically aware, extremely well informed by primary sources, and placed within the wider context of church history—whilst simultaneously being relatively short. This is a great book for anyone who would like to know more about the Pentecostal movement. Both in terms of its history and beliefs, it provides insight helpful to people within and outside of the Pentecostal churches. For anyone looking for a great introductory text to the Pentecostal movement, this is that text."

—Helgi Gudnason,
Pastor, Filadelfia Pentecostal Church, Iceland

"Jonathan has written an expansive book covering a vast scope of Pentecostal theology and understanding worldwide. But he has done so succinctly without losing depth or rigor. These 40 questions will give the reader an accurate overview of Pentecostal belief and practice in several areas, while also correcting errors from within and caricatures often directed toward Pentecostals. These 40 questions will benefit Pentecostal churches and small groups that wish to deepen their understanding and strengthen their biblical convictions."

—Jamie Lavery,
Pastor, Elim Church Crawley, UK

40 QUESTIONS ABOUT Pentecostalism

Jonathan Black

Benjamin L. Merkle, Series Editor

40 Questions About Pentecostalism

Published by Kregel Academic, an imprint of Kregel Publications, 2450 Oak Industrial Dr. NE, Grand Rapids, MI 49505-6020.

This book is a title in the 40 Questions Series edited by Benjamin L. Merkle.

For a complete list of titles in the 40 Questions series, go to 40questions.net.

ISBN 978-0-8254-4824-9

Library of Congress Cataloging-in-Publication Data

Name: Black, Jonathan, 1982– author.
Title: 40 questions about Pentecostalism / Jonathan Black.
Other titles: Forty questions about Pentecostalism
Description: First edition. | Grand Rapids, MI: Kregel Academic, [2024] | Series: 40 questions | Includes bibliographical references and index.
Identifiers: LCCN 2024001970 (print) | LCCN 2024001971 (ebook) | ISBN 9780825448249 (print) | ISBN 9780825471278 (epub) | ISBN 9780825471261
Subjects: LCSH: Pentecostal churches—History. | Pentecostalism—History.
Classification: LCC BX8762 .B54 2024 (print) | LCC BX8762 (ebook) | DDC 269/.4—dc23/eng/20240226
LC record available at https://lccn.loc.gov/2024001970
LC ebook record available at https://lccn.loc.gov/2024001971

Printed in the United States of America

24 25 26 27 28 / 5 4 3 2 1

To Richard Hasnip and Ollie Ward—
friends and colleagues,
gifts from the Lord both to me
and to our students

Contents

Part 4: Questions About the Gifts of the Holy Spirit

Part 5: Questions About the Church and the Second Coming

Abbreviations

AC	The Apostolic Church
ACC	Australian Christian Churches (formerly Assemblies of God, Australia)
ACVG	"The Vision Glorious: A Confession of the Faith of the Apostolic Church" (UK)
AdDDF	Déclaration de Foi des Assemblées de Dieu de France
AG	Assemblies of God (USA)
AoG	Assemblies of God (UK and elsewhere)
BFP	Bund Freikirchlicher Pfingstgemeinden (Germany)
Brazil DdF	Declaração de Fé das Assembleias de Deus no Brasil
CAC	Christ Apostolic Church
CoGiC	Church of God in Christ
CoP	Church of Pentecost
Elim SFT	Elim Pentecostal Church (UK) Statement of Foundational Truths
FDF	The Foursquare Declaration of Faith
IPHC	International Pentecostal Holiness Church
PAOC	Pentecostal Assemblies of Canada
PAOCSET	Pentecostal Assemblies of Canada Statement of Essential Truths
RCCG	Redeemed Christian Church of God
Romanian CF	Apostolic Pentecostal Church of God of Romania Confession of Faith
VPE	Verenigde Pinkster- en Evangeliegemeenten (The Netherlands)
WAGFSF	World Assemblies of God Fellowship Statement of Faith

Introduction

Pentecostalism is not always well understood, even by Pentecostals. It is my hope that this book will help bring clarity. I write it as a lifelong Pentecostal, yet I also write it as a lifelong conservative evangelical—for these are not opposing traditions. In other words, I'm writing for evangelicals, some of whom will be Pentecostals and some of whom won't. In these pages, I want to show both groups what we hold in common and what is distinct about Pentecostals among our fellow evangelicals.

Some of the questions in this book will focus more on showing you *what* Pentecostals believe. This is especially the case on topics where there is confusion, and here I'll give plenty of evidence from Pentecostals all over the world. Other questions will focus more on demonstrating *why* Pentecostals believe what they believe. In these questions you'll find fewer footnotes and more Scripture. I hope that the answers to both sorts of questions will benefit Pentecostals and non-Pentecostals alike.

Many books on Pentecostalism focus on the United States. However, Pentecostalism is not an American movement but a global one. Therefore, I've sought to bring in voices from every continent. I've tracked down Pentecostal confessions of faith and doctrinal writings from as many countries as possible and have tried to include a good representation of the global movement. A few non-English language Pentecostal movements have produced English translations of their confessions of faith (notably the Creed of the Pentecostal Movement in Iceland and the Main Articles of Faith of the Pentecostal Church of Finland). For most confessional documents beyond the Anglosphere, however, you will have to make do with my translations.

Finally, not every Pentecostal will agree with everything I've written. As I'm sure will become clear as you read, there is considerable variety among Pentecostals in various areas. Furthermore, many people in Pentecostal churches have been influenced by the later charismatic and neo-charismatic movements (and can even, at times, be more familiar with the beliefs of those movements than the beliefs of classical Pentecostalism). I have endeavored to represent the mainstream of classical Pentecostalism while also giving you a glimpse of some of the major variants. Hopefully, from all this you will gain a good idea of the heart of the movement.

PART 1

Introductory Questions

SECTION A

Historical Questions

QUESTION 1

What Is Pentecostalism?

A little more than a century ago, there was no such thing as Pentecostalism. Today, some hail it as the second largest grouping of Christians in the world, with more than 500 million adherents. Of course, this number depends very much upon the definition of Pentecostalism. Whatever the precise number of Pentecostals in the world might be (for it has to be admitted that it is not a simple thing to count), it is clear that Pentecostalism has become a significant and growing part of Christianity around the world, with Pentecostals now outnumbering Baptists, Anglicans, Lutherans, Presbyterians, and Reformed believers.[1]

Difficulties with Defining Pentecostalism

One of the reasons why counting Pentecostals is so difficult is that there are many different definitions of Pentecostalism. Some scholars use the word to refer to anyone who believes that the extraordinary gifts of the Holy Spirit are still available in the church today, including not only churches traditionally known as Pentecostal but all charismatic and continuationist (those who believe that "sign gifts" such as tongues and prophecy are still in operation today) Christians, whether or not they would call themselves Pentecostal. For them, the 500-million statistic includes not only people who attend Pentecostal churches but also charismatics in the Roman Catholic Church; members of Oneness churches (who deny the doctrine of the Trinity); empowered evangelicals (like the Association of Vineyard Churches, where people might believe in the present supernatural work of the Holy Spirit in signs and wonders but reject the Pentecostal idea of baptism in the Holy Spirit);

1. With a careful distinction between "Pentecostals" and "renewalists," the number of classical Pentecostals in the world in 2010 was 178 million, with an annual growth rate of 2.6 percent. See Jason Mandryk, *Operation World*, 7th ed. (Downers Grove, IL: InterVarsity Press, 2010), 3.

and many, many more. Many of these "renewalists" would not call themselves Pentecostal, nor would they be considered Pentecostals by most Pentecostal churches. Although they share a common emphasis on the present-day miraculous work of the Holy Spirit, they do not share the same theology. The only people who call all these groups Pentecostal are scholars, and even they do not all agree with the label.

While many academics have adopted such broad phenomenological and sociological definitions of Pentecostalism, others have pointed out problems with this approach. Robert Menzies writes, "As a Pentecostal, when I read sociologically-oriented books about Pentecostals, even those that contain many significant and helpful insights, I feel that something is lacking. I often feel that the picture presented of what it means to be a Pentecostal is a caricature, an image that, while partially true, contains many exaggerations and distortions."[2] Simon Chan argues that these broad phenomenological definitions of Pentecostalism are actually "a redefinition of Pentecostalism itself." The choice, Chan tells us, is between defining Pentecostalism "in terms of actual historical links with a movement which calls itself Pentecostal" (and thus history and theology will be key to the definition) or "in terms of a cluster of religious experiences understood phenomenologically" (in which case the focus will be practice rather than theology).[3]

Yet, theology is essential to identity. After all, both Roman Catholics and Southern Baptists receive Communion, yet their theological understanding of what happens when they receive Communion is a major dividing line between the two communities. With the emergence of Pentecostalism in the early twentieth century, it was not the experience of the baptism of the Holy Spirit that was new but the theological explanation of that experience. As Chan concludes, "I do not think that it is legitimate to call a movement Pentecostal solely on the basis of common experiences. There is, after all, no such thing as a religious experience without any theological interpretation."[4]

A Theological Approach to Pentecostalism

So, if we are not going to redefine Pentecostalism but, rather, portray it in a way that corresponds to the faith of Christians who call themselves Pentecostals and churches that recognize one another as part of the Pentecostal movement, we need to define Pentecostalism theologically. Pentecostal worship looks very different around the world; yet, despite this wide variety of styles and practices, there is a common theological core. Part

---

2. Robert P. Menzies, *Pentecost: This Is Our Story* (Springfield, MO: Gospel Publishing House, 2013), 16.
3. Simon Chan, "Whither Pentecostalism," in *Asian and Pentecostal: The Charismatic Face of Christianity in Asia*, eds. Allan Anderson and Edmond Tang (Oxford: Regnum, 2005), 577.
4. Chan, "Whither Pentecostalism," 579.

of this theological core is shared with other orthodox Christians in many other traditions, while some of it is unique to Pentecostalism, but both the similarities and differences are important. If it were possible to hold to the aspects of Pentecostal faith that are distinctive without holding on to what's held in common with other orthodox and evangelical Christians, it would no longer be classical Pentecostalism. Classical Pentecostalism is a faith rooted in the authority of Scripture and the centrality of Jesus Christ and his saving work, not merely in a spiritual experience.

One of the earliest Pentecostal leaders, the Norwegian minister Thomas Ball Barratt, tried to come up with a definition of Pentecostalism to help people understand what this new movement was about:

> [Pentecostals] all believe in the authority of the Word of God, in Jesus Christ as their Saviour, Head and King. They are mostly baptised in water since believing, they all believe in the necessity of a clean heart and a holy life, in the possibility of being baptised in our day, as on the Day of Pentecost, in the Holy Ghost, and the greater number believe, that tongues, in connection with the baptism, is a proof of the presence of the Holy Ghost, and are to be expected now as at first in Jerusalem, or at least prophetic utterances and worship in the Spirit. . . . All the great truths of any importance, held by the evangelical denominations, are to be found in the tenets of this Movement, as well as this great truth concerning the Baptism in the Holy Ghost, and the signs following.[5]

Here, one of the pioneers of Pentecostalism insists that both the Pentecostal distinctive of the baptism in the Holy Spirit and the great truths of evangelical Christianity (including the Trinity, the authority of Scripture, Christ's atoning work, and salvation through faith in Christ) are essential to Pentecostal identity.

Writing in the twenty-first century, the British Pentecostal scholar William Kay makes the same point: "Pentecostalism is the marriage of a spiritual experience called 'baptism in the Holy Spirit' with evangelical doctrines."[6] The authority of Scripture, the centrality of Jesus Christ and his atoning work, the need for personal repentance and faith in Jesus, and the necessity of holiness in life are all just as important as the baptism and gifts of the Holy Spirit for a true understanding of Pentecostalism. Robert Menzies sums up this Pentecostal emphasis on evangelical doctrine:

---

5. Thomas Ball Barratt, *In the Days of the Latter Rain*, rev. ed. (London: Elim Publishing, 1928), 149.
6. William K. Kay, *Pentecostalism* (London: SCM, 2009), xvii.

> It is impossible to understand Pentecostals apart from these core Evangelical convictions. At its heart, the Pentecostal movement is not Spirit-centered but Christ-centered. The work of the Spirit, as Pentecostals understand it, centers on exalting and bearing witness to the Lordship of Christ. . . . Pentecostals are often pictured as extremely emotional and experientially driven, but this is a caricature of the real image. In reality, Pentecostals are "people of the Book." . . . The Christ-centered and Bible-driven nature of the Pentecostal movement should not be missed.[7]

The Biblical Foundation of Pentecostalism

Pentecostals do believe in distinct spiritual experiences (including the baptism and gifts of the Holy Spirit). Yet the very reason they believe in these experiences is because they see them in the Bible. The Pentecostal approach is not *the Bible plus experience* but rather *biblical experience*. Pentecostals want their experience to line up with what they see in Scripture. Therefore, for Pentecostals, experience is not in any way supposed to be an authority competing with Scripture. All Christian experience must be tested by and measured against God's Word, for God's word in Scripture is always our ultimate authority. As Thomas Zimmerman, former general superintendent of the Assemblies of God in the United States, put it, "The Holy Spirit is the river, but the Spirit will only flow within the banks of Scripture."[8] The common slogan used by the Elim Pentecostal Church in the UK proclaims Pentecostalism to be a movement that stands "foursquare upon the Word of God,"[9] summing up this Pentecostal view of Scripture's authority over spiritual experience.

Confidence in the authority of the inerrant Scriptures is a hallmark of classical Pentecostalism. Donald Gee, highly regarded around the world as a great Pentecostal teacher and leader, emphasizes that "the Scriptures are our infallible guide."[10] Back in Azusa Street, William Seymour wrote of Scripture as "the only and the sufficient rule of faith and practice." He emphasized, "God

---

7. Menzies, *Pentecost*, 14.
8. Quoted in George O. Wood, foreword to Anthony D. Palma, *The Holy Spirit: A Pentecostal Perspective* (Springfield, MO: Logion, 2001), 10.
9. This slogan was emblazoned on banners at Elim conventions, such as those at the Royal Albert Hall in London, and frequently used in Elim publications. "Foursquare" refers to the experience of Christ as Savior, Healer, Baptizer in the Spirit, and Soon Coming King, but this experiential knowledge of Christ rests solidly upon the Word of God in Scripture.
10. Donald Gee, "To Seekers After the Baptism in the Holy Ghost," *Elim Evangel* (May 1923): 87. British writers tend to use "infallible" in the same sense that Americans use the word "inerrant."

calls us to follow the Bible."[11] Seymour was criticized for his "protestant orthodoxy," yet he was not swayed from it. For Seymour, this orthodox Protestant approach to the Bible was essential to Pentecostalism. He warned strongly against any temptation to let spiritual experiences take the place of Scripture's authority: "When we leave the word of God and begin to go by signs and voices we will wind up in Spiritualism. God's word is God's law. The Holy Spirit came to give us power to stand on the infallible word."[12] Pentecostals must never "pin our faith on outward manifestations. We are to go by the word of God. Our thought must be in harmony with the Bible or else we will have a strange religion."[13] So, Pentecostals share with our other evangelical brothers and sisters this understanding of the authority of Scripture, along with a central role for Scripture in our worship and piety.

The Evangelical Heart of Pentecostalism

The Pentecostal expectation of experiences in line with Scripture, however, does not begin with the baptism in the Holy Spirit. It begins with salvation. When William Seymour described what was going on in the Azusa Street Revival in a letter in July 1906, he wrote, "People are getting saved. . . . Praise [the] Lord, Amen."[14] Taking the gospel to people all over the world so that people would be saved by Jesus has always been much more important to Pentecostals than enjoying spiritual experiences. In fact, in the very same letter, Seymour writes of how missionaries had already been sent out from Azusa Street to India, Jerusalem, Africa, and China (and this was only a few months after the beginning of the revival). Even the experience of the baptism of the Holy Spirit is understood by Pentecostals in connection with evangelism and mission. So, salvation in Jesus (and telling others of that salvation in Jesus) stands at the heart of Pentecostalism.

The salvation of which Pentecostals want to tell the world has been accomplished by Christ through his death on the cross in our place and his resurrection from the dead. Pentecostals are "messengers of this precious atonement," for "salvation lies in the Blood of Jesus."[15] Early Pentecostals saw their unity not only in the experience of the baptism of the Spirit but also in Christ's blood.[16] Therefore, the blood of Jesus has always been central to Pentecostal preaching, worship, and piety.

---

11. William J. Seymour, *The Doctrines and Discipline of the Azusa Street Apostolic Faith Mission*, reprinted in Gastón Espinosa, *William J. Seymour and the Origins of Global Pentecostalism: A Biography and Documentary History* (Durham, NC: Duke University Press, 2014), 223–24.
12. Seymour, *Doctrines and Discipline*, 219.
13. Seymour, quoted in Espinosa, *William J. Seymour*, 141.
14. Seymour, "Letter to Warren Faye Carothers," in Espinosa, *William J. Seymour*, 161.
15. William J. Seymour, "The Precious Atonement," in Espinosa, *William J. Seymour*, 166; see also Seymour, *Doctrine and Discipline*, 219.
16. Barratt, *In the Days of the Latter Rain*, 217.

Pentecostals, then, not only emphasize the experience of the baptism and gifts of the Spirit, but root their faith and piety in the Bible, proclaim a salvation accomplished by Christ on the cross, desire to see people come to personal faith in Jesus, and so send (and go as) missionaries all over the world to tell people of the salvation found in Christ alone. In other words, Pentecostals are evangelicals, for these are the four aspects of David Bebbington's definition of evangelicalism (biblicism, crucicentrism, conversionism, and activism).[17] Therefore, as Robert Menzies shows, "The term, Pentecostal, is not only compatible with the adjective, Evangelical, but incomprehensible apart from it. Thus, to be Pentecostal is, by definition, to be Evangelical."[18]

But among evangelicals, Pentecostals are also distinctive. While their evangelical identity is essential, so is their emphasis on the experience of the baptism in the Holy Spirit as something distinct from being born again. That is, after all, how they get the name "Pentecostal"—from their belief that the baptism of the Spirit which the disciples received on the day of Pentecost is still available for believers today.[19]

Summary

So, how can we sum up what Pentecostals believe? Pentecostals are orthodox, evangelical Christians who believe that the Scriptures encourage every believer to receive the baptism in the Holy Spirit, understood as an experience distinct from regeneration and marked by "signs following" (including the gifts of the Holy Spirit listed in 1 Corinthians 12:8–10).[20] The faith of Pentecostals is founded upon the word of God in Scripture and is centered upon Christ and him crucified, who now pours out from the Father's right hand the Holy Spirit of promise upon his church, just as he did in the book of Acts.

REFLECTION QUESTIONS

1. Do you think doctrine is essential to identity?

---

17. David Bebbington, *Evangelicalism in Modern Britain: A History from the 1730s to the 1980s* (Grand Rapids: Baker, 1989), 2–3.
18. R. P. Menzies, *Christ-Centered: The Evangelical Heritage of Pentecostal Theology* (Eugene OR: Cascade, 2020), 146.
19. Donald Gee, *The Pentecostal Movement* (London: Victory Press, 1941), 7–8; see also Tony Richie, *Essentials of Pentecostal Theology* (Eugene, OR: Resource Publications, 2020), 2.
20. This definition deliberately draws upon and adapts the definition given by R. P. Menzies; see *Christ-Centered*, 145. The main difference between my definition and that of Menzies is that he specifically includes "speaking in tongues" as the sign of the baptism in the Holy Spirit, whereas I have only referred to "signs following." This reflects geographical and denominational differences that will be explained more in question 20.

2. How would you define Pentecostals, in your own words?

3. How do you think your own history with Pentecostals, charismatics, and other continuationist Christians will affect your interaction with the material in the rest of this book?

4. On what is the faith of Pentecostals centered?

5. Do you agree with William Seymour's warning that if we "pin our faith on outward manifestations [rather than Scripture] . . . we will have a strange religion"?

QUESTION 2

What Were the Precursors to Pentecostalism?

Many movements and families of churches can trace their origins back to a single person or event in the history of Christianity. Lutherans can look back to Martin Luther in the sixteenth century for their beginnings; most Methodists can trace their history back to the ministry of John Wesley in the eighteenth century; and Anglicans cannot deny that a series of acts of Parliament under King Henry VIII and then under Queen Elizabeth I established the Church of England (and its daughter churches) as a distinct tradition. Yet, for Pentecostals there is no clear equivalent. While there were some very significant and influential figures at the beginning of the movement, there was no single founder of Pentecostalism; nor was there a single place where Pentecostalism began.

Historians have given much consideration to questions surrounding Pentecostal origins. Some trace the movement to events in Kansas in 1901. Others see the origins in Los Angeles in 1906. Yet, as Allan Anderson has argued, this "'made in the USA' assumption is one of the great disservices done to worldwide Pentecostalism."[1] Instead of looking solely to the United States, we should recognize that Pentecostalism has origins in multiple countries. These arose together and influenced one another (often quite quickly), further reinforcing one another. As such, the histories we will consider in this and the next few chapters will overlap.

This perspective is not new. If anything, it is the original understanding of Pentecostal origins, especially outside of the United States. The great early British Pentecostal leader Donald Gee, who had traveled extensively around the Pentecostal world (and probably knew its variety better than nearly

1. Allan Anderson, "Revising Pentecostal History in Global Perspective," in *Asian and Pentecostal*, eds. Allan Anderson and Edmond Tang (Baguio City: Regnum, 2005), 152.

anyone else of his generation) took this multiple-origins view of the beginnings of the movement: "The Pentecostal Movement does not owe its origin to any outstanding personality or religious leader, but was a spontaneous revival appearing almost simultaneously in various parts of the world. . . . The outstanding leaders of the Pentecostal Movement are themselves the products of the Movement. They did not make it; it made them."[2] In the United States, Frank Bartleman, who was present at Azusa Street, wrote that Pentecostalism "was rocked in the cradle of little Wales. It was brought up in India following, becoming full grown in Los Angeles later."[3] If even a participant in the Azusa Street revival points us to other parts of the world, it would be remiss of us not to turn to Wales and India over the course of these next chapters, as well as to Los Angeles—along with Topeka, Toronto, Oslo, London, Sunderland, and elsewhere. Yet first, we need to consider some earlier developments that were important precursors to the rise of the movement.

The American Holiness Movement

In the United States, a series of nineteenth-century revivals among Methodists eventually led to the emergence of the Holiness movement, which sought to restore the earlier Wesleyan emphasis on entire sanctification (or Christian perfection). Eventually this led to separate Holiness churches emerging outside of mainline Methodism in the last two decades of the nineteenth century.[4]

The Holiness movement emphasized John Wesley's teaching on Christian perfection, understood as a second blessing of entire sanctification, distinct from justification, to be received at some moment in the Christian life.[5] They frequently referred to this sanctification experience as the "baptism in the Holy Spirit."[6] In reality, however, their teaching owed more to John Fletcher (1729–1785) than to John Wesley, for it was Fletcher who transformed Wesley's view of Christian perfection (as "the culmination of a life of holiness") into "a

---

2. Donald Gee, *The Pentecostal Movement* (London: Victory Press, 1941), 3.
3. Frank Bartleman, *Azusa Street: An Eyewitness Account* (Gainesville, FL: Bridge-Logos, 1980), 22.
4. Vinson Synan, *The Holiness-Pentecostal Tradition: Charismatic Movements in the Twentieth Century* (Grand Rapids: Eerdmans, 1997), 41–43.
5. Melvin E. Dieter, "Wesleyan-Holiness Aspects of Pentecostal Origins: As Mediated Through the Nineteenth-Century Holiness Revival," in *Aspects of Pentecostal-Charismatic Origins*, ed. Vinson Synan (Plainfield, NJ: Logos International, 1975), 59. In fact, Wesleyan Holiness teaching had moved quite far beyond Wesley's own view on Christian perfection. Geoffrey Butler suggests that comparisons between Wesley's teaching and what would emerge in Pentecostalism are in reality "due to surface level commonalities." See Geoffrey Butler, "Wesley, Fletcher, and the Baptism of the Holy Spirit: A Pentecostal Analysis," *Journal of Pentecostal Theology* 30 (2021): 189.
6. Synan, "Pentecostal Roots," in *The Century of the Holy Spirit: 100 Years of Pentecostal and Charismatic Renewal*, ed. Vinson Synan (Nashville: Thomas Nelson, 2001), 15.

crisis experience . . . available to every Christian."[7] This would pave the way for the doctrine of subsequence (in which the baptism of the Holy Spirit is seen as an experience distinct from and subsequent to regeneration; chapter 19 outlines this doctrine more fully).

In the nineteenth century, this Holiness teaching—along with the language of baptism in the Spirit as a distinct, post-conversion crisis experience—was spread widely by Wesleyans such as Phoebe Palmer and Oberlin Perfectionists such as Asa Mahan.[8] Palmer in particular popularized an emphasis on the baptism of the Spirit as an instantaneous crisis experience through her teaching of a "shorter way" to perfection through placing "all on the altar."[9]

In the United States (although not always in other countries) the earliest leading figures in the emergence of Pentecostalism came from Wesleyan Holiness backgrounds, including both Charles Parham and William Seymour. Several Wesleyan Holiness denominations or groups of churches also became Pentecostal denominations as the revival spread through their ranks, including the Church of God in Christ, the Church of God, the Fire-Baptized Holiness Church, and the Pentecostal Holiness Church (the last two merging in 1911 to become what is now the International Pentecostal Holiness Church).

Wesleyan Holiness teaching had a significant role to play in the development of an understanding of the baptism in the Holy Spirit as a distinct experience from conversion. However, although some early Pentecostals came directly from a Wesleyan Holiness background, much of the influence of these teachings was mediated to Pentecostalism from other parts of the evangelical world.

Late-Nineteenth-Century Holiness and Revival Emphases in American Reformed Evangelicalism

In the late nineteenth century, an emphasis on the baptism in the Holy Spirit also emerged among non-Wesleyan evangelicals. Edith Waldvogel has argued that there were three general ways in which this differed from the emphasis given to the matter in Wesleyan Holiness circles. First, she writes, "The context in which Reformed evangelicals expressed their teaching was strongly doctrinal and primarily premillennialist." The conviction of the imminent return of Christ gave a strong incentive both for holiness and for evangelistic effectiveness. Second, they rejected the Wesleyan concept of a "second blessing"

7. Butler, "Wesley, Fletcher, and the Baptism of the Holy Spirit," 189.
8. Synan, "Pentecostal Roots," 26–28; see also Donald W. Dayton, "From Christian Perfection to the 'Baptism of the Holy Ghost,'" in *Aspects of Pentecostal-Charismatic Origins*, ed. Vinson Synan (Plainfield, NJ: Logos International, 1975), 41–53. Mahan's theology was essentially Wesleyan, although he himself was a Congregationalist minister, which may account for his influence beyond Wesleyan circles.
9. Synan, *Holiness-Pentecostal Tradition*, 17. See also Dieter, "Wesleyan-Holiness Aspects," 62.

of entire sanctification. Third, they incorporated (to a much greater extent than Wesleyans) "a practical emphasis on divine healing."[10]

Prominent figures in these types of Reformed evangelical circles in the United States were Dwight Moody, R. A. Torrey, A. J. Gordon, and A. B. Simpson.[11] Waldvogel argues,

> Though these men did not function as a formal group or espouse a well-defined program, their remarkably similar spiritual odysseys formed a basis for a distinct understanding of the evangelical message: each ultimately accepted baptism by immersion, became convinced of Christ's premillennial advent, espoused divine healing and . . . became associated with foreign missionary efforts, and stressed the necessity of a close relationship between the believer and the Holy Spirit. The conservative evangelical doctrinal framework into which they incorporated their particular emphases was similar to that which would later characterize the Assemblies of God [and other Pentecostals who did not adhere to Wesleyan Holiness teaching].[12]

Like later "Finished Work" Pentecostalism (an expression which is often used to refer to the varieties of classical Pentecostalism which do not hold to Wesleyan Holiness doctrines), these evangelicals "rejected two central tenets of the contemporary Holiness message: (1) they denied that sanctification was instantaneous, and (2) they contended that sanctification was not the baptism with the Holy Spirit."[13] Instead, they saw sanctification as progressive and the baptism in the Spirit as an enduement of power for service.

In 1907, a significant number of leaders from A. B. Simpson's Christian and Missionary Alliance who had accepted the Pentecostal experience left the movement and became leaders of newly emerging Pentecostal assemblies. Several of these, including Frank Boyd, D. W. Kerr, William Evans, and J. Roswell Flower, went on to become figures of great importance in the early years of the Assemblies of God.[14] Thus, right from the beginning, there were significant non-Wesleyan voices and influences among Pentecostals.

---

10. Edith L. Waldvogel, "The 'Overcoming' Life: A Study in the Reformed Evangelical Contribution to Pentecostalism," *Pneuma* 1, no. 1 (1979): 8.
11. William W. Menzies, "The Non-Wesleyan Origins of the Pentecostal Movement," in *Aspects of Pentecostal-Charismatic Origins*, ed. Vinson Synan (Plainfield, NJ: Logos International, 1975), 87–90.
12. Waldvogel, "The Overcoming Life," 9.
13. Waldvogel, "The Overcoming Life," 9.
14. Menzies, "Non-Wesleyan Origins," 89; Charles W. Nienkirchen, *A. B. Simpson and the Pentecostal Movement* (Peabody, MA: Hendrickson, 1992), 83–84.

British Evangelical Influences on Emerging Pentecostalism

The evangelical context from which British Pentecostalism emerged had many overlapping features with the United States, but even more significant differences. While both John Wesley and John Fletcher had ministered in England, there was not a distinct Wesleyan Holiness movement in the United Kingdom comparable to that in the United States. "What is striking," Ian Randall notes, "when the emergence of British Pentecostalism is compared with the development of Pentecostalism in North America, is the absence of strong Wesleyan holiness influences in Britain."[15] In fact, although a few small organizations (such as Reader Harris's Pentecostal League of Prayer) attempted to keep it alive, older Wesleyan sanctification teaching had largely died out in Britain—being "confined to the margins of English religious life"—by the beginning of the twentieth century.[16]

Holiness was a very important theme among British evangelicals, but in a non-Wesleyan way. Three (at times overlapping) movements had significant influence on the emergence of Pentecostalism in the United Kingdom: the Welsh Revival tradition (flowing from Calvinistic Methodism), the Keswick Conventions and their accompanying spirituality, and Brethrenism. We will give our attention to the impact of the Welsh Revival in the next chapter, but here let us consider the other two.

Keswick

The Keswick Convention has been held in the town of Keswick in the Lake District since 1875 and was instrumental in the development of an emerging non-Wesleyan holiness movement. Keswick had much in common with and was influenced by the North American Higher Life movement; yet it remained distinctively British in character and departed from its North American counterpart theologically in a number of respects.[17] Keswick and the smaller "Keswick" conventions held in various parts of the country (e.g., Welsh Keswick in Llandrindod Wells, and later Portstewart Keswick in County Londonderry) and empire (e.g., the Keswick conventions organized by Andrew Murray in South Africa) were significant influences upon British evangelical life and thought. Although the main Keswick Convention was, before the First World War, a largely upper-middle-class gathering, it "drew

---

15. Ian M. Randall, "Old Time Power: Relationships between Pentecostalism and Evangelical Spirituality in England," *Pneuma* 19, no. 1 (Spring 1997): 59.
16. David Bebbington, *Holiness in Nineteenth-Century England* (Carlisle: Paternoster, 2000), 72. Even Reader Harris was, however, a member of the Church of England rather than part of a distinct Holiness denomination. Thus, even what remained of Wesleyan Holiness in the UK had significant differences from the Holiness churches in the United States.
17. James Robinson, *Pentecostal Origins: Early Pentecostalism in Ireland in the Context of the British Isles*, Studies in Evangelical History and Thought (Milton Keynes: Paternoster, 2005), 10.

together a mix of British conservative evangelicals . . . and can properly be understood as representing the conservative evangelical mainstream."[18] Many of Britain's earliest Pentecostal leaders already attended the Keswick Convention or Keswick in Wales.[19]

Many Keswick teachers emphasized the need for a baptism in the Holy Spirit (distinct from and subsequent to conversion). A distinction was made between being "indwelt" by the Holy Spirit at conversion and being "filled" with the Holy Spirit at a later point. Unlike the American Wesleyan Holiness teachers, they did not equate the baptism of the Spirit with "entire sanctification." Rather, Andrew Murray taught that the experience of the baptism in the Spirit subsequent to regeneration was "specially given as power for work."[20] Thus, the understanding of the baptism of the Holy Spirit that spread through the influence of Keswick spirituality was that it was an empowering experience rather than a sanctifying experience.

Brethren Primitivism

Yet Pentecostalism was also a primitivist movement, seeking to restore what they saw as significant aspects of New Testament church life. In Britain, Brethren assemblies were already a significant feature of evangelicalism, and they too shared this desire to restore the New Testament pattern of church life. As Pentecostalism began to emerge there were some overlaps between these two movements. Occasionally an assembly would divide into two—one Pentecostal and one Brethren (as in Penygroes). At other times what had begun as a Brethren assembly would become Pentecostal, including an assembly in Manchester (of which J. Nelson Parr was a member) that went on to become Britain's largest Pentecostal church for many decades. For much of the twentieth century, the weekly British Pentecostal Breaking of Bread services looked almost identical to those in Brethren assemblies, except for the operation of the gifts of the Spirit (and the audible participation of women in Pentecostal worship). Ian Randall concludes that British Pentecostals were "indebted to Brethren sources for elements in their form of church life and at least in part for their simple belief in what was often called 'the old Book.'"[21]

Summary

Pentecostalism emerged through neither one event nor the influence of one significant person. Rather, a number of theological currents came together in various parts of the world, resulting in a strong anticipation of an

---

18. Randall, "Old Time Power," 55.
19. E.g., Alexander Boddy, J. Nelson Parr, D. P. Williams, George Jeffreys, W. F. P. Burton. See Randall, "Old Time Power," 59; and Chris Palmer, "Wales and Embryonic Pentecostalism," *Journal of the European Pentecostal Theological Association* 34, no. 2 (2014): 176.
20. Andrew Murray, *The Spirit of Christ* (London: James Nisbet, 1888), 324.
21. Randall, "Old Time Power," 60.

experience of the baptism of the Holy Spirit subsequent to conversion among many different groups of evangelical Christians. While much attention has been given to the Wesleyan Holiness aspects of Pentecostal origins, large parts of Pentecostalism were not direct descendants of the Wesleyan Holiness movement. Developments within the Reformed evangelical world in North America and among British evangelicals (including Keswick spirituality and Brethren primitivism) played important roles in the emergence of much of Pentecostalism.

REFLECTION QUESTIONS

1. How did early Pentecostals like Frank Bartleman and Donald Gee understand the origins of the Pentecostal movement?

2. Why might it be a disservice to focus exclusively on events in the United States in telling the story of Pentecostal beginnings?

3. Why might so much attention have been given to the Wesleyan Holiness movement in considerations of the origins of Pentecostalism?

4. How did Reformed evangelicals in the United States contribute to the emergence of Pentecostalism?

5. Why is British evangelicalism significant for the beginnings of Pentecostalism?

QUESTION 3

What Role Did Wales and India Play in the Emergence of Pentecostalism?

Around the world, revivals were taking place in the first few years of the twentieth century that would feed into the emergence of Pentecostalism. Although several of the most well-known revivals took place in the United States, several powerful revivals also took place in other parts of the world, independently of Azusa Street or Topeka. The most significant of these was the Welsh Revival of 1904–1905. The Welsh Revival served as a catalyst for revivals in India and elsewhere, and gave birth to Pentecostalism in Wales. It also prepared people in England, Los Angeles, and elsewhere to seek a similar outpouring of the Holy Spirit.

The Welsh Revival

The Welsh Revival of 1904–1905 was not the first Welsh revival but the latest in a long series of revivals dating back to 1735. The first Welsh revival—under the ministries of such figures as Howell Harris, Daniel Rowland, and William Williams (Pantycelyn)—produced Calvinistic Methodism, a movement that was to have an enduring and significant influence on Welsh Christianity. From this movement a long series of revivals broke out. Testimonies from the original Calvinistic Methodist Revival point to powerful post-conversion experiences of the baptism in the Holy Spirit as a seal of assurance. Howell Harris, for example, wrote: "I felt suddenly my heart melting within me like wax before the fire with love to God my Saviour; and also felt not only love, peace, etc., but longing to be dissolved, and to be with Christ. Then was a cry in my inmost soul, which I was totally unacquainted with before, Abba, Father! Abba, Father! I could not help calling God my Father; I knew that I was His child, and that He loved me and heard me."[1]

1. Howell Harris, *A Brief Account of the Life of Howell Harris* (Trefecca: n.p., 1791), 15.

These post-conversion experiences were spoken of as the baptism *of fire* or *of power*.[2] There are also possible accounts of speaking in tongues. For example, William Williams (Pantycelyn) wrote of witnessing a man upon whom the Spirit fell whose "tongue spoke unusual words, his voice was raised, his spirit was aflame."[3]

The Calvinistic Methodists were strongly influenced by the Puritan tradition, and their view of the baptism of the Spirit as the sealing assurance of the Holy Spirit was in line with earlier Puritan writers such as Thomas Goodwin.[4] Other Puritans, like Isaac Ambrose, wrote of such experiences in terms very similar to later Pentecostal testimonies: "This day in the evening the Lord in his mercy poured into my soul the ravishing joy of his blessed Spirit. O how sweet was the Lord unto me? I never felt such a lovely taste of heaven before: I believe this was the joyful sound, the kisses of his mouth, the sweetnesses of Christ, the joy of his Spirit, the new wine of his kingdom; it continued with me about two days."[5] The spirituality of the first Welsh revival was carried on in Calvinistic Methodism and on into the wider world of late-nineteenth and early-twentieth-century Welsh evangelicalism.[6] Thus, while the revival of 1904–1905 touched many churches outside of the Calvinistic Methodist movement, the spirituality of the revival was, to a large extent, forged within the Calvinistic Methodist spiritual tradition.[7]

Where American Pentecostals look back to Azusa Street or Topeka, British Pentecostals look back to the Welsh Revival of 1904–1905 as their point of origin.[8] Many of the early Pentecostal leaders were saved during

---

2. D. Martyn Lloyd-Jones, "Howell Harris and Revival," in *The Puritans: Their Origins and Successors* (Edinburgh: Banner of Truth, 1987), 290.
3. William Williams, *The Experience Meeting*, trans. Mrs. Lloyd-Jones (Bridgend: Evangelical Movement of Wales, 1973), 8–9.
4. Cf. Thomas Goodwin, "Sermons XV-XVII," in *The Works of Thomas Goodwin* (Edinburgh: James Nichol, 1861), 1:227–67; Thomas Goodwin, "A Child of Light Walking in Darkness," in *The Works of Thomas Goodwin*, 3:231–350; Thomas Goodwin, "Exposition of Various Portions of the Epistle to the Ephesians," in *The Works of Thomas Goodwin*, 2:391–414. Andrew Murray also draws on Goodwin in his teaching on the Holy Spirit. See Andrew Murray, *The Spirit of Christ* (London: James Nisbet, 1888), 86.
5. Isaac Ambrose, diary, May 20, 1641, as recorded in Isaac Ambrose, *Media: The Middle Things, in Reference to the First and Last Things* (London, 1650), 71, quoted in Tom Schwanda, *Soul Recreation: The Contemplative-Mystical Piety of Puritanism* (Eugene, OR: Pickwick, 2012), 178.
6. For a long time, all Methodism in Wales was Calvinistic Methodism; therefore, in earlier sources, the term Calvinistic was unnecessary. This might confuse modern readers who could assume Methodist implies Wesleyan theology. Wesleyan Methodism did not enjoy any success in Wales until much later. Thus, the Methodist Fathers of Wales were all Calvinistic Methodists.
7. Eifion Evans, *The Welsh Revival of 1904*, 3rd ed. (Bridgend: Bryntirion, 1987), 170.
8. Khuyhung Cho, "The Importance of the Welsh Revival in British Pentecostalism," *Journal of the European Pentecostal Theological Association* 30, no. 1 (2010): 32.

the revival (including D. P. Williams, George Jeffreys, Stephen Jeffreys, and Donald Gee), and many people experienced the baptism in the Holy Spirit and spiritual gifts, including visions, prophecy, singing in the Spirit, speaking in tongues, and spontaneous prayer.[9] Eifion Evans (a non-Pentecostal historian) argues that the main reason for "the rise of a vigorous Pentecostalism" in the aftermath of the revival was "the prominence given to Pentecostal manifestations during the revival."[10] Throughout the Welsh Revival, there was an emphasis on the Pentecostal power of the Holy Spirit. Evan Roberts, the most prominent minister of the revival, taught the need for a personal experience of the baptism in the Spirit.[11] Donald Gee, in his assessment of the Welsh Revival, insisted that "it is impossible, and would be historically incorrect, to disassociate the Pentecostal Movement from that remarkable visitation of God's Spirit."[12]

One of the most remarkable "Pentecostal" moments in the revival actually took place in England rather than Wales. A large Welsh contingent had traveled to Keswick for the 1905 convention, and while there three hundred of them gathered for an all-night prayer meeting. English convention attenders were appalled and considered the Welsh prayer meeting "out of control" due to people speaking in tongues.[13]

Joseph Smale, a minister from Los Angeles, visited Wales to witness the Welsh Revival. His experience led him to gather people to pray for revival in Los Angeles when he returned. His account of the Pentecostal phenomena he saw and experienced during the revival in Wales led to a wider acceptance of Pentecostal ideas among these Christians in Los Angeles, even before the Azusa Street Revival. Alexander Boddy, an Englishman, also visited Wales during the revival. He too was prompted to return to his home church and begin a prayer meeting for the revival to spread to England.

---

9. For evidence of speaking in tongues during the Welsh Revival from a non-Pentecostal source, see Brynmor Pierce Jones, *The King's Champions: Revival and Reaction 1905–1935*, enlarged ed. (Cwmbran: Christian Literature Press, 1986), 62. For evidence from a participant in the revival who would later go on to be a significant Pentecostal leader, see D. P. Williams, *The Prophetical Ministry in the Church* (Penygroes: Apostolic Church, 1931), 98–99, and *Souvenir Exhibiting the Movements of God in the Apostolic Church* (Penygroes: Apostolic Church, 1933), 9.
10. Evans, *Welsh Revival*, 190. Evans downplays the "distinctly Pentecostal emphases" of the revival as "rarer occurrences and incidental features," see *Welsh Revival*, 192. However, the evidence of D. P. Williams and Brynmore Pierce Jones (see previous note) would suggest that, although they might not have occurred everywhere, these Pentecostal features were not rare.
11. Evans, *Welsh Revival*, 192; Noel Gibbard, *Fire on the Altar: A History and Evaluation of the 1904–05 Welsh Revival* (Bridgend: Bryntirion Press, 2005), 169–77.
12. Donald Gee, *The Pentecostal Movement* (London: Victory Press, 1941), 5–6.
13. For a brief account, see Allan Anderson, "Review of Dyfed Wyn Roberts, ed., *Revival, Renewal and the Holy Spirit*," *Pneuma* 32, no. 2 (2010): 285.

After the revival subsided, groups that came to be called "children of the revival" continued to meet across Wales. Seeking to keep the revival fire burning, many of these groups displayed Pentecostal features and were eventually organized into Pentecostal assemblies.[14] One particularly significant example of this was in the village of Penygroes in Carmarthenshire. Sarah Jones, who lived just outside the village, had been baptized in the Spirit and had begun to speak in tongues during the revival. Reports conflict over whether this happened in 1904 or very early in 1906, but it was certainly prior to the first Pentecostal baptisms in the Spirit in England in 1907 and also prior to Azusa Street, where the revival did not begin until later in 1906. Jones was known for exercising several gifts of the Spirit, including prophecy and healing, in addition to tongues. Even Evan Roberts came to visit Jones.[15] A group of children of the revival in the village of Penygroes maintained a strong emphasis on the baptism and gifts of the Holy Spirit and would become the mother assembly of the Apostolic Church, a church with twenty million members around the world today.[16]

Another Pentecostal group in Wales, predating any contacts with England or America, was to be found in Pen-y-Fai (near Bridgend). There, in the Welsh Baptist church, a Mr. Tomlinson was baptized in the Spirit during the sermon one Sunday morning in 1906 and "began to speak in a new unlearned tongue, and fell to the floor."[17] The minister, Pastor Hill, recognized this as the work of God and so began meetings for people to seek the baptism of the Holy Spirit, where "many came into this experience of the Spirit's fullness."[18]

---

14. James Robinson, *Pentecostal Origins: Early Pentecostalism in Ireland in the Context of the British Isles*, Studies in Evangelical History and Thought (Milton Keynes: Paternoster, 2005), 14.
15. Gibbard, *Fire on the Altar*, 182.
16. Already during the revival itself, people in Penygroes, including D. P. Williams (who would go on to become the first president of the Apostolic Church), witnessed speaking in tongues; see Williams, *Souvenir*, 9; Thomas Napier Turnbull, *What God Hath Wrought: A Short History of the Apostolic Church* (Bradford: Puritan Press, 1959), 18. Williams recounts that "the great outpouring of the Holy Spirit" in the 1904 revival was a "manifestation of power beyond human management," in which "many were heard speaking with tongues and prophesying. So great was the visitation in Penygroes and the districts that nights were spent in the churches. Many witnessed to God's healing power in their bodies" (*Prophetical Ministry*, 98–99). Rees Evans, another participant in the revival in the village, tells us that in Penygroes itself the revival did not die out in 1905, but rather "these flames of enthusiasm carried on for about seven years," which would mean that there was no clear distinction between the end of the Welsh Revival and the beginning of Pentecostalism in Penygroes. See Rees Evans, *Precious Jewels From the 1904 Revival in Wales* (Penygroes: n.p., 1963), 6.
17. David R. J. Ollerton, *The Revival's Children: Early Welsh Pentecostalism in the Growth of Bethlehem Pentecost Church, Cefn Cribwr* (Bridgend: n.p., 1980), 14.
18. Ollerton, *The Revival's Children*, 14.

India: The Mukti Mission

In March 1905, a revival broke out in the Khasi Hills in Assam (now in Meghalaya state) in the northeast of India. Welsh Calvinistic Methodist missionaries and the Indian Christians with whom they worked had been praying for a great outpouring of the Holy Spirit for three years.[19] They were encouraged in their prayers when news reached them of the revival in Wales. Several thousand people came to faith in Christ, and the revival involved prophecies, visions, and miracles.

A few months later, revival came to the Mukti Mission in Kedgaon, in what is now Maharashtra state in the west of India. Pandita Ramabai had founded Mukti as a self-sufficient community for dispossessed women and children. In January 1905 she issued a call for prayer, and 550 women began meeting to pray twice each day. At the end of June 1905, the revival began with people being baptized in the Holy Spirit. Among them were several missionaries who had come to Mukti to work with Ramabai, including the American Minnie Abrams. Prophecies and miracles were also a feature of the Mukti Revival. Soon, reports of similar revivals were coming from various places across India.

In the spring and summer of 1906 several people in Manmad and Bombay (now Mumbai) spoke in tongues, and the same happened at Mukti later in the year. Writing in 1907, Ramabai described how people were speaking "in various unknown tongues as the Spirit teaches them to speak, and gradually get to a place where they are in unbroken communion with God."[20] Ramabai and Abrams saw great value in tongues but did not see speaking in tongues as indispensable evidence of baptism in the Spirit. Abrams wrote that "all may and should receive this sign, yet we dare not say that no one is Spirit-baptized who has not received this sign."[21]

This, again, was a Pentecostal revival that began before the Azusa Street Revival. News of the events in India were reported in the earliest British and American Pentecostal publications. Through these reports, Abrams's book *The Baptism of the Holy Ghost and Fire* (1906), and her travels, the revival in India, like the Welsh Revival, was influential in the emergence of Pentecostalism in other regions. For example, Abrams sent a copy of her book

---

19. The Welsh Calvinistic Methodists had also begun to use the word "Presbyterian," and so were known by both names.
20. Pandita Ramabai, as quoted in R. V. Burgess, "Ramabai, Sarasvati Mary (Pandita)," in *New International Dictionary of Pentecostal Charismatic Movements*, eds. Stanley M. Burgess and Eduard M. van der Maas (Grand Rapids: Zondervan, 2002), 1018. Burgess is quoting from an article written by Ramabai in the *Mukti Prayer-Bell* in 1907, but he does not provide a reference.
21. Minnie Abrams, "A Message from Mukti," *Confidence* (September 15, 1908): 14. Many early Pentecostal leaders in Europe, as well as William Seymour in the United States, later came to hold this position.

to a former classmate in Chile, which was a significant factor in the emergence of Pentecostalism in that country. Although the events at Mukti had an impact far beyond its own region, Ramabai and the Mukti Mission later "backed out of the Pentecostal movement and interpreted the revival there as part of the larger evangelical awakening in the first decade of the twentieth century."[22]

Summary

Before the revival at Azusa Street in Los Angeles, significant revivals in other parts of the world, which would have a major impact on the emergence of Pentecostalism, had already begun. The Welsh Revival of 1904–1905 was steeped in the spirituality of the long Welsh Calvinistic Methodist revival tradition, which could ultimately trace the roots of its understanding of the subsequent experience of the Holy Spirit back to the Puritan emphasis on the Spirit's sealing work of assurance. British Pentecostalism (and in those countries where Pentecostalism spread from Britain) traces its origins directly to this revival. The revivals in India were influenced by reports of the revival in Wales, and both the Welsh and Indian revivals had an impact on Azusa Street.

REFLECTION QUESTIONS

1. How does the Welsh Revival connect Pentecostalism with Puritanism?
2. Which aspects of the Welsh Revival could be described as Pentecostal?
3. In what ways does British Pentecostalism find its origins in the Welsh Revival?
4. What were the significant features of the Indian revivals for the emergence of Pentecostalism?
5. How did Pandita Ramabai and Minnie Abrams understand the connection between speaking in tongues and the baptism in the Holy Spirit?

---

22. Michael Bergunder, *The South Indian Pentecostal Movement in the Twentieth Century*, Studies in the History of Christian Missions (Grand Rapids: Eerdmans, 2008), 24.

QUESTION 4

How Did Pentecostalism Begin in the United States?

A few years before the revival broke out in Wales, a series of events began in the United States which, like the influence of the Welsh Revival, would eventually feed into the events at Azusa Street in Los Angeles.

Topeka

Charles Fox Parham (1873–1929) was a Holiness preacher who had experienced divine healing while he was a college student. In the summer of 1900, he spent twelve weeks travelling round various Holiness centers in the United States. During this trip, at the Bible school of Frank Sandford in Shiloh in Maine, Parham witnessed people speaking in tongues.[1] After returning to his home in Topeka, Kansas, Parham established a Bible school where he taught Holiness doctrine. In December 1900, Parham challenged his thirty-four students to find "the Bible evidence of the Baptism of the Holy Ghost." Notably (as he himself admits), he had already led them to Acts 2 when he set this task.[2]

We have two accounts of what happened next. According to Parham, the students unanimously and independently agreed that speaking in tongues was the indisputable scriptural evidence of the baptism in the Spirit. He then relays that, at the New Year's Eve Watchnight Service (December 31, 1900), Agnes Ozman asked him to lay hands on her and pray for the baptism of the Spirit with the "biblical sign." Parham recounts that after praying for Ozman,

1. James R. Goff, Jr., *Fields White unto Harvest: Charles F. Parham and the Missionary Origins of Pentecostalism* (Fayetteville: University of Arkansas Press, 1988), 73.
2. Charles Fox Parham, *Apostolic Faith* 2 (July 1926): 2; quoted in Goff, *Fields White unto Harvest,* 66.

"a halo seemed to surround her head and face, and she began speaking in the Chinese language, and was unable to speak English for three days."[3]

Agnes Ozman's own account is somewhat different. She dates her experience to the evening of January 1, 1901, writing, "I did not know that I would talk with tongues when I received the Baptism."[4] Further, she does not mention any previous consensus among the students about the "biblical sign," but rather she says she found biblical support for her experience only *after* it had happened.[5] Here is Ozman's description of what happened when she was prayed for on January 1: "It was as hands were laid upon my head that the Holy Spirit fell upon me and I began to speak in tongues, glorifying God. I talked several languages, and it was clearly manifest when a new dialect was spoken. I had the added joy and glory my heart longed for, and a depth of the presence of the Lord within that I never knew before. It was as if rivers of living water were proceeding from my innermost being."[6] Later, she writes that she came to understand this as similar to what happened to the disciples in Ephesus in Acts 19:6.[7]

However, this New Year's prayer meeting was not the first time Ozman had spoken in tongues. She wrote that during a period of prayer and fasting three weeks earlier, the Lord "gave us blessed times of refreshing [and] while three of us girls were in prayer, I spoke three words in another tongue. While I did not understand this manifestation then as I do now, yet it was a very precious and sacred experience, and was treasured up in our hearts. Not feeling satisfied with the above experience and having a great burden within, which I knew God could relieve, I decided, January 1, 1901, to obey the Word and have hands laid upon me and prayer offered that I might receive the baptism in the Spirit."[8] Yet, in Ozman's estimation, something new did happen on January 1. Not only did she speak in tongues, but, as she writes, "heaven's glory filled [her] soul." Afterward she encouraged people "not to seek for tongues but for the baptism in the Holy Spirit."[9]

After some time, however, Ozman's experience led her into "spiritual darkness." She explained: "I did as I see so many others are doing in these days, rested and revelled in tongues and other demonstrations instead of resting alone in God."[10] This experience of spiritual darkness did not turn Ozman

---

3. Parham, *Apostolic Faith* 2; quoted in Goff, *Fields White unto Harvest*, 67.
4. Agnes O. LaBerge, *What God Hath Wrought* (Chicago: Herald, 1921), 28–29. LaBerge was Ozman's married name.
5. LaBerge, *What God Hath Wrought*, 29.
6. Stanley H. Frodsham, *With Signs Following: The Story of the Latter Day Pentecostal Revival* (Springfield, MO: Gospel Publishing House, 1926), 11.
7. Agnes Ozman, "The First One to Speak in Tongues," *Latter Rain Evangel* (January 1909): 2.
8. Ozman, "First One," 2.
9. Ozman, "First One," 2.
10. Ozman, "First One," 2.

against her Pentecostal experience but rather led her to see that the gifts of the Holy Spirit must be kept in their proper place. Resting and rejoicing in the gifts, rather than the Giver, is the path to spiritual darkness.

The discrepancies between Parham's and Ozman's accounts of these events has, as Parham's biographer James Goff noted, "cast some doubt upon Parham's true role in the development of Pentecostal theology."[11] Some claim Parham was the originator of the teaching that speaking in tongues is the initial evidence of the baptism in the Spirit. However, both Parham's and Ozman's accounts "downplay the direct hand Parham had in formulating this crucial tongues-as-evidence position and passing it on to the Bethel community."[12] Yet Goff argues that Parham had actually "solidified the Holy Spirit baptism confirmed by 'mission tongues' idea by the time he opened Bethel Bible College" in 1900, convinced that he had "a new message for world evangelism."[13]

Parham's Ministry and Influence After Topeka

Whatever the actual sequence of events at the turn of the twentieth century in Topeka, a revival was *not* the result. Enthusiasm for Parham's teaching quickly diminished. In late 1903, however, his teaching on tongues as the sign of the baptism in the Spirit alongside an emphasis on divine healing resulted in a large number of conversions and healings in Galena, Kansas. There, several hundred people were baptized in the Spirit, accompanied by the experience of speaking in tongues. Parham quickly established a church at a rural crossroads in Keelville, where the first Apostolic Faith meeting hall was built.[14] This enabled Parham to then open a new Bible school in Houston, Texas, in 1905. The school remained very small, with only about twenty-five students.[15] One of the students who heard Parham's teaching here, however, was William Seymour.[16]

By 1906, a number of Apostolic Faith assemblies had been established in Texas and Kansas, which Parham organized into a federation with himself as

---

11. Goff, *Fields White unto Harvest*, 71–72.
12. Goff, *Fields White unto Harvest*, 72.
13. Goff, *Fields White unto Harvest*, 74. Another recent biographer is uncertain, noting the difference between Parham's earlier and later accounts. See Larry Martin, *Charles Fox Parham: The Unlikely Father of Modern Pentecostalism* (New Kensington, PA: Whitaker House, 2022), 55.
14. Goff, *Fields White unto Harvest*, 90–94.
15. Robert Owens, "The Azusa Street Revival: The Pentecostal Movement Begins in America," in *The Century of the Holy Spirit: 100 Years of Pentecostal and Charismatic Renewal*, ed. Vinson Synan (Nashville: Thomas Nelson, 2001), 44.
16. Seymour, an African American, was not allowed to join the classes due to racial segregation laws but was permitted only to listen through an open door or window. As Gastón Espinosa points out, this "affirmed the letter but violated the spirit of the Jim Crow segregation laws in Houston." See Gastón Espinosa, *William J. Seymour and the Origins of Global Pentecostalism* (Durham, NC: Duke University Press, 2014), 50.

"projector." Yet, by 1907 Parham's influence had been destroyed by scandal, leaving him isolated from the emerging Pentecostal movement. When he died in 1929, he was virtually unknown among the second generation of Pentecostals.

Despite Parham's later obscurity, he did make some significant contributions to the emergence of the Pentecostal movement. First, it was Parham who introduced the doctrine of speaking in tongues as the initial physical evidence of the baptism in the Holy Spirit.[17] Although not all Pentecostals would accept the doctrine of initial physical evidence, the close connection established by Parham between speaking in tongues and the baptism in the Holy Spirit would serve to give emerging Pentecostalism a distinct identifying mark in an era when the expectation of a post-conversion baptism in the Holy Spirit was much more widely held among various types of evangelicals. Second, Parham placed a strong missionary emphasis on the baptism in the Spirit, even though he himself did not send out any missionaries. This centrality of missions to Pentecostalism would continue to grow, even as Parham's initial theory of "missionary tongues" was rejected.

Los Angeles

In 1904 an English minister, Joseph Smale, was pastoring a Baptist church in Los Angeles and returned home to the United Kingdom for a break. While there, he met Evan Roberts and witnessed the Welsh Revival. Upon returning to California, Smale started holding daily meetings in the hope that the revival would come to Los Angeles. After nineteen weeks the church board objected, and Smale left the Baptist pastorate to form a new church in the city. In the First New Testament Church (as this new congregation was known), Smale taught about the baptism of the Spirit and encouraged members to seek the experience. Eventually, on Easter Sunday 1906, Jennie Moore (who would later marry William Seymour) was baptized in the Spirit and spoke in tongues at Smale's church. Initially this caused some confusion (Bartleman describes the reaction as "a great stir"), as Smale and the church had not been expecting tongues. But by June, the church had adopted a position of full freedom in the Spirit in its services.[18]

News of the Welsh Revival had also reached another minister in Los Angeles, the itinerant evangelist Frank Bartleman. Bartleman wrote to Evan Roberts to ask the people of Wales to pray for the people of California. Roberts wrote back, encouraging Bartleman to hold daily meetings to seek revival.[19]

---

17. This doctrine is covered in question 20.
18. For Bartleman's account, see Frank Bartleman, *Azusa Street: An Eyewitness Account* (Gainesville, FL: Bridge-Logos, 1980), 49. For an academic account of Smale's role in the emergence of Pentecostalism, see Tim Welch, *Joseph Smale: God's Moses for Pentecostalism* (Milton Keynes: Paternoster, 2013).
19. Bartleman, *Azusa Street*, 18.

When revival broke out at Azusa Street, Bartleman wrote eyewitness accounts of what took place.

William J. Seymour

William Joseph Seymour arrived in Los Angeles from Houston on February 22, 1906. He had been attending Parham's Bible school in Houston, where, as an African American, he was not legally allowed to sit in the same classroom with the white students and, so, sat in the hallway and listened to the classes through an open door.[20] From Parham, Seymour imbibed Holiness teaching with the addition of the baptism of the Holy Spirit as a "third experience" distinct in time and nature from both conversion and entire sanctification.[21] Having moved to Los Angeles to take up the pastorate of a small Holiness congregation, Seymour preached his very first sermon on Acts 2:4, identifying speaking in tongues as the biblical evidence of the baptism in the Spirit. Although he had not yet experienced the baptism of the Spirit himself, he was convinced of its necessity. A week later, Seymour found himself locked out of the church before the evening service due to his teaching.[22]

Finding himself not only churchless but homeless in a new city, Seymour was invited to stay with a couple from the church. They began to pray together, and other members from the church started to join them. Soon the prayer meeting outgrew the house and moved to the home of another member of the church on North Bonnie Bray Street.[23] On April 6, the group (all African American) began to fast as well as pray for the baptism in the Spirit. They planned to fast for ten days while praying and meditating on Acts 2:1–4 until they had the same experience. Only three days later, on April 9, people began to be baptized in the Spirit, accompanied by speaking in tongues.[24] Seymour himself received the Pentecostal baptism on April 12, after a night spent in prayer. He and a white man spent the night praying side by side and received the baptism in the Spirit together.[25]

The meetings moved to the front porch, where a racially mixed crowd gathered to hear Seymour preach from a makeshift pulpit. As the crowds grew

---

20. Synan, *Holiness-Pentecostal Tradition*, 93.
21. Synan, *Holiness-Pentecostal Tradition*, 93. While this teaching is still held by some Wesleyan Holiness Pentecostals (particularly in the United States), it is not accepted by the majority of Pentecostals and is completely unknown in many other parts of the world. The mainstream of American Pentecostalism rejected this three-experience view in the years between William Durham's teaching of the Finished Work view in 1910 and the drawing-up of the Assemblies of God Statement of Fundamental Truths in 1916.
22. Cecil M. Robeck, Jr., *The Azusa Street Mission and Revival: The Birth of the Global Pentecostal Movement* (Nashville: Thomas Nelson, 2006), 62–63.
23. Robeck, *Azusa Street*, 64–65.
24. Espinosa, *William J. Seymour*, 54–55.
25. Espinosa, *William J. Seymour*, 56.

over the next few days, the porch collapsed (although no one was hurt).[26] A larger venue was needed. The group found an abandoned African Methodist Episcopal Church building on Azusa Street, which had most recently been used as stables.

Azusa Street

The first person baptized in the Spirit at Azusa Street received the baptism even before meetings began. On Friday, April 13, as people from the Bonnie Bray Street meetings were working to prepare the building for use, a Mexican American day worker was pulled aside from his work by an African American woman who, after a lively discussion, prayed for him. He was overcome by the power of the Spirit and fell to his knees in tears amid the mess of building work. He then invited many Spanish-speakers to the meetings (both Mexican Americans and Mexican immigrants). Eyewitness reports say that hundreds accepted the invitation and attended. These Spanish speakers then quickly took the message to Spanish-speaking communities across the city, throughout California, and into northern Mexico.[27]

After the Azusa Street Mission opened at Easter of 1906, Seymour conducted meetings three times each day, seven days each week (with the services often continuing so long they blended into one another). There were very regular reports of people being converted and baptized in the Spirit during the meetings, as well as people being healed and demons being cast out. After the services, people would gather upstairs to "tarry" for the baptism in the Holy Spirit. (The historic Pentecostal practice of "tarrying" involved spending time in prayer and quiet meditation while waiting for the Lord to pour out his Spirit.)[28] No musical instruments were used to accompany worship in Azusa Street.[29]

People were drawn to Azusa Street from across the United States and beyond, with many significant leaders receiving the baptism of the Holy Spirit there and taking the Pentecostal message back to their home churches—and sometimes, as in the cases of Gaston Barnabas Cashwell and Charles Harrison Mason, to whole denominations.[30] As the revival reached its peak, between eight hundred and fifteen hundred people attended the Mission on Sundays.[31]

---

26. Robeck, *Azusa Street*, 69; Vinson Synan, *The Holiness-Pentecostal Tradition: Charismatic Movements in the Twentieth Century* (Grand Rapids: Eerdmans, 1997), 96.
27. Espinosa, *William J. Seymour*, 59.
28. Espinosa, *William J. Seymour*, 60–61.
29. Bartleman, *Azusa Street*, 64.
30. Ithiel C. Clemmons, *Bishop C. H. Mason and the Roots of the Church of God in Christ* (Largo, MD: Pneuma Life, 1996), 46; see also Stanley H. Frodsham, *With Signs Following: The Story of the Pentecostal Revival in the Twentieth Century*, rev. ed. (Springfield, MO: Gospel Publishing House, 1941), 41–43.
31. Espinosa, *William J. Seymour*, 68.

Visitors came to the revival in Azusa Street from around the world. Very soon, missionaries were also being sent out from Azusa Street. Together with the wide circulation of the revival's magazine, *The Apostolic Faith*, this ensured that Azusa Street would become one of the most influential international centers of the Pentecostal movement. Espinosa argues that "Seymour and Azusa along with those they influenced were the single most important catalyst for the origins and spread [of Pentecostalism] prior to 1912 globally."[32] Yet, Seymour himself saw the revival in Azusa Street as the latest in a series of revivals, the most recent having been the Welsh Revival of the previous year. When reports of the Mukti Revival in India reached Los Angeles, Seymour reported this as a parallel revival.[33] Wales, Azusa Street, and Mukti were all seen as part of one larger whole.

Summary

Both Topeka and Los Angeles played an important role in the emergence of Pentecostalism in the United States and, via Azusa Street, beyond. While racism stopped Seymour from entering the classroom in Houston, he would later see racial and ethnic barriers broken down through the love of the powerful outpouring of the Holy Spirit during the revival at Azusa Street. The revival in Los Angeles drew together early Pentecostal leaders from around the United States and other countries, and was also a catalyst in sending out Pentecostal missionaries to other parts of the world.

REFLECTION QUESTIONS

1. What can we learn from Agnes Ozman's experience of spiritual darkness?
2. How did Charles Fox Parham contribute to the beginnings of Pentecostalism?
3. How had Christians in Los Angeles been prepared for revival before it began?
4. How did William Seymour contribute to the emergence of Pentecostalism?
5. What was the Pentecostal practice of tarrying?

---

32. Espinosa, *William J. Seymour*, 70.
33. Espinosa, *William J. Seymour*, 56.

QUESTION 5

How Did Pentecostalism Begin in Canada, Norway, England, and Chile?

We have already seen that Pentecostalism began to emerge organically from the Welsh Revival in Wales, as well as looked at two of the most significant aspects of the emergence of Pentecostalism in the United States. However, there were many other countries where Pentecostalism began somewhat organically, without American missionaries or significant American influence. In this chapter we shall give our attention to just a few.

Canada: Toronto's East End Revival

Topeka and Los Angeles might be the most famous points of origin for Pentecostalism in North America, but they were not alone. In Canada there was also a Pentecostal revival in 1906, which the evidence suggests was completely independent of what was happening in the United States. The East End Mission was established in the city of Toronto in May 1906 by James and Ellen Hebden, an English couple who had moved to Canada a year and a half earlier. Originally established as a healing mission, it was to be transformed into a Pentecostal work after November 17, 1906, when Ellen Hebden was baptized in the Spirit, accompanied by speaking in tongues. Over the next few months, seventy to eighty people had the same experience in the East End Mission. News spread across Canada and into the United States, and people began to travel to Toronto seeking the baptism in the Spirit. The Hebdens published Canada's first Pentecostal magazine, organized Canada's first Pentecostal conventions and camp meetings, and sent out Canada's first Pentecostal missionary.[1]

1. Adam Stewart, "From Monogenesis to Polygenesis in Pentecostal Origins: A Survey of the Evidence from the Azusa Street, Hebden and Mukti Missions," *Penteco Studies* 13, no. 2 (2014): 156–57.

There is no connection between the Hebdens and William Seymour, nor is there any evidence that the Hebdens had any knowledge of the Azusa Street revival. Rather, "both Ellen's Spirit baptism and the early Pentecostal movement in Canada, appear to have originated independent of any influence from Pentecostalism in the United States."[2] As in Britain, the Hebdens' major theological influences came from Keswick spirituality rather than the Wesleyan Holiness movement.[3]

Norway: Thomas Ball Barratt in Kristiania (Oslo)

A holiness movement developed in Scandinavia out of Lutheran Pietism, with some influence from Methodist theology. For these Scandinavian Christians, the Christian life was seen as one of continual growth in grace.[4] As was the case in Britain, Wesleyan Holiness teaching had little impact in Scandinavia: "The Holiness Movement in Scandinavia was never like that in the U.S.A. even though it was influenced by American theologians and mission practitioners. In Scandinavia, the North American sources were read through the lenses of the Lutheran State church traditions, especially German and Scandinavian Pietism. It was also influenced by the Baptists, Free Baptists, and Brethren. The issues in contention in the North American context generally did not have currency here. American perfectionism as applied to spirituality (for example the distinction between 'entire sanctification' and 'gradual sanctification') had minimal influence."[5]

In September 1906, a Norwegian Methodist minister, Thomas Ball Barratt, read a copy of the first issue of *The Apostolic Faith* (the magazine produced at Azusa Street), while staying in New York. Inspired by what he read, he wrote letters to Azusa Street and received replies from people involved in the revival there (though, significantly, not from William Seymour). He immediately began to seek this experience of the baptism of the Holy Spirit. On October 7 he had a powerful experience of the Holy Spirit. Although he did not speak in tongues then, on November 15, at a service with some African American believers in New York, a woman named Lucy Leatherman—who had just returned from Azusa Street—prayed for him, and he did. However, this was the full extent of his connection with the Los Angeles revival. Barratt himself never went to Azusa Street. His own theological interpretation of his experience was also somewhat different from the current understanding at Azusa Street. He interpreted speaking in tongues as a "seal" of his baptism in the Spirit rather than as the ability to speak a foreign language.[6]

---

2. Stewart, "Monogenesis to Polygenesis," 160.
3. Stewart, "Monogenesis to Polygenesis," 160.
4. David Bundy, *Visions of Apostolic Mission: Scandinavian Pentecostal Mission to 1935*, Studia Histroico-Ecclesiastica Upsaliensia 45 (Uppsala: Uppsala Universitet, 2009), 86.
5. Bundy, *Visions of Apostolic Mission*, 85.
6. Bundy, *Visions of Apostolic Mission*, 169.

Barratt wrote an essay on the baptism in the Spirit, which he sent to William Seymour for publication. However, the manuscript was rejected due to theological differences. In it, Barratt rejected the necessity of tongues as the sign of the baptism in the Spirit. As David Bundy has pointed out, in this essay we see the first indications of some divergences between European and American Pentecostalism.[7]

Upon his return to Kristiania (present-day Oslo), Barratt taught on the baptism in the Holy Spirit in his church, and soon daily services were being held with two hundred to three hundred people in attendance. This mission was eventually formally organized into a Pentecostal church in 1910.[8] However, even before Barratt's mission was formally organized, an earlier Pentecostal assembly had been established in Skien by a then-Baptist pastor, Carl Magnus Seehus, whose wife Ida Betea Seehus had been baptized in the Spirit accompanied by speaking in tongues while praying by herself in 1905. Initially, her husband was skeptical of her experience, but after hearing the reports of Barratt's ministry in Oslo he embarked upon a major systematic Bible study of the theme and concluded that it was indeed of God. When many in their Baptist church rejected the teaching, Seehus began what was possibly the first officially established Pentecostal assembly in continental Europe.[9]

In January 1907, shortly after his arrival back in Norway and the beginning of his Pentecostal meetings, Barratt wrote a description of what was happening:

> God is wonderfully demonstrating His power here in the Norwegian capital. . . . Folk from all denominations are rushing to the meetings. Over twenty have received their Pentecost and are speaking in tongues. Several have . . . had heavenly visions. Some have seen Jesus at our meetings, and the tongues of fire have been seen over my head again by a free-thinker, convincing him of the power of God. Many are seeking salvation and souls are being gloriously saved. . . . Some of the languages spoken are European. One man was thrown on his back, a preacher, last Sunday morning . . . and when he rose he spoke in four languages, one of these was English. He could speak none of them before. After that, he

---

7. Bundy, *Visions of Apostolic Mission*, 170–71.
8. Bundy, *Visions of Apostolic Mission*, 176–77.
9. Karl Inge Tangen, "Pentecostal Movements in Norway," in *Global Renewal Christianity: Volume 4 Europe and North America*, eds. Vinson Synan and Amos Yong (Lake Mary, FL: Charisma House, 2017), 199.

> prophesied and invited sinners to come to Christ. Numbers threw themselves down and cried for salvation.[10]

Ministers from several European countries, many of whom would go on to be major early Pentecostal leaders, traveled to Oslo to witness the revival. Alexander Boddy was overwhelmed by what he experienced there. "My four days in Christiania cannot be forgotten," he wrote. "I stood with Evan Roberts at the Tonypandy meetings [during the Welsh Revival], but never have I witnessed such scenes as in Norway, and soon I believe they will be witnessed in England."[11] Barratt himself also traveled to Sweden, Denmark, Germany, the United Kingdom, Palestine, Syria, Lebanon, India, the Netherlands, Finland, Iceland, Italy, Switzerland, Latvia, and Poland, spreading the Pentecostal message.[12]

Although Barratt was encouraged to seek the baptism in the Spirit by reading two issues of their magazine and some letters from Azusa Street, he rarely referred to Azusa Street or American Pentecostalism when he returned to Norway. As Bundy points out, "American Pentecostal writings and narratives of American Pentecostal experiences are remarkably absent throughout the Nordic countries during this period."[13] There was a connection to Azusa Street in Barratt's baptism in the Spirit and what happened afterward in Norway, but it was at a distance, in much the same way that people in Los Angeles had been inspired by what they had read at a distance about the Welsh Revival.

England: Pentecost in Brixton

Very early in the New Year of 1907, in a house on Akerman Road in Brixton, a district in south London, Mrs. Catherine Price was kneeling down in prayer, quietly worshipping the Lord. Deeply stirred by accounts of the Welsh Revival and the recent news of what was happening on Azusa Street, Catherine and her husband had been seeking the Lord together in prayer every evening for an outpouring of the Holy Spirit.[14] As she worshipped her Savior, she had a vision of Jesus on the cross:

> It was dark. He extended His arms to me and said, "Come to Me." Oh! the unutterable love and compassion in His voice. I obeyed and groaned in the Spirit. . . . Then the darkness

10. T. B. Barratt, "In Norway, 29th January, 1907," *Apostolic Faith* 1, no. 6 (February–March 1907): 1.
11. Alexander Boddy, "Tongues in Norway: A Pentecostal Experience," *Leaflets on Tongues,* no. 6.
12. Bundy, *Visions of Apostolic Mission*, 180–226.
13. Bundy, *Visions of Apostolic Mission*, 487.
14. T. E. H., "Echoes from Heathfield," *Confidence* 9, no. 10 (October 1916): 167.

> fled, and I was raised up with Him in glory. Involuntarily, I threw up my arms to praise Him, and suddenly they seemed charged with electricity, and a power came upon me and I praised him in another tongue. He immediately gave the interpretation, which was "Glory to Jesus—the bleeding Lamb." The next morning the Holy Ghost came in mighty power . . . speaking in four or five languages, sometimes giving the interpretation. For one and a half hours this continued. . . . The glory of God filled my soul.[15]

This was the first baptism in the Spirit accompanied by speaking in tongues of the Pentecostal revival in England. Catherine Price had read about people speaking in tongues, but she had not had any contact with any other center of Pentecostal revival.[16]

The next evening, she went to a church meeting and felt a great burden to give a testimony of what had happened. However, when she opened her mouth, she yet again started speaking in another language. The minister asked her if she knew the language she was speaking, and when she replied that she did not, he told her that if it were from the Lord, the Lord would give the interpretation if she asked for it. So she did ask the Lord, and then gave an interpretation. The result was "conviction, confession, and wholehearted yieldedness to the Lord Jesus all over the hall."[17] Later that year, Catherine Price opened her house for prayer meetings, which became the first Pentecostal meetings in London.

England: The Boddys and Sunderland

In the north of England, the Reverend Alexander Boddy (1854–1930), vicar of Monkwearmouth in Sunderland, and his wife Mary had been seeking the baptism in the Holy Spirit for several years. Mary Boddy had been healed from asthma in 1899 and since then had prayed for people for healing, while Alexander anointed them with oil.[18] Alexander Boddy visited Wales during the revival and upon his return home began to pray with his wife and a group of parishioners for the revival to spread to the northeast of England. When Boddy heard news of Azusa Street, he wanted to find a way to visit. However,

15. Catherine Price's testimony, quoted in A. A. Boddy, "The Pentecostal Movement," *Confidence* 3, no. 8 (August 1910): 195.
16. Neil Hudson, "The Earliest Days of British Pentecostalism," *Journal of the European Pentecostal Theological Association* 21 (2001): 51–52.
17. Donald Gee, *The Pentecostal Movement: A Short History and an Interpretation for British Readers* (London: Victory Press, 1941), 23.
18. Timothy B. Walsh, *To Meet and Satisfy a Very Hungry People: The Origins and Fortunes of English Pentecostalism, 1907–1925*, Studies in Evangelical History and Thought (Milton Keynes: Paternoster, 2012), 38.

he then heard of the revival in Oslo and traveled there instead. Hugely impressed by what he saw of the power of God in Oslo, Boddy invited T. B. Barratt to come to Sunderland in September 1907.

When Barratt came to Sunderland, each day he would preach a gospel message and at the end invite only those who were seeking the baptism in the Holy Spirit to remain behind in the hall for a tarry meeting. On September 11, 1907, Barratt prayed for Mary Boddy, who said she felt nothing at all but "knew God had come" and so continued to worship, and found that her words had turned to tongues, accompanied by a vision of the blood of Jesus.[19] A pastor was baptized in the Spirit the following night, speaking in tongues and prophesying that "the prophets of the Lord have gone astray, they have spurned the holy blood."[20] Both in Brixton and in Sunderland the baptism of the Holy Spirit was strongly associated with the centrality of the blood of Jesus. Alexander Boddy was not baptized in the Spirit until December 2, 1907, after Barratt had returned to Norway. Boddy estimated that he was the fiftieth person to speak in tongues in Sunderland.

From Barratt's visit until the outbreak of the First World War, Boddy's church in Sunderland became a major center for Pentecostalism in the United Kingdom and beyond.[21] Boddy started a series of annual Whitsun (i.e., Pentecost) conventions and established a magazine, *Confidence: A Pentecostal Paper for Great Britain*. The magazine connected British Pentecostals with one another and provided news of where and how the revival was spreading, in the UK and around the world. The Whitsun Convention drew together many of the emerging leaders of British Pentecostalism, as well as Pentecostal leaders from Germany and the Netherlands, providing a basis for some European Pentecostal consensus in the coming years.[22] As Neil Hudson has noted, this "Western European emphasis presented British Pentecostalism with distinctives that differed from their American counterparts."[23]

Like other early Pentecostals in Britain, Boddy was influenced by the Welsh Revival and Keswick.[24] Unlike most other British Pentecostal leaders,

---

19. Mary Boddy, "Testimony of a Vicar's Wife," *Apostolic Faith* 1, no. 11 (October–January 1908): 1.
20. T. B. Barratt, "How Pentecost Came to Great Britain in 1907," *Redemption Tidings* 9, no. 11 (November 1933): 4.
21. Hudson, "Earliest Days," 53.
22. Hudson, "Earliest Days," 61–67.
23. Hudson, "Earliest Days," 66.
24. Kimberley Ervin Alexander has attempted to use Boddy to argue for Wesleyan roots for British Pentecostalism. See Kimberley Ervin Alexander, "Alexander A. Boddy, the Pentecostal League of Prayer, and the Wesleyan Roots of British Pentecostalism," in *Holiness and Pentecostal Movements: Intertwined Pasts, Presents, Futures*, eds. David Bundy, Geordan Hammond, and David Sang-Ehil Han (University Park: Pennsylvania State University Press, 2022), 72–95. While it is incontrovertible that Boddy was, for a time, a member of Reader Harris's Pentecostal League of Prayer, the conclusion that "the

he was, and continued to be, a priest in the Church of England. This was a significant factor in the waning of Boddy's influence as the British Pentecostal denominations emerged.

Chile

Willis Hoover was an American Methodist minister in Chile. His wife Mary was a close friend and former classmate of Minnie Abrams, who in 1907 sent Mary a copy of her book, *The Baptism of the Holy Ghost and Fire*. Mary then began writing to Pentecostal leaders around the world, and in 1909 she and her husband were both baptized in the Spirit. Many members of Hoover's congregation and two nearby congregations also received this Pentecostal experience. This led to the establishment of the Methodist Pentecostal Church of Chile in 1910. Although the Hoovers had correspondence with various Pentecostal leaders, Chilean Pentecostalism began without the influence of missionaries from overseas or visits to Azusa Street or another revival center. The isolation of Chile from other early Pentecostal centers is also seen in the fact that Chilean Pentecostals retained infant baptism, which was almost universally rejected by classical Pentecostals in the rest of the world.

Summary

Pentecostalism is not an exclusively American-originated phenomenon. While some early Pentecostal leaders in other parts of the world (like T. B. Barratt) had some knowledge of Azusa Street or some indirect connections, others (like James and Ellen Hebden) appear to have had no knowledge of the Los Angeles revival. In each of these cases, even when there was some knowledge of the American revival, the Pentecostal movement emerged in its own way and without direct American influence. Canada, Norway, England, and Chile—not to mention Wales, in addition to many other countries—each had their own Pentecostal revivals leading to the establishment of their own forms of Pentecostalism, which, while having much in common with the American movement, also had their own distinctive features.

---

earliest and most influential published expression of Pentecostalism in England may be categorized as Wesleyan Holiness Pentecostal, as much as many of the American expressions may be so categorized" is much too great a leap. Even if it were true that Boddy himself thought like an American Wesleyan Holiness Pentecostal, he expressed it in such a way that no other British Pentecostal leader picked it up from him. None of the three British Pentecostal denominations that emerged in the early years (the Apostolic Church, Elim, and the Assemblies of God) took the Wesleyan Holiness position, and none of their leaders argued for such a position. Wesleyan Holiness Pentecostalism was an American phenomenon and was unknown in Britain until much later.

REFLECTION QUESTIONS

1. How did the theological background of Canadian, Norwegian, and British Pentecostalism differ from that of Azusa Street?

2. In what ways was Azusa Street influential at a distance?

3. In Brixton and Sunderland we see an association between the baptism of the Holy Spirit and the blood of Jesus. Why might the blood of Jesus be significant for the baptism in the Holy Spirit?

4. Did any of these early Pentecostals in Canada, Norway, Britain, or Chile set out with the intention of beginning a Pentecostal church?

5. What role did the Welsh Revival play in the beginnings of Pentecostalism in England?

SECTION B

Theological Questions

QUESTION 6

How Do Pentecostals View the Bible?

Pentecostals are Bible people. "It is all right to have the signs following, but not to pin our faith on outward manifestations," wrote William Seymour. "We are to go by the word of God. Our thought must be in harmony with the Bible or else we will have a strange religion."[1] Even the Pentecostal experience of the baptism of the Holy Spirit should lead us not away from the Bible but back to it, for, as Seymour always strongly maintained, the baptism of the Holy Spirit "means to be flooded with . . . a love for the truth as it is in God's Word."[2]

This has not changed. Richard Massey concludes, "As regards the inspiration and authority of the Bible, the Pentecostal churches are still firmly within the conservative evangelical tradition. . . . The line from B. B. Warfield through to J. I. Packer is firmly held, concluding with the affirmation that 'what Scripture says, God says.'"[3] It is impossible to avoid "the central position of the Bible in all aspects of Pentecostal belief and practice."[4] The statements of faith of Pentecostal denominations of every type, all over the world, declare their faith in the inspiration and supreme authority of the Scriptures, while the lives of Pentecostal believers demonstrate their love of, and reliance upon, God's written Word.

The Inspiration of Scripture

The article on the Bible in the Confession of Faith of the Apostolic Church in Francophone Switzerland sums up what classical Pentecostals worldwide believe about the inspiration of Scripture: "The Bible is the written Word of God, inspired by Him, infallible and normative for faith and life. It is also at the

1. William J. Seymour, *Doctrines and Disciplines of the Azusa Street Apostolic Faith Mission* (Los Angeles: Apostolic Faith Mission, 1915), 92.
2. Seymour, *Doctrines and Disciplines*, 92.
3. Richard D. Massey, "The Word of God: Thus Saith the Lord," in *Pentecostal Perspectives*, ed. Keith Warrington (Carlisle: Paternoster, 1998), 64.
4. Massey, "Word of God," 79.

same time a human word, for the Holy Spirit inspired human beings to write, taking fully into account their personality and cultural and historical context. We recognise the verbal and plenary inspiration of the Holy Scriptures."[5]

Pentecostals do not ignore the human authors of Scripture and the contexts in which they lived and wrote. Scriptural inspiration is not (except in some very particular instances which are noted as such in Scripture itself) a divine dictation, but rather "God chose to transmit His Word by human instruments, delighting to use human means whenever possible to accomplish His purposes."[6] In this understanding, the "Pentecostal sits easily with conservative evangelical colleagues about how inspiration works and what it effects,"[7] holding to "the 'supervisory' or 'concursive' theory . . . which implies God working in and through the human faculties and personalities of the writers."[8]

Inspiration applies to the whole of the Bible in its very words in the original languages, not only to the ideas expressed in Scripture (Ps. 119:160; Matt. 5:18; Luke 16:17; 2 Tim. 3:16). Therefore, "the Bible does not simply contain the Word of God, but is, in reality, the . . . very Word of God inspired by the Holy Spirit."[9] This is what the confessional statement above called "verbal and plenary inspiration."[10]

The Authority of Scripture

As the fully inspired Word of God himself, the Bible is God's own voice, speaking with his authority. This is expressed in the declaration of faith of the French Assemblies of God: "The Scriptures . . . hold their inspiration and authority from God alone; they are infallible and the only norm for the life and faith of the Church. Therefore, neither customs nor decrees, neither visions nor miracles, nor any other revelation or tradition can ever modify or add to the Scriptures. All things must be examined, regulated and reformed according to Scriptures which contain everything which is necessary for salvation and for the edification of the Church."[11] As "our highest authority," no

5. Église Apostolique Suisse Romande, *Confession de Foi*, Article 5; all translations, unless otherwise noted, are my own.
6. Anthony D. Palma, *The Holy Spirit: A Pentecostal Perspective* (Springfield, MO: Logion, 2001), 84.
7. Massey, "Word of God," 66.
8. Massey, "Word of God," 67. For comparable accounts from the United States and France, see French L. Arrington, *Christian Doctrine: A Pentecostal Perspective* (Cleveland, TN: Pathway Press, 1992), 1:59; and André Thomas-Brès, *La Foi Donnée aux Saints Une Fois Pour Toutes* (Grézieu la Varenne, France: Viens et Vois, 1986, reédition, 2016), 17.
9. Pentecostal Assemblies of Canada, "Statement of Fundamental and Essential Truths (2014)," 5.1.
10. For another example of the explicit use of the language of "verbal and plenary inspiration," see IPHC "Articles of Faith," 5.
11. AdDDF, 2.

modifications or additions can be made to Scripture.[12] The French Assemblies of God confessional statement above is clear that visions, miracles, and any other revelation are just as much excluded as ecclesiastical or cultural customs, government or church decrees, or human traditions from being considered on par with or wielding authority over Scripture. Rather, "every word and experience is to be measured by the teaching of Holy Scripture. The overarching authority of Scripture—a tenet which found renewal in the Reformation—is affirmed by Pentecostals."[13]

The Bible's authority is God's own authority. Thus, Pentecostals "do not worship a book, but the living God." For, in trusting in the absolute authority of Scripture, they are "trusting God, who speaks to us by the Bible and who opens our understanding by the Holy Spirit."[14]

The Truthfulness of Scripture

In the declaration of faith that she drew up for the Foursquare Church, Aimee Semple McPherson wrote, "We believe that the Holy Bible is the Word of the living God; true, immutable, steadfast, unchangeable, as its author, the Lord Jehovah."[15] Pentecostals root their understanding of the nature of Scripture in the nature of the God who speaks in Scripture. Therefore, Pentecostals believe in the entire truthfulness of Scripture; the Bible must be true because it is the Word of the God who is truth (Num. 23:19; 2 Sam. 7:28; Isa. 65:16; Titus 1:2). As the Church of God theologian French Arrington put it: "The truthfulness of the Bible is compatible with the character of God. God has always been truthful; otherwise He would not be God. To ascribe error to Scripture (as it was originally given) does not do justice to the character of God. A fully reliable and authoritative Bible agrees with what we know about God's character."[16]

Thus, Pentecostals "believe in the inerrancy of the Holy Scripture."[17] The French Pentecostal André Thomas-Brès explains inerrancy as the Bible's freedom from error in any domain.[18] In other words, the Bible's truthfulness is

---

12. ACC, "Doctrinal Basis," 4.4. Explicit warnings are given against adding to or taking away from Scripture in the Indian Pentecostal Church of God Statement of Faith, 1; and Elim Pentecostal Church of New Zealand Statement of Faith, 1.
13. Arrington, *Christian Doctrine*, 1:31.
14. Der Kommentar zum Glaubensbekenntnis BewegungPlus, 6.
15. FDF, 1.
16. Arrington, *Christian Doctrine*, 1:31. Cf. Apostolic Church, *Fundamentals of the Apostolic Church* (Penygroes: Apostolic Publications, n.d.), 24; and John R. Higgins, "God's Inspired Word," in *Systematic Theology*, ed. Stanley M. Horton, rev. ed. (Springfield, MO: Gospel Publishing House, 1995), 103.
17. Pentecostal Theological Institute Bucharest, "Confession of Faith," 2. See also ACC, "Doctrinal Basis," 4.4; Church of God of Prophecy, preamble to "Statement of Faith"; PAOCSET, "Bible"; and Elim SFT, "The Bible."
18. Thomas-Brès, *La Foi Donnée*, 23.

not limited to matters of faith or doctrine. In everything that the Bible affirms, it is "reliable,"[19] "true,"[20] and "infallible."[21] This "perfect infallibility of authoritative revelation of God is secured in every part of the Scriptures, the words containing Truth in infinite perfection and fullness," for "inspired individuals were so controlled by the Holy Spirit that what they wrote was the Word of God without human error."[22] This is the doctrine of scriptural inerrancy. Pentecostals of all denominations can wholeheartedly raise their voices to sing with their brothers and sisters from the Church of God in Christ, "I know the Bible's right."[23]

The Sufficiency of Scripture

In the Scriptures we have everything we need for salvation and godliness. The Bible is "all-sufficient in its provision, and comprehensive in its sufficiency."[24] Pentecostals are not waiting for a new revelation to give them something necessary that isn't contained in Scripture, for "God does not grant new revelations that are contrary or additional to inspired biblical truth."[25]

Yet, like the churches of the Reformation, Pentecostals are not anti-confessional but declare their faith in tenets, articles of religion, statements of fundamental truths, and confessions of faith, often alongside the ancient creeds of the Christian church.[26] Would such documents not constitute a "decree" or "tradition" competing with the sufficiency of Scripture? For some early

---

19. Pentecostal Movement in Iceland, "Creed," 1.
20. PAOCSET, "Bible"; Apostolische Kirche Deutschland, "Das Glauben Wir," 5.
21. AGSFT, 1; CoP, "Tenets," 1; Christian Churches Ireland (AoG), "Statement of Faith," 1; Pentecostal Church in Poland, "Confession of Faith," 1; WAGFSF, 1; *Église Apostolique Suisse Romande*, "Confession de Foi," 5; AdDDF, 2; VPE, "Geloofsbasis," 5; Assemblee di Dio in Italia, "Articoli di Fede," 1; Schweizerische Pfingstmission, "Glaubensbekenntnis," 1. Pentecostals often use the older term "infallible" with the same meaning as "inerrant" (as is clear from context). This is true outside North America, where there has not been the same debate over these terms and where English is not the language in use. In the United Kingdom, "infallible" is still the term preferred by most evangelicals, but with exactly the same meaning as "inerrant" in North America. It is also true for North American denominations whose statements of faith were written before the North American inerrancy debates (e.g., the Assemblies of God). Where the American inerrancy debates have reached, "Pentecostals have come out strongly on the side of inerrancy, pointing out that this applies to the text as originally given and to the text rightly interpreted. In other words . . . they would align themselves with the Chicago Statement on Biblical Inerrancy"; see Massey, "Word of God," 68.
22. AC, "Fundamentals," 24; J. B. Clyne, *Asked and Answered: A Catechism of Apostolic Principles* (Bradford: Puritan Press, 1953), 6.
23. Ithiel C. Clemens, Appendix B to *Bishop C. H. Mason and the Roots of the Church of God in Christ* (Largo, MD: Pneuma Life, 1996), 168.
24. Apostolic Church, "Fundamental Truths," 8.
25. PAOC, "Statement of Fundamental and Essential Truths (2014)," 5.1. For the relationship between prophecy and the sufficiency of Scripture, see question 29.
26. The Apostolic Church, the Pentecostal Church in Poland, the Pentecostal Church of Finland, and the Pentecostal Assemblies of Canada are all among the Pentecostal

Pentecostals (particularly in North America), this was a concern that delayed their adoption of statements of faith. However, most Pentecostals have understood that the authority of the creeds and confessions of faith are subject to and derivative of Scripture's supreme authority. As the Pentecostal Church in Poland states at the beginning of its confession of faith, the faith contained in the confession (and the Apostles' Creed and Nicene Creed, which explicitly stand alongside it) is based "on what is written in God's unchanging and ever-relevant Word as recorded in the Holy Scriptures."[27] The various Pentecostal confessions of faith are not authorities set above Scripture, competing with Scripture's sufficiency. Rather, they are summaries of the sufficient teaching of the authoritative Scriptures. The authority of the confessional statements rests upon the supreme authority and sufficiency of Scripture on which they rely.

As the French Assemblies of God put it, "all things must be examined, regulated and reformed according to Scriptures which contain everything which is necessary for salvation and for the edification of the Church."[28] That is an expression of the sufficiency of Scripture and what it means for the life of the church.

The Power of Scripture

Pentecostals do not see the Bible as simply a book *about* God. Pentecostals read the Bible as the "living and active" Word of God, "sharper than any two-edged sword, piercing to the division of soul and of spirit, of joints and of marrow, and discerning the thoughts and intentions of the heart" (Heb. 4:12). The Bible is a powerful book. As one early British Pentecostal teacher put it, "the Scriptures are continually able to give and do everything that man needs for time and eternity."[29]

> The secret of all spiritual growth lies in true knowledge, trust and continuance, day by day, in the Scriptures, to the very end. Let us grow in grace, and in spiritual knowledge, established in grace and in truth, our minds saturated with the truth of the Scriptures, our wills subjugated or submitted

---

denominations that explicitly state their adherence to the historic creeds of the church. The International Pentecostal Holiness Church explicitly holds to the Apostles' Creed.

27. See Pentecostal Church in Poland, preamble to "Confession of Faith." Similar statements are made as a preamble to various documents; see Apostolic Church, "Tenets"; Pentecostal Church of Finland, "The Main Articles of Faith of the Pentecostal Church of Finland"; ACC, "Doctrinal Basis"; Church of God of Prophecy, "Statement of Faith"; the AGSFT (which is shared by other national Assemblies of God denominations derived from American missionary work); Indian Pentecostal Church, "Scripture," in "Statement of Faith"; CoGiC, "What We Believe"; and RCCG, "Beliefs."
28. AdDDF, 2.
29. T. V. Lewis, "The Written Word," in *The Enduring Word: A Report of the Apostolic Church International Convention*, August 1944 (Penygroes: Apostolic Publications, 1944), 143–44.

> to the will of God as made known to us through the Word Written, with our consciences always sensitive to the Light of the Word. Oh for a solitary and prayerful study of the Word; thus shall we be mighty in the Scriptures. Let us give ourselves to the ministry of the Word of God, and to prayer.[30]

Reading and preaching the Bible are not simply about information transfer. Rather, the author of Scripture meets us in gracious power in his Word, to save and to transform.[31] God works in power by his Word, and Pentecostals expect to know the fruit of God's powerful Word in their lives. "God's Word is also a mirror to show us ourselves as we are or may be. . . . The laver in which to wash away our sins and defilement. . . . The lamp and light to guide us in the right path. . . . The fire, hammer and sword to be used in the warfare of life."[32]

One of the most distinctive Pentecostal confessional statements on Scripture is Aimee Semple McPherson's declaration of faith for the Foursquare Church:

> We believe that the Holy Bible is the Word of the Living God, immutable, steadfast, unchangeable, as its author, the Lord Jehovah, that it was written by holy men of old as they were moved upon and inspired by the Holy Spirit; that it is lighted lamp to guide the feet of a lost world from the depths of sin and sorrow to the heights of righteousness and glory, an unclouded mirror that reveals the face of a crucified Savior, a plumb line to make straight the life of each individual and community, a sharp two-edged sword to convict of sin and evil doing; a strong cord of love and tenderness to draw the penitent to Christ Jesus, a balm of Gilead, in-breathed by the Holy Spirit that can heal and quicken each drooping heart, the only true ground of Christian fellowship and unity, the loving call of an infinitely loving God, the solemn warning, the distant thunder of the storm of wrath and retribution that shall overtake the unheeding, a sign post that points to Heaven, a danger signal that warns from Hell, the divine,

---

30. Lewis, "Written Word," 147.
31. Hugh Dawson, "The Word of the Lord Endureth Forever," in *The Enduring Word: A Report of the Apostolic Church International Convention*, August 1944 (Penygroes: Apostolic Publications, 1944), 53.
32. S. A. Jamieson, *Pillars of Truth* (Springfield, MO: Gospel Publishing House, 1926), 14; cf. Arrington, *Christian Doctrine*, 1:29.

> supreme and eternal tribunal by whose standards all men, nations, creeds, and motives shall be tried.[33]

McPherson takes most of this article of the declaration to set out the power and efficacy of the Scriptures. What she describes is not an instruction manual or textbook of doctrines. What she describes is a book through which the saving God himself is at work in powerful and effective ways. This is how Pentecostals understand the Scriptures. Pentecostals go to the Bible for blessing, growth, and fruitfulness. "If you are to grow and flourish what must you do?" asks a Zimbabwean Apostolic catechism. And the answer it supplies: "Take delight in God's Word and meditate in it continually."[34]

Meeting Jesus in His Word

Such blessing is found in meditating on the Scriptures because in the Scriptures we meet with Jesus. Right at the heart of the article on the Bible in the Foursquare declaration is the confession that Scripture is "an unclouded mirror that reveals the face of a crucified Saviour . . . a strong cord of love and tenderness to draw the penitent to Christ Jesus."[35] Jesus, who died and rose for us, meets with us in his love and tenderness through the words of Scripture. To the question, "What is the chief purpose of the Bible?" a British Apostolic catechism responds, "To reveal Jesus Christ as the Son of God and the Saviour of men."[36] God's purpose in giving us the Bible is "to draw [us] into vital and loving relation with God."[37]

Bishop C. H. Mason of the Church of God in Christ described what happens when Pentecostals come to the Bible: "From the Scriptures Jesus spoke to the minds of the people, and they looked at Him and marveled. Jesus showing forth the wisdom of God." [38] As Pentecostals read, hear, and meditate on the word, they "delight to see Jesus" and meet him there as the "great God at hand."[39] In drawing near to God's written Word, they draw near to the eternal Word.

Summary

Pentecostals love the Bible because it is the powerful Word of the God of grace and in reading and meditating upon it we meet with Jesus, the living

33. FDF, 1.
34. R. J. Joel Lewis, *Question & Quotation: Belief and Behaviour* (Bulawayo, Zimbabwe-Rhodesia: The Apostolic Church, 1979), 17. Cf. Jamieson, *Pillars of Truth*, 14.
35. FDF, 1.
36. Clyne, *Asked and Answered*, 5.
37. Jamieson, *Pillars of Truth*, 13.
38. C. H. Mason, Appendix A "A Prayer and a Vision of Bishop C. H. Mason," in Ithiel C. Clemens, *Bishop C. H. Mason and the Roots of the Church of God in Christ* (Largo, MD: Pneuma Life, 1996), 144.
39. Mason, "Prayer and Vision," 144.

Word. The Lord transforms us by his Word and calls us to hear and trust his Word at all times. He has inspired every word of the Scriptures; therefore, the Scriptures carry his authority and are without error, for they are the Word of the God of truth.

REFLECTION QUESTIONS

1. What does it mean to say that the Scriptures are inspired by God?
2. Why is the Bible our highest authority?
3. In what way is Scripture powerful?
4. What did William Seymour say about the relationship between the baptism in the Holy Spirit and the Bible?
5. Why should we meditate on God's Word? Do you take time each day to meditate on Scripture?

QUESTION 7

How Do Pentecostals View Jesus?

There is nothing more central to the Pentecostal faith than Jesus Christ. He is "the substance of the Bible," "the sum of our redemption," and "at the centre of everything."[1] For Pentecostals around the world, "the sweetest and most precious name is the name of Jesus."[2] Back in the 1930s, when Norwegian Pentecostals opened a brand-new building for their central assembly in Oslo, they wanted to make that very clear:

> There is a name which is at the center of our divine service, and that name, seen in large letters on the front of the platform, is—JESUS. Everything centers around this one point—this holy name of JESUS. Our preaching is centered around this name. Many are of the opinion that we Pentecostal people are always in a state of ecstasy, because we, like the first Christians, speak in tongues and believe in miracles. But the main points of our doctrine, our speaking in tongues and interpretation, our prophesying, our song and music, our meetings, all are centered around Jesus.[3]

Jesus, not the baptism or gifts of the Spirit, is at the center of Pentecostalism. Even the way Pentecostals speak about the "foursquare gospel" points back to the centrality of Christ, for Pentecostals do not simply believe in salvation, healing, the baptism in the Spirit, and the second coming; they believe in Jesus the Savior, Jesus the healer, Jesus the baptizer in the Spirit, and Jesus the

1. W. R. Thomas, *L'Emmanuele* (Naples: Edizioni Ricchezze di Grazia, 1965), 7, 92, 97.
2. Thomas, *L'Emmanuele*, 102.
3. William S. Johnson, Opening of the Filadelfia Temple (speech), Oslo, 1938, quoted in Stanley H. Frodsham, *With Signs Following: The Story of the Pentecostal Revival in the Twentieth Century*, rev. ed. (Springfield, MO: Gospel Publishing House, 1941), 72.

soon-coming King. The gospel is not merely good news about blessings Jesus provides; the gospel is the good news of Jesus himself.

God in the Flesh

Jesus is God the Son, "co-existent and co-eternal with the Father."[4] He is "not a secondary deity, a god, or a being like God, but God himself, of the very same essence as the Father."[5] Through him and for him all things were created (John 1:3; Col. 1:16) and in him all things hold together (Col. 1:17). In ancient times, he was seen by Abraham and Isaiah (John 8:56; 12:41), and it was he who delivered the children of Israel out of Egypt (1 Cor. 10:1–2; Jude 5). Yet, in the fullness of time, he came into the world to be "born of woman" in order to redeem us and bring us into the family of God (Gal. 4:4–5). For us, and for our salvation, "he was willing to leave the glory that he had with the Father before the world was, and to be 'born of the Virgin Mary.'"[6] In "the condescension of the Almighty in the incarnation: not the poverty of the manger, but the advent into the human race," he humbled himself in a way far beyond our "power to describe," as he came "to partake of human weakness, always to be the son of man, always the kinsman redeemer of a fallen and lost race."[7] Christianity is rooted in the incarnation of Jesus, for, as one early Hong Kong Pentecostal publication put it, "the incarnation . . . grants the fountain of life."[8] Pentecostals are very clear: "Doubt the incarnation, then you doubt Christianity."[9]

The articles of faith of the International Pentecostal Holiness Church set out with detail what the incarnation entails: "We believe that the Son, who is the Word of the Father, the very and eternal God, of one substance with the Father, took man's nature in the womb of the blessed virgin; so that two whole and perfect natures, that is to say, the Godhead and the manhood were joined together in one Person, never to be divided, whereof is one Christ, very God and perfect man."[10]

Notice a few significant details here. First, the eternal Son took on human nature. The one person of Jesus Christ *is* the person of God the Son; he is the same Son before and after the incarnation. Second, the one person of the incarnate Son exists in "two whole and perfect natures." Therefore, Christ is not part God and part man. Nor is there anything insufficient in

---

4. FDF, 2.
5. Noel Brooke, "The Eternal Deity of Christ," *Pentecostal Holiness Advocate* (January 31, 1970): 14.
6. Alexander Boddy, "Christ in His Holy Land," *Confidence* 2, no. 10 (October 1909): 238.
7. "Latter Rain Blessings," *The Bridegroom's Messenger* 3, no. 55 (February 1, 1910): 4.
8. "Truth: Burning Heart," trans. Connie Au, *Pentecostal Truths* 3, nos. 7–8 (July–August 1910): 1.
9. "The Birth of Christ and Its Message to Us," *The Pentecostal Evangel* (December 20, 1924): 4.
10. IPHC, "Articles of Faith," 2.

either his deity or his humanity. (They are whole and perfect.) He is also not a mixture between a divine nature and a human nature (which would be neither whole and perfect man nor whole and perfect God). Rather, he is "very . . . God" (i.e., "of one substance with the Father") and "perfect man" (i.e., of the same nature as us, except that, unlike us, his humanity is not fallen and sinful). Third, these two natures in one Person are "joined . . . never to be divided." Thus, Jesus is not sometimes acting as God, and sometimes acting as man; every act of Christ is an act of the one incarnate person. Furthermore, Jesus will never cast off our nature. He has united humanity to himself forever. Neither nature can be abandoned; neither nature can be laid aside.

He Humbled Himself

In recent years, a controversial teaching about the incarnation of Jesus has had an impact in some charismatic and Pentecostal circles. Bill Johnson, the pastor of Bethel Church in Redding, California, and an influential charismatic speaker and writer, has taught that Jesus "laid His divinity aside as He sought to fulfil the assignment given to Him by the Father."[11] For Johnson, this means that Christ "had no supernatural capabilities whatsoever! While He is 100 percent God, He chose to live with the same limitations that man would face once He was redeemed. . . . He performed miracles, wonders, and signs as a man in right relationship to God . . . not as God."[12] This view of Christ's self-emptying (Phil. 2:7) is neither orthodox nor a standard Pentecostal position. Rather, orthodox Pentecostals have always warned, any claim that Jesus laid aside his deity "would mean the destruction of the whole fabric of Christianity."[13]

Most early Pentecostals understood the self-emptying of Christ in Philippians 2:7 not as a giving up of divine attributes, but in terms of the Lord of Glory humbling himself to "serve [his] inferior."[14] An early Pentecostal Bible college principal clarified that "the phrases that follow, 'the form of a servant' and 'likeness of man,' must be considered as explaining its meaning. It does not mean that the Lord emptied himself of his Deity or Godhood."[15] Mary Boddy reflected on this in Sunderland, seeing Christ's self-emptying in terms of the substitutionary nature of his life and work in taking on our sin and

---

11. Bill Johnson, *When Heaven Invades Earth: A Practical Guide to a Life of Miracles* (Shippensburg, PA: Destiny Image, 2003), 79.
12. Johnson, *When Heaven Invades*, 29.
13. "Fundamental Truths," *The Apostolic Church: Its Principles and Practices* (Penygroes: Apostolic Church, 1937), 191.
14. D. W. Kerr, "The Mind of Christ," *Pentecostal Evangel* (January 17, 1925): 2.
15. A. L. Greenway, *Philippians: Analytical Bible Study Course* (Manchester: Puritan Press, n.d.), 2:18.

being "numbered with the transgressors."[16] An early American Pentecostal, Gustav Sigwalt, explained it by writing that Christ "humbled Himself down to us, identifying Himself with us in our low estate."[17] British Pentecostals wrote of this as a "veiling [of] His inherent glory."[18] The early British Assemblies of God leader L. F. W. Woodford was very clear that "by the mystery of the Incarnation He did not surrender any of the perfections of His Divine nature and character."[19]

One British Pentecostal publication surveyed and assessed a variety of kenotic and semi-kenotic Christologies and demonstrated why all such theories are incompatible with orthodox Christianity, concluding that Christ not only possessed but also "exercised His Own inherent attributes, as the Second Person of the Trinity" during his incarnate ministry on earth.[20] Early Pentecostal leaders taught firmly that in the incarnation "all those marvellous attributes of Jehovah were made manifest in the Lord Jesus Christ."[21] Christ's miracles were very explicitly viewed by Pentecostals as demonstrations of his divine attributes.[22] A major British Pentecostal doctrinal handbook clearly sets out that divine attributes are "positively predicated of Christ," for we must always see that the "one person [of Christ] is the only-begotten of the Father, the divine Logos, who took upon Himself human nature" and we must never give "the slightest ground to multiply or divide the person; nor to confound the natures."[23] In the United States, Carl Brumback taught that Christ's "mediatorial service implies no change in His essential and eternal nature . . . and that is an eternal fact which it would be impossible for Him to change—for any cause."[24] As the early Welsh Pentecostal leader D. P. Williams put it, "It was impossible for Him to lay aside His Divine Nature and Attributes."[25]

Contemporary Pentecostals still agree: "Jesus emptied himself by his assuming the nature of a servant. . . . Jesus, the second [person] of the Trinity,

---

16. Mary Boddy, "The New Creation 3," *Confidence* 3, no. 2 (February 1910): 38.
17. Gustav Sigwalt, "Humility," *Pentecostal Holiness Advocate* 1, no. 10 (July 5, 1917): 3.
18. E. C. W. Boulton, "Editorial," *Elim Evangel* 5, no. 9 (September 1924): 189; cf. E. C. W. Boulton, "The Incarnation," *Elim Evangel* 6, no. 24 (December 15, 1925): 285; John H. Carter, "Studies on the Fundamental Truths 2," *Redemption Tidings* 2, no. 2 (February 1926): 11; D. P. Williams, *The Trinity* (Penygroes: Apostolic Church, n.d.), 2:24.
19. L. F. W. Woodford, "Studies on the Person and Work of Christ 7: His Perfect Life," *Redemption Tidings* 15, no. 15 (July 14, 1939): 2.
20. Robert Clarke, *The Christ of God* (London: Elim, 1949), 35.
21. E. C. W. Boulton, "Daily Readings and Meditations," *Elim Evangel* 9, no. 2 (January 16, 1928): 21; cf. Boulton, "The Incarnation," 286.
22. E.g., Thomas, *L'Emmanuele*, 13; see also W. Gornold, "Principal G. Jeffreys Opens New Tabernacle at Hove," *Elim Evangel* 10, no. 13 (July 26, 1929): 197.
23. W. A. C. Rowe, *One Lord, One Faith* (Bradford: Puritan Press, n.d.), 63.
24. Carl Brumback, *God in Three Persons* (Cleveland, TN: Pathway, 1959), 139.
25. Williams, *Trinity*, 2:23.

does not lay aside his deity. God cannot divorce himself from his very nature."[26] In France, André Thomas-Brès is emphatic that to suppress either the divinity or the humanity of the person of Christ "is to reject the teaching of the Word of God." While some of Christ's divine attributes were "veiled" during much of his ministry on earth, he nevertheless still shared "equally all the attributes" that belong to the Father "throughout the whole of his earthly ministry," and furthermore, these attributes were "manifested in the course of his ministry."[27] These Pentecostal voices hold fast to orthodox Christology. It is very clear that Jesus could not have laid aside his deity.

As Johnson sees a laying aside of divinity in Christ's incarnation, he accounts for Christ's divine works in his earthly ministry with an anointing of the Holy Spirit in a way that suggests Christ is a model of living under such an anointing for Christians to emulate. "The anointing is what linked Jesus, the man, to the divine, enabling Him to destroy the works of the devil. . . . If the Son of God was that reliant upon the anointing, His behavior should clarify our need for the Holy Spirit's presence upon us to do what the Father has assigned."[28] In this, Jesus is portrayed as the perfect example for us to follow in our attempts to climb up to God, rather than as God himself who has stooped down and entered into our humanity to rescue us from our death in sin and trespasses.[29]

The theology expressed in Johnson's teaching raises several significant problems. First, although Johnson tries to attenuate his claim that Jesus "laid His divinity aside" by insisting that he is "100 percent God," he sees him as the sort of "God" who "had no supernatural capabilities whatsoever." This is a redefinition of the nature of God. A "God" with no supernatural capabilities is a God who does not share in the divine attributes. The divine attributes are the very essence of God: God *is* his attributes. A God who does not share in the divine attributes does not share in the being of God. Jesus could not lay aside his divinity without ceasing to be God.

This would not only be a Christological problem, but a Trinitarian problem as well; if the Son were to cease to be God, God would cease to be triune. None of this is compatible with a God who does not change (Mal. 3:6). The Welsh apostolic leader D. P. Williams argues from the fact that Jesus is "the Immutable, the Unchangeable One" to demonstrate that "there can be no

26. David Demchuk, "Philippians," in *Full Life Bible Commentary to the New Testament*, ed. French L. Arrington and Roger Stronstad (Grand Rapids: Zondervan, 1999), 1103.
27. André Brès-Thomas, *La Foi Donné aux Saints Une Fois Pour Toutes* (Grézieu le Varenne: Viens et Vois, 2016), 85–86, 88.
28. Johnson, *When Heaven Invades*, 79–80.
29. There are striking parallels here with the connections between Nestorianism and Pelagianism. Johnson's Christology is not Nestorian, although it does display some Nestorian tendencies.

possibility" of any laying aside of his divinity.[30] Such a change would not be compatible with the essential grammar of Trinitarian orthodoxy, for it would necessitate a denial of the eternal Father-Son relationship, the consubstantiality of the three persons, the unity of the divine will, and the inseparability of the Trinity's external operations.

Second, Johnson seeks to highlight the relationship between Christ and the Holy Spirit; yet the way he does this actually diminishes their relationship. For Johnson, it is an external anointing with the Spirit which "linked Jesus, the man, to the divine." However, this understanding ignores the Trinitarian relationship between the Spirit and the Son. The Scriptures tell us that the Holy Spirit is "the Spirit of Christ" (Rom. 8:9; 1 Peter 1:11) or "the Spirit of [God's] Son" (Gal. 4:6). Thus, he is Christ's own Spirit, not merely an external influence upon Christ.

As Cyril of Alexandria put it in his ninth anathema against Nestorius: "If anyone says that the One Lord Jesus Christ was glorified by the Spirit, using the power that came through him as if it were foreign to himself, and receiving from him the power to work against unclean spirits and to accomplish divine signs for men, and does not rather say that the Spirit is his very own, through whom he also worked the divine signs, let him be anathema."[31] This was not only accepted as the standard of Christian orthodoxy by the ancient church at the Council of Ephesus (AD 431), but continued to be upheld by later councils. Neither was it forgotten by early Pentecostals. D. P. Williams likewise highlighted that the Spirit of Christ, "the One that anointed Him on the banks of Jordan," is the Spirit of the Son, "proceeding from Him" from all eternity.[32] We cannot look at the role of the Holy Spirit in the earthly life and ministry of Christ in isolation from the eternal, Trinitarian relationship between the Son and the Spirit.

Exalted Above the Heavens, Yet Closer Than a Brother

This same Jesus, who humbled himself to take on the form of a servant and die the death of the cross, is now risen, glorified, and "ascended far above all the heavens, that he might fill all things" (Eph. 4:10). Indeed, "God has highly exalted him" (Phil. 2:9). Therefore, Pentecostals bow in adoration before Jesus as King of Kings and Lord of Lords, enthroned at the right hand of the Father and sovereign over all creation. Before he ascended into heaven, Jesus said to his disciples that "all authority in heaven and on earth" had been given to him (Matt. 28:18). Thus, Pentecostals have confidence in Jesus as the one to whom they can bring every need, and offer their prayers boldly to the

30. Williams, *Trinity*, 2:23.
31. Cyril of Alexandria, "The Third Letter of Cyril to Nestorius," in John McGuckin, *Saint Cyril of Alexandria and the Christological Controversy* (Crestwood, NY: St Vladimir's Seminary Press, 2004), 274.
32. Williams, *Trinity*, 2:70.

Father in Jesus's name: "There can be no doubting . . . the final supremacy of the God-man, nor the full sway of His dominion."[33] At all times, we can trust in the reality of Christ's "supreme authority and his mediation in the presence the Father in [our] favour."[34]

Yet, the highly exalted King of Kings and Lord of Lords is also the "friend who sticks closer than a brother" (Prov. 18:24).[35] The Lord of Glory is also the believer's "dearest Friend,"[36] as well as the church's Bridegroom. Believers are "those souls who love the Bridegroom,"[37] and the Holy Spirit guides the Bride "to the arms of the Bridegroom."[38]

The same Christ who is exalted to the Father's right hand dwells in our hearts by faith (Eph. 3:17). Although Christ is on the throne of heaven, "spiritually, in his divine representative, the Holy Spirit, he lives in our hearts."[39] Therefore, believers can know precious and intimate fellowship with Christ their gracious and loving Lord. "This means we can taste the sweetness of Christ, listen to his voice, behold and gaze upon the glory of Christ, feel the presence of Christ . . . follow the footsteps of Christ, and constantly enjoy communion with Christ."[40] Pentecostals long for "sweet, close communion with Jesus."[41] And the Christ whose communion we enjoy, we find to be full of compassion, mercy, and grace for us (Heb. 4:14–16), for "Jesus Christ really is the same yesterday, today, and forever."[42]

Summary

Along with the whole of Christ's church, Pentecostals believe in and worship the Lord Jesus Christ, the incarnate God. The orthodox Christology that Pentecostals believe and teach is summed up in the confession of the Apostolic Church in the UK:

> Our Lord Jesus Christ, the Eternal Word and Son of the Father, has, by His incarnation in the womb of the Virgin

33. Greenway, *Philippians*, 2:24.
34. AdDDF, 4.
35. Pentecostals frequently apply this verse to Jesus. E.g., John Leech, "A Sinful Woman Saved," *Confidence* 8, no. 7 (July 1915): 126; Moses Prostchansky, "Russian Testimony," *Christian Evangel* (November 21, 1914): 3; and Gustav Sigwalt, "Wausau, Fla.," *Pentecostal Holiness Advocate* (October 18, 1917): 8.
36. Sigwalt, "Wausau, Fla.," 8.
37. Pastor Friemel, "Whit-Monday," *Confidence* 4, no. 6 (June 1911): 134.
38. Aimee Semple McPherson, "The Bride in Her Veil of Types and Shadows," *The Bridal Call* 2, no. 10 (March 1919): 4.
39. Thomas, *L'Emmanuele*, 67.
40. Thomas, *L'Emmanuele*, 67.
41. Loraine Bushby, "Testimony of a Young Epworth Leaguer," *The Bridal Call* 5, no. 5 (October 1921): 26.
42. "Pentecostal News: London," *Confidence* 2, no. 2 (February 1909): 48. Cf. Hebrews 13:8.

> Mary, taken on true humanity, so that He is both one with the Father, sharing in His nature as true God, and one with us, sharing in our nature as true Man. In the Incarnate Son, the glory of the invisible God is seen, full of grace and truth. He has not set aside what He was, but for our sake has also taken on what we are so that in the unity of His One Person, all that He does He does as the God-Man.[43]

Yet this highly exalted, incarnate God draws near to us in love, dwells within those who trust in him, and meets with us in loving communion.

REFLECTION QUESTIONS

1. What does it mean that the Word became flesh?
2. Why was it not possible for Jesus to lay aside his divinity?
3. How can we better understand what it meant for Jesus to humble himself?
4. Where is Jesus now?
5. Why is Jesus so central to Pentecostal theology?

---

43. ACVG, 3.

QUESTION 8

What Do Pentecostals Believe Concerning the Trinity?

Apart from debates about the *filioque*, the Trinity is a doctrine that unites the entire Christian church: Protestant, Catholic, Eastern Orthodox, Oriental Orthodox, and the Church of the East.[1] To depart from the doctrine of the Trinity would be to depart from orthodox Christianity of any sort. Yet, due to a strange quirk of North American Pentecostal history, the question "What do Pentecostals believe concerning the Trinity?" is one we need to look at carefully.

The New Issue

In April 1913, an unwise statement was made from the pulpit during a baptismal sermon at a camp meeting in Arroyo Seco, California. Robert McAlister, a Canadian Pentecostal leader, commented in his sermon that the apostles baptized in the name of Jesus rather than in the name of the Father, Son, and Holy Spirit, thereby igniting a huge controversy among American and Canadian Pentecostals. What was intended as a throwaway comment startled many in the congregation. McAlister immediately tried to roll back what he had said, but it was too late. One minister who had been listening, John G. Schaepe, was so inspired by the comment that he stayed up through the night to pray and study the Scriptures on the topic. In the middle of the night, he ran through the camp shouting that he had received a new revelation about baptism in the name of Jesus.

As a result, many who had been previously baptized in the name of the Father, Son, and Holy Spirit were re-baptized in the name of the Lord Jesus

1. The *filioque* is the understanding of the Western Churches (i.e., Protestant and Catholic) that the Holy Spirit proceeds from the Father and the Son (a doctrine that is not shared by the Eastern Churches).

Christ. These re-baptisms began a year after the original camp meeting at Arroyo Seco. Two ministers, Frank Ewart and Glenn Cook, rebaptized one another in a baptismal tank that they had set up in a tent for public meetings in Belvedere, California. This divisive teaching and baptismal practice became known as "the New Issue." The New Issue did not affect Wesleyan Holiness Pentecostals or Pentecostals outside North America, so even from the outset it was confined to a small portion of the movement.

This new baptismal practice quickly led to a new view of God among its adherents. The leaders of the New Issue were teaching that *Jesus* was "the name of the Father and of the Son and of the Holy Spirit" (Matt. 28:19). As a result, they quickly rejected the doctrine of the Trinity. "Those who have been doctrinated . . . with the 'three person God' idea are bewildered," wrote G. T. Haywood, one of the major Oneness leaders, in 1915. "There is but one God and he has been manifested in a threefold manner. And this threefold manifestation was not intended to establish a three person God idea."[2] Three manifestations of the one God who is the Lord Jesus Christ was to become the central Oneness teaching.

Oneness Pentecostalism

Oneness is not the same as Unitarianism. While Unitarians deny the deity of Christ, Oneness Pentecostals stress that "the whole fullness of deity dwells bodily" in Jesus (Col. 2:9). They reject understanding the Father, Son, and Holy Spirit as persons, which they argue would compromise strict monotheism: "Oneness theologians by and large consign the Trinity exclusively to the realm of divine self-disclosure in the world. There is seldom a hint of the threefold nature of God—only an affirmation of a threefold revelation."[3] The statement of faith of the United Pentecostal Church (one of the largest Oneness denominations) expresses this: "There is one God, who has revealed Himself as Father; through His Son, in redemption; and as the Holy Spirit, by emanation. Jesus Christ is God manifested in flesh. He is both God and man."[4]

Oneness teaching sees the Father, Son, and Holy Spirit as three manifestations of God by which he has revealed himself in history (and denies that God exists eternally as the three persons of the Father, Son, and Holy Spirit). As a result, Oneness teaching has often been regarded by Trinitarians as a form of Modalism (or Sabellianism). David Reed's assessment is that "while the movement's views conform most closely to historic modalism, there are voices in the tradition that are suggestive of a kind of economic Trinitarian thought."[5]

---

2. G. T. Haywood, "The One True God," *Meat in Due Season* 1, no. 9 (December 1915): 3.
3. David A. Reed, *In Jesus' Name: The History and Beliefs of Oneness Pentecostals* (Blandford Forum, UK: Deo, 2008), 261.
4. "About God," Our Beliefs, The United Pentecostal Church International, accessed on August 9, 2022, https://www.upci.org/about/our-beliefs.
5. Reed, *In Jesus' Name,* 272.

Yet, while there has been variety within Oneness teaching, what emerges most clearly is that "since 1916 Oneness Pentecostalism has consciously moulded its identity as an anti-Trinitarian movement."[6]

Although historically Oneness was a North American issue, it has since spread around the world. Recent estimates for the number of Oneness adherents vary between fourteen and twenty million people.[7] Thus, while Oneness adherents make up a small minority compared to Trinitarian Pentecostals, they are a significant movement in their own right. Major Oneness denominations include the United Pentecostal Church and the Pentecostal Assemblies of the World.

The Mainstream Pentecostal Response to Oneness

Although some scholars look on Oneness as merely variety within the Pentecostal world, that has not been the way mainstream Pentecostal churches have viewed the matter. The strong language of Bishop C. H. Mason, the first presiding bishop and chief apostle of the Church of God in Christ (the largest Pentecostal denomination in the United States), against Oneness was typical of the orthodox Pentecostal perspective: "The 'One in the Godhead people' are undertaking to show God His wrong sayings. . . . Danger! He is an antichrist that denieth the Father and the Son. So, to say that Jesus is not the Son of God [but rather the name of the Godhead] is to make God a liar."[8] As Oneness teaching is intimately connected to the baptismal formula, Mason turns his attention to it as well: "Baptizing in the name of Jesus. Is it right? Yes. But it is only right when it is done like Jesus said to do it . . . in the name of the Father and of the Son and of the Holy Ghost. This is the only way that Jesus commanded it to be done."[9] For Mason, and other orthodox Pentecostals, Oneness cannot be taken seriously as a Pentecostal option, but must be regarded as a serious departure from biblical truth. In the Assemblies of God, S. A. Jamieson notes that "Sabellius was the father of this heretical doctrine."[10] A generation later Carl Brumback, in a book refuting Oneness teaching and endorsed by the leaders of six of North America's largest Pentecostal denominations, had as severe an assessment of Oneness as Mason: "The Oneness group itself is a composite of the most heretical teachings that ever plagued the Church, ancient or modern."[11] For these orthodox Pentecostal leaders, Oneness is not an acceptable alternative variety of Pentecostalism; it is serious heresy.

6. Reed, *In Jesus' Name*, 272–73.
7. Reed, *In Jesus' Name*, 339.
8. C. H. Mason, "The Sonship of Jesus," *Year Book of the Church of God in Christ for the Year 1926* (Chicago: Church of God in Christ, 1926), 33.
9. Mason, "Sonship," 32.
10. S. A. Jamieson, *Pillars of Truth* (Springfield, MO: Gospel Publishing House, 1926), 22.
11. Carl Brumback, *God in Three Persons* (Cleveland, TN: Pathway Press, 1959), 22.

Pentecostals and the Trinity

Before "the New Issue" broke out, right back at the very beginning of the Pentecostal revival, an Englishwoman summed up what is central to Pentecostals in a testimony she sent to Azusa Street of her baptism in the Spirit. Her testimony ends with an interpretation of tongues, which she writes "was all about the precious, precious Blood. Glory to the Triune God! Glory to the Lamb upon the throne."[12] The blood of Jesus, the risen Lamb upon the throne, and the glory of the triune God are the foundation of our faith and the basis of our salvation. All the distinctives of Pentecostalism, to be truly Pentecostal, must flow from the cross and glorify the Trinity.

While they have always marveled in recognition of the profound mystery "altogether beyond the power of our poor finite minds to comprehend it fully," orthodox Pentecostals have also always been firmly convinced that this doctrine is the foundation of the whole of the Christian faith and of our salvation.[13] "From the beginning, God the Father, God the Son, and God the Spirit have, in the mystery of the Trinity, dwelt together in undiminishing rapture and unsurpassable love."[14] Salvation must be seen to be Trinitarian, for "the Trinity brings about redemption."[15] Alexander Boddy expresses the Trinitarian nature of salvation, writing that "through the precious Blood poured out," those who "stand now in the victory of [their] mighty Saviour, the Lord Jesus," can say "the Triune God is my Fortress around me. The Triune God is the Garrison within me."[16] His wife Mary writes of the Trinity at the center of all things and our highest calling as the worship of the triune God. "We bow before [the Father] in deep wonder, and worship as the Holy Spirit unfolds to our innermost spirit the beauties of the holiness and power and divinity of our Blessed Saviour, Christ the Lord."[17] Early Pentecostals frequently spoke of the baptism and gifts of the Holy Spirit in explicitly Trinitarian terms. The baptism in the Spirit is the outpouring of "the Blessed Third Person of the Holy Trinity."[18] It is "God the Holy Spirit, the Third Person of the Trinity, coming upon and into the believer in such fullness."[19]

---

12. M. J. D., "A Wonderful Baptism in England," *Apostolic Faith* 1, no. 11 (October 1907–January 1908): 2.
13. John H. Carter, "Studies on the Fundamental Truths 2," *Redemption Tidings* 2, no. 2 (February 1926): 10, 12.
14. Percy G. Parker, "The Name in Which to Pray," *Elim Evangel* 9, no. 16 (September 1, 1928): 250.
15. "The Holy Spirit the Same Now as at Pentecost," *Elim Evangel* 7, no. 22 (November 15, 1926): 267.
16. Alexander Boddy, "The Indwelling and Abiding Trinity," *Confidence* 5, no. 6 (June 1912): 125.
17. Mary Boddy, "Behold I Make All Things New," *Confidence* 8, no. 8 (August 1915): 150–52.
18. "A Visitor's Summing Up of the Sunderland Convention," *Confidence* 5, no. 6 (June 1912): 137.
19. Donald Gee, "Studies on the Fundamental Truths 6," *Redemption Tidings* 2, no. 6 (June 1926): 14.

The gifts of the Holy Spirit manifest the operation of the Trinity (1 Cor. 12:4–6).[20]

In one of the earliest Pentecostal doctrinal books, S. A. Jamieson sets out the orthodox Trinitarian teaching: "In the Godhead the three persons are the same in substance, of one and the same indivisible essence. There is but one God and He is indivisible. . . . The distinction between these three is only a personal distinction."[21] When we speak of the first, second, or third person of the Godhead, "the Father is mentioned first, as He is neither begotten nor preceded. The Son is second in order because He is eternally begotten by the Father. . . . The Spirit is third, as he proceedeth from the Father and the Son."[22] The eternal generation of the Son constitutes the Father-Son relationship so that, as Bishop C. H. Mason points out, Jesus "is not the Father of God but the Son of God, nor is He His own father, for no son has ever begotten himself, but all sons have fathers that beget them."[23] Without this relation of eternal generation, the Father could not "be genuinely called Father."[24] The Son is begotten of the Father from all eternity, for the Son is "very God, very life of His life, very nature of His nature, very divinity of His divinity," sharing the Father's own life, nature, and power.[25]

These relations of origin, the eternal generation of the Son and the procession of the Holy Spirit, are vital elements of the doctrine, as it is these relations of origin that distinguish one person of the Trinity from another.[26] They cannot be distinguished by attributes, for they each share fully in the same divine nature, and they cannot be distinguished by what they do, for the external operations of the Trinity are indivisible. D. P. Williams rooted all theology in the eternal generation of the Son, teaching that "the basic doctrine of the Christian faith," from which all else flows, is "that God is the Father, and that He has a Son within His essence eternally."[27]

The American Assemblies of God included a long section on "the essentials as to the Godhead" in its original statement of fundamental truths in 1916, to combat the Oneness heresy specifically. Part of this statement took up the issue of the eternal relations of origin, underscoring the importance of this teaching:

---

20. A. E. Saxeby, "Signpost Bible Studies: Notes on 1 Corinthians," *Elim Evangel* 2, no. 1 (December 1920): 13; see also Saxeby, "Concerning Spiritual Gifts," *Elim Evangel* 7, no. 20 (October 15, 1926): 243; and Donald Gee, "Gifts of the Spirit," *Redemption Tidings* 4, no. 2 (February 1928): 12.
21. Jamieson, *Pillars of Truth,* 17.
22. Jamieson, *Pillars of Truth,* 17–18.
23. Mason, "Sonship," 31.
24. Brumback, *God in Three Persons,* 120.
25. Hattie Hammond, "Constraining Love," *Redemption Tidings* 13, no. 8 (April 9, 1937): 1.
26. D. P. Williams, *The Trinity* (Penygroes: Apostolic Church, n.d.), 1:51.
27. Williams, *Trinity,* 1:77.

> Christ taught a distinction of Persons in the Godhead which he expressed in specific terms of relationship, as Father, Son and Holy Ghost. . . . Accordingly, therefore, there is that in the Father which constitutes Him the Father and not the Son; there is that in the Son which constitutes Him the Son and not the Father; and there is that in the Holy Ghost which constitutes him the Holy Ghost and not either the Father or the Son. Wherefore the Father is the Begetter; the Son is the Begotten; and the Holy Ghost is the one proceeding from the Father and the Son.[28]

It is because of these eternal relations of origin that the triune God is the eternal God who is love. As Welsh Apostolic leader Thomas Rees put it, "If God were not a Trinity, on whom could His love have been lavished, when there was no-one eternally existent but only Himself? . . . Therefore to deny the distinction of Father, Son and Holy Ghost in the eternal Being of God is to make the love of God dependent on things created, and that would contradict the self-existence and the self-sufficiency of God."[29] This comes from Jesus's own words in his great High Priestly Prayer on the night of his arrest, in which he speaks of how the Father "loved [him] before the foundation of the world" (John 17:24). Pentecostals very explicitly share with their brothers and sisters across the rest of the Christian church a robust and biblical faith in the triune God, as confessed in the ancient creeds.

Pentecostals and the Creeds

Pentecostals are often mistaken for being anti-creedal. But this is far from the truth for mainstream Pentecostalism. Instead, Carl Brumback's attitude is more representative of the Pentecostal approach to the historic creeds of the church: "What a debt we owe to those men who spelled out with such exactness and clarity the basic truths of the Trinitarian faith in the Nicene and Athanasian Creeds! These classic statements enabled the Church to avoid the danger of drifting into an extreme position."[30] For Brumback, the Athanasian Creed is "the bulwark of the doctrine of the Trinity."[31] This is not a single individual getting carried away. Brumback's

---

28. AG, "A Statement of Fundamental Truths Approved by the General Council of the Assemblies of God," in *Minutes of the General Council of the Assemblies of God* (St. Louis, MO: General Council of the Assemblies of God, October 2–7 1916), 13.b–c. This is now included (with a very minor linguistic update) in section 2 of the current AGSFT as well as in versions in use in many other countries.
29. Thomas Rees, *The Unity of the Godhead and the Trinity of Persons Therein* (Bradford: Puritan Press, 1954), 18.
30. Brumback, *God in Three Persons*, 97.
31. Brumback, *God in Three Persons*, 103.

God in Three Persons was endorsed by the leaders of the Church of God, the Pentecostal Assemblies of Canada, the Assemblies of God, the Church of the Foursquare Gospel, the Pentecostal Holiness Church, and the Open Bible Standard Churches. It was written by an Assemblies of God author and published by the official press of the Church of God. So Brumback's enthusiasm for the Nicene and Athanasian Creeds appears to have sat easily with Pentecostal denominational leaders.

A few years earlier, the Pentecostal Assemblies of Canada had produced a catechism that explicitly drew on the language of the Athanasian and Nicene Creeds and included all three ecumenical creeds as an appendix.[32] The aim of the catechism was to "set forth the beliefs of the Pentecostal movement" and be a contribution to Pentecostalism as a whole (not only to the Pentecostal Assemblies of Canada).[33] Question 18 of the catechism points to the Athanasian, Nicene, and Apostles' Creeds as "the three Creeds which have come down from the early days of Christianity and belong to the universal Christian Church."[34] The next question tackles the relationship between holding to the creeds alongside the doctrine of *sola scriptura*, showing how the creeds "give expression to the truths contained in the Holy Scriptures; and do not claim to teach anything contrary to, or beyond, the Scriptures," while question 20 highlights "the value of the Creeds to us today."[35] The questions on the Trinity use language drawn from the Athanasian Creed.[36] The three ecumenical creeds are deeply woven into this Pentecostal catechism, and especially into its articulation of the doctrine of the Trinity.

Two decades earlier in the United Kingdom, the Apostolic Church noted in its council that the three creeds "direct the Church and protect it from errors that would have driven the Church here and there."[37] For the Apostolic Church, "it would be better for us to lose an assembly or a mission field than to lose the doctrines that the Lord has laid down" in the creeds.[38]

The Pentecostal Holiness Church also highlights the importance of the ecumenical creeds. The Definition of Chalcedon was considered "parallel in importance with the Nicene Creed."[39] And in 1921, the fourth general council debated which wording of the Apostles' Creed should be used in the

---

32. The three ecumenical Creeds are the Apostles' Creed, the Nicene Creed, and the Athanasian Creed.
33. J. Eustace Purdie, *Concerning the Faith* (Toronto: Full Gospel Publishing House, 1951), Foreword.
34. *Concerning the Faith*, 11.
35. *Concerning the Faith*, 11–12.
36. *Concerning the Faith*, 15.
37. Minutes of the Apostolic Church General Council, 1929.
38. Minutes of the Apostolic Church General Council, 1929. In context this statement refers to the tenets of the Apostolic Church as well as the three creeds.
39. G. F. Taylor, "Christ Our Saviour," *Pentecostal Holiness Advocate* (April 3, 1919): 2.

Pentecostal Holiness Church.[40] The Church of God in Christ explicitly holds to the Apostles' Creed, Nicene Creed, and the Definition of Chalcedon.[41] In the Assemblies of God, Myer Pearlman decried those who were "insisting that the church discard the ancient time-honored creeds."[42] While a few Pentecostal churches appear to have had more of an aversion to creeds, this has never been the case for Pentecostalism as a whole.[43]

Summary

Classical Pentecostals share with all other Christians a strong faith in the triune God. When the Oneness heresy arose, orthodox Pentecostals were firm in their opposition to this anti-Trinitarian teaching. Rather, they have always maintained that the doctrine of the Trinity is the very heart of the Christian faith and the truth from which all other Christian doctrine flows.

REFLECTION QUESTIONS

1. What is the doctrine of the Trinity?

2. What is the problem with Oneness teaching?

3. What are the eternal relations of origin that distinguish the three persons of the Trinity?

4. Do Pentecostals find value in the ancient creeds?

5. Why are the creeds important if we hold to the principle of *sola scriptura*?

---

40. Minutes of the Fourth General Council of the Pentecostal Holiness Church, 24–25. The debate was whether the term "Catholic" or "Christian" should be used.
41. *Church of God in Christ Standardized Ordination Curriculum* (Memphis, TN: Church of God in Christ Publishing House, 2012), 14–16.
42. Myer Pearlman, "Christian Creed and Life: What of the Value and Danger of Creeds?," *Pentecostal Evangel* (September 7, 1929): 6.
43. The Church of God and the Church of God of Prophecy appear to have had more of an aversion to the creeds. But this anticreedalism is more characteristic of these two related denominations than of Pentecostalism as a whole.

PART 2

Questions About Salvation

QUESTION 9

Why Is the Blood of Jesus So Central to Pentecostalism?

If Pentecostals were going to appeal to some sort of evidence that God was at work in the movement, you might have expected them to look to miraculous signs. Yet, that was not the proof that early Pentecostals tended to offer. "The proof of the divine origin of this movement," they commonly insisted, "is that Christ is honoured and the Blood of the Cross extolled."[1] From the beginning, the blood of Jesus has been a central Pentecostal theme. All the way back to the beginnings of Pentecostalism on both sides of the Atlantic, the precious blood was proclaimed as of central importance. In the Welsh Revival, emphasis on the blood of Jesus continued "a long revival tradition in Wales," going back to the Calvinistic Methodists.[2] The songs of the Welsh Revival were "in the key either of the sufferings of Jesus in the Garden or on Calvary, or the gracious wonder of His atoning love."[3] At Azusa Street, eyewitness accounts tell us, "there was great emphasis on the work of Christ and a tremendous exaltation of the blood of Christ and the Cross."[4] From the very beginnings of English Pentecostalism, the blood of the Lamb was the focus of worship, and "a large part of the meetings was spent on our knees, praying, singing, or in silence praying to God's Lamb,

1. W. T. Greenstreet, "Revival Tidings from Near and Far: Pentecost in Poland," *Redemption Tidings* 9, no. 5 (May 1933): 15.
2. Ben Pugh, "Power in the Blood: The Significance of the Blood of Jesus to the Spirituality of Early British Pentecostalism and Its Precursors," (PhD diss., University of Bangor, 2009), 134.
3. H. Elvet Lewis, "The Heart of the Revival," *British Weekly* (February 2, 1905), quoted in Eifion Evans, *The Welsh Revival of 1904* (Bridgend: Bryntirion, 1987), 167.
4. Stanley M. Horton, "The Pentecostal Perspective," in *Five Views on Sanctification*, ed. Stanley N. Gundry (Grand Rapids: Zondervan, 1987), 108.

whose Blood was so precious."[5] A century later G. E. Patterson, the presiding bishop and chief apostle of the Church of God in Christ (the largest Pentecostal denomination in the United States), was still preaching (and leading congregations in singing of) the precious blood of Jesus, just like countless numbers of unknown Pentecostal pastors in churches large and small all over the world.[6] Ben Pugh sums up the centrality of Christ's blood to the movement: "The Blood is almost as definitive of Pentecostal origins as the Spirit."[7] Jesus "poured out His blood for you and for me" and so we "trust that precious blood of Jesus for our salvation—the blood alone!"[8]

The front cover of one of the earliest editions of the American Assemblies of God magazine was devoted to "the Precious Blood of Christ." Summing up why Pentecostals loved this theme so dearly, "The Blood," the cover article proclaimed, "is the theme of the Word of God from the first book, in which we see God making coats of skin—involving the shedding of blood—for Adam and his wife, until the last, with its revelation of the Slain Lamb and the Courts of Heaven resounding with the praises of those whom He has loved and washed from their sins in His own Blood." It then lists the benefits that are found in the blood of Jesus alone: safety, atonement, life, access to God, redemption, the forgiveness of sins, sanctification, and victory. Those who "deny the blood" thereby "reject the only means of safety, of atonement, of life, of access to God, of forgiveness of sins, of holiness and of victory."[9] This is what Pentecostals mean by the power of the blood.

But Pentecostals recognize not only the power of the blood—they also recognize (and loudly proclaim) the *necessity* of the blood of the Jesus. "We believe that the measure of truly divine blessing that any movement experiences depends upon its attitude to this vital and precious subject," wrote a British Pentecostal leader in the 1960s, warning that "evangelical bodies and testimonies that deteriorate in the faith and proclamation of the essential truth concerning the Blood of Christ proceed surely to their death."[10] A Pentecostalism without the blood would be a Pentecostalism that had departed from its most important message.

---

5. T. B. Barratt, "The Conference in Sunderland," *Confidence* 1, no. 4 (July 1908): 5.
6. To give one example, more than a million people have watched Bishop G. E. Patterson's sermon "There Is Power in the Blood" on YouTube in the last eighteen months. See G. E. Patterson, "There Is Power in the Blood," YouTube, March 6, 2021, 38:36, https://youtu.be/ddwqA803r0Y.
7. Pugh, "Power in the Blood," 187.
8. Dotun Davies, *Blessed: Living in the Fullness of God's Blessings* (Liverpool: TAC, 2019), 15, 17.
9. "The Precious Blood of Christ," *Weekly Evangel* (January 20, 1917), front cover.
10. W. A. C. Rowe, *One Lord, One Faith* (Bradford: Puritan Press, n.d.), 87.

The Centrality of the Cross

Here we should clarify that to speak of the blood of Jesus is to speak of his atoning death for us.[11] It is not a red liquid that is powerful; it is the blood of the incarnate God poured out for his people in death. Christ's atoning work on the cross isn't simply one aspect of the Pentecostal faith among many—it is right at the heart of all that Pentecostals believe. Harold Horton, one of the most significant early Pentecostal Bible teachers in the English-speaking world (and beyond), insisted that "the cross must be all."[12] The Holy Spirit "will honour . . . the simple proclamation of the naked truth that Jesus saves through the blood of the cross."[13] Summing up the centrality of the cross for Pentecostals, Horton writes, "The nearer we get to this splendid glory of the . . . cross the more the glory of the Lord surrounds us."[14] The great first-generation Welsh Pentecostal leader D. P. Williams also insisted on the centrality of the glory of the cross to the Pentecostal message: "We preach Christ Crucified. It is the Sword—the Word of God. . . . This is our Victory—the ministry concerning the Blood."[15] And this message of the cross is central to the whole of the Pentecostal message, for "it is only on the ground of the Blood that the Holy Ghost does His work."[16] For Pentecostals, "the heart is the cross . . . wisdom with blood on it; goodness with blood on it; mercy with blood on it; power with blood on it."[17] Glory is only found through the blood of Jesus.

W. R. Thomas, who went from Britain to pioneer a major Pentecostal work in Italy between the two world wars, expresses how the Pentecostal understanding of the work of the Holy Spirit is rooted in the cross of Jesus: "The Holy Spirit always leads us to Calvary; he exalts the blood of Christ and manifests himself only where Christ's atoning and substitutionary death is fully and humbly acknowledged."[18] That is why Harold Horton insists that even the nine supernatural gifts of the Holy Spirit are "designed by God to enhance the glory of the cross," not to distract or detract from it in any way.[19]

---

11. Leon Morris, *The Apostolic Preaching of the Cross*, 3rd rev. ed. (Grand Rapids: Eerdmans, 1965), 112–26; Alan Stibbs, *His Blood Works: The Meaning of the Word "Blood" in Scripture* (Fearn, Ross-shire: Christian Heritage, 2011), 77–83.
12. Harold Horton, "The Naked Splendour of the Cross," *Redemption Tidings* 19, no. 22 (October 22, 1943): 3.
13. Horton, "Naked Splendour of the Cross," 1.
14. Horton, "Naked Splendour of the Cross," 1.
15. D. P. Williams, "The Weapons of Our Warfare," *Riches of Grace* 15, no. 3 (April 1940): 25–26.
16. D. P. Williams, "Return of a Pure Language," *Riches of Grace* 1, no. 9 (1920): 28.
17. D. P. Williams, "Exposition," *Riches of Grace* 11, no. 1 (September 1935): 41.
18. W. R. Thomas, *Il Paracleto: La Persona e l'Opera dello Spirito Santo* (Naples: Edizioni Ricchezze di Grazia, 1961), 2.
19. Harold Horton, "The Naked Splendour of the Cross (Part 2)," *Redemption Tidings* 19, no. 23 (November 5, 1943): 4.

Atoning Blood

The Scriptures proclaim that in Christ "we have redemption through his blood, the forgiveness of our trespasses, according to the riches of his grace" (Eph. 1:7). Therefore, we are "justified by his blood" (Rom. 5:9). For Pentecostals, this justification through the blood of the Jesus is at the root of all the blessings of the blood: "The shedding of the precious Blood of Christ is the powerful basis and means by and through which, is provided *all* that a sinner can need. Justification is the sinner's first great need and paves the way for all the blessings of salvation that follow."[20] The blood of Jesus alone is "the wide-open golden gate of grace," and so it is the only way into "divine favour and fellowship." It is only justification through the atoning blood of Jesus that brings us into "the enjoyment of all other favours."[21] This finished work of Jesus in shedding his blood on the cross, by dying in our place, is the only way to be saved. "We can find salvation only in the blood sacrifice of Christ. . . . Our salvation is in Christ's blood, not in our good deeds."[22]

Rather than relying on our good deeds, we rely wholly on Jesus and his shed blood for us. This means that the benefits of the blood are applied by faith alone: "Everything, literally everything, depends upon the precious Blood of Christ; but none of this can be ours unless by faith we lay hold personally of its reality and effectiveness. The shed Blood of the Paschal Lamb was unavailing unless it was sprinkled actually on the door posts and lintels. The same is true spiritually, the Blood of Christ must be taken and applied by faith."[23] This Exodus-Passover imagery of applying the blood to the door posts and lintels of our hearts goes back to the very earliest days of Pentecostalism as a way to describe faith as our personal reliance on the shed blood of the Lamb of God. In England, Pentecostals were taught to pray, "I praise Thee . . . that Thou didst bear all my sins, and didst bear away my sin. I sprinkle Thy Blood on the Lintel and Doorposts of my heart, and I am safe from the destroyer. I thank Thee again for this sign of Victory and this red mark of ownership. I belong to Thee my Crucified Saviour, whose Blood cleanses from all sin."[24] At Azusa Street, Christian believers were described as "people that are living under the Blood."[25] True saving faith is sheltering under the shed, atoning blood of Jesus (Rom. 3:25).

---

20. Rowe, *One Lord, One Faith*, 90–91.
21. Rowe, *One Lord, One Faith*, 93.
22. Davies, *Blessed*, 18.
23. Rowe, *One Lord, One Faith*, 93.
24. Alexander Boddy, "Pleading the Blood," *Confidence* 1, no. 5 (August 1908): 5–6.
25. "Questions Answered," *Apostolic Faith* 1, no. 11 (October–January 1908): 2. For the predominance of this expression in publications from Azusa Street, see Pugh, "Power in the Blood," 172.

Cleansing Blood

We are justified by Christ's blood, yet in that acceptance in Christ we are also blessed with every spiritual blessing in him (Eph. 1:3). Therefore, it should not surprise us that the Scriptures connect the blood of Jesus with every aspect of our salvation in Christ. This includes our sanctification.

Those who are in Christ Jesus have been sanctified by "the blood of the covenant" (Heb. 10:29). Hebrews is not referring here to the ongoing process of sanctification but something that has already taken place, for "we have been sanctified through the offering of the body of Jesus Christ once for all" (Heb. 10:10). Thus, our definitive (or positional) sanctification is through the blood of Jesus. God "already sees us [believers in Christ] as holy because of Christ's cleansing blood."[26] In definitive sanctification, "as a result of the finished work of Christ the penitent is changed from a defiled sinner into a holy worshiper."[27]

However, the efficacy of the blood of Jesus is not limited to the moment of conversion. "There is also a continuous aspect to sanctification by the blood."[28] For, "if we walk in the light, as he is in the light, we have fellowship with one another, and the blood of Jesus his Son cleanses us from all sin" (1 John 1:7). The next verses connect this ongoing cleansing to confession of sin (1 John 1:8–2:2). Myer Pearlman summed this up for his Pentecostal readers: "consciousness of sin mars fellowship with God; confession and faith in the eternal sacrifice of Christ removes the barrier."[29] Throughout this life, Christians will constantly need the cleansing power of Christ's blood. Our progressive sanctification is no less dependent on the blood than is our justification.

Victory by the Blood

Closely connected to the sanctifying power of the blood is the theme of victory. Early Pentecostals spoke frequently of victory through the blood, yet this wide image could encompass a number of different ideas.

First, the blood of Jesus is powerful for victory over temptation. It is Christ who has triumphed over sin through his death in our place on the cross, and so in the spiritual warfare of the Christian life believers fight against sin and temptation only in the power of "the finished work of Christ on Calvary."[30] In this battle, we march "forth to new conquests in His name beneath His blood-stained banner, ever living a patient, sober, unselfish, godly life that

26. David Petts, *The Holy Spirit: An Introduction* (Mattersey: Mattersey Hall, 1998), 57. For more on definitive or positional sanctification, see question 13.
27. Myer Pearlman, *Knowing the Doctrines of the Bible* (Springfield, MO: Gospel Publishing House, 1937), 255.
28. Pearlman, *Knowing the Doctrines*, 255.
29. Pearlman, *Knowing the Doctrines*, 255.
30. Donald Gee, "Studies on the Fundamental Truths: 7," *Redemption Tidings* 2, no. 7 (July 1926): 14.

will be a true reflection of the Christ within."[31] Believers see Calvary as "a glorious place of victory as well as a place of forgiveness," for "the poured-out Blood speaks to us of complete victory over sin."[32] It is only by the blood of Jesus that we "overcome [our] untiring, cunning adversary,"[33] for it is "faith in His Blood" which will withstand "temptations from below and around."[34] That is why Pentecostals often "plead the blood" when praying against temptation, for "the mention of the Blood stirs all Heaven. It is poison to the Hosts of Hell."[35] When the world, the flesh, or the devil present temptations, we should run to the precious blood of Jesus. "When Satan presents anything to you, just tell him you are under the blood. Just plead the blood, and he will flee.... When the Holy Ghost is working, keep your eyes centered upon Jesus, and when the devil presents a thought, just rebuke him and plead the blood."[36]

Second, Jesus, through his shed blood, has won the victory over the forces of darkness and causes us to share in his victory. An article in *The Apostolic Faith* drew on Matthew 7:9–11 and Luke 11:11–13 to point to how our heavenly Father protects us from the devil's work: "Never let the hosts of hell make you believe that while you live under the blood, honoring the blood, and pleading through the blood for blessings from the throne, that God will let Satan get through the blood and put a serpent into you. There is no way for Satan to make his way through the blood."[37]

The early Pentecostals confidently proclaimed that "the blood of Jesus prevails against every force and power of the enemy."[38] Trusting in Jesus and sheltering under his blood, there is no need to fear demonic powers, for "evil spirits cannot come under the Blood, any more than the Egyptians could pass through the Red Sea.... The Blood gives you power over all the power of the enemy. But we must have Christ within us."[39] The blood is not an abstract source of power. We can rely upon the power of the shed blood of Jesus because, through faith, Jesus who shed his blood for us dwells in us and we dwell in him.

Access by the Blood

Pentecostals are confident that they can draw near into the heavenly holy of holies by the blood of Jesus (Heb. 10:19–22). It is through Christ's death for our sins that we have access into the presence of God with our prayers, requests, and worship, and that we draw near to God in close communion.

---

31. FDF, 8.
32. Boddy, "Pleading the Blood," 3–4.
33. Boddy, "Pleading the Blood," 4.
34. Alexander Boddy, "Born from Above," *Confidence* 2, no. 4 (April 1909): 96.
35. Boddy, "Pleading the Blood," 6.
36. "Jesus, O How Sweet the Name," *Apostolic Faith* 1, no. 11 (October 1907–January 1908): 4.
37. "If We Ask Our Father for Bread," *Apostolic Faith* 1, no. 4 (December 1906): 3.
38. "Pentecost with Signs Following," *Apostolic Faith* 1, no. 4 (December 1906): 1.
39. "Questions Answered," *Apostolic Faith* 1, no. 11 (October 1907–January 1908): 2.

One early Pentecostal writer described this boldness to enter into the holiest as the "best of all" the benefits of the blood.[40]

Older Pentecostals often speak of "pleading the blood" as they come to the Lord with their prayers and worship. This pleading the blood, early Pentecostals explained, simply meant "presenting the Atonement to the Father in the power of the Holy Ghost."[41] In other words, they were consciously relying on and giving thanks for Christ's finished work on the cross in all their prayers, intercession, and worship. Pentecostals sing of the blood and mention the blood frequently in their prayers, as it is only by the shed blood of Jesus that we have been rescued from our sin, brought near to God, and welcomed into his presence.

Summary

The precious shed blood of Jesus is at the heart of Pentecostal faith and Pentecostal worship because it is only through Christ's death in our place on the cross that we are saved. The Pentecostal emphasis on the baptism and gifts of the Holy Spirit is not a distraction from the centrality of Christ's blood, but rather "the Holy Spirit always exalts Jesus, and His precious blood. As He is exalted and faithfully preached, God is restoring the old time power."[42]

REFLECTION QUESTIONS

1. What do we mean when we talk about the blood of Jesus?
2. Why is the blood of Jesus such a central theme for Pentecostals?
3. How does Christ's blood bring about our salvation?
4. In what ways is victory found through the blood of Jesus?
5. What does it mean to "plead the blood"?

---

40. S. A. Jamieson, *Pillars of Truth* (Springfield, MO: Gospel Publishing House, 1926), 92.
41. "Sunderland International Pentecostal Congress, Whitsun, 1909: A Record in Detail," *Confidence* 2, no. 7 (July 1909): 159.
42. Frank Bartleman, *How Pentecost Came to Los Angeles* (Los Angeles: n.p., 1925), 151.

QUESTION 10

Do Pentecostals Believe in Penal Substitution?

The good news Pentecostals preach and believe is centered on the cross of Christ. Jesus suffered under Pontius Pilate and died on a cross outside the walls of Jerusalem. Yet it is not simply that Jesus died, but that he "died for our sins" (1 Cor. 15:3). The death of Jesus on the cross accomplished something; for through his death on the cross Jesus saves.

The French Assemblies of God sum up what Pentecostals believe about the power of Christ's atoning death on the cross in their declaration of faith: "[Christ] died by crucifixion in order to fulfil the Scriptures and according to the determined purpose of God. We believe in the sacrifice of his perfect life offered up once-for-all on the cross and by which we receive the forgiveness of our sins and reconciliation with God, that we might have eternal life."[1] Or, as the Dutch Pentecostal Churches succinctly confess, "Through his suffering and death on the cross, he made an eternal atonement for all who believe in him."[2]

Penal Substitution at the Cross

At the heart of the Pentecostal understanding of the cross is the fact that Jesus died in our place, taking the punishment we deserved for our sins. This is the doctrine of penal substitution: Christ died as our substitute (in our place), bearing the penalty of sin (the punishment we deserved).

Jesus himself said that he "came not to be served but to serve, and to give his life as a ransom for many" (Matt. 20:28; Mark 10:45). The use of "for" (*anti*) here carries the specific substitutionary meaning of "instead of" or "in the place of."[3] Jesus came to give his life as the ransom price for sinners; he

1. AdDDF, 4.
2. VPE, "Geloofsbasis," 3.
3. Leon Morris, *The Apostolic Preaching of the Cross*, 3rd ed. (Grand Rapids: Eerdmans, 1965), 34.

died in their place. This is a substitutionary death. But it is also a penal death, for the ransom price that Jesus paid is the penalty for sin.

Paul writes that "Christ redeemed us from the curse of the law by becoming a curse for us—for it is written, 'Cursed is everyone who is hanged on a tree'" (Gal. 3:13). The curse he writes of is the punishment sinners deserve for their sin (Gal. 3:10). Thus, by his death on the cross, Jesus has taken on our curse in order to set us free from it. The curse he takes at the cross is the penalty for our sins, and he bears this penalty in our place. This is penal substitution.[4]

Penal Substitution and Propitiation

What is this curse or penalty for sin? The death that Christ died is the penalty that he paid for our sins, for indeed, "the wages of sin is death" (Rom. 6:23). As John Stott explains, "The Bible everywhere views human death not as a *natural* but as a *penal* event," for "death (both physical and spiritual) is seen as a divine judgment on human disobedience."[5] This death is not only physical but also spiritual and judicial, and as such it is the expression of God's wrath against sin (Rom. 1:18). The wrath of God is not an irrational outburst of anger but rather "his steady, unrelenting, unremitting, uncompromising antagonism to evil in all its forms and manifestations."[6] As Leon Morris points out: "Those who object to the conception of the wrath of God should realize that what is meant is not some irrational passion bursting forth uncontrollably, but a burning zeal for the right coupled with a perfect hatred of everything that is evil." Rather, his is "a love which is so jealous for the good of the loved one that it blazes out in fiery wrath against everything that is evil."[7] God's wrath is, in the words of the Scottish theologian Donald Baillie, "identical with the consuming fire of inexorable love in relation to our sins."[8]

Therefore, in order to take our place in bearing the penalty for our sins, Jesus had to take our place in bearing the wrath of God through his death on the cross. This is what the Bible calls "propitiation." It is a sacrifice that takes away the wrath of God. In his epistle, John tells us that Christ's work of propitiation is the manifestation of God's love for us: "In this the love of God was made manifest among us, that God sent his only Son into the world, so that we might live through him. In this is love, not that we have loved God but that he loved us and sent his Son to be the propitiation for our sins" (1 John 4:9–10). This is

---

4. For further scriptural support for the doctrine of penal substitution, see Jonathan Black, *Apostolic Theology: A Trinitarian, Evangelical, Pentecostal Introduction to Christian Doctrine* (Luton: Apostolic Church, 2016), 256–67.
5. John Stott, *The Cross of Christ*, 20th anniversary ed. (Nottingham: InterVarsity Press, 2006), 77.
6. Stott, *Cross of Christ*, 202.
7. Morris, *Apostolic Preaching*, 209.
8. D. M. Baillie, *God Was in Christ* (London: Scribners, 1948), 189.

why Christ came into the world and took on our "flesh and blood," in order "to make propitiation for the sins of the people" (Heb. 2:14, 17).

The fact that Christ's death was the propitiation for our sins (Rom. 3:24–26; 1 John 2:1–2) means that in his death he bore the penalty for our sins, God's wrath, which was our due. Therefore, propitiation involves penal substitution, for as our propitiation Jesus took the punishment in our place.

A proper Trinitarian theology is important to help us understand the doctrines of propitiation and penal substitution. It is not a matter of an angry Father lashing out at a loving Son. Both the love and the wrath belong to the triune God. And so, "It is God himself who in holy wrath needs to be propitiated, God himself who in holy love undertook to do the propitiating, and God himself who in the person of [the] Son died for the propitiation of our sins. Thus God took his own loving initiative to appease his own righteous anger by bearing it his own self in [the person of the] Son when he took our place and died for us."[9]

It is God himself, in the person of God the Son, who has taken on our humanity, who died as our propitiation and penal substitute. And God the Son, who is our penal substitute, is "head of the body" and "one with all the members of the body," and so "he can bear the moral responsibility, the guilt for their sin, and they can enjoy the moral responsibility, the reward, for his righteousness."[10] Our understanding of penal substitution must be rooted in both a good Trinitarian theology and a strong understanding of the union of believers with Christ.

Penal Substitution: The Heart of the Pentecostal Gospel

All over the world, from the very beginning of the movement, Pentecostals have proclaimed the good news of salvation through Christ's penal substitutionary death on the cross.[11] In the UK, Pentecostals have always seen penal substitution as "the very heart of the gospel."[12] The *Catechism upon the Tenets of the Apostolic Church*, for example, taught that Christ, "as our Substitute, by His Atonement, [made] full reparation and satisfaction to God the Father for the sin of mankind," and that "the sins of

9. Stott, *Cross of Christ*, 204.
10. Stephen R. Holmes, *The Wondrous Cross: Atonement and Penal Substitution in the Bible and History* (London: Paternoster, 2007), 97.
11. I am providing lots of evidence in this section, as some academics have recently tried to claim that Pentecostals either do not or should not believe in penal substitution. While space only permits a small amount of the vast evidence, this doctrine has in fact always been central to classical Pentecostalism.
12. W. R. Thomas, *The Virgin Birth, Sinless Life and Atoning Death of Our Lord Jesus Christ* (Bradford: Puritan Press, n.d.), 17. For more detail on penal substitution in British Pentecostalism, see Jonathan Black, "'The Very Heart of the Gospel': Penal Substitution in British Pentecostalism," *Journal of Pentecostal and Charismatic Christianity* 42, no. 2 (2022): 93–109.

mankind [were] imputed to Christ, as the Divine Sacrifice and Substitute for us."[13] An Apostolic children's catechism states that Jesus "died for, or in the place of mankind," explaining that "Jesus made propitiation for sin" by offering his "pure and perfect life on the altar in our place." Through this substitutionary and propitiatory death "God's justice was satisfied and sinners were saved from God's judgment." [14] D. P. Williams, the founding apostle of the Apostolic Church, taught that Jesus "took upon Himself the awful consequences of our sins" and suffered "the wrath of divine justice" for us, as our substitute and surety.[15] The confession of faith of the Apostolic Church UK states: "In offering Himself up to the Father through the Eternal Spirit on Calvary's cross in His atoning death, [Christ] shed His blood and died for our sin, bearing in our place the full penalty which we deserved. Christ has redeemed us from the curse of the law by bearing the curse for us in His work of propitiation."[16] In the first officially published explanation of the article on the atonement in the British Assemblies of God *Statement of Fundamental Truths*, John Carter teaches that "the sufferings and death of Christ were vicarious—i.e., in the place of others. . . . God, in Christ, took the sinner's place and bore the full penalty of his sin. . . . Justice therefore is now satisfied, the penalty for sin has been borne."[17]

British Pentecostal pioneers in other countries were also explicit about the centrality of penal substitution. In Italy, W. R. Thomas wrote that "the Lord Jesus died as our Substitute bearing our punishment."[18] While Garfield Vale, a British missionary to Congo, taught that "through His sufferings and death" Jesus "paid the penalty for our sins and perfectly satisfied the demands of Divine Justice. . . . It is a penalty paid in order to deliver the guilty." Christ's death was a "substitution . . . by paying all the incurred penalties."[19]

In the United States, Pentecostals across denominations also taught penal substitution. In the very earliest years of the movement, Albert Copley taught that Christ died as a propitiation for those who stood condemned by their sins. "This is substitution. Jesus Christ took the place of the ungodly, died the death that he should have died, i.e., of a guilty sinner. . . . By tasting death for every man, He appeased the wrath of God." Copley also made clear that

13. *Catechism upon the Tenets of the Apostolic Church* (Penygroes: Apostolic Church, n.d.), 3.3.16; 3.3.24.
14. Kongo Jones, *Holwyddoreg ar Fywyd ein Harglwydd Iesu Grist* (Penygroes: Eglwys Apostolaidd, n.d.), 8.1 (p. 28), 8.9–10 (p. 31).
15. D. P. Williams, "The Priesthood of Our Lord Jesus Christ," *Herald of Grace* 5, no. 3 (March 1945): 48–49.
16. ACVG, 3.
17. John Carter, "Studies on the Fundamental Truths No. 4," *Redemption Tidings* 2, no. 4 (April 1926): 13.
18. W. R. Thomas, *L'Emmanuele* (Naples: Edizioni Ricchezze di Grazia, 1965), 37.
19. Garfield Vale, "Topical Studies on Doctrinal Topics: Atonement," *Redemption Tidings* 9, no. 1 (January 1933): 7.

this was not a novel teaching for his Pentecostal readers: "With this truth," he wrote, "we are well acquainted."[20]

Pentecostals continued to be well acquainted with this vital truth. Stanley Frodsham, a significant early Assemblies of God leader, taught that "Jesus . . . came down from the glory and on our behalf he paid the death penalty due to us for breaking the law. . . . At Calvary he took our sin, and now he gives us his own righteousness. . . . The shedding of [his blood] has fully paid the penalty for all our sins."[21] In the first major Assemblies of God overview of Christian doctrine (a book that has been translated into several languages, is still in print, and is still used in Pentecostal Bible colleges all over the world), Myer Pearlman sets out a penal substitutionary understanding of the atonement: "In the Person of His Son, God Himself took the penalty. . . . Having assumed human nature, He was able to identify Himself with mankind and so suffer their penalty. He died in our stead; He took the penalty that was ours."[22]

The Foursquare Church, from its earliest days, taught that "Christ took our place in His death. We were under the sentence of death because of sin. Christ in His death on the cross became our substitute and bore for us the penalty of sin . . . that we might be made the righteousness of God."[23] The Foursquare Declaration of Faith teaches penal substitution very explicitly: "We believe that while we were yet sinners Christ died for us, the Just for the unjust; freely, and by divine appointment of the Father, taking the sinner's place, bearing his sins, receiving his condemnation, dying his death, fully paying his penalty."[24]

Wesleyan Holiness Pentecostals also taught penal substitution from the beginning. In 1908, Hattie Barth wrote in the Pentecostal journal *The Bridegroom's Messenger* that Christ "fulfilled every demand of the law, became our substitute, paid the penalty that we might go free. Every demand of justice having been satisfied."[25] Church of God writers held to penal substitution too. An early Church of God publication taught that "our Lord Jesus Christ took upon Himself our nature (sin excepted) and became the substitute for the human family that he might bear the penalty due their sin (both natural or Adamic and actual)."[26] More recently, Church of God theologian French Arrington set out a very clear doctrine of penal substitutionary atonement in

---

20. A. S. Copley, "Pauline Sanctification," *The Pentecost* 2, no. 6 (May 1910): 6.
21. Stanley Frodsham, "The Ten Commandments," *The Christian Evangel* (February 8, 1919): 10.
22. Myer Pearlman, *Knowing the Doctrines of the Bible* (Springfield, MO: Gospel Publishing House, 1937), 206, 208.
23. F. E. R., "Healing in the Atonement," *The Bridal Call* 7, no. 5 (October 1923): 11.
24. FDF, 4.
25. Hattie Barth, "Justification, Sanctification, and the Baptism of the Holy Ghost," *The Bridegroom's Messenger* 1, no. 6 (January 1908): 2.
26. J. M. Stanfield, "Degeneracy of the Human Race," *Church of God Evangel* 6, no. 31 (July 31, 1915): 3.

his three-volume *Christian Doctrine: A Pentecostal Perspective*: "Christ paid the full penalty for our disobedience. He bore the judgment of death we deserved. . . . In His crucifixion Jesus was our substitute, bearing the penalty of our sins in His own body on the cross. The word *substitute* means that Jesus carried our sins so we will never have to suffer the penalty for our transgressions. . . . He died *in the place of* those who should have died."[27] Just like the Pentecostals in the UK, Arrington is convinced the fact "that Jesus died as our substitute is the heart of the gospel."[28]

This is not just the opinion of some Pentecostal writers in Britain and North America. This is the ubiquitous teaching of classical Pentecostals all over the world. Pentecostal confessions of faith around the world testify to the firm faith of Pentecostals in Christ's substitutionary atoning death.[29] The Nigerian Apostolic writer Dotun Davies teaches that "men are acquitted because a loving Saviour took their place and accepted the sentence of death on a Cross. . . . Christ assumes the penalty of our transgressions and acquits us."[30] In Pakistan, the Full Gospel Assemblies Bible College teaches, "We believe in the atoning sacrifice of Christ on the cross: dying in our place, paying the price of sin and defeating evil, so reconciling us with God."[31] Dutch Pentecostals confess their belief that "on the cross, Jesus, as substitute . . . bore the penalty for sin and effected reconciliation and peace with God for everyone who believes in him."[32] The Hungarian Pentecostal Church confesses that the Lord Jesus Christ "took the penalty for us, in our place in his death on the cross for our sins."[33] Romanian Pentecostals confess that Jesus died for our sins,

---

27. French Arrington, *Christian Doctrine: A Pentecostal Perspective* (Cleveland, TN: Pathway Press, 1993), 2:63, 73.
28. Arrington, *Christian Doctrine*, 2:74.
29. E.g., WAGFSF, 2.b; Assembleias de Deus em Portugal, "Declaração de Fé," 1; Apoštolská Církev Vyznání (Confession of Faith of the Czech Apostolic Pentecostal Church), 4; Apoštolská Cirkev na Slovensku *Čomu veríme* (Confession of Faith of the Apostolic Pentecostal Church of Slovakia), 2; Freie Christengemeinde Österreich, "Doctrinal Principles," 3; Estonian Christian Pentecostal Church, "Basic Principles," 3; AGSFT, 3.d; Mosaik (The Danish Pentecostal Movement), "Declaration of Faith," 2; L'Église Apostolique Belge, "Confession de Foi de," 2; Assemblee di Dio in Italia, "Articoli di Fede," 4; Christian Churches Ireland, "Statement of Faith," 3; BFP, Creed, 3; Elim SFT, 3. Some Pentecostal academics argue that these could refer to non-penal forms of substitution; however, the historical context for the adoption of the wording of substitutionary atonement—in comparison with how the same wording is used for penal substitution among other late-nineteenth and early-twentieth-century evangelicals, and official publications from Pentecostal denominations explaining their confessions—all demonstrate that by substitutionary atonement Pentecostals have always understood what theologians would more precisely call penal substitution.
30. Dotun Davies, *Blessed: Living in the Fullness of God's Blessings* (Liverpool: TAC, 2019), 12.
31. Full Gospel Assemblies Bible College (Pakistan), "Statement of Faith," 6.
32. VPE, "Geloofsbasis," 7.
33. Magyar Pünkösdi Egyház, "Hitvallásunk," 2.2.

"bearing the punishment that the sinner deserved."[34] In Brazil, the declaration of faith of the Assemblies of God teaches that Christ's death was the "propitiation for our offences" and a "substitutionary death" involving the "transfer of guilt from the sinner to the victim." As such, "his death was in our place" as "the act that appeases divine wrath."[35] As the wrath of God is the penalty for sin, this is a clear statement of penal substitutionary atonement.

Penal Substitution and *Christus Victor*

Pentecostals affirm, uphold, and proclaim the doctrine of penal substitutionary atonement. That does not mean, however, that it is the only aspect of what Jesus accomplished at the cross that they affirm. In the last chapter, for example, we looked at the connection between the blood of Jesus and victory. Christ's victory at the cross (*Christus Victor*) has always been a significant Pentecostal theme. Yet *Christus Victor* and penal substitution are not in competition as two mutually exclusive or alternative understandings of the atonement. Rather, Christ triumphs at the cross through bearing the penalty in our place. He is our victor *because* he is our penal substitute. Christ's victory is rooted in his work of propitiation (Gal. 1:4; Heb. 2:14–17).[36] Our penal substitute is the one who tramples down death, hell, sin, and the devil through the conquest of the cross. For the story of Scripture is the "unfolding story of victory through sacrifice."[37]

Summary

From the movement's beginning right down to today, Pentecostals all over the world have been united in their faith in Jesus as our penal substitute who died on the cross in our place, bearing the full penalty for all our sins. This is the heart of the gospel which Pentecostals believe and proclaim.

REFLECTION QUESTIONS

1. What is the penalty for sin?
2. Why do we need a penal substitute?
3. How is Jesus our propitiation?

---

34. Romanian CF, 10.
35. Brazil DdF, 5.1, 5.2, 5.4.
36. Black, *Apostolic Theology*, 276–79. See further, Joshua M. McCall, *The Mosaic of Atonement: An Integrated Approach to Christ's Work* (Grand Rapids: Zondervan, 2019), 314–17.
37. Jeremy R. Treat, *The Crucified King: Atonement and Kingdom in Biblical and Systematic Theology* (Grand Rapids: Zondervan, 2014), 129.

4. Why do Pentecostals see penal substitution as “the very heart of the gospel”?
5. How do penal substitution and *Christus Victor* fit together?

QUESTION 11

How Do Pentecostals Understand Justification?

Jesus is the Savior. That is the heart of the Pentecostal faith. Yes, Jesus is also the healer, baptizer in the Holy Spirit, and soon-coming King, but all of that depends first and foremost on the fact that he is the Savior. There is nothing more central to the faith of Pentecostals than salvation in Jesus. This question, then, focuses on one aspect of the salvation found in Christ: justification.

Justification by Grace Alone

Pentecostals are heirs of the Reformation, holding with great conviction to the Reformation doctrine of justification by grace alone through faith alone.[1] In India, Pentecostals confess that "justification [is] wrought by the grace of God, and faith in the Lord Jesus Christ," which is in harmony with Pakistani Pentecostals, who believe "in the justification of sinners by the grace of God through faith in Jesus Christ."[2] The Methodist Pentecostal Church of Chile "firmly teaches and upholds the biblical doctrine of justification by faith alone," emphasizing that justification is "by faith in Jesus Christ and not by works of the law."[3] The Italian Apostolics likewise stress that justification is "not by our works" but only "through the atoning sacrifice of Jesus Christ, the Eternal Son of God incarnate to redeem humanity."[4]

In North America, the International Pentecostal Holiness Church is equally emphatic: "We believe, teach and firmly maintain the scriptural doctrine of

1. P. C. Nelson, *Bible Doctrines*, rev. ed. (Springfield, MO: Gospel Publishing House, 1981), 33; see also Guy P. Duffield and Nathaniel M. Van Cleave, *Foundations of Pentecostal Theology* (Los Angeles, CA: Foursquare Media, 2008), 225.
2. Indian Pentecostal Church of God, "Statement of Faith," 5; Full Gospel Assemblies Bible College (Pakistan), "Statement of Faith," 8.
3. Iglesia Metodista Pentecostal de Chile, "Declaración de Fe," 8.
4. Chiesa Apostolica in Italia, "Articoli di Fedi," 4.

justification by faith alone." Further, the two largest Pentecostal denominations in the United States, the Church of God in Christ and the Assemblies of God, both also confess their belief in this Reformation doctrine.[5] The declaration of faith of the Foursquare Church states that those "who call upon [Christ] may be justified by faith" and that this "salvation of sinners is wholly through grace."[6] Acts Churches New Zealand and Acts Global Churches of Australia likewise confess that salvation is received "by grace and through faith in Christ alone."[7] Thus, Pentecostals all over the world are united in this Reformation belief in justification by grace alone through faith alone.

But why do Pentecostals around the world hold to this Reformation doctrine? For Pentecostals, the answer to that question can only be because they see it taught in Scripture. Paul highlights this gracious nature of our justification, writing that we are "justified by his grace as a gift, through the redemption that is in Christ Jesus" (Rom. 3:24; cf. Titus 3:7). Grace and the saving work of Christ are inseparable, for "God gives his grace freely in Jesus, who was given for us and is offered to us in the gospel."[8] It is this grace of God in Christ that *alone* justifies sinners. Our works cannot be added to Christ's finished work, for "a person is not justified by works of the law but through faith in Jesus Christ . . . because by works of the law no one will be justified" (Gal. 2:16). Rooted in the Scriptures, Pentecostals very clearly teach that "justification cannot be worked for, nor merited. It is only received through God's grace."[9]

Declared Righteous

The Church of God in Christ clarifies that justification is a "judicial act of God in which He, on the basis of the righteousness of Jesus Christ . . . removes the guilt of sin and restores the sinner to all filial (son and daughter) rights as a child of God." This "takes place outside the sinner," and "God declares the sinner righteous."[10] In justification, a Canadian Pentecostal catechism tells us, "God declares one righteous, who has no righteousness of his own, [and] accepts him as such," and this "only . . . on the ground of the work our Lord Jesus Christ completed on the cross of Calvary."[11]

5. IPHC, "Articles of Faith," 8; CoGiC, "Salvation," in "What We Believe"; AGSFT, 5a.
6. FDF, 5–6.
7. Acts Churches New Zealand, "Statement of Belief," 3; Acts Global Churches (Apostolic Church Australia), "Statement of Faith," 3; see also ACC, "Doctrinal Basis," 4.8.
8. Jonathan Black, *Apostolic Theology: A Trinitarian, Evangelical Pentecostal Introduction to Christian Doctrine* (Luton: Apostolic Church, 2016), 406.
9. Duffield and Van Cleave, *Foundations*, 231.
10. "Articles of Faith," in *Official Manual with the Doctrines and Discipline of the Church of God in Christ* (Memphis, TN: CoGiC, 1991), 56–57. Cf. AdDDF, 5; Pentecostal Church of Finland, "The Main Articles of Faith of the Pentecostal Church of Finland," 4.
11. *Concerning the Faith* (Toronto: Full Gospel Publishing House, 1951), q. 217–18 (pp. 38–39).

The biblical words for "justify" in both Hebrew and Greek refer to a legal (or forensic) declaration.[12] It is the language of a courtroom judgment, where the accused is declared righteous (not made righteous). This declaratory nature can also be seen in that the opposite of justification in the New Testament is condemnation (e.g., Rom. 8:33–34). Condemnation is not a transformative process; it is the declaration of a verdict. The parallel between it and justification demonstrates that justification, likewise, cannot be a process of transformation either. Furthermore, other expressions used in Scripture as equivalents to justification are also forensic. Whoever has been justified "does not come into judgment" (John 5:24), is reconciled to God (2 Cor. 5:19–20), and does not have sin imputed but has righteousness imputed instead (Rom. 4:5–8). Thus, in Scripture justification is clearly a forensic declaration.

This is very important, for it means that justification is not an ongoing process of transformation. In that case, it would be more like progressive sanctification, in which we are conformed more and more to the image of Christ in holiness. We cannot become more justified (or less justified). If it were a process, it could depend in part on something in us; justification would in some measure be dependent upon our level of sanctification, and thus these two aspects of salvation would be confused.[13] In that case, it would not be by grace *alone*. That would be more like the Roman Catholic understanding of justification.[14] Pentecostals, however, hold to the Reformation doctrine in which justification and sanctification are clearly distinguished. Justification is an instantaneous declaration. Unlike regeneration or sanctification, justification does not involve a change inside of us. Rather, it is an external and objective declaration that gives us a new standing as righteous in God's sight.

Imputed Righteousness

The Redeemed Christian Church of God, which originated in Nigeria, highlights the imputation of Christ's righteousness in justification: "We are able to stand before God as though we have never sinned . . . clothed with a white garment which is the righteousness of Christ."[15] This imputation that is at the heart of the doctrine of justification is also explicit in the doctrinal statement of the Elim Pentecostal Church in the UK, which confesses that "the sinner is pardoned and accepted as righteous in God's sight" through

---

12. Matthew Barrett, *40 Questions About Salvation* (Grand Rapids: Kregel, 2018), 195.
13. For Pentecostals and other Protestants, our sanctification depends on our justification, but our justification does not depend on our sanctification. We partake of both through our union with Christ, but the two must never be confused or conflated, or we will run into difficulties.
14. In Roman Catholic theology, "justification is not only the remission of sins, but also the sanctification and renewal of the interior man" (*Catechism of the Catholic Church*, 2019; *Council of Trent, Decree on Justification*, chap. 7).
15. RCCG, "Justification and Our Garment," in "Beliefs."

"faith in the Lord Jesus Christ" and that "this justification is imputed by the grace of God because of the atoning work of Christ, is received by faith alone and is evidenced by the fruit of the Spirit and a holy life."[16]

Imputation is the positive side of justification, in which God reckons (or credits) the righteousness of Christ to our account. In justification "God counts righteousness apart from works" (Rom. 4:6). This is "the righteousness of God through faith in Jesus Christ for all who believe" (Rom. 3:22), imputed to us as a gift of God's grace. This is not "a righteousness of my own that comes from the law, but that which comes through faith in Christ, the righteousness from God that depends on faith" (Phil. 3:9). In other words, this righteousness is not something inherent in us. Rather, we receive this righteousness from God through faith in Christ, as a "free gift" (Rom. 5:17).

But it is not simply a righteousness that we receive from outside of ourselves as God's free gift. This righteousness comes to us through "one man's obedience" (Rom. 5:19). The status of righteousness that God gives us through faith in Christ is ours on the basis of someone else's obedience. Where we were disobedient, Christ obeyed for us; and now, through faith in Christ, we benefit from his perfect obedience—his righteousness for us. Christ's righteousness—his full obedience for us—is credited to the account of those who trust in him. This is what we mean by the imputation of Christ's righteousness.[17]

Christ not only died on the cross for us but lived a perfectly righteous, sinless life for us, in which he "fulfilled all the obligations of the law."[18] Christ took "the penal curse of the law upon himself [and] acts as a substitute for sinners, in which our sin is reckoned to be his."[19] But in this great exchange, God not only declares "the sinner to be 'not guilty' but as 'righteous.' This is done by God, not only imputing our guilt to Christ, but by imputing Christ's righteousness to us."[20] As Myer Pearlman put it, "man's only hope is to have a righteousness which God will accept—a 'righteousness of God.' Since man naturally lacks this righteousness, it must be provided for him; it must be an imputed righteousness."[21] This righteousness that God imputes to us is Christ's

---

16. Elim SFT, 6; cf. Hungarian Pentecostal Confession (Magyar Pünkösdi Egyház Hitvallásunk), 6.2
17. For fuller Pentecostal accounts of imputation, see Black, *Apostolic Theology*, 397–403; and Duffield and Van Cleave, *Foundations*, 228–29. For more in-depth accounts from non-Pentecostal authors (but sharing the same doctrine), see Barrett, *40 Questions About Salvation*, 211–26; Michael Horton, *Justification* (Grand Rapids: Zondervan, 2018), 2:321–66; and Thomas Schreiner, *Faith Alone: The Doctrine of Justification* (Grand Rapids: Zondervan, 2015), 170–90.
18. *Introducing the Apostolic Church: A Manual of Belief, Practice and History* (Penygroes: Apostolic Church, 1988), 144.
19. *Introducing the Apostolic Church*, 144.
20. *Introducing the Apostolic Church*, 144.
21. Myer Pearlman, *Knowing the Doctrines of the Bible* (Springfield, MO: Gospel Publishing House, 1936), 236.

obedience for us.[22] As a result, "not a single thing stands against the sinner's account; Christ's righteousness is imputed fully and effectually."[23] Thus, our justification relies entirely upon "the absolute righteousness and utter obedience and sacrifice of [the] only-begotten and incarnate Son."[24] Christ himself, to whom we are united through faith, is the believer's righteousness (1 Cor. 1:30; 2 Cor. 5:21).

A British Apostolic catechism sums up the Pentecostal (and Reformation) understanding of the doctrine:

> Q. What is justification?
>
> A. Justification is that act of God's grace which imputes to the sinner the righteousness of Christ, whereby he is accepted as righteous in God's sight.[25]

The Canadian catechism explains that the righteousness that is imputed in justification is the righteousness of "Christ's sinless and perfect life on earth which fulfilled every demand of the holy law of God in thought, word, and deed."[26]

Yet, this Reformation doctrine of justification through the imputation of Christ's righteousness is not confined to catechisms and confessional documents. It fills popular Pentecostal writing and preaching. In the early days of the American Assemblies of God, it was hailed as "amazing truth. . . . His righteousness imputed to us that we might be made the righteousness of God in Him—if we but accept His proffered mercy."[27] We should "not expect to stand before the Throne in any other" righteousness than Christ's "imputed righteousness. . . . His righteousness is laid on me."[28] Our own righteousness is nothing but "filthy rags, a word that in the Hebrew means something unmentionable, unspeakably loathsome to us. That is what our righteousness is in God's sight. We get imputed righteousness through and in Christ, and praise God for it."[29] As an article in *The Pentecost* put it in 1910, believers "are clothed with a righteousness which is acceptable to a holy God. Christ once dead, but now the living one, is made unto us righteousness."[30]

---

22. French L. Arrington, *Christian Doctrine: A Pentecostal Perspective* (Cleveland, TN: Pathway, 1993), 2:212.
23. W. A. C. Rowe, *One Lord, One Faith* (Bradford: Puritan Press, n.d.), 92.
24. Rowe, *One Lord, One Faith*, 91–92.
25. Clyne, *Asked and Answered*, 18.
26. *Concerning the Faith*, 39, q. 220.
27. "Our Acquittal," *Weekly Evangel* (March 27, 1915): 3.
28. "The Message of Easter," *Weekly Evangel* (April 7, 1917): 4.
29. "The Waiting Bridegroom," *Weekly Evangel* (January 12, 1918): 2.
30. "Lessons from Genesis," *The Pentecost* 2, no. 5 (April 1, 1910): 3.

In the UK, the great Pentecostal missionary pioneer of the Congo Evangelistic Mission, Willie Burton, preached of the robe of "the spotless God-wrought righteousness of Christ" imputed to all who believe. "Sinful as thou art, only believe on the Lord Jesus Christ: and thou shalt stand spotless before the throne of God, arrayed in the garments of a righteousness which He has provided."[31] The congregation at an early Elim convention heard in no uncertain terms that "the Bible tells us that we are saved by imputed righteousness."[32] Donald Gee, an important early British Pentecostal leader who became a noted Pentecostal thinker around the world, wrote of this imputation in response to a question sent in by a reader of *Redemption Tidings*: "This robe of imputed righteousness is consistently viewed in the Scriptures as being given by God to his people: it is neither a natural possession of their own nor the result of their own good works. To despise or neglect the provision of the spotless robe of Christ's imputed righteousness must inevitably result in the soul being unfit for the heavenly feast and the sight of the King in his beauty."[33]

The Norwegian Pentecostal pioneer T. B. Barratt wrote that "by faith in the atonement, we are imputed the righteousness of Christ without works."[34] These are merely a few examples, but they demonstrate that Pentecostal belief in justification by faith alone through the imputation of Christ's righteousness is neither geographically nor denominationally limited. This is a common theme to classical Pentecostals as a whole and vital to their understanding of salvation.

Justifying Faith

But what is faith? This is a crucial question when it comes to understanding justification by faith alone, but also one that has taken on a fresh importance for Pentecostals in the light of the distorted understanding of faith seen in the Word of Faith movement.[35] Classical Pentecostals understand faith as "a certain conviction wrought in the heart by the Holy Spirit, as to the truth of the Gospel and a heart trust in the promises of God in Christ."[36] This definition includes the three classical elements of the Protestant understanding of faith: *notitia* (understanding of the message of the gospel), *assensus* (believing that the contents of the gospel message are true), and *fiducia* (trusting in the gospel for oneself).

This faith comes by the Word of God,[37] and "has no independent merit apart from its object—the Lord Jesus Christ. . . . All the merits are in Christ

31. W. F. P. Burton, "Christ's Seamless Robe," *Elim Evangel* 4, no. 11 (November 1923): 228.
32. F. T. Ellis, "God's Record," *Elim Evangel* 4, no. 9 (September 1923): 172.
33. Donald Gee, "Answers to Questions," *Redemption Tidings* 5, no. 11 (November 1929): 17.
34. T. B. Barratt, "Holiness," *Redemption Tidings* 5, no. 6 (June 1929): 4.
35. We will look at the Word of Faith movement in question 14.
36. *CoGiC*, "Salvation," in "What We Believe."
37. *Concerning the Faith*, q. 201 (p. 36)

alone; faith is but the empty hand that reaches out and lays hold upon the fullness provided in Christ."[38] To have faith in Christ means to "throw oneself completely upon the merits of Christ's Blood and finished work, and depend . . . on that, and that alone, for salvation."[39] In order to help clarify that faith is simply resting and relying on Jesus who died for us (rather than something we do in order to merit God's favor), Pentecostals often speak of "justification . . . through the finished work of Christ" or being "justified . . . through his precious blood."[40] Aimee Semple McPherson describes this very Protestant Reformation understanding of faith shared by classical Pentecostals beautifully in the declaration of faith she wrote for the Foursquare Church: "We have no righteousness or goodness of our own wherewith to seek divine favor, and must come, therefore, throwing ourselves upon the unfailing mercy and love of Him who bought us and washed us in His own blood, pleading the merits and the righteousness of Christ the Savior, standing upon His word and accepting the free gift of love and pardon."[41] The focus in McPherson's declaration is on Christ, not on us; because faith is simply resting and relying on Jesus the Savior. And through resting and relying on the Savior, the believer has "imputed to him the righteousness of the Redeemer."[42]

Summary

God justifies sinners by declaring them righteous in Christ through clothing them with Christ for righteousness. So justification is something that God does *outside* of us, *for* us. Yet, justification is not the entirety of God's great salvation. For Pentecostals also believe that God works *in* us to transform us and make us a new creation in Christ Jesus through the new birth.

REFLECTION QUESTIONS

1. If justification were a lifelong process of transformation inside of us instead of an instantaneous declaration outside of us, could we ever have assurance that we are right with God?
2. Why must the righteousness that justifies be one that is imputed to us?

---

38. *Concerning the Faith*, q. 202–3 (p. 36)
39. *Concerning the Faith*, q. 207 (p. 37)
40. Apostolic Church, "Tenets," 4; FDF, 6; see also Gereja Bethel Indonesia, "Confession of Faith," 5. This is in keeping with the Reformation emphasis in Pentecostal soteriology. T. F. Torrance points to John Knox's preference for "justification through the blood of Christ"; see Torrance, "Justification," in *Theology in Reconstruction* (London: SCM, 1965), 151.
41. FDF, 5.
42. FDF, 7.

3. What is saving faith?

4. How does the doctrine of justification by grace alone bring you comfort and assurance?

5. How does the doctrine of justification by grace alone through faith alone foster humility?

QUESTION 12

How Do Pentecostals Understand the New Birth?

"You must be born again," said Jesus to Nicodemus (John 3:7). Around the world, Pentecostals have joined with their other evangelical brothers and sisters in echoing these words of Christ. The only way to be saved is to be born again, and this new birth (or *regeneration*) is the gracious work of God by his Holy Spirit, not a human work (John 3:5–8). The source of this new life is in Jesus Christ. In God's mercy, it is "through the resurrection of Jesus Christ from the dead" that we are "born again to a living hope" (1 Peter 1:3), and by this new birth God has "made us alive together with Christ" (Eph. 2:5). This takes place as the Holy Spirit works through God's Word as the gospel is proclaimed (1 Peter 1:23; James 1:18).

What Pentecostals Believe About the New Birth

Believers in Christ are "born anew from above through the joint work of the Word and the Holy Spirit. Regeneration is the beginning of a new, spiritual reality and state in a person's life."[1] Through the new birth, the Holy Spirit dwells "in the heart of the person who converts. . . . Through him, the believer confesses Christ as Lord, [and] he enables him to live in true communion with God and his brothers and sisters."[2] Like justification, regeneration (or the new birth) is "instantaneous and complete."[3] Human beings cannot be saved without this "operation of the Holy Spirit," which is "absolutely essential" due

1. Hungarian Pentecostal, "Confession of Faith," 6.4; for other examples of this emphasis on being born again by the Holy Spirit through Christ, see Gereja Bethel Indonesia, "Confession of Faith," 5; Romanian CF, 8c (p. 10); Fundamentals of the Apostolic Church, 2b.
2. The Apostolic Church in Hungary, "Larger Confession of Faith," 6a.
3. WAGFSF, 4.

to the "utter depravity of human nature" as a result of the fall.[4] This "total corruption" (or "depravity") means that human nature is "burdened with a tendency to sin" and "inclines to evil continually" as it "remains under the dominion of sin" and "subject to God's wrath and condemnation" and to "spiritual death."[5] As Aimee Semple McPherson sums it up, "In consequence of [Adam's fall], all mankind are sinners . . . shapen in iniquity and utterly void by nature of that holiness required by the law of God, positively inclined to evil, guilty and without excuse, justly deserving the condemnation of a just and holy God."[6] In other words, all humanity is dead in sin and our only hope is to be raised to new life in Christ by the Holy Spirit through the word of the gospel. As the confession of the Apostolic Church UK puts it, "The only way to be set free from this sin and guilt is to turn out from ourselves and our sin, and up to Christ in repentance through God's gracious gift of the new birth of regeneration."[7]

Repentance and the New Birth

Repentance is inseparable from the new birth, for in regeneration the Holy Spirit turns us away from death in sin to Christ for life. Repentance is not merely regret or sorrow for sin (2 Cor. 7:10). Rather, as Ghanaian Pentecostal theologian Eric Nyamekye explains, it is "a complete change of life, a radical change which causes one to begin a new life altogether."[8] To repent involves "turning away from acts that lead to death, and . . . turning towards God."[9] However, repentance is not a human work by which we earn God's favor. On the contrary, "repentance is an effect or sign of our faith in the finished work of Christ on the cross."[10] It is a gift of God that flows from the cross of Christ, and that flows out in our lives from the Spirit's gift of the new birth and faith in Jesus.

Although repentance begins when we are born again, it does not end there. Nyamekye clarifies that "it also involves a continuous sense of limitedness by which we should always acknowledge our weaknesses and willingly determine to turn to the power of God for help."[11] We need to continue re-

4. WAGFSF, 4; Assemblee di Dio in Italia, "Articoli de Fede," 7; CoGiC, "Statement of Faith," 5; AC, "Tenets," 2.
5. Brazil DdF, 9.6 (p. 58); CoP, "Tenets," 3; CoGiC, "Sin," in "What We Believe"; Hungarian Pentecostal Confession of Faith, 5; Iglesia Evangélica Pentecostal de Chile, "Los Articulos de Fe," 7; AdDDF, 3; Elim SFT, 5; PAOC, "Statement of Fundamental and Essential Truths (2014)," 4.
6. FDF, 3.
7. ACVG, 3.
8. Eric Nyamekye, "Repentance, Justification and Sanctification," in *Tenets of the Church of Pentecost*, ed. Opoku Onyinah (Accra, Ghana: Church of Pentecost, 2019), 167.
9. Nyamekye, "Repentance," 170.
10. Nyamekye, "Repentance," 170.
11. Nyamekye, "Repentance," 171.

penting every time we see sin in our lives, for it "is in doing so that we bear the fruit of our repentance. This means that spiritual poverty, a sense of limitedness and dependency on the grace of God, must continue with us throughout our Christian journey."[12] This Pentecostal understanding of the Christian life as a life of repentance is explicit in a British Pentecostal confession: "The necessity for repentance does not end at conversion, but rather, the whole life of believers should be a life of repentance. The depths of our sin mean that this repentance will encompass every area of our lives. Therefore, as we grow in likeness to Christ throughout the Christian life, we should never fear or flee from His call to repentance. We must not ignore the Holy Spirit's convicting work, but pray that our eyes would be opened to the extent of our sin and turn from it back to our Saviour."[13]

Two Ways of Speaking of the New Birth

Although the new birth is a very important concept for Pentecostals, it can also sometimes be a confusing concept in Pentecostal theology, in that the term can be used in two different ways.[14] This can be seen in the statement of faith of the World Assemblies of God Fellowship, where flowing from the new birth, "the believing sinner is regenerated, justified, and adopted into the family of God, becomes a new creation in Christ Jesus, and heir of eternal life."[15] To readers from some other evangelical traditions this might look incoherent—regeneration leading to regeneration—but that is not what is meant. Instead, in Pentecostal theology the new birth in its wider sense is more analogous to the concept of union with Christ in Reformed theology.

This larger concept of the new birth is the Holy Spirit indwelling, uniting believers to Christ, and bringing us into a life of communion with God.[16] Thus, Danish and Irish Pentecostals can even simply confess that "salvation is also known as the new birth."[17] The declaration of faith of the Brazilian Assemblies of God states that "salvation in Jesus Christ is . . . a spiritual rebirth" in which "the sinner is immediately and simultaneously saved, justified and adopted as a child of God," resulting in "the process of sanctification until his final glorification in the day of Christ."[18] The doctrine and faith of the

12. Nyamekye, "Repentance," 171.
13. ACVG, 3.
14. Although this twofold way of speaking about regeneration may not be very common in current evangelical theology, historically it is not unique to Pentecostals. See, e.g., Joel M. Beeke and Paul M. Smalley, *Reformed Systematic Theology: Volume 3, Spirit and Salvation* (Wheaton, IL: Crossway, 2021), 401.
15. WAGFSF, 4.
16. The Apostolic Church in Hungary, "Larger Confession of Faith," 6a.
17. Mosaik (Danish Pentecostal Movement), "Declaration of Faith," 5; Christian Churches Ireland, "Statement of Faith," 5.
18. Brazil DdF, 10.2 (p. 63).

Congregação Cristã no Brasil not only speaks of the whole of salvation under the rubric of "regeneration or the new birth," but equates this with being "in Christ Jesus," thus explicitly demonstrating that the new birth is indeed a Pentecostal way of speaking of union with Christ. Those who receive the new birth are in Christ and "have him for Wisdom, Righteousness, Sanctification, and Redemption."[19]

New Life in Christ

When we realize that the new birth is, for Pentecostals, all about union with Christ, we can see even more clearly that the Pentecostal focus is not on salvation as something that comes from Jesus, but rather on Jesus the Savior. Salvation is found in Jesus himself; it is not just something he gives us or does for us. The Lord is salvation. The early Welsh Pentecostal leader D. P. Williams put it like this:

> This new order of life can only be participated in through faith and vital union with the living Christ. The Incarnation brought our Human Nature into oneness with God, and the Redemption through Christ by His Death and Resurrection has made a way for our personalities to be implanted with the seed of Life Eternal that can only be found and possessed in the Death and Resurrection of Christ our Lord. This is the plan and plane of the New Race, the New Humanity in Christ. It is by Divine Conception and birth, and that birth operates in and through the Death and Resurrecting Power of our Lord, whereby the power of His Endless Life manifests itself in the gift to the contrite soul of the same Endless Life. That Life within the soul proceeds onward to an ultimate goal of perfection to bring forth fruit unto righteousness and holiness.[20]

The new birth isn't only about the beginning of the Christian life. It is a "vital union with the living Christ" that encompasses the whole of the Christian life all the way to the "ultimate goal of perfection" in the resurrection. This is a participation in the divine nature, as Christ gives "of Himself by the ministry of the Word and of the Holy Spirit," "as we commune with Him . . . [and as] we drink his blood [and] eat his flesh" in the Breaking of Bread.[21]

19. Congregação Cristã no Brasil, "Doctrine and Faith," 5.
20. D. P. Williams, "Editorial: Our Life Out of Death," *Riches of Grace* 11, no. 4 (March 1936): 306–7; for this doctrine articulated in a confessional statement, see *Fundamentals of the Apostolic Church,* 2b.
21. D. P. Williams, "Exposition," *Riches of Grace* 3, no. 1 (March 1927): 46; see also D. P. Williams, "The Three Spheres of Activity in the Governance of God," *Riches of Grace* 11, no. 1 (September 1935): 205.

So, unlike justification, regeneration effects a change *in* us. In the narrower sense, regeneration "is the change from the state of depravity, or spiritual death, to that of spiritual life."[22] In the larger sense, the new birth "is a spiritual change wrought in the soul by the Holy Spirit, by which man becomes the possessor of the Divine nature, and is made a new creature in Christ Jesus." It is a participation in new divine life in Christ, which "is according to the nature of the Seed imparted incorruptible, and produces fruit according to its own nature, which is in holiness and godliness (Gal. 5:22, 23)."[23]

Harold Horton, the British Pentecostal Bible teacher famed around the world for his early book on the gifts of the Spirit, wrote of the new birth in the same way: "The redeemed of the Lord are not only saved unto everlasting life; they are the children of God. . . . We are not merely accepted of God; we are begotten of God. Our relationship to God is not one of divine courtesy but of divine life. We are born of God. Our divine Parentage is as real as, but infinitely more enduring than, our human parentage. As children of God we are partakers—now—of His mighty, miraculous super-nature. Beloved, now are we the sons of God, partakers of His divine nature (2 Peter i, 4; 1 John iii, 2)."[24]

On the other side of the ocean, at the Central Bible Institute of the Assemblies of God, Adolph Gouthey taught that spiritual life comes through being made a partaker of the divine nature in being born from above, which results in "the constant indwelling of Christ."[25] At the Assemblies of God General Council, Joseph Tunmore preached of being made partakers of the divine nature as the new life in Christ: "This life is [Christ] himself, and you have no life apart from him."[26] Samuel Jamieson, in one of the first Assemblies of God doctrinal books, wrote that in regeneration sinners are "united to Christ by a living bond" and, "through their relation to Christ," made partakers of the divine nature. "To this end Jesus took on himself . . . the nature of man, that we might put on his divine nature. . . . Christians are made partakers in Christ of the divine nature."[27] The new birth, union with Christ, and participation in the divine nature all go together and encompass salvation.

Yet, at times Pentecostals could also distinguish regeneration from union with Christ and see it as merely one aspect of salvation. For example, Myer Pearlman in his enduringly influential doctrinal handbook (which is still used in translation in multiple languages around the world to this day) sets out justification, regeneration, and sanctification as a triple "grace procured by the atoning death of Christ" and "three blessings [which] flow from our union

---

22. AC, "Fundamental Truths," 2.3.
23. J. B. Clyne, *Asked and Answered: A Catechism of Apostolic Principles* (Bradford: Puritan Press, 1953), 11; AC, "Fundamentals," 2b.
24. Harold Horton, *The Gifts of the Spirit*, 3rd ed. (Luton: Assemblies of God, 1949), 13.
25. A. P. Gouthey, "Things Pertaining to Life," *Pentecostal Evangel* (April 23, 1927): 2.
26. Joseph Tunmore, "The Essentials to Pentecost," *Christian Evangel* (November 2, 1918): 2.
27. S. A. Jamieson, *Pillars of Truth* (Springfield, MO: Gospel Publishing House, 1926), 34, 38.

with Christ."[28] However, this does not stop Pearlman from later writing that "regeneration involves spiritual union with God and with Christ through the Holy Spirit; and this spiritual union involves a Divine indwelling," by which we are "partakers of the Divine nature."[29]

This twofold understanding of the new birth means that Pentecostals expect it to result in powerful transformation. As the Foursquare Declaration of Faith puts it:

> We believe that the change which takes place in the heart and life at conversion is a very real one; that the sinner is then born again in such a glorious and transforming manner that the old things are passed away and all things are become new; insomuch that the things once most desired are now abhorred, while the things once abhorred are now held most sacred and dear; and that now having imputed to him the righteousness of the Redeemer and having received of the Spirit of Christ, new desires, new aspirations, new interests, and a new perspective on life, time and eternity, fills the blood-washed heart so that his desire is now to openly confess and serve the Master, seeking ever those things which are above.[30]

This is not just an invisible transfer from death in sin to life in Christ. This is "a new nature" that "produces fruit according to its own nature, which is in holiness and godliness (Gal. 5:22, 23)."[31] Those who are born again are "a new creation" (2 Cor. 5:17) with new desires, a new outlook on life, and new motivations and goals.

Summary

Being born again is the only way to be saved. Due to the fall, we are all born dead in sin and so we need Christ to raise us to new life by his Holy Spirit through the gospel word. This new birth can be considered in two ways. In the narrower sense, regeneration refers to the change that takes place within us as the Holy Spirit lifts us out of death in sin and grants us new life in Christ. In the wider sense, the new birth describes the whole of our salvation and all the benefits we receive in union with Christ, as partakers of the divine nature.

---

28. Myer Pearlman, *Knowing the Doctrines of the Bible* (Springfield, MO: Gospel Publishing House, 1937), 221.
29. Pearlman, *Knowing the Doctrines*, 248.
30. FDF, 7.
31. AC, "Fundamentals," 2b.

REFLECTION QUESTIONS

1. Why do we need to be born again?
2. How pervasive are the effects of sin in the lives of fallen human beings?
3. What is repentance?
4. What does it mean to be a partaker of the divine nature?
5. In what two ways do Pentecostals consider the new birth?

QUESTION 13

What Do Pentecostals Believe About Sanctification?

From the very beginning, Pentecostals of all kinds have placed a great deal of emphasis on the importance of holiness. "Christ [is] our sanctification through the Word,"[1] wrote the Northern Irish Pentecostal theologian Alexander Ferran. Wesleyan Holiness Pentecostals speak of Jesus as our sanctifier. Finished Work Pentecostals speak of Christ as our sanctification. But all Pentecostals agree that Christlikeness is essential.

Historical Approaches to Holiness Among Pentecostals

It was a disagreement over sanctification that led to the first major division among Pentecostal groups. The earliest American Pentecostals came from Wesleyan Holiness backgrounds, and so added a Pentecostal understanding of the baptism in the Spirit to their prior Wesleyan framework. Yet, within a few years of the beginning of the movement, a large number of Pentecostals rejected this Wesleyan Holiness understanding.

Wesleyan Holiness Pentecostals and Entire Sanctification

Wesleyan Holiness Pentecostals already believed in *entire sanctification* as a work of the Holy Spirit that was distinct from and subsequent to conversion or justification. Maintaining their emphasis on the necessity of holiness, the newly emerging Wesleyan Holiness Pentecostals added the baptism in the Spirit as another distinct experience, now subsequent to entire sanctification. Sanctification, therefore, was viewed as a "second work," and the baptism of the Spirit as "the gift of God on a sanctified life."[2] It was necessary to receive

1. Alexander Ferran, *Justification and Sanctification* (Bradford: Puritan Press, n.d.), 19.
2. J. Benjiman Wiles, *Becoming Like Jesus: Toward a Pentecostal Theology of Sanctification* (Cleveland, TN: Center for Pentecostal Theology Press, 2021), 273. As Wiles notes, the

the experience of sanctification before receiving the baptism in the Spirit. Thus, Wesleyan Holiness Pentecostals held to a three-step process: justification, sanctification, then the baptism in the Spirit.

For Wesleyan Holiness Pentecostals, sanctification "was deemed a definite, instantaneous experience wrought by faith in the blood of Christ and available to the justified believer. . . . The result was the immediate and complete removal of the Adamic nature from the justified believer," which then prepared the believer to receive the baptism in the Holy Spirit.[3] It did not lead to complete sinlessness, for "the possibility of resisting the Holy Spirit was present in the sanctified life," yet it did remove "hindrances to growth and the tendency to sin with which the merely justified believer struggled."[4] Further growth was possible through deeper levels of consecration, but this "maturity" was distinguished from the "purity" given by the sanctification experience.[5]

Wesleyan Holiness Pentecostals saw justification and sanctification as God's twofold manner of dealing with the twofold problem of sin: "the sin principle or Adamic sin, and actual transgression, the daily acts of sin committed by us in our unregenerate state."[6] Actual transgressions are dealt with first in justification, while the sin principle is removed "by a distinct act of grace," which is "subsequent to regeneration. . . . The Old Man's death and removal is a distinct experience, different from conversion and subsequent to it."[7] It is this distinct experience that Wesleyan Holiness Pentecostals call "sanctification," "purity," "full salvation," or the "second work of grace."[8]

In all of this, these early Pentecostals were simply following the established theology of the Wesleyan Holiness movement, with the addition of their new understanding of the baptism in the Holy Spirit. However, it was not the experience of all early Pentecostals. When Mrs. Elmer Fisher, a Baptist, was taken by her husband to the Azusa Street Mission at the beginning of the revival in the spring of 1906 and saw people being baptized in the Spirit, she said, "I already have this." In 1880 she had known "an unusual anointing of the Holy Spirit and began to speak in a language she had never learned."[9] Immediately afterward, the Lord gave her the interpretation of the

---

baptism in the Spirit was never considered by Pentecostals to be an additional work of grace, even within the Wesleyan Holiness Pentecostal stream.

3. Wiles, *Becoming Like Jesus*, 274.
4. Wiles, *Becoming Like Jesus*, 274–75.
5. Wiles, *Becoming Like Jesus*, 275.
6. W. H. Turner, *The Finished Work of Calvary or the Second Blessing—Which?* (Franklin Springs, GA: Pentecostal Holiness Church, 1947), 10.
7. J. H. King, *From Passover to Pentecost*, 3rd ed. (Franklin Springs, GA: Pentecostal Holiness Church, 1955), 22–23.
8. Turner, *Finished Work*, 12–13.
9. Stanley M. Horton, "The Pentecostal Perspective," in *Five Views on Sanctification*, ed. Stanley N. Gundry (Grand Rapids: Zondervan, 1987), 106.

tongue as well. From then until she came to Azusa Street in 1906 she had continued to pray in tongues in private. When she told her story, people at the mission were confused, as she was a Baptist and did not hold to Wesleyan Holiness teaching about sanctification; nor had she had a distinct experience of sanctification that could be understood in a Wesleyan Holiness way. Mrs. Fisher did not argue over the question, but her story demonstrates that from the very beginning there were Pentecostals who did not fit or hold to the Wesleyan Holiness model.[10]

The Finished Work Teaching on Sanctification

In 1910, the question of whether Pentecostals should accept the Wesleyan Holiness teaching on sanctification as a distinct experience subsequent to conversion became a major issue of debate. In May 1910, Albert Sidney Copley published an article entitled "Pauline Sanctification," arguing that Wesleyan Holiness teaching came from "a mistaken, or an incomplete view of the work of Calvary."[11] Copley's theology of sanctification was rooted in union and identification with Christ and "the finished work of Christ."[12] He argued for a position that "echoed Reformation thought more than the dominant [Wesleyan] holiness-pentecostal heritage."[13]

Copley's role has largely been forgotten; the name most closely associated with Finished Work teaching today is William Durham. The controversy was sparked, the story goes, at a convention in Chicago in May 1910, by a sermon Durham preached entitled "The Finished Work of Christ." A member of the Church of God (probably A. J. Tomlinson) later wrote that this sermon "caused the first schism in the hitherto unified ranks of the Pentecostal Movement" by "nullify[ing] the blessing of sanctification as a second definite work of grace."[14] However, there is no historical evidence that this supposedly dramatically divisive sermon was ever preached.[15] Copley's article seems to be the earliest sustained critique of the "second work" sanctification teaching, although other Pentecostals already clearly did not accept the Wesleyan Holiness position.[16]

10. Horton, "The Pentecostal Perspective," 106–7. Mrs. Fisher was Stanley Horton's grandmother. Horton's mother, too, was baptized in the Spirit at Azusa Street without a prior sanctification experience.
11. A. S. Copley, "Pauline Sanctification," *The Pentecost* 2, no. 6 (May 1, 1910): 6.
12. Copley, "Pauline Sanctification," 6–7.
13. Christopher J. Richmann, "William H. Durham and Early Pentecostalism: A Multifaceted Reassessment," *Pneuma* 37 (2015): 231.
14. "History of Pentecost," *The Faithful Standard* (November 1922): 8.
15. Richmann, "William H. Durham and Early Pentecostalism," 227–29.
16. E.g., Mary Lindley, "The Beginning of Days for Me," *The Pentecost* 2, no. 2 (January 1, 1910): 1–3.

Durham, however, became a major figure in the spread of Finished Work teaching. Through his magazine *Pentecostal Testimony*, as well as his preaching in various centers of Pentecostal revival, Durham spread the message that "the Bible does not teach that [sanctification] is a second definite work of grace."[17] Unlike conversion and the baptism in the Spirit, "not one single case is recorded [in the Bible] where any one got sanctified as a second, instantaneous work of grace."[18] Instead, Durham taught, sanctification is rooted in union with Christ and worked out through identification with him. "In conversion, we come into Christ, our Sanctifier, and are made holy. . . . When one really comes into Christ he is as much in Christ as he will ever be. He is in a state of holiness and righteousness. . . . In conversion we become identified with Christ and come into a state of sanctification, and we are continually exhorted to live the sanctified life in the Holy Spirit."[19]

Thus there is a positional aspect to sanctification that takes place at conversion through our union with Christ, and an ongoing, progressive aspect to sanctification as the holiness of Christ is worked out in our lives: "Instead of telling folks that there is an experience that removes the necessity for bearing the daily cross, they should have been taught that the Christian life is a battle from conversion to glorification."[20] Therefore, there is no need "to seek for any intermediate experience" of sanctification between conversion and receiving the baptism in the Holy Spirit.[21]

In the Bible, "there is absolutely no reference ever made to any intermediate experience of any kind. The reason of this is, there is none to refer to."[22] The baptism of the Spirit is available to believers after conversion, without an experience of sanctification in between. Douglas Jacobsen evaluates Durham's teaching as "a stirring call to the pentecostal community to be clearer in its thinking [and] more consistent in its living. . . . His theology represented a strenuous attempt to identify the essential beliefs of the movement and to eliminate all forms of error and sloppy thinking."[23]

Although Durham died in July 1912 and so did not live long enough to fully elaborate Finished Work theology, more than half a million copies of his writings had been distributed in the last two years of his life, spreading

---

17. William Durham, "Sanctification," *Pentecostal Testimony* 1, no. 8 (1911): 1.
18. Durham, "Sanctification," 1.
19. Durham, "Sanctification," 2.
20. Durham, "Sanctification," 2.
21. William Durham, "The Great Revival at Azusa Street Mission—How It Began and How It Ended," *Pentecostal Testimony* 1, no. 8 (1911): 3.
22. William Durham, "The Two Great Experiences or Gifts," *Pentecostal Testimony* 1, no. 8 (1911): 5.
23. Douglas Jacobsen, *Thinking in the Spirit: Theologies of the Early Pentecostal Movement* (Bloomington: Indiana University Press, 2003), 163.

his teaching widely across the Pentecostal world.[24] This also enabled Finished Work Pentecostals to develop their sanctification teaching in various directions. Few stuck rigidly to Durham's Finished Work teaching, with most moving either in the direction of Keswick theology or toward a more classical Reformed view of sanctification.[25] Nonetheless, following in the footsteps of Copley and Durham, Finished Work Pentecostals make up the vast majority of Pentecostals worldwide.

Mainstream Pentecostal Teaching on Sanctification

While a minority of Pentecostals still hold to the Wesleyan Holiness view, it has long been forgotten by the Pentecostal mainstream. Most Pentecostals around the world see sanctification as a "process,"[26] recognizing that it is "the work of the Holy Spirit in the believer, through which the character of Jesus Christ is increasingly shaped in his life. It is therefore not a one-time, single, specific event, but a process that begins at rebirth and lasts until the end of the earthly life."[27] As William Menzies concludes, in this Pentecostals "reflect a basic affinity for the Reformed position" on sanctification.[28]

Two articles from Pentecostal confessional statements on sanctification (that of the Foursquare Declaration of Faith and that of the World Assemblies of God Fellowship), complement one another to provide quite a full articulation of mainstream Pentecostal teaching on holiness. The first declares:

> We believe that having been cleansed by the precious blood of Jesus Christ and having received the witness of the Holy Spirit at conversion, it is the will of God that we be sanctified daily and become partakers of His holiness; growing constantly stronger in faith, power, prayer, love and service, first as babies desiring the sincere milk of the Word; then as dear children walking humbly, seeking diligently the hidden life, where self decreases and Christ increases; then as strong men having on the whole armor of God, marching forth to new conquests in His name beneath His blood-stained banner, ever living a patient, sober, unselfish, godly life that will be a true reflection of the Christ within.[29]

---

24. Wiles, *Becoming Like Jesus*, 101.
25. William W. Menzies, "The Spirit of Holiness: A Comparative Study," *Paraclete* 2, no. 3 (Summer 1968): 14.
26. Romanian CF, 11.
27. Hungarian Pentecostal Confession, 6.5; cf. Central Gospel Assemblies of Pakistan, "Statement of Faith," 19; Hungarian Apostolic Confession, 5b; Apostolic Church in Slovakia, "Confession," 8.
28. Menzies, "Spirit of Holiness," 16.
29. FDF, 8.

Cleansing, we see here, takes place at conversion when, the previous article of the declaration tells us, the heart is "blood-washed" through new birth.[30] Now, sanctification flows out of this regeneration, in "daily" and "constant" growth. This is a lifelong, progressive sanctification, as believers are conformed more and more to the image "of the Christ within."

The World Assemblies of God Fellowship statement of faith emphasizes another significant aspect of Pentecostal teaching: "Sanctification is an act of separation from that which is evil, and of dedication unto God. In experience it is both instantaneous and progressive. It is produced in the life of the believer by his appropriation of the power of Christ's blood and risen life through the person of the Holy Spirit. He draws the believer's attention to Christ, teaches him through the Word and produces the character of Christ within him."[31] Here we see not only that we are sanctified in Christ through the Spirit by the Word, but also that there are two aspects to this sanctification: "instantaneous and progressive." The renowned Apostolic doctrinal writer W. A. C. Rowe likewise wrote that "sanctification comprehends the instantaneous act and a continual process."[32] Yet the "instantaneous" aspect of sanctification here is not the Wesleyan second work of grace. Rather, it is the cleansing by the precious blood of Jesus in the new birth of which the Foursquare declaration speaks. As Myer Pearlman, one of the most influential teachers of Pentecostal doctrine, puts it, "Sanctification is: (1) Positional and instantaneous. (2) Practical and progressive."[33] In the *positional* sense, sanctification is "simultaneous with justification." Pearlman turns to the words of the Westminster Shorter Catechism to define progressive sanctification as "the work of God's free grace, whereby we are renewed in the whole man after the image of God, and are enabled more and more to die unto sin, and live unto righteousness."[34] Like the later World Assemblies of God Fellowship statement, Pearlman teaches that the means of sanctification are the blood of Christ, the Holy Spirit, and the Word.[35]

Rather than a "second work" of grace, the majority of Pentecostals hold to an instantaneous *definitive* (or *positional*) sanctification at the time of justification and regeneration, followed by *progressive* sanctification

30. FDF, 7.
31. WAGFSF, 8.
32. W. A. C. Rowe, *One Lord, One Faith* (Bradford: Puritan Press, n.d.), 94.
33. Myer Pearlman, *Knowing the Doctrines of the Bible* (Springfield, MO: Gospel Publishing House, 1937), 252.
34. Pearlman, *Knowing the Doctrines*, 253; *Westminster Shorter Catechism*, q. 35.
35. Pearlman, *Knowing the Doctrines*, 254–57. For a contemporary Pentecostal articulation of definitive and progressive sanctification by the blood of Christ, the Holy Spirit, and the Word of God, see Jonathan Black, *Apostolic Theology: A Trinitarian, Evangelical, Pentecostal Introduction to Christian Doctrine* (Luton: Apostolic Church UK, 2016), 417–30; see also Guy P. Duffield and Nathaniel M. Van Cleave, *Foundations of Pentecostal Theology* (Los Angeles: Foursquare Media, 1983), 242–51.

of increasing growth in Christlikeness, flowing out from our union with Christ. This emphasis on both definitive and progressive sanctification among Pentecostals is very similar to the teaching of the Reformed theologian John Murray.[36] Both Murray and Stanley Horton write of the cross as the key to our *positional* or *definitive* sanctification from their respective Reformed and Pentecostal perspectives, and both root this instantaneous aspect of sanctification in union with Christ. For both, also, the life of progressive sanctification is only possible because of this definitive beginning in union with Christ.[37] The outworking of holiness—progressive sanctification—is rooted in our definitive sanctification through union with Christ in his death and resurrection. "To a large extent, the progress of sanctification is dependent upon the increasing understanding and appropriation of the implication of that identification with Christ in his death and resurrection. Nothing is more relevant to progressive sanctification than the reckoning of ourselves to be dead to sin and alive to God through Jesus Christ (cf. Rom. 6:11)."[38] Those words sound like they should be from a Pentecostal sermon; but they are in fact from the Reformed Murray. Therefore, developments toward a more precise understanding of sanctification among Pentecostals have brought Pentecostals and Reformed theologians even closer together in their understanding of holiness.

Summary

While many early Pentecostals believed in (and the Wesleyan Holiness minority of Pentecostals still believe in) entire sanctification as a second work of grace to be received after conversion and before the baptism in the Holy Spirit, the vast majority of Pentecostals around the world today reject this position. Instead, the mainstream Pentecostal understanding of sanctification is very similar to that of Reformed evangelicals, with a major emphasis on the ongoing nature of progressive sanctification throughout this life.

---

36. On the development of John Murray's teaching on definitive sanctification, see David D. Cho, *The Ground of Holy Life: A Reformed Response to the Holiness Movement in America with Progressive and Definitive Sanctification* (Eugene, OR: Resource, 2021), 156–81. Both Murray and Finished Work Pentecostals were reacting to Keswick teaching in different ways, but appear to have come to similar solutions. Murray did not fully develop his position on definitive justification until the 1960s. Pentecostals had been making this distinction between definitive and progressive sanctification much earlier, though the position was not fully developed until the beginning of the 1960s.
37. See Horton, "The Pentecostal Perspective," 116; John Murray, "Sanctification," *Christianity Today* (May 11, 1962), 30; and John Murray, "Definitive Sanctification," *Calvin Theological Journal* 2 (1967): 13.
38. John Murray, "The Pattern of Sanctification," in *Collected Writings of John Murray* (Edinburgh: Banner of Truth, 1977), 2:311.

REFLECTION QUESTIONS

1. How do Wesleyan Holiness Pentecostals understand the relationship between sanctification and the baptism of the Holy Spirit?
2. What was the "Finished Work" controversy?
3. What is *positional* or *definitive* sanctification?
4. What is *progressive* sanctification?
5. Read again the article on sanctification from the Foursquare Declaration of Faith above. In which aspects of sanctification described there do you see God at work in your life, and in which do you see the need to pray for God to work?

QUESTION 14

Do Pentecostals Affirm the Prosperity Gospel?

Many people outside the classical Pentecostal world associate Pentecostals with the prosperity gospel. It is true that *some* people in Pentecostal churches believe this teaching; however, many people in non-Pentecostal churches do too. Moreover, many Pentecostals reject prosperity teaching just as strongly as many non-Pentecostals. It is not part of the theology of classical Pentecostalism, and in fact many classical Pentecostal denominations, pastors, and theologians specifically teach that the "prosperity gospel" is a serious error (although it is unfortunately true that some pastors and churches have adopted aspects of prosperity teaching).

Prosperity theology has become a major movement with widespread influence across the Christian church, with 46 percent of (self-identified) American Christians (not just Pentecostals) in 2007 agreeing or mostly agreeing with the statement "God will grant material prosperity to all believers who have enough faith."[1] A decade later, 69 percent of American Protestant churchgoers were found to agree with the statement "God wants me to prosper financially."[2] Thus, aspects of prosperity teaching have entered the popular theology of a large proportion of believers *across denominations and traditions*. As Kate Bowler points out in her investigation of the history of the American prosperity movement, "The prosperity gospel cannot be conflated with fundamentalism, Pentecostalism, evangelicalism, the religious right, the so-called black church, or any of the usual suspects (though it certainly overlaps with each)."[3]

1. Pew Research Center, "Spirit and Power: A 10-Country Survey of Pentecostals" (Washington, DC: Pew Research Center, 2007), 147.
2. Lifeway Research, *Churchgoers Views—Prosperity* (July 2018), 6.
3. Kate Bowler, *Blessed: A History of the American Prosperity Gospel* (Oxford: Oxford University Press, 2013), 4.

The historical sources that would converge into prosperity teaching are complex. However, the contemporary prosperity *movement* largely finds its origins in the teachings of Kenneth Hagin. Hagin founded Rhema Bible Training Center in 1974. By the year 2000, more than 16,500 students had graduated. He also spread his teaching internationally via radio, cassette tapes, a monthly magazine, and books. More than sixty-five million books have been distributed by his ministry, most of them written by Hagin himself.[4] While Hagin originally had been ordained as an Assemblies of God pastor, he broke ties with the denomination and established his own independent ministry organization as he developed his prosperity teachings—teachings the Assemblies of God rejected.[5] Hagin's prosperity teachings were further spread by figures such as Kenneth Copeland, Charles Capps, and Frederick Price. In subsequent decades, prosperity teaching has been adapted in various directions by innumerable others.

Although I've used the term "prosperity gospel" here, there are several other ways of describing the same (or a very similar) set of beliefs and teachings. Many of these terms, such as "health and wealth teaching," "success theology," or "name it and claim it," are often used by opponents of the movement, but rejected by its adherents. While "prosperity theology" is the term most often used by scholars, the most common description used by adherents is "Word of Faith."[6] I shall use the language of "prosperity" as it can be applied not only to full-blown Word of Faith teaching, but also to diluted versions that reject some of the more esoteric Word of Faith beliefs.

What Is the "Prosperity Gospel"?

At its essence, prosperity teaching is summed up in the idea that "God wants to heal and transform us so that we can live healthy and prosperous lives in order to help others more effectively."[7] The teaching is centered on the

---

4. Ted Olsen, "Weblog: Kenneth Hagin, 'Word of Faith' Preacher, Dies at 86," *Christianity Today*, September 1, 2003, https://www.christianitytoday.com/ct/2003/septemberweb-only/9-22-11.0.html.
5. For the Assemblies of God rejection of prosperity teaching, see the position paper adopted by the general presbytery August 19, 1980, "The Believer and Positive Confession," Assemblies of God website, https://ag.org/Beliefs/Position-Papers/The-Believer-and-Positive-Confession.
6. For an evaluation of some of these terms, see Mikael Stenhammar, *The Worldview of the Word of Faith Movement: Eden Redeemed* (London: T&T Clark, 2022), 5–8.
7. "Hillsong Statement of Faith" in the Hillsong College Student Handbook, September 1, 2020, Hillsong College Policies and Procedures Online Manual, https://trainers.hillsong-college.edu.au/hillsong-statement-of-faith. The most recent version of the Hillsong global governing principles has been modified to replace the word "prosperous" with "blessed." See "Hillsong Global Governing Principles," Hillsong Church website, https://hillsong.com/policies/global-governing-principles. Hillsong began as part of the Assemblies of God Australia (now Australian Christian Churches) but has since separated. Thus, Hillsong is a

promise of healing and prosperity, and the consequent rejection of suffering. However, this is often further embedded in a larger web of beliefs concerning how these (supposed) promises are to be received. Kate Bowler argues that prosperity teaching has four central themes: faith, wealth, health, and victory.[8] Key to this is an idiosyncratic concept of faith as "a power that unleashes spiritual forces and turns the spoken word into reality."[9] Word of Faith leaders put forward a concept of "the God-kind of faith" based on a particular reading of Mark 11:22, which, Kenneth Hagin claims, "Greek scholars tell us . . . should be translated "Have the God-kind of faith."[10] This, they argue, is the type of faith by which God spoke the world into being: "That is the God-kind of faith. God believed what He said would come to pass and it did."[11] Believers, then, are to exercise this "God-kind of faith" by "believing with the heart and saying it with the mouth."[12] Brian Houston of Hillsong Church expresses this word of faith teaching for a different cultural moment: "Faith needs to be spoken. It needs to be heard, because when it is heard it has power."[13]

These spoken declarations of faith can, then, according to the prosperity teachers, bring about wealth, health, and victory. Hagin writes that by these "positive confession[s] . . . our lips can make us millionaires."[14] For Brian Houston, abundant life now includes financial blessing, for "God can bless your business and bring abundant resources your way."[15] Hagin insists that "it is God's will for His children to prosper," for "Christ has redeemed us from the curse of poverty" as well as "the curse of sickness" and "the curse of death."[16] Discussing Christ's curse bearing and the blessing of Abraham in Galatians 3, Hagin argues that "just as the curse is threefold in nature, so was Abraham's blessing. First, it was a material, financial blessing. Second, it was

---

movement that originated within a classical Pentecostal denomination but departed from classical Pentecostalism both institutionally and theologically.

8. Bowler, *Blessed*, 7.
9. Bowler, *Blessed*, 7.
10. Kenneth E. Hagin, *New Thresholds of Faith*, 2nd ed. (Tulsa, OK: Kenneth Hagin Ministries, 1990), 80. Hagin does not supply any evidence of Greek scholars who would uphold his translation.
11. Hagin, *New Thresholds*, 81. This concept of God having faith is not only novel, but undermines the entire classical Christian understanding of the nature of God. Hagin's claim here is simply incompatible with historic Christian faith.
12. Hagin, *New Thresholds*, 82.
13. Brian Houston, *There Is More: When the World Says You Can't, God Says You Can* (Colorado Springs: Waterbrook, 2018), 63.
14. Hagin, *New Thresholds*, 83.
15. Houston, *There Is More*, 37. Houston clarifies that financial blessing is not the only aspect of abundant life. Houston has also written a book entitled *You Need More Money: Discovering God's Amazing Financial Plan for Your Life* (Sydney: Brian Houston Ministries, 1999).
16. Hagin, *New Thresholds*, 54–55.

a physical blessing. Third, it was a spiritual blessing."[17] Therefore, he writes, "We as Christians need not suffer financial setbacks; we need not be captive to poverty or sickness."[18] Healing and prosperity are both seen to be in the atonement in the same way as salvation, and thus available to all believers in just as certain a way as salvation.[19] Hagin clarifies further that prosperity means that God wants believers to "eat the best; He wants them to wear the best clothing; He wants them to drive the best cars; He wants them to have the best of everything."[20]

Because, for prosperity teachers, health is to be found in the blessing of the atonement in the same way as wealth and salvation, and because it can be spoken into being through a positive confession, healing is seen as a guarantee. Kenneth Hagin, for example, teaches that believers are to

> refuse to allow disease or sickness in our bodies, because we ARE healed. We know that the pain, sickness, or disease that seems to be in our bodies was laid on Jesus. He bore it. We do not need to bear it. All we need to do is agree with God and His Word and accept the fact that he "himself took our infirmities, and bore our sicknesses" and "with his stripes we are healed." We simply *know* it, so we thank God. We don't have to have anybody lay hands on us. We don't have to have any manifestation of the gifts of the Spirit. We simply thank the Father for our perfect deliverance.[21]

The result of this teaching is that many prosperity adherents are encouraged to deny the symptoms of illness. John Avanzini teaches: "You may experience symptoms of sickness. They may manifest themselves in pain or in some inability. Your mind will want to *reason* from these symptoms that you are sick and may even become sicker. . . . When symptoms come, you must cast down thoughts of sickness because they contradict the knowledge you have about God. His Word says you are already healed."[22]

To admit the symptoms, or even ask for prayer more than once, may be called a negative confession.[23] This can result in those who are sick and not healed being blamed for their lack of healing. Benny Hinn, for example, said,

---

17. Hagin, *New Thresholds*, 55.
18. Hagin, *New Thresholds*, 57.
19. For healing in the atonement, see question 31.
20. Hagin, *New Thresholds of Faith*, 57.
21. Kenneth E. Hagin, *Seven Things You Should Know About Divine Healing* (Tulsa, OK: Kenneth Hagin Ministries, 1983), 54.
22. John Avanzini, *It's Not Working, Brother John: 25 Things That Close the Windows of Heaven* (Tulsa, OK: Harrison House, 1992), 144.
23. Bowler, *Blessed*, 151.

"We know that in the presence of God there is healing, and I would give all that I have to see people healed, so I really believe it is the fault of the person. They have failed to enter into God's presence and allow Him to touch them."[24]

In addition to wealth and health, the prosperity gospel promises victory rather than suffering.[25] This does not mean there is no place for suffering of any kind. Some of the older prosperity preachers distinguished between "suffering sickness and disease" (which believers "have no business suffering") and "suffering wrongfully" because one is a Christian in an unbelieving world.[26] However, such caveats are not always clear or present.

Finally, we should consider the place of Jesus within the prosperity gospel. In his recent examination of the worldview of the movement, Mikael Stenhammar highlights the "exalted anthropology" of Word of Faith teaching, which leads to "a low functional Christology."[27] Prosperity teachers see believers as "a form of super human."[28] Yet, this downplays the believer's need for Christ. "Jesus' ongoing significance in Word of Faith theology is primarily as a passive Helper for the believer to implement their restored authority according to his set example . . . thus downplaying the believer's need for a dynamic and submissive relationship with him."[29]

How Do Pentecostals Respond to the "Prosperity Gospel"?

Prosperity teaching did not properly emerge until about a half century after Pentecostalism. Yet, even from the beginning, standard Pentecostal teaching was contrary to the prosperity gospel. As a 1909 Pentecostal publication put it: "Adversity, in the state of things in the present life, has far less danger for us than prosperity. Both, when received in the proper spirit, may tend to our spiritual advancement. But the tendency of adversity, in itself considered, is to show us our weakness, and to lead us to God; while the natural tendency of prosperity, separate from the correctives and directions of divine grace, is to inspire us with self-confidence and to turn us away from God."[30] More recently, major Pentecostal denominations such as the Assemblies of God have produced position papers rejecting Word of Faith teachings.[31] We will give more attention to Pentecostal perspectives on healing and suffering in questions 30–32. But for now we will focus on prosperity itself.

---

24. Sherry Andrews, "Anointed to Heal," *Charisma* (April 1979): 14–17; quoted in Bowler, *Blessed*, 151.
25. Bowler, *Blessed*, 179.
26. Kenneth E. Hagin, *Must Christians Suffer?* (Tulsa, OK: Kenneth Hagin Ministries, 1982), 2–3.
27. Stenhammar, *Worldview*, 254–55.
28. Stenhammar, *Worldview*, 256.
29. Stenhammar, *Worldview*, 257.
30. "Adversity," *Latter Rain Evangel* (February 1909): 12.
31. AG, "Believer and Positive Confession," August 1980.

The chief Pentecostal objection to the prosperity gospel is that it is not a faithful account of the Bible's teaching. Those who teach that God wills all believers to prosper financially rely on a small number of proof texts. However, these are not representative of the Bible's overall teaching on God's will. Perhaps the most significant proof text for prosperity teaching is 3 John 2: "Beloved, I pray that you may prosper in all things and be in health, just as your soul prospers" (NKJV). Hagin teaches that this verse shows that "God wants his children to prosper" and that this is a promise "regarding financial blessing."[32] However, that is not at all what this verse is saying. The Greek word translated "prosper" here never refers to financial prosperity. The ESV does not use the word "prosper" here and so avoids this potential misinterpretation: "Beloved, I pray that all may go well with you and that you may be in good health, as it goes well with your soul" (3 John 2). The text is not telling us that God wants all Christians to prosper financially, but rather that John is praying that things are well with Gaius—much like we might begin an email by writing, "I hope you're well." In fact, as the distinguished Pentecostal New Testament scholar Gordon Fee points out, this was simply "the *standard* form of greeting in a personal letter in antiquity."[33]

The New Testament perspective on financial prosperity is quite different. Christ himself warned that "it is easier for a camel to go through the eye of a needle than for a rich person to enter the kingdom of God" (Matt. 19:24). Those who have, Jesus instructs, should share with those who do not (Luke 3:11), and he pronounces woes against the rich and those who are full, after blessing the hungry and the poor (Luke 6:20–25). The desire for financial prosperity, Paul warns, is a temptation and snare that will "plunge people into ruin and destruction" (1 Tim. 6:9). Rather, the "standard is sufficiency: and surplus is called into question."[34]

Pentecostal responses to prosperity teaching give attention to the overall teaching of the Bible on God's will, rather than relying on individual proof texts. The Assemblies of God position paper on the matter emphasizes that "the desire of the heart is not always the criterion by which the will of God is determined." Rather, the paper states, "There are times when the enjoyable or the pleasurable may not be the will of God."[35] Pentecostals are encouraged to compare Scripture with Scripture, which demonstrates that "positive verbal expressions do not always produce happy effects, nor do negative statements always result in unhappy effects."[36] Pentecostals are clear that "doctrine will

32. Hagin, *New Thresholds*, 54.
33. Gordon D. Fee, *The Disease of the Health and Wealth Gospels* (Vancouver: Regent College Publishing, 1985), 10.
34. Fee, *Disease*, 44.
35. AG, "Believer and Positive Confession," 4.
36. AG, "Believer and Positive Confession," 3.

be sound only as it is developed within the framework of the total teaching of Scripture."[37] Therefore, we must recognize that a faithful Christian life will involve suffering (see question 32).

Pentecostals also see the Bible's teaching on faith very differently to the Word of Faith concept of "the God-kind of faith." For Pentecostals, "faith is a personal confidence and reliance upon God." It is a response to God's grace in Christ and "has no independent merit apart from its object—the Lord Jesus Christ."[38] Rather than a power that believers use to speak prosperity and health into being, faith is "leaping toward or going out to God in trust . . . and throw[ing] oneself completely upon the merits of Christ's blood and finished work."[39] This is a significant difference between Pentecostal and Word of Faith teachings. For Pentecostals, "faith is not a work."[40] Instead, it is "rest[ing] and rely[ing] upon Christ Jesus."[41] However, the Word of Faith teaching turns faith into a work through which God responds to us when we exercise it correctly.[42] Such a concept of faith veers away from Christian orthodoxy into semi-Pelagianism.

When the object of faith is shifted either to prosperity (or health) or to the positive confession itself, Jesus is no longer central. This is in line with the low-functioning Christology inherent in Word of Faith teaching noted above. However, Jesus Christ is absolutely central to the Pentecostal faith. While it could be argued that Jesus has brought believers into their position of authority to exercise faith, this reduces the Pentecostal teaching on the living relationship between Christ and the Christian to a mechanistic connection. For Pentecostals Jesus is himself the healer and the one through whom we bring our needs to the Father in prayer, trusting in his gracious provision. He is not merely a mechanism which we can now bypass. The living union with Christ that is so vital to Pentecostal faith is lost in Word of Faith teaching.

Summary

While there are some Pentecostals who have adopted prosperity teaching, it is not a classical Pentecostal teaching. Rather, when prosperity teachings are added to Pentecostal faith, they distort it into something that is quite different from the Christ-centered, biblical nature of classical Pentecostalism.

---

37. AG, "Believer and Positive Confession," 3.
38. *Concerning the Faith* (Toronto: Full Gospel Publishing House, 1951), Qs. 194, 201, 202 (pp. 35–36).
39. *Concerning the Faith*, Qs. 205, 207 (p. 37).
40. French Arrington, *Christian Doctrine: A Pentecostal Perspective* (Cleveland, TN: Pathway Press, 1993), 2:205.
41. ACVG, 4; cf. Myer Pearlman, *Knowing the Doctrines of the Bible* (Springfield, MO: Gospel Publishing House, 1937), 225–26.
42. Kenneth Copeland, *The Laws of Prosperity* (Fort Worth, TX: Kenneth Copeland Ministries, 1974), 41.

REFLECTION QUESTIONS

1. How would you summarize the "prosperity gospel"?
2. How does the Word of Faith understanding of faith differ from the classical Pentecostal understanding of faith?
3. Does 3 John 2 teach that it is the will of God for all believers to prosper financially?
4. What is the New Testament attitude toward wealth?
5. In what ways does the prosperity gospel undermine the gospel of Jesus Christ?

PART 3

Questions About the Baptism of the Holy Spirit

QUESTION 15

What Does the Old Testament Say About the Outpouring of the Holy Spirit?

The baptism in the Holy Spirit is Pentecostalism's "central distinctive."[1] As Bible people, Pentecostals insist that all their theology and practice must come from the Word of God. The question for Pentecostals, Carl Brumback reminds us, must always be, "Is the doctrine according to the Scriptures? That is the crux of the matter."[2] Therefore, if we are to examine this central Pentecostal distinctive of the baptism in the Spirit, we must begin with the Scriptures. We will start in the Old Testament by looking at the anointing of the Holy Spirit (in ways that are distinct from salvation), before tracing the promise of the future outpouring of the Spirit.

The Anointing of the Spirit in the Old Testament

The Holy Spirit was active in the world before the day of Pentecost. Throughout the Old Testament we see a wide range of activities empowered by the Spirit, distinct from and in addition to his salvific work. In fact, Douglas Oss points out that in the Old Testament "the empowering work of the Spirit is much more evident than the inner-transforming [work]."[3]

A particularly clear way in which we see this empowering work of the Spirit in the Old Testament is in prophecy. In the book of Numbers, we have a powerful example of this when the Lord put his Spirit on seventy elders of the

1. Frank D. Macchia, *Baptized in the Spirit: A Global Pentecostal Theology* (Grand Rapids: Zondervan, 2006), 19; see also David Petts, "The Baptism in the Holy Spirit: The Theological Distinctive," in *Pentecostal Perspectives*, ed. Keith Warrington (Carlisle: Paternoster, 1998), 98.
2. Carl Brumback, *God in Three Persons* (Cleveland, TN: Pathway, 1959), 19.
3. Douglas Oss, "A Pentecostal/Charismatic View," in *Are Miraculous Gifts for Today? Four Views*, ed. Wayne Grudem (Leicester: InterVarsity Press, 1996), 245.

children of Israel "and as soon as the Spirit rested on them, they prophesied" (Num. 11:25). When they realized that Eldad and Medad, who were not with the other elders, were prophesying in the camp because "the Spirit rested on them" (v. 26), Moses declared his desire that all the Lord's people might be prophets and "that the LORD would put his Spirit on them!" (v. 29). Here Moses links prophecy very explicitly to the Holy Spirit coming upon people.

This is a pattern we see repeated throughout the Old Testament. After Samuel anoints Saul to be king, he tells Saul that he will encounter a group of prophets and "the Spirit of the LORD will rush upon you, and you will prophesy with them and be turned into another man" (1 Sam. 10:6), which takes place just as Samuel had said (v. 10). Later, "the Spirit of God came upon the messengers of Saul, and they also prophesied" (1 Sam. 19:20). In his last words, David prophetically tells us that "the Spirit of the LORD speaks by me; his word is on my tongue" (2 Sam. 23:2). During David's reign, "the Spirit clothed Amasai" to prophesy (1 Chron. 12:18), while later in Judah's history "the Spirit of the LORD came upon Jahaziel the son of Zechariah" to prophesy to King Jehoshaphat (2 Chron. 20:14–15); and, further, "the Spirit of God clothed Zechariah the son of Jehoiada the priest" to prophesy, to the people (2 Chron. 24:20). The power of the prophets to prophesy and to write the books of the prophets was also by the Holy Spirit (Ezek. 11:5; Mic. 3:8).

However, prophecy is not the only way in which we see the Spirit's anointing in the Old Testament. Throughout the book of Judges, we see the Holy Spirit's anointing upon those raised up to lead God's people. When the Lord raised up Othniel, "the Spirit of the LORD was upon him" to judge Israel (Judg. 3:10). "The Spirit of the LORD clothed Gideon" to lead the Israelites in their hour of need (Judg. 6:33–34). "The Spirit of the LORD was upon Jephthah" while he judged Israel (Judg. 11:29). Later "the Spirit of the LORD rushed upon" Samson to perform miraculous feats (Judg. 14:6, 19; 15:14–15). The Spirit coming upon individuals to equip them to lead God's people also carries on beyond the judges, for when Samuel anointed David as God's choice of future king over Israel, "the Spirit of the LORD rushed upon David from that day forward" (1 Sam. 16:13).

Such anointing stretches back before the entrance into the Promised Land as well, for "Joshua the son of Nun was full of the spirit of wisdom, for Moses had laid his hands on him" (Deut. 34:9). The Spirit of wisdom is none other than the Spirit of the Lord himself—the Holy Spirit (Isa. 11:2). But here we see part of the reason for the Spirit's anointing upon the judges and kings: they needed the Lord's wisdom to lead his people. When Joseph told Pharaoh his dream, interpreted it, and then gave wise counsel in light of it, Pharaoh recognized that "the Spirit of God" was in Joseph (Gen. 41:38). Centuries later, a similar (though confused) pagan recognition of God's Spirit in Daniel is made due to the wisdom of God displayed in him (Dan. 5:11). The Lord also filled Bezalel with wisdom in practical "ability and intelligence, with knowledge and all craftsmanship" for the artistic design and craftmanship required for the construction of the tabernacle (Exod. 31:3; 35:30–35). Bezalel, along with Oholiab, was also "inspired" by the Spirit of God to teach these skills to others (Exod. 35:34). On the subject of their teaching abilities, Stanley Horton (a leading Pentecostal theologian of the late twentieth century) writes, "The Spirit would supply them with supernatural help in connection with the practical tasks of preparing materials for the tabernacle. . . . Bezalel and Aholiab were not to depend on their natural abilities and skills alone."[4]

What clearly emerges from our consideration of the anointing and outpouring of the Holy Spirit upon individuals in the Old Testament is that the Holy Spirit came upon people in ways that were not salvific. The Holy Spirit came upon people to speak through them in prophecy; to empower them to lead and guide God's people; and to give wisdom, knowledge, skill, and ability; as well as to enable them to teach others. Thus, we see how an empowering and equipping work of the Holy Spirit, distinct from salvation, is very evident in the Old Testament.

The Promise of the Spirit in the Old Testament

In the Old Testament we not only see examples of the Holy Spirit's work, but we also read promises of the future outpouring of the Spirit. Yet these promises are of three kinds: there are promises of the Holy Spirit's inner-transforming (salvific) work, promises of the Holy Spirit's empowering and equipping work, and promises of assurance by the Spirit.

The Spirit and the Promise of Inward Transformation

Through the prophet Ezekiel, the Lord speaks of a coming day when he will give his people a new heart and put "a new spirit . . . within them" (Ezek. 11:19). This new heart and new spirit, the Lord says, will "cause you to walk in my statutes and be careful to obey my rules" (Ezek. 36:26–27). When the Lord puts his Spirit within his people, they will live (Ezek. 37:14). Thus, the Lord promises new life, a transformed heart, and a new obedience by his Spirit. This is a promise of salvation and inward transformation, and it corresponds to the promise of the new covenant made in Jeremiah 31:31–34. So the Old Testament looks forward to the days of the new covenant in which the Lord will give life and salvation by the Holy Spirit. However, these are not the only types of promise of the Spirit's work among God's people in the coming new covenant age.

The Spirit and the Promise of Empowering and Equipping

On the day of Pentecost, Peter takes up Joel's prophecy of the Spirit's outpouring. This promise of the Spirit is quite different from those of Ezekiel.

---

4. Stanley M. Horton, *What the Bible Says about the Holy Spirit* (Springfield, MO: Gospel Publishing House, 1976), 26.

> And it shall come to pass afterward,
> that I will pour out my Spirit on all flesh;
> your sons and your daughters shall prophesy,
> your old men shall dream dreams,
> and your young men shall see visions.
> Even on the male and female servants
> in those days I will pour out my Spirit. (Joel 2:28–29)

Although Joel does speak of salvation for those who call on the name of the Lord a few verses later (v. 32), the focus of the Spirit's work here is not on salvation. Rather, the result of the Spirit's outpouring will be prophecy, dreams, and visions. Furthermore, this outpouring of the Spirit will not be limited to a particular group among God's people. It is for sons and daughters, young and old, and for people of every rank in society, including servants. Joel does not point to the new heart, new spirit, and new obedience of the new covenant. Rather, he points to the other aspect of the Spirit's work, which we have already seen in the Old Testament: his empowering and equipping, especially, here for prophecy. As we have seen above, the Spirit came upon a small number of particular individuals to speak in prophecy in the Old Testament; however, now Joel speaks of a coming day when this aspect of the Spirit's work will not be limited to a privileged few, but available to all God's people.

This is a promise of the Spirit's charismatic empowerment, not of the new birth through the Spirit. Moses had already anticipated this in Numbers 11, after the prophecies of Eldad and Medad: "Would that all the Lord's people were prophets, that the Lord would put his Spirit on them!" (Num. 11:29). Anthony Palma, an American Assemblies of God scholar, calls this "Moses' intense desire" with the reminder that "Moses himself [was] a prophet."[5] Parallel to the promise of inward transformation through the new birth by the Spirit, we find in the Old Testament a promise of prophetic empowerment for the people of God.

The Spirit and the Promise of Assurance

Yet, the Old Testament also contains a third group of promises that are neither promises of salvation nor promises of empowerment.[6] We can see this in Isaiah 44, where the Lord promises to pour out his Spirit in blessing, as "water on the thirsty land, and streams on the dry ground" (v. 3). The result will be that

---

5. Anthony D. Palma, *The Holy Spirit: A Pentecostal Perspective* (Springfield, MO: Gospel Publishing House, 2001), 135.
6. For further detail on this third group of promises, see Jonathan Black, *Apostolic Theology: A Trinitarian, Evangelical, Pentecostal Introduction to Christian Doctrine* (Luton: Apostolic Church, 2016), 435–39.

> This one will say, "I am the LORD's,"
> another will call on the name of Jacob,
> and another will write on his hand, "The LORD's,"
> and name himself by the name of Israel. (v. 5)

Although they already belong to the Lord, now, through the outpouring of the Spirit, there is a fresh recognition of this belonging. Through the outpoured Spirit, they will confidently identify themselves as the Lord's people and speak with assurance that they are indeed his own. Thus, by pouring out the Holy Spirit upon his people, the Lord assures them that they truly are his.

Later, Isaiah will show the connection between this outpouring of the Spirit upon the Lord's people and speaking words from God: "My Spirit that is upon you, and my words that I have put in your mouth, shall not depart out of your mouth, or out of the mouth of your offspring, or out of the mouth of your children's offspring" (Isa. 59:21). The Spirit who assures us that we are the Lord's people is the Spirit who puts his words in our mouths.

Ezekiel also connects the outpouring of the Holy Spirit with assurance, for the Lord says that his people "shall know that I am the LORD their God" (Ezek. 39:28). This takes place when he will "pour out [his] Spirit upon the house of Israel," which will also mean that he "will not hide [his] face anymore from them" (Ezek. 39:29). As God pours out his Spirit into the hearts of his people, the Holy Spirit assures us that God's face is not hidden from us.

Summary

In the Old Testament we see examples of the outpouring of the Holy Spirit and promises of the more widespread future outpouring of the Spirit. The Holy Spirit anointed prophets; raised up and empowered leaders for God's people; and gave wisdom, practical ability, and the ability to teach others. The prophets promised that in the future the Spirit would transform within, empower and equip God's people, and grant them assurance. Thus, both in history and in prophecy, the Old Testament points us both to the Holy Spirit's salvific role and also to an outpouring of the Spirit upon God's people that is distinct from regeneration, involving both assurance and equipping.

REFLECTION QUESTIONS

1. What are some examples of the Spirit's anointing in the Old Testament, and what are the results?

2. Do these examples demonstrate that the Holy Spirit is poured out on God's people for purposes apart from regeneration?

3. What does the Holy Spirit's role in the work of Bezalel and Oholiab teach us about the outpouring of the Spirit?
4. What are the three types of promise we find in the Old Testament concerning the future outpouring of the Holy Spirit?
5. How do you understand the promises from Isaiah and Ezekiel in the final section?

QUESTION 16

What Does the New Testament Say About the Outpouring of the Holy Spirit?

In the last chapter we looked at what we learn from the Old Testament about the outpouring of the Holy Spirit. In this chapter we will turn our attention to the New Testament.

The Promise of the Spirit in the Gospels

The promise of the baptism in the Holy Spirit bookends Christ's earthly ministry, appearing at the beginning on the lips of John the Baptist (Matt. 3:11; Mark 1:8; Luke 3:16; John 1:33), and at the end on the lips of Christ himself (Acts 1:5; cf. Luke 24:49).

John the Baptist on the Promise of the Spirit

John preached about the one who "will baptize you with the Holy Spirit" (Mark 1:8). He also identified the baptizer in the Holy Spirit as the Messiah (Luke 3:15–17) and as the one who would bring God's judgment on those who do not repent (Matt. 3:7–12). When he baptized Jesus in the Jordan, John saw that it was Jesus who is the baptizer in the Holy Spirit and bore witness to this: "I saw the Spirit descend from heaven like a dove, and it remained on him. I myself did not know him, but he who sent me to baptize with water said to me, 'He on whom you see the Spirit descend and remain, this is he who baptizes with the Holy Spirit'" (John 1:32–33).

In the teaching of John the Baptist recorded in the Gospels, Jesus's identity as the baptizer in the Spirit is given even more prominence than his identity as the Lamb of God (John 1:29, 36). John pointed to Jesus as the one who was coming both to take away our sins *and* to baptize us in the Holy Spirit.

Jesus on the Promise of the Spirit

Before his ascension to the right hand of the Father, Jesus tells his disciples that they "will be baptized with the Holy Spirit not many days from now" (Acts 1:5). He calls this "the promise of the Father" and tells them to wait in Jerusalem for it (Acts 1:4). Thus, when at the end of Luke's gospel Jesus tells his disciples to "stay in the city until [they] are clothed with power from on high" because he is "sending the promise of [his] Father" (Luke 24:49), the comparison with Acts 1 shows us that the promise of "power from on high" in Luke is the being "baptized with the Holy Spirit" in Acts. The baptism in the Holy Spirit is, then, one of the last things to which Jesus draws his disciples' attention before ascending. And this promise is important enough that they are to wait to receive it before doing anything else.

However, this is not the first time Jesus speaks of the outpouring of the Spirit. In John 7, for example, Jesus teaches about the Spirit in terms of "rivers of living water" that will flow out of the heart (John 7:38–39). Importantly, John adds here that "as yet the Spirit had not been given, because Jesus was not yet glorified" (John 7:39). Thus, Jesus is talking about something new, over and above the experience of the Spirit by Old Testament believers. After Jesus was glorified in his resurrection and ascension, he would pour out the Holy Spirit in a new way. Jesus must return to the Father before the Spirit can come in this way (John 16:7).

The largest part of Christ's teaching concerning the Holy Spirit took place on the night of his arrest, recorded in John 14–16. Not only does Jesus speak to his disciples about the coming of the Holy Spirit just before his ascension but also just before he goes to the cross. This focus on the coming of the Holy Spirit before Christ's departure from his followers in both his death and his ascension highlights its significance.

The first portion of Jesus's teaching on the coming of the Holy Spirit, in the upper room that night, is found in John 14:15–28. Here he calls the Spirit "another Helper" (v. 16), indicating that this will be another Helper of the same kind as Jesus himself.[1] The Holy Spirit's ministry to believers, therefore, is not of a different sort to Christ but rather stands in continuity with his work. Christ is the first "helper," and so this other helper of the same sort will represent Christ to his people. Already this helper is known by the disciples, for "he dwells with" them; but now Jesus promises that he is coming to "be in you" (v. 17). When he does, he will be more than merely Christ's representative. For by the Holy Spirit Christ himself will come to his people (v. 18) and manifest himself to them (v. 21). The Lord Jesus "himself comes to us in the

1. See Stanley M. Horton, *What the Bible Says About the Holy Spirit* (Springfield, MO: Gospel Publishing House, 1976), 123–24; and Craig S. Keener, *The Gospel of John: A Commentary* (Grand Rapids: Baker Academic, 2003), 2:972.

Holy Spirit, for the Holy Spirit mediates both the Father and the Son to us (John 14:18, 20, 23)."[2]

The Spirit will also "teach [them] all things and bring to [their] remembrance all that [Christ has] said to [them]" (v. 26). As D. A. Carson points out, "The Spirit's ministry in this respect was not to bring qualitatively new revelation, but to complete, to fill out, the revelation brought by Jesus himself."[3] With this, Pentecostals fully agree: Christ's promise here "guaranteed the accuracy of [the apostles'] preaching and . . . theology, thus giving us assurance of the inerrancy of the New Testament" and also points us to the Spirit's ongoing teaching ministry "not by bringing new revelation, but by bringing new understanding, new comprehension, new illumination."[4] Craig Keener demonstrates that this also involves empowerment "to enable them to continually reapply the teaching of Jesus to ever new situations."[5]

In the next chapter, Jesus makes a related promise that the Spirit "will bear witness about me" (John 15:26). Like the promise that the Spirit will teach them and bring what Christ has said to remembrance, Jesus begins this promise by speaking of the Spirit as the helper who comes from the Father and the Son (15:26; cf. 14:26). This highlights both the significance and the connection between these two statements. It is in bearing witness about Christ that the Spirit teaches and brings what Christ has said to his people's remembrance. Jesus further reinforces this point in chapter 16: "When the Spirit of truth comes, he will guide you into all the truth, for he will not speak on his own authority, but whatever he hears he will speak, and he will declare to you the things that are to come. He will glorify me, for he will take what is mine and declare it to you. All that the Father has is mine; therefore I said that he will take what is mine and declare it to you" (John 16:13–14). The teaching of the Spirit is not divided from the teaching of Christ, for the Father, Son, and Holy Spirit are one God—the holy and consubstantial Trinity. Everything the Spirit does will glorify Christ, and in glorifying Christ will glorify the Father.

This helps us to understand Jesus's surprising statement, "it is to your advantage that I go away, for if I do not go away, the Helper will not come to you. But if I go, I will send him to you" (John 16:7). It is not that the Spirit is somehow greater than Christ; rather, it is because the Spirit glorifies Christ and takes what is Christ's and declares it to his people that the coming of the Spirit is to our advantage. In this glorification of Christ, the Spirit draws us to gaze upon the glory of the triune God.

---

2. Horton, *What the Bible Says*, 123.
3. D. A. Carson, *The Gospel According to John*, Pillar New Testament Commentary (Nottingham: Apollos, 1991), 505.
4. Horton, *What the Bible Says*, 121.
5. Keener, *John*, 2:982.

These passages from John 14–16 do not exhaust Jesus's teaching on the Holy Spirit; however, they do demonstrate that there are significant aspects of Jesus's teaching on the coming of the Holy Spirit that are not exhausted in regeneration. The exalted Savior pours out his Spirit not only to give new life, but also to give us knowledge and understanding of Scripture, to enable us to apply God's Word to new situations, to testify to Christ, and to bring Christ's presence to us by the Spirit. The outpoured Holy Spirit is the Spirit of revelation, who opens our eyes to greater understanding of the revelation of Christ in Scripture and who testifies to Christ in us and through us.

One other gospel passage is particularly significant for our consideration of the promise of the outpouring of the Holy Spirit. In Luke 11, Jesus asks: "What father among you, if his son asks for a fish, will instead of a fish give him a serpent; or if he asks for an egg, will give him a scorpion? If you then, who are evil, know how to give good gifts to your children, how much more will the heavenly Father give the Holy Spirit to those who ask him!" (Luke 11:11–13). Here, Pentecostal New Testament scholar William Simmons notes, "It is God's benevolent will to give the Holy Spirit to all who ask him."[6] However, what is particularly noteworthy is the encouragement to ask. In the parallel passage in Matthew 7:11, Jesus says that our "Father who is in heaven [will] give good things to those who ask him." Thus, the gift of the Holy Spirit is a good thing. (The contrast with serpents and scorpions in Luke's account already makes that clear.) Therefore, those who are already the children of the heavenly Father are to come to him and ask for the good gift of his Holy Spirit. As Stanley Horton sums up, "If we come persistently asking Him, He will give us what we ask for, not something bad, not something less than the best, but the Holy Spirit himself."[7]

The Anointing of the Spirit in the Early Church

We see the anointing of the Spirit and its results in the life of the early church throughout the book of Acts. Given that we will trace through several of the accounts of people being baptized in the Spirit in Acts in questions 19 and 20, we will focus here on a different passage from Acts and a few significant passages in the Epistles in order to highlight the Spirit's anointing in the early church.

Acts 4

As recorded in Acts 4, the result of a prayer meeting is that "the place in which they were gathered together was shaken, and they were all filled with the Holy Spirit and continued to speak the word of God with boldness" (Acts

---

6. William A. Simmons, *The Holy Spirit in the New Testament: A Pentecostal Guide* (Downers Grove, IL: InterVarsity Press, 2021), 41.
7. Horton, *What the Bible Says*, 104.

4:31). What is particularly of note here is that those who were here filled with the Holy Spirit included Peter and John, who had already been filled with the Spirit on the day of Pentecost (Acts 2:4). Thus, it is clear that the baptism in the Holy Spirit is not a "once-for-all sanctifying or empowering work."[8] Rather, as Pentecostals have always emphasized, there is a need to be "refilled," which is "the traditional expression to indicate that the empowering work of the Spirit, with diverse manifestations, is something that happens repeatedly in the life of a believer."[9] Douglas Oss explains that, in Pentecostal understanding, the baptism in the Holy Spirit is "the first experience of the Spirit's empowering work, which inaugurates a life characterized by continued anointings with the Spirit. It is not of the same once-for-all nature as regeneration."[10] As Paul tells the Ephesians, believers should continually "be filled with the Spirit" (Eph. 5:18).

The Epistles

Paul asks the Galatians, "Did you receive the Spirit by works of the law or by hearing with faith?" (Gal. 3:2). This is a rhetorical question; we are supposed to understand clearly that the answer is "by hearing with faith." Yet, "the entire argument runs aground if this appeal is not also to a reception of the Spirit that was dynamically experienced."[11] The Pentecostal New Testament scholar Gordon Fee points out, "Even though Paul seldom mentions any of the visible evidences of the Spirit in such contexts as these, here is the demonstration that the experience of the Spirit in the Pauline churches was very much the same as that described and understood by Luke [in Acts]—as visibly and experientially accompanied by phenomena that gave certain evidence of the presence of the Spirit of God. . . . Such an understanding alone makes the present rhetoric possible at all."[12] A few verses later, Paul asks again, "Does he who supplies the Spirit to you and works miracles among you do so by works of the law, or by hearing with faith?" (Gal. 3:5). This is still a rhetorical question, and the same answer is implied. This time, however, Christ's giving of the Spirit is explicitly connected with his working miracles among his people. Paul is pointing the Galatians to an experiential reality. They *know* they have received the Spirit by hearing with faith. Something tangible happened. And something tangible still happens as the Lord continues to supply his Spirit and work miracles among them. Essentially Paul is saying, "Surely the miracle-working presence of

8. Douglas Oss, "A Pentecostal/Charismatic View," in *Are Miraculous Gifts for Today? Four Views*, ed. Wayne Grudem (Leicester: InterVarsity Press, 1996), 243.
9. Oss, "Pentecostal/Charismatic View," 243.
10. Oss, "Pentecostal/Charismatic View," 243.
11. Gordon Fee, *God's Empowering Presence: The Holy Spirit in the Letters of Paul* (Peabody, MA: Hendrickson, 1994), 382–83.
12. Fee, *God's Empowering Presence*, 383–84.

the Holy Spirit is evidentiary proof that they have been justified by faith alone, without circumcision or the works of the law."[13]

He makes a further link between the distinct experiences of justification and this receiving of the Spirit in verses 13–14. By his death on the cross, Christ has "redeemed us from the curse of the law by becoming a curse for us" (Gal. 3:13). Yet, the result of this curse-bearing by Christ in his death is twofold: Jesus died so that in him "the blessing of Abraham might come to the Gentiles" and "so that we might receive the promised Spirit through faith" (Gal. 3:14). The blessing of Abraham is justification by faith alone. Therefore, Christ died on the cross, both so that we might be justified through faith in him, and so that we might be baptized in the Holy Spirit. "Receiving the Holy Spirit is not based on our own goodness and piety. It is the work of Christ that atones for our sins and cleanses us from unrighteousness. . . . Because of his sacrifice we need only ask in faith to receive the Holy Spirit."[14]

Paul also connects receiving the Holy Spirit with experiencing the reality of our adoption into God's family: "Because you are sons, God has sent the Spirit of his Son into our hearts, crying, 'Abba! Father!'" (Gal. 4:6). This is an experience that causes us to recognize that we are the well-loved adopted children of God. "We are caught up into the love of Christ and filled with joy as we begin to glimpse the significance of our divine adoption."[15] In Ephesians, Paul expresses this concept as being "sealed with the promised Holy Spirit, who is the guarantee of our inheritance" (Eph. 1:13–14).

Paul also emphasizes that this is an experience of God's love, for "God's love has been poured into our hearts through the Holy Spirit who has been given to us" (Rom. 5:5). Here he "portrays love descending on us like a downpour. . . . Paul assumes that this downpour of love is a vivid enough experience for believers that it can serve as a source of assurance about the future work of God in their lives."[16]

Biblical Terminology for the Baptism in the Holy Spirit

The book of Acts uses a variety of expressions interchangeably for the empowering work of the Holy Spirit that Pentecostals call the baptism in the Holy Spirit. Of these, five are used for what happens on the day of Pentecost and also used in at least one other incident in the book of Acts. These are: "baptized in the Holy Spirit" (Acts 1:5; 11:16); the Spirit coming upon or falling upon (1:8; 8:16; 10:44; 11:15; 19:6); "filled with the Holy Spirit" (2:4;

---

13. Simmons, *Holy Spirit*, 118.
14. William Simmons, "Galatians," in *Full Life Bible Commentary to the New Testament*, eds. French L. Arrington and Roger Stronstad (Grand Rapids: Zondervan, 1999), 993.
15. Robert P. Menzies, *Speaking in Tongues: Jesus and the Apostolic Church as Models for the Church Today* (Cleveland, TN: CPT Press, 2016), 163.
16. Van Johnson, "Romans," in *Full Life Bible Commentary to the New Testament*, eds. French L. Arrington and Roger Stronstad (Grand Rapids: Zondervan, 1999), 725.

9:17); the pouring out of the Spirit (2:17–18; 10:45); and the gift of the Spirit (2:38; 10:45; 11:17). One further expression, receiving the Spirit (8:15–20; 10:47; 19:2), is used to describe what happens to Cornelius and his household (which Peter also describes as being baptized in the Spirit) and for two other instances in Samaria and Ephesus (both of which are also described by another term used on the day of Pentecost). These six expressions, then, all describe the empowering anointing with the Holy Spirit that Pentecostals call the baptism in the Holy Spirit.[17]

Summary

In the New Testament, both John the Baptist and Jesus promise that Christ will baptize in the Holy Spirit. Jesus teaches that the Holy Spirit will not only give new life but also give us knowledge and understanding of Scripture, enable us to apply God's Word to new situations, testify to Christ, and bring Christ's presence to us by the Spirit. Furthermore, Jesus encourages his disciples to pray to receive this good gift. Paul also writes of an experience of the Holy Spirit as a result of Christ's atoning work and connects this with an awareness of our adoption and of God's love poured out in our hearts. Throughout the New Testament, a number of different expressions are used for this baptism in the Holy Spirit.

REFLECTION QUESTIONS

1. What do the promises of John the Baptist and Jesus tell us about the baptism in the Holy Spirit?

2. What was the purpose of the Spirit's coming that Jesus spoke of on the night of his arrest?

3. What is the significance of Luke 11:11–13 for our understanding of the baptism of the Holy Spirit?

4. What does the experience of the disciples in Acts 4:31 teach us about the baptism in the Holy Spirit?

5. Reflect on each of the expressions the New Testament uses for this experience. What does each tell us about the nature of this experience?

---

17. The expression Pentecostals use most often, "baptize in the Spirit," is the most common biblical expression for this empowerment, being used by John the Baptist in the Gospels, as well as in the book of Acts.

QUESTION 17

What Is the Pentecostal Doctrine of the Baptism of the Holy Spirit? (Part 1)

In the last two questions we have examined a large amount of the Bible's teaching related to the outpouring of the Holy Spirit to empower God's people and assure them that they are indeed his. In the next few questions we will look at some of the key features of how Pentecostals have assembled this biblical material into their doctrine of the baptism in the Holy Spirit. We will begin this question by considering the theological question of what the baptism of the Spirit actually is. The Foursquare Declaration of Faith provides us with a helpful introduction to the Pentecostal understanding of the baptism in the Spirit:

> We believe that the baptism of the Holy Spirit is the incoming of the promised Comforter in mighty and glorious fullness to endue the believer with power from on high; to glorify and exalt the Lord Jesus; to give inspired utterance in witnessing of Him; to foster the spirit of prayer, holiness, sobriety; to equip the individual and the Church for practical, efficient, joyous, Spirit-filled soul-winning in the fields of life; and that this being still the dispensation of the Holy Spirit, the believer may have every reason to expect His incoming to be after the same manner as that in which He came upon Jew and Gentile alike in Bible days, and as recorded in the Word, that it may be truly said of us as of the house of Cornelius: the Holy Ghost fell on them as on us at the beginning.[1]

1. FDF, 10.

The Spirit Glorifies Christ

Pentecostals look to Jesus as the baptizer in the Holy Spirit (John 1:33). It is the risen and ascended Savior who pours out the Holy Spirit from the Father's right hand (Acts 2:33). Therefore, the baptism in the Holy Spirit draws our attention to Christ in a powerful way, for he is its source. Only the one who died for us, rose again for us, and ascended into heaven for us can pour out the Holy Spirit upon us. Thus, the baptism in the Spirit depends on, and so ever points us to, the glory of Christ's cross and empty tomb. It is the one who has raised his nail-pierced hands in blessing over his people (Luke 24:50–51) who pours out the Spirit from heaven; the baptism in the Holy Spirit truly flows from the cross (Gal. 3:13–14).

Jesus promised that the Holy Spirit would glorify him (John 16:14). He is the Spirit of Christ (Rom. 8:9; 1 Peter 1:11) who always points us to Christ. Even before receiving the baptism of the Spirit, the Holy Spirit is at work in our lives to convict us of our sin, draw us to Christ for salvation, and regenerate us and unite us to Christ through faith (John 3:5; 16:8; 1 Cor. 6:17). It is the Holy Spirit who works through the gospel to open our eyes to our guilt and the reality of our sinful state, and to show us the glory of Christ and his finished work for our salvation. It is the Holy Spirit who raises us from our death in trespasses and sins to new life in union with Christ. Therefore, without the Holy Spirit, we could not be Christians (Rom. 8:9–11).

Here we must be very clear. The Holy Spirit dwells in every true believer (Rom. 8:9). Pentecostals do not believe that we do not have the Holy Spirit until we receive the baptism of the Spirit. The baptism of the Holy Spirit is not the first time we encounter the Holy Spirit. All Christians have received the Holy Spirit in salvation; then, in the baptism in the Spirit we receive the Holy Spirit in a different way, for a different purpose.[2] Yet, both in the Spirit's indwelling in salvation and in the Spirit's outpouring in the baptism of the Spirit, the Holy Spirit always glorifies Jesus in all that he does.

The Purpose of the Spirit's Outpouring

If the Holy Spirit already lives in all those who are saved, what is distinctive about the baptism of the Holy Spirit? In questions 19 and 20 we will consider some distinctive features of the manner in which we receive the Holy Spirit in the Pentecostal baptism, but here let's focus on its purpose.

2. For examples of Pentecostal confessional documents that clearly teach that all believers have received the Holy Spirit at conversion, see ACVG, 5; AdDDF, 6; Hungarian Pentecostal Confession of Faith (Magyar Pünkösdi Egyház, "Hitvallásunk)," 9; Pentecostal Movement in Norway, "Basis of Faith," 5; Pentecostal Church of Finland, "Main Articles of Faith," 5.

The Upward Sweep of the Spirit: Regeneration and Union with Christ

To help us consider the difference between regeneration and the baptism in the Holy Spirit, it will help us to think in terms of directions. Regeneration is an upward movement. The Holy Spirit lifts us out of our death in sin, unites us to Christ, and seats us with him in the heavenly places (Eph. 2:4–6). Thus, in conversion, the Holy Spirit catches us up in an upward sweep. This is a full salvation, for in it we are blessed "with every spiritual blessing" in Christ (Eph. 1:3). Therefore, nothing needs to be added to what is ours in Christ. There is nothing lacking in the salvation we have received in Jesus.

The Downward Sweep of the Spirit: Baptism in the Holy Spirit

Thus, it is incorrect to speak of the baptism in the Holy Spirit as a "second blessing." This is not how Pentecostals understand the experience.[3] Every blessing is ours in Christ, and so there is no place for a second blessing (Eph. 1:3). Rather, the baptism of the Holy Spirit is connected to what we have already received in salvation in Christ. Donald Gee, the internationally renowned early British Pentecostal theologian, described it as "the Divine consummation of the initial experience of every repentant sinner who turns to the Saviour and by faith in Him receives remission of sins."[4]

The baptism of the Spirit is a revelatory experience which Gee describes as making Christ "intensely real" to the believer, or as "a new discovery of the Living Christ."[5] For Bishop C. H. Mason of the Church of God in Christ, this fresh revelation of Christ in the baptism of the Spirit was so intense that he could describe it as receiving "Him, Jesus my Lord in the Holy Ghost."[6] Mason had already received the Lord Jesus in salvation; then at Azusa Street he received this powerful revelation of Christ in the baptism of the Holy Spirit. As D. P. Williams explains, the baptism in the Spirit brings "inward consciousness and evidence" of the fact that the living Christ is already dwelling in our hearts.[7] This is not the addition of something that was lacking in our salvation, but rather an opening of our eyes to the glory and wonder of what is already ours in Jesus.

---

3. Some Wesleyan Holiness Pentecostals speak of a "second blessing" of sanctification, although the majority of Pentecostals reject this concept too; see question 13. However, classical Pentecostals, including Wesleyan Holiness Pentecostals, do not speak of the baptism in the Holy Spirit as a "second blessing." Donald Gee, an internationally significant representative of the mainstream Pentecostal position, explicitly rejects ideas of the baptism in the Spirit as a "second blessing." See Donald Gee, "Studies on the Fundamental Truths: 6," *Redemption Tidings* 2, no. 6 (June 1926): 13.
4. Gee, "Studies," 13.
5. Donald Gee, *Pentecost* (Springfield, MO: Gospel Publishing House, 1932), 9–10, 22.
6. J. O. Patterson, German Ross, and Julia Atkins, eds., *History and Formative Year of the Church of God in Christ: Excerpts and Commentary from the Life and Works of Bishop C. H. Mason* (Memphis, TN: Church of God in Christ, 1969), 17.
7. D. P. Williams, "Editorial: Church Unity," *Riches of Grace* 12, no. 2 (November 1936): 242.

Although we already have a full salvation in Christ, we are not always aware of just how full and glorious it is. We know objectively what is ours when we are born again because the Bible tells us. Regeneration can sometimes involve a dramatic conversion experience, but it can also happen quietly in a way that we only recognize after the fact. The baptism in the Holy Spirit, however, is always a tangible experience. It is something that people can see and recognize (Acts 8:18).[8] Just as the Holy Spirit has swept us upward into union with Christ in salvation, now in the Pentecostal baptism he sweeps down upon us, bringing us a tangible experience of the reality of the blessings that are already ours in Christ.

In the baptism of the Holy Spirit, Christ, by his Spirit, opens our eyes to what is already objectively true. In the words of Donald Gee, "The finest fruit of a genuine Baptism in the Holy Spirit is the new and wonderful revelation it brings of the Lord Jesus Christ, the Risen Saviour, the Lover of the Soul."[9] As the love of God is poured out in our hearts in this baptism (Rom. 5:5), this is not the beginning of God's love to us, but rather an authentication and assurance of the reality that we are already the well-beloved children of God. It is a wonderful experience of what is already true. The baptism of the Spirit is, as the major Italian Pentecostal leader W. R. Thomas reminds us, "not a vague blessing" but rather an assuring, loving "demonstration of our salvation, an assurance of our sanctification, a foretaste of our glorification with Christ in eternity."[10] Donald Gee describes it as an "outstanding moment of God-consciousness" in which "the believer is surrounded by God; filled with God; bathed in Divine Love; touched by Divine power; drunk with Divine ecstasy."[11] This is a powerful opening of our eyes to the reality of the love of God toward us in Christ by the Spirit.

---

8. We will consider this more in question 20.
9. Gee, "Studies," 10–15.
10. William Roger Thomas, *Il Paracleto: La persona e l'opera dello Spirito Santo* (Grosetto: Ediz. Ricchezze di Grazia, 1961), chapter 7.
11. Gee, "Studies," 13. Gee is almost apologetic about the last expression "drunk with Divine ecstasy," but insists that it is a biblical description, pointing later in the article to Acts 2:13. He lived long before abuses in some extreme charismatic circles occurred, which have been justified as "drunkenness in the Spirit." For Gee, this was a reference to the overwhelming power and joy of the Spirit (p. 14), not an excuse for indecency and disorder in the worship of God. Furthermore, while stressing the overwhelming nature of the baptism in the Spirit, Gee also warns that "a real overwhelming in the Spirit of God can be missed by too much emphasis being placed upon the outward manifestations of His coming, as though they were the principal thing, and really represented that for which we were seeking. It cannot be too emphatically stated that all manifestations of the Spirit, such as tongues [and] prophecy . . . have absolutely no value, but rather the reverse, unless they come spontaneously from the overflowing and overwhelming of the believer in God." See Donald Gee, "The Baptism in the Holy Ghost," *Redemption Tidings* 3, no. 6 (June 1927): 3.

Immersion in the Triune God of Love

The first indication the New Testament gives us of the nature of this experience is when John the Baptist prophesies that Jesus will baptize in the Spirit (Matt. 3:11; Mark 1:8; Luke 3:16; John 1:33). John was baptizing, and he spoke of Jesus baptizing. Therefore, his hearers would have formed their conception of what Jesus was going to do in parallel with what John was doing. As Donald Gee put it: "As they watched John immersing in the waters of Jordan day after day they would form a very clear idea of what baptism in water entailed, and they would rightly conclude that this wonderful coming baptism in the Spirit must be somehow or another similar. To their minds it would inevitably mean something overwhelming, something real, something tangible; something they would be conscious of themselves and something others could without fail observe also."[12] Yet, Gee also warns that we cannot

> magnify these outward evidences at the expense of a just appreciation of the great central verity of . . . God the Holy Spirit, the Third Person of the Trinity, coming upon and into the believer in such fulness that an overwhelming of the whole being, including the physical, is only what should be expected. . . . The Baptism that Jesus gives is surely as real as the baptism in water instituted by John for repentance. Rightly conceived it is a wonderful parallel. The Strong Son of God immersing the believer into the very fulness of the Divine Love that henceforth there may [be] an altogether new power to be one of His witnesses.[13]

Therefore, the baptism in the Holy Spirit is "an immersion in God."[14] When we are baptized in the Spirit, we are "immersed in the Trinity."[15] "O Wonder of all wonders! That the very Substance and Essence and Nature of God, who is a consuming Fire, should actually come in to make our bodies and the Church of God an habitation for the Fire of His Love. He is the house-warmer, the Comforter, the Grace that consumes, the power that imparts Divine Energy; the Light that illuminates and transforms, lifting up the soul to the realm of God."[16]

12. Gee, "Studies," 14.
13. Gee, "Studies," 14.
14. Gee, "Studies," 14; cf. D. P. Williams, "The Inception of the World-Wide Missionary Cause," *Apostolic Church Missionary Herald* 1, no. 7 (April 1925): 210.
15. Jonathan Black, *Theosis of the Body of Christ* (Leiden: Brill, 2020), 229. Cf. Jonathan Black, *Apostolic Theology: A Trinitarian, Evangelical, Pentecostal Introduction to Christian Doctrine* (Luton: Apostolic Church, 2016), 451–52.
16. Williams, "Inception," 211.

Paul connects the outpouring of God's Spirit with the outpouring of his love: "God's love has been poured into our hearts through the Holy Spirit who has been given to us" (Rom. 5:5). Italian Pentecostal theologian Luigi Roncavasaglia describes this as "a testimony of love" and an "immersion in . . . the love of God which illuminates the mystery of the cross . . . [and] seals my position of sonship."[17]

This outpouring of God's love in the outpouring of the Spirit brings both "a new personal sense of his great love in Christ for my own soul" and also "a fresh realisation of the Divine love for *all* men."[18] In the baptism of the Spirit, the soul is "drawn out in love to the Lord, and in this new deeper love for the Heavenly Bridegroom will be found the true spring at last for love of others."[19] Thus, it is both a love that assures us of our adoption as well-beloved children of God and sends us out to make God's love in Christ known to others. It is an assuring love and an equipping love. And this is not a momentary ecstasy. Rather, the Holy Spirit has been poured out to stay, and so this love should have an enduring effect. There should be "an ever-ripening" of love as the fruit of the Spirit in our lives.[20]

Donald Gee warns that "this new capacity for Divine Love being shed abroad in the heart is often produced at the baptism of the Holy Spirit by the human spirit being utterly broken as never before."[21] The baptism of the Spirit is not a man-centered, self-aggrandizing experience. It should never be thought of as a badge of spiritual superiority. Rather, it is "a baptism that overwhelms the natural with God, and humbles man utterly to the dust."[22]

Summary

All believers receive the Holy Spirit when they are born again, when they are blessed with "every spiritual blessing in Christ" (Eph. 1:3). However, Pentecostals believe that believers also receive the Holy Spirit in a different way subsequently, bringing a tangible experience of the reality of the blessings which are ours in Christ. This experience brings us a powerful assurance of our adoption as well-beloved children of God and sends us out with assurance to make God's loving salvation in Christ known to others.

---

17. Luigi Roncavasaglia, *Edificherò La Mia Chiesa: Contribuo Per Un'Ecclesiologia* (Grosseto: Edizioni Ricchezze di Grazia, 1997), 131.
18. Gee, "The Baptism in the Holy Ghost," 3.
19. Gee, "The Baptism in the Holy Ghost," 3.
20. Gee, "The Baptism in the Holy Ghost," 3.
21. Gee, "The Baptism in the Holy Ghost," 3.
22. Gee, "The Baptism in the Holy Ghost," 2.

REFLECTION QUESTIONS

1. What biblical basis do you see for the statement at the beginning of this chapter from the Foursquare Declaration?

2. How does the Holy Spirit glorify Christ in our salvation?

3. Why should the baptism in the Holy Spirit not be thought of as a "second blessing"?

4. How does the baptism of the Holy Spirit relate to assurance of salvation?

5. In what way does the outpouring of God's love in our hearts in the baptism of the Holy Spirit empower us?

QUESTION 18

What Is the Pentecostal Doctrine of the Baptism of the Holy Spirit? (Part 2)

We have seen that the baptism in the Holy Spirit is a powerful way in which God assures us of his great love toward us and of the reality of the blessings that are ours in our union with Christ. In this way it is a fulfilment of the Old Testament promises of an outpouring of the Holy Spirit that would bring a fresh recognition and assurance of our belonging to the Lord (see question 15). As Christ pours out the Spirit into our hearts, this filling with the Holy Spirit assures us that God's face is not hidden from us. Rather, by the Spirit we know the smile of God in the face of Jesus Christ. Thus, the baptism of the Holy Spirit functions as an assuring seal of our adoption to sonship as well-beloved children of God.

Seal of Sonship and Guarantee of Inheritance

To the Corinthians, Paul writes, "It is God who establishes us with you in Christ, and has anointed us, and who has also put his seal on us and given us his Spirit in our hearts as a guarantee" (2 Cor. 1:21–22). Later, in the same letter, Paul reminds them that God "has given us the Spirit as a guarantee" (2 Cor. 5:5). In being anointed with the Spirit, believers receive the Spirit as a seal and a guarantee. In Ephesians Paul explains this further, telling us that in Christ, believers are "sealed with the promised Holy Spirit, who is the guarantee of our inheritance until we acquire possession of it, to the praise of his glory" (Eph. 1:13–14). In receiving the Spirit, we are "sealed for the day of redemption" (Eph. 4:30).

The idea of the guarantee in these Scriptures is a first installment that guarantees the rest will come. Thus, not only does the baptism of the Holy Spirit serve to assure us of our future inheritance, but it gives us a foretaste of that future inheritance here and now. Through the outpouring of the Holy Spirit, we taste "the powers of the age to come" (Heb. 6:5). Stanley Horton explains that this guarantee demonstrates that "our inheritance is more than a hope. Now in the midst of the corruption, decay, and death of the present age, we enjoy in and through the Holy Spirit the actual beginning of our inheritance."[1]

In both 2 Corinthians and Ephesians, this foretaste and guarantee is connected with the sealing of the Spirit. In the New Testament, the idea of a seal is an authentication or acknowledgment of ownership. A seal was placed on a document to authenticate it as genuine. A seal could be placed on an object to show to whom it belonged. The Father "set his seal" on Jesus as the acknowledgement and authentication that Jesus is indeed the Son of God (John 6:27). Whoever receives Christ's testimony "sets his seal to this, that God is true" (John 3:33). This is an acknowledgement of the authenticity of the truth of God's word. So, when we are sealed with the Spirit, this is "a mark of recognition that we are indeed sons."[2] Thus, the baptism (or sealing) with the Spirit is "an experiential assurance of sonship."[3]

We can see this idea expressed in another way in Galatians 4:6: "And because you are sons, God has sent the Spirit of his Son into our hearts, crying, 'Abba! Father!'" The Lord pours out his Spirit into the hearts of those who are already his sons, causing them to cry out to him in a fresh recognition of the reality of their relationship with the Father through the Son.[4] As Martyn Lloyd-Jones puts it, "The baptism with the Spirit is the highest form of assurance of salvation that anybody can ever receive, and . . . with this assurance comes power."[5] Romanian Pentecostals explain the baptism of the Spirit as "a seal for the day of redemption, a guarantee of the inheritance, power from above for the service of confessing the full Gospel."[6]

---

1. Stanley M. Horton, *What the Bible Says about the Holy Spirit* (Springfield, MO: Gospel Publishing House, 1976), 237.
2. Horton, *What the Bible Says*, 238.
3. Jonathan Black, *Apostolic Theology: A Trinitarian, Evangelical, Pentecostal Introduction to Christian Doctrine* (Luton: Apostolic Church, 2016), 453. D. Martyn Lloyd-Jones argues that Scripture uses the terms "baptized" and "sealed" with the Spirit synonymously for the same experience of baptism of the Spirit, but with a differing focus for each term. "Baptized" is used "when it is purely a question of witness and testimony," while "sealed" is used "more in terms of our inheritance and the certainty that is given to us that we are the heirs of God." See Lloyd-Jones, *Joy Unspeakable: The Baptism and Gifts of the Holy Spirit* (Eastbourne: Kingsway, 2008), 333.
4. Many of the adopted sons of God are, of course, daughters. The Bible uses the language of sonship for all believers—male and female—to emphasize both that we all share fully in the same inheritance and also that the relationship we have been brought into is Christ the Son's own relationship with his Father. The salvation that is ours in Christ does not differ depending on our sex. Paul makes this very clear in the previous chapter: "for in Christ Jesus you are all sons of God, through faith. For as many of you as were baptized into Christ have put on Christ. There is neither Jew nor Greek, there is neither slave nor free, there is no male and female, for you are all one in Christ Jesus" (Gal. 3:26–28).
5. Lloyd-Jones, *Joy Unspeakable*, 333.
6. Romanian CF, 16.

The Outward Flow of the Spirit: Power for Witness

The powerful assurance of the love of God in Christ and of our sonship in the well-beloved Son, which we receive by the Holy Spirit in the baptism, results in power for service and especially power to testify to Christ. Jesus promised that his disciples would be "clothed with power from on high" (Luke 24:49). He also explained that this power that they would receive "when the Holy Spirit has come upon you" would make them his "witnesses in Jerusalem and in all Judea and Samaria, and to the end of the earth" (Acts 1:8). The connection between the power of the Holy Spirit here and witness for Christ shows us that this is power for evangelism. The Holy Spirit empowers believers to speak boldly of Christ and his saving work for us.

We see this in practice on the day of Pentecost, when the believers in the upper room are baptized in the Spirit and then go out to suddenly proclaim the gospel, publicly and powerfully. As a result, thousands came to Christ as Savior and Lord. Later, when the disciples were forbidden by the authorities from speaking of Christ, the church gathered to pray for boldness to continue speaking (Acts 4:29–30). The Lord responded by pouring out the Holy Spirit afresh upon them, and, as a result of this filling, they "continued to speak the word of God with boldness" (Acts 4:31).

This is not simply power. Jesus warns that power by itself is of no use (Matt. 7:22–23). Without knowing and being known by Christ, power is a danger rather than a benefit (Matt. 7:23; Acts 19:13–17). "It is not a power that somehow associates itself with Christ (cf. Acts 19:13–17), nor a power for the sake of Christ, which we can wield as our own work to gain divine favour (cf. the reliance on what they have done in Christ's name in Mt 7:22–23). Rather it is the power of Christ himself as he comes to his church through his Spirit."[7] The power comes when the Spirit comes, for it is the Holy Spirit himself who is this power for witness. As the Holy Spirit pours out the love of God in our hearts, assuring us of our sonship and of God's great love for us, he emboldens us to speak about Jesus. As the Spirit pours out God's love in our hearts, that causes us to respond in love both to God and in Christlike love to our neighbor. Such Christlike love sends us to speak to others in love so that they too may know the saving love of God in Christ. As one early Pentecostal leader wrote: "When the Holy Ghost comes down, He lays upon the spirit of the believer the burden of the whole wide world . . . making you to weep, and cry, and sob for the salvation of others, even the ends of the earth."[8]

---

7. Black, *Apostolic Theology*, 454.
8. D. P. Williams, "The First Missionary Prayer Meeting," *Apostolic Church Missionary Herald* 1, no. 5 (April 1924): 138.

The Gracious Gift of the Outpoured Spirit

It is the crucified, risen, and ascended Christ who baptizes in the Holy Spirit (Acts 2:23–24, 32–33). Therefore, this is a gift of his grace, as a result of his cross (Gal. 3:13–14). As such, the baptism of the Holy Spirit cannot be earned. We do not receive it as a reward for our works, but only as a result of Christ's work. Therefore, we must receive the baptism in the Spirit through faith in Christ (Gal. 3:2, 5).[9] As the early American Pentecostal G. F. Taylor put it: "The blessings of God come to us through faith . . . spiritual graces come to us alone by faith. We say that the Holy Ghost is received by appropriating faith. . . . It must be faith for the Baptism alone."[10] The Romanian Pentecostal confession of faith teaches that the baptism of the Spirit is "received on the basis of faith following the new birth."[11]

The focus here is on the Lord himself. Ithiel Clemmons, a bishop in the Church of God in Christ, reminds Pentecostals that the goal must be "always a baptism by the Holy Spirit rather than a show of power by speaking in tongues. . . . The gift of the Holy Spirit—not the gifts that the Spirit bestows—should be the primary focus of the believer's quest."[12] Likewise, D. P. Williams warned an earlier generation of Pentecostals, "if we put our trust in the gifts and not in the Giver, we shall soon become prodigals from our Father's home."[13]

Receiving the Baptism in the Holy Spirit

Because the baptism in the Holy Spirit is a gracious gift given by the ascended Lord, it must be received as a gift. David Petts warns against being held back from receiving the baptism of the Spirit by a sense of unworthiness or feeling "the need to achieve a certain level of holiness before [asking] God for the gift of his Spirit."[14] Rather than looking at our unworthiness, we should instead trust in God's work of justification. Receiving God's good gift of the baptism in the Holy Spirit "depends not on our own righteousness but on Christ's atoning work on the cross."[15] In justification, "God has declared us righteous despite our unworthiness and it is only in that righteousness with which he has credited us that we are fit to receive the Spirit."[16]

Relying on Christ's work for us in his death and resurrection, and on Christ's righteousness imputed to us, we can come to the Lord expectantly

---

9. For further discussion of this, see Black, *Apostolic Theology*, 466–68.
10. G. F. Taylor, "Basis of Union XVI: The Baptism of the Holy Ghost," *Pentecostal Holiness Advocate* (January 24, 1918): 5.
11. Romanian CF, 16.
12. Ithiel C. Clemmons, *Bishop C. H. Mason and the Roots of the Church of God in Christ* (Largo, MD: Pneuma Life, 1996), 55–56.
13. D. P. Williams, "Grace and Apostleship (II)," *Riches of Grace* 15, no. 9 (October 1940): 97.
14. David Petts, *The Holy Spirit: An Introduction* (Mattersey: Mattersey Hall, 1998), 80.
15. Petts, *Holy Spirit*, 80.
16. Petts, *Holy Spirit*, 83.

when we ask to receive this good gift. Such believing prayer is the expression of our faith in the Lord for this promise of the baptism in the Spirit. Jesus's promise in Luke 11:13 encourages us to ask with expectation, for there he promises both that "if we ask for the Holy Spirit God will give us the Holy Spirit" and that our heavenly Father "will not let us receive 'stones' or 'scorpions' or 'snakes'" when we ask him for the good gift of his Spirit.[17] Therefore we can have assurance both that the Lord is willing to give this gift and that we have no need to fear.

The Danish Pentecostal leader Sigfrid Beck summarizes what those who seek the baptism in the Holy Spirit need: they must have experienced true conversion to Christ and been adopted as sons of God; they must truly desire the baptism in the Spirit (John 7:37–39); they should pray in faith and ask for it; and they should continue to persevere in prayer until they receive it, living their lives always in submission to the Lord.[18] Those who seek the baptism of the Spirit should draw close to the Lord in prayer with "assured faith and thanksgiving."[19]

Summary

Pentecostals believe that all Christians receive the Holy Spirit when they are born again. However, they do not believe this is the same as the baptism in the Holy Spirit. As the confession of faith of the Apostolic Church UK puts it, "When Christ baptises us in the Holy Spirit, we receive the Spirit in another way, pouring out God's love in our hearts, assuring us that we are His children, and empowering us to serve Him and proclaim to others the good news of salvation in Jesus."[20] This "foretaste of the age to come" is promised to all believers (Acts 2:39),[21] and it is a gracious gift poured out by the Lord Jesus as a result of his death on the cross, his resurrection, and his ascension. Therefore, this gift can only be received through faith (Gal. 3:2, 5), which Jesus teaches us to express in believing prayer (Luke 11:13).

REFLECTION QUESTIONS

1. In what way is the baptism in the Holy Spirit a seal and a guarantee?

2. Why do Pentecostals connect the baptism in the Holy Spirit with power for evangelism?

---

17. Petts, *Holy Spirit*, 83.
18. Sigfrid Beck, *Le Baptême dans le Saint Esprit*, trans. Théo Lachat (Lillebonne: Editions Foi et Victoire, 1955), 19–28.
19. Beck, *Le Baptême dans le Saint Esprit*, 31.
20. ACVG, 5.
21. ACVG, 5.

3. Why is power by itself insufficient? Where does Jesus warn us about this?
4. How is the gracious gift of the baptism of the Holy Spirit received?
5. How is the baptism of the Holy Spirit connected to the work of Christ?

QUESTION 19

What Is the Pentecostal Doctrine of Subsequence?

All Christians believe in the baptism in the Holy Spirit. What makes Pentecostals different from other evangelical Christians is that they do not believe that this baptism in the Spirit is the same as being born again. This is the Pentecostal doctrine of subsequence: the understanding that the baptism of the Holy Spirit is a distinct experience from conversion. This does not mean that someone cannot get saved and be filled with the Spirit at the same time. For example, Cornelius and his household experienced both simultaneously, as recorded in Acts 10:44–48. The subsequence aspect of Pentecostal doctrine is logical and theological rather than chronological. It underscores that the baptism in the Spirit is dependent upon regeneration. In other words, you cannot be baptized in the Spirit without having been born again. Yet, as baptism in the Spirit and regeneration are not identical, there may be (and frequently is) a time interval between the two. Some might be baptized in the Spirit at the very moment they get saved, some might be filled with the Spirit a short time later, and some might have been Christians for a long time before receiving the Pentecostal baptism. This is why some Pentecostals have suggested that separability might be a more helpful word than subsequence, as it more clearly conveys the intent of the doctrine. As Anthony Palma points out, "The emphasis of responsible Pentecostals has always been on theological separability, not temporal subsequence."[1]

Theology and the Book of Acts

Pentecostals turn immediately to the book of Acts to demonstrate the doctrine of subsequence. But before we turn to Acts, we first need to think about

1. Anthony D. Palma, *The Holy Spirit: A Pentecostal Perspective* (Springfield, MO: Logion, 2001), 132. Subsequence, however, remains the more familiar term, and so that is why this question uses it.

whether that's a legitimate move to make. Are all narrative accounts in Scripture necessarily normative for Christian doctrine and experience? John Stott has famously argued, "This revelation of the purpose of God in Scripture should be sought primarily in its *didactic*, rather than its *descriptive* parts. More precisely, we should look for it in the teaching of Jesus, and in the sermons and writings of the apostles, rather than in the purely narrative portions of the Acts. . . . What I *am* saying is that what is descriptive is valuable only in so far as it is interpreted by what is didactic."[2] If Stott is correct in this argument, then we would have to concede that we could not look to the narrative accounts of the baptism in the Spirit in the book of Acts for a doctrine of subsequence.

However, Pentecostal scholars have pointed to Paul's teaching on the nature of Scripture and its authority as a counterargument to Stott. Paul writes to Timothy that "all Scripture is breathed out by God and profitable for teaching" (2 Tim. 3:16; cf. Rom. 15:4), making no distinction between genres. Furthermore, he specifically states that scriptural narratives were written to teach Christians. Writing of the experiences of the children of Israel in the wilderness after the exodus from Egypt, Paul tells us that "these things happened to them as an example, but they were written down for our instruction" (1 Cor. 10:11). Today, this recognition that scriptural narratives were written with a theological as well as historical purpose is widespread among evangelical Christians.[3]

Grant Osborne, for example, in the first edition of his widely read book on hermeneutics writes, "Narrative is not as direct as didactic material, but it does have a theological point and expects the reader to interact with that message."[4] Therefore, as Pentecostal scholar Roger Stronstad concludes, "The historical accounts of the activity of the Holy Spirit in Acts provide a firm foundation for erecting a doctrine of the Spirit which has normative implications for the mission and religious experience of the contemporary church."[5]

Narrative Accounts of Subsequence in Acts[6]

Acts 2:1–4: The Day of Pentecost

The events of the day of Pentecost have traditionally formed an important pattern for Pentecostals. After all, that's where Pentecostalism gets its name. However, there are complications in directly applying the events of the

2. John Stott, *The Baptism and Fullness: The Work of the Holy Spirit* (Downers Grove, IL: InterVarsity Press, 2006), 5.
3. A key book in opening up this recognition among Evangelical scholars was I. Howard Marshall, *Luke: Historian and Theologian* (Grand Rapids: Zondervan, 1970).
4. Grant Osborne, *The Hermeneutical Spiral: A Comprehensive Introduction to Biblical Interpretation* (Downers Grove, IL: InterVarsity Press, 1991), 172.
5. Roger Stronstad, *The Charismatic Theology of St Luke* (Peabody, MA: Henrickson, 1984), 9.
6. For the equivalence between the various terms used for the baptism of the Holy Spirit in these accounts, see question 16.

upper room in Acts 2 to Christians today. Yes, the 120 who gathered in the upper room were already believers before they received the baptism in the Holy Spirit. However, this was something new, which Jesus had already told them could not occur until after he ascended and was glorified (Luke 24:49; John 7:39; 16:7; Acts 1:4–8). Therefore, these believers could not have been baptized in the Spirit at the moment of their conversion. Thus, by itself, what happened on the day of Pentecost is insufficient to establish a doctrine of subsequence, for the day of Pentecost is a unique event.

Yet, later in Acts, the events of the day of Pentecost are repeated on other occasions, suggesting they do reveal how God works in the lives of Christians.[7] Therefore, although they are not enough by themselves to establish a doctrine of subsequence, they should be understood in relation to the other Pentecost-like outpourings of the Spirit in the book of Acts.

Acts 8:14–20: The Samaritan Believers

The clearest example of subsequence in the book of Acts is found in Samaria in Acts 8. The Samaritans had already "received the word of God" (v. 14), and enough time had passed for them to be baptized in water, for the news of their conversion to be sent to Jerusalem, and for Peter and John to be sent down from Jerusalem to Samaria. Yet in all this time, the Holy Spirit "had not yet fallen on any of them" (v. 16). It was only when the apostles finally "laid their hands on them [that] they received the Holy Spirit" (v. 17). This is an example not only of a logical or theological subsequence, but also of a clear chronological subsequence. Hence, I. Howard Marshall, as a non-Pentecostal, calls verse 16 "perhaps the most extraordinary statement in Acts."[8]

Some scholars have tried to argue that the Samaritans were not truly converts to Christianity until the apostles came and prayed for them; they speculate that there was something defective about their faith, and thus the Spirit fell on them at the moment of their true conversion.[9] Yet this does not fit the evidence. Luke specifically tells us that these Samaritans had "received [*dechomai*] the word of God" (v. 14), and receiving the word is an expression he uses elsewhere in Acts to speak of conversion (Acts 2:41; 11:1). Furthermore, unlike in Ephesus in Acts 19, the apostles do not re-baptize the Samaritans. Thus, Peter and John see nothing defective about their baptism or the faith that led to it. As Howard Ervin concludes, "Obviously, these two representatives of the apostolic college in Jerusalem were satisfied that these Samaritan disciples were born again in consequence of the Holy Spirit's

---

7. Roger Stronstad, *Spirit, Scripture and Theology: A Pentecostal Perspective*, 2nd ed. (Baguio City, Philippines: Asia Pacific Theological Seminary Press, 2018), 36.
8. I. Howard Marshall, *The Acts of the Apostles* (Grand Rapids: Eerdmans, 1980), 157.
9. See James D. G. Dunn, *Baptism in the Holy Spirit* (London: SCM Press, 1970), 55–68; and Anthony A. Hoekema, *Holy Spirit Baptism* (Grand Rapids: Eerdmans, 1972), 36–37.

regenerative work, accomplished through Philip's preaching of the gospel."[10] The text does not support a denial of subsequence on this occasion.[11]

Richard Gaffin argues that the Pentecostal outpouring in Samaria is an extension of Pentecost. The focus, then, is not on the experience of individual believers, but on Samaria receiving the baptism of the Spirit. A similar extension, he argues, occurs with the Gentiles in Acts 10:45, thus fulfilling the programmatic statement of Jesus in Acts 1:8.[12] However, this understanding of the development from Acts 2 to Acts 8 to Acts 10 as an extension of Pentecost from Jerusalem to Samaria to the uttermost parts of the earth breaks down in Acts 19, where a similar Pentecostal experience is described in Ephesus, which cannot fit into this programmatic pattern. This extension of Pentecost argument does not fit all the occurrences of subsequence in Acts and so does not provide a strong reason to accept it as a valid theological description for what happens to the Samaritans in Acts 8.

Acts 9:17: Saul of Tarsus

Three days after Saul met Jesus on the road to Damascus the Lord sent Ananias to lay hands on him to "be filled with the Holy Spirit" (Acts 9:17). This is not the extension of Pentecost to another group of people but rather an example of one individual who is baptized in the Spirit a few days after encountering the Lord.[13] (Luke uses this same terminology of being "filled" with the Spirit for the baptism in the Spirit in Acts 2:4.)

Acts 10:44–48: Cornelius and His Household

The reception of the baptism in the Holy Spirit by Cornelius and his household while Peter was still preaching the gospel to them shows that a doctrine of theological subsequence (or separability) does not necessitate chronological subsequence. Pentecostals do not object to both salvation and baptism in the Spirit happening simultaneously; they simply maintain that they are two distinct things that may happen at the same time.

Acts 19:1–7: The Ephesian Disciples

Paul's visit to Ephesus is significant in two ways: in the pattern of subsequence, and in the nature of the question that Paul asks the Ephesian disciples. When Paul arrives, he finds about a dozen "disciples" (v. 1). Some

---

10. Howard Ervin, *Spirit Baptism: A Biblical Investigation* (Peabody, MA: Hendrickson, 1987), 73.
11. Cessationist scholars such as Richard Gaffin agree that this is an example of subsequence, although he disagrees that it teaches a doctrine of subsequence. See Richard Gaffin, *Perspectives on Pentecost: New Testament Teaching on the Gifts of the Holy Spirit* (Phillipsburg, NJ: P&R, 1979), 27.
12. Gaffin, *Perspectives on Pentecost*, 23–27.
13. Gaffin does not consider this text in *Perspectives on Pentecost.*

interpreters argue that these were disciples only of John the Baptist.[14] It is of note that nearly every other time the word "disciple" is used in Acts (and it is used thirty times), it refers to a disciple of Christ. There is only one exception, in Acts 9:25, where the phrase is "his disciples," with the word "his" making clear that these are Saul's disciples (although Saul's disciples were also Christ's disciples). Thus, the word "disciples" used in Acts without any clear reference to someone else, suggests very strongly that these disciples in Ephesus were Christ's disciples.

However, even if they had only been disciples of John the Baptist and not actually Christians, there is still a clear example of subsequence: after hearing Paul's teaching, they are baptized, and then Paul laid his hands on them and "the Holy Spirit came on them" (vv. 5–6). So even if they were only born again while listening to Paul, there was still a time gap, albeit small, which allowed for them to be baptized in water after believing, and then to be baptized in the Spirit. There may not have been much of a chronological gap between the two experiences (conversion and baptism in the Spirit), but it is a gap nonetheless, demonstrating that these were two distinct and separable events. Pentecostals do not demand a significant time delay between regeneration and baptism in the Spirit; they merely teach a theological subsequence, and even such a short chronological subsequence as this demonstrates that.

We not only see subsequence in the experience of the Ephesian disciples, but Paul teaches it when he asks: "Did you receive the Holy Spirit when you believed?" (v. 2). The mere fact of asking such a question indicates that it is possible to believe without having received the Holy Spirit in this particular way. While many discussions have swirled around the Greek grammar and precise translation of this verse, its implications for the doctrine of subsequence do not actually depend on any of those things.[15] If all Christians are automatically baptized in the Holy Spirit when they are born again, Paul's question wouldn't make any sense. The simple fact that he asks it at all points to the separability of believing in Christ and receiving the baptism of the Spirit.

Throughout the book of Acts, Pentecostals see a pattern of subsequence and separability in accounts of people being baptized in the Holy Spirit. While the day of Pentecost alone, as a unique event in the history of redemption, is not enough to establish a doctrine of subsequence, the repeated pattern throughout the book highlights that this is part of the theology that Luke intends to teach. And as Anthony Palma notes, "Luke's historiography is ultimately not his own, but that of the Holy Spirit."[16] So, in the way Pentecostals understand Scripture, if Luke intends to teach it, the Holy Spirit intends it too.

---

14. See, for example, Marshall, *Acts*, 305.
15. For a summary of these discussions see Palma, *Holy Spirit*, 125–30.
16. Palma, *Holy Spirit*, 94.

Praying for the Spirit

Jesus taught his disciples to pray and ask for the Holy Spirit as a good gift from God (Luke 11:9–13; cf. Matt. 7:7–11). He was speaking to believers and so encouraging those who already believe to ask for the gift of the Spirit. Taken together with the examples in Acts, this supports a doctrine of subsequence.

Summary

Pentecostals read the book of Acts as a model for the life of the church today, and so see the repeated pattern of people being baptized in the Spirit subsequent to being born again as teaching the distinction between these two experiences (which they refer to as the doctrine of subsequence). This approach to Acts has found growing support from New Testament scholarship, which has increasingly pointed to Luke's intent to teach theology through narrative. The doctrine of subsequence does not mean that there must be a long (or even any) delay between conversion and baptism in the Spirit, but only that these are two distinct and separable events (and thus baptism in the Spirit is theologically, or logically, subsequent to regeneration).

REFLECTION QUESTIONS

1. In what ways does Luke use narrative to teach about the role of the Holy Spirit in the life of believers?

2. How do you understand what happened in Samaria in Acts 8?

3. What does the experience of Cornelius and his household mean for the Pentecostal understanding of the baptism in the Holy Spirit?

4. Do you think "subsequence" is a helpful term? Can you think of a better way to explain what Pentecostals mean by this?

5. What is the significance of Jesus's words in Luke 11:13 for the Pentecostal doctrine of the baptism in the Holy Spirit?

QUESTION 20

Is the Baptism in the Holy Spirit Followed by Signs?

What did the Welsh Revival, the Mukti Revival, Agnes Ozman in Topeka, Sarah Jones in Penygroes, the Azusa Street Revival, and Catherine Price in London all have in common? Not only baptism in the Spirit, but baptism in the Spirit accompanied by speaking in tongues. The connection between the baptism in the Spirit and speaking in tongues is what initially set Pentecostals apart from many other evangelicals who were also seeking the baptism in the Spirit at the beginning of the twentieth century. As Robert Menzies puts it, "The link between speaking in tongues and baptism in the Holy Spirit has marked the modern Pentecostal movement since its inception and without this linkage it is doubtful whether the movement would have seen the light of day, let alone survived."[1]

But notice I have used the word "connection" rather than a stronger word like "evidence." In this chapter we are going to examine this connection by looking at what signs we can see accompanying the baptism of the Holy Spirit in the book of Acts. Only then will we be able to consider the question of whether speaking in tongues is the initial evidence of the baptism in the Spirit.

Narrative Accounts of Signs Following the Baptism of the Spirit in Acts

The Scriptures themselves point us to the question of signs or evidence of the baptism in the Holy Spirit. "The evidence that a person had been filled with the Spirit was so clear that the apostles could tell the church in Acts 6:3 to choose seven men *known to be* full of the Spirit."[2]

---

1. Robert P. Menzies, *Pentecost: This Is Our Story* (Springfield, MO: Gospel Publishing House, 2013), 67–68.
2. David Petts, *The Holy Spirit: An Introduction* (Mattersey: Mattersey Hall, 1998), 72.

Acts 2: The Day of Pentecost

In Acts 2 we read of the first baptisms in the Spirit on the day of Pentecost. Three miraculous signs took place that day: "a sound like a mighty rushing wind" (v. 2), "divided tongues as of fire" resting on each of the disciples in the upper room (v. 3), and speaking in tongues (v. 4). However, of these three phenomena, only one took place when the disciples were baptized in the Spirit. The sound of the mighty wind and the tongues of fire preceded their baptism in the Spirit. "Only one, speaking in tongues, is recorded as a direct result of their having been filled."[3]

This is also the only time in Acts that we have an account of the sound of the rushing wind or the tongues of fire. "Nowhere else in Acts are they mentioned again in conjunction with people being filled with the Spirit."[4] These two signs are presented by Luke as unique phenomena to mark that particular moment, emphasizing "the greatness of the occasion in salvation history, and did not occur again when others were filled with the Spirit."[5]

After the crowds heard the disciples proclaiming the wonderful works of God in their own languages, they asked "What does this mean?" (v. 12). Peter responded by pointing them to Joel's prophecy of the outpouring of the Holy Spirit (vv. 17–21). Considering Peter's response, David Petts points out, "It is important to realise that Peter's answer must be understood in the light of the crowd's question. The question was about tongues. It was therefore about tongues that Peter was speaking when he replied and quoted the prophecy from Joel. The speaking in tongues about which the crowd were asking was the sign that God's promise had been fulfilled."[6] Peter teaches that speaking in tongues on the day of Pentecost is the promised sign of the outpouring of the Holy Spirit. Thus, the day of Pentecost provides not only an example of tongues accompanying the baptism of the Spirit but the teaching that connects the two.

Acts 8:14–20: The Samaritan Believers

When the Samaritan believers are filled with the Spirit in Acts 8, there is no explicit mention of speaking in tongues. However, the baptism in the Spirit of these Samaritans was clearly seen, for "Simon saw that the Spirit was given through the laying on of the apostles' hands" (Acts 8:18) and what he saw impressed him to such a degree that he offered money to buy the power to bestow the baptism of the Spirit (Acts 8:19). Even without the sign of speaking in tongues, Simon saw something that he thought would further his career

3. Petts, *Holy Spirit*, 73.
4. Anthony D. Palma, *The Holy Spirit: A Pentecostal Perspective* (Springfield, MO: Gospel Publishing House, 2001), 137.
5. French L. Arrington, *Christian Doctrine: A Pentecostal Perspective* (Cleveland, TN: Pathway, 1994), 3:64.
6. Petts, *Holy Spirit*, 74.

as a magician. Simon had already seen "signs and great miracles performed" (v. 13), but it was only now that he saw the baptism of the Holy Spirit that he wanted to buy the power to perform what he saw. Therefore, there must have been an externally visible manifestation or sign that accompanied the baptism of the Holy Spirit. Luke does not tell us exactly what this sign was, but he certainly shows us that there was a sign (or signs) of some sort, which were perceptible to others and somehow more impressive to the former sorcerer than the signs and great miracles he had already seen.

Acts 9:17: Saul of Tarsus

Again, Luke does not mention a specific sign when Saul (Paul) is filled with the Spirit. However, in this case, Saul's actual baptism in the Spirit is not recorded. Therefore we do not have a description of what happened. We do know that the apostle Paul later wrote of how he spoke "in tongues more than all of you" (1 Cor. 14:18). So we know that (1) Paul was baptized in the Spirit when Ananias laid hands on him, and that (2) Paul spoke in tongues. However, we have no explicit connection between the two.

Acts 10:44–48: Cornelius and His Household

The Holy Spirit fell on Cornelius and his household while Peter was still speaking to them. Peter and his fellow Jewish believers were "amazed" at this because it was clear to them that "the gift of the Holy Spirit was poured out even on the Gentiles" (v. 45). But how was that clear to them? Luke tells us exactly how they knew it: "For they were hearing them speaking in tongues and extolling God" (v. 46). Speaking in tongues was the clear sign for Peter and his companions that these Gentile believers had been baptized in the Holy Spirit. When Peter goes back to Jerusalem and tells the church about what has happened, he says, "The Holy Spirit fell on them just as on us at the beginning" (Acts 11:15). The outward likeness between these two events—the day of Pentecost and the baptism in the Spirit of Cornelius and his household—was that on both occasions everyone who was baptized in the Spirit spoke in tongues.

Acts 19:1–7: The Ephesian Disciples

When the Ephesian disciples received the baptism in the Spirit, the same sign was evident: "When Paul had laid his hands on them, the Holy Spirit came on them, and they began speaking in tongues and prophesying" (Acts 19:6). David Petts argues that "it is significant that tongues is mentioned first here. The natural way to understand this is simply that it happened first. They spoke in tongues and then they prophesied."[7]

---

7. Petts, *Holy Spirit*, 75.

In each of these instances from the book of Acts, apart from the case of Saul in Acts 9:17 where the actual event is not described, there is some clear outward sign that accompanies or follows the baptism in the Holy Spirit.

Is Speaking in Tongues the Initial Physical Evidence of the Baptism in the Holy Spirit?

Especially in North America, Pentecostalism is commonly associated with the doctrine of initial physical evidence. This is set out in the American Assemblies of God statement of fundamental truths: "The baptism of believers in the Holy Spirit is witnessed by the initial physical sign of speaking with other tongues."[8] The teaching can be traced back to Charles Parham's Bible School in Topeka (see question 3). The doctrine of initial physical evidence, as Douglas Oss explains, means that "if there is no manifestation of tongues, then there has been no Spirit-baptism."[9] It is not just that speaking in tongues will be the first sign of the baptism in the Spirit; it is the essential sign. In its absence, the Pentecostal baptism did not take place.

However, this is not a doctrine shared by all Pentecostals around the world. Many early European Pentecostals rejected the initial physical evidence doctrine. Alexander Boddy was very clear that "there are differences of views about the tongues in the Pentecostal Movement. There are brethren who feel that this is the scriptural evidence of the Baptism of the Holy Ghost, and we also have dear honoured servants of God . . . [who] do not all insist upon the tongues as exclusively the sign."[10] His wife Mary worried that overemphasis on tongues as *the* sign would "dishonour and damage" God's work by confusing people as to the true nature of the baptism in the Spirit. She argued that when people are baptized in the Spirit, they "will speak in tongues *if they expect to do so*," but not that it was an essential, necessary evidence. "Merely speaking in tongues is not necessarily a convincing sign."[11]

For Gerrit Polman in the Netherlands, there was a much more significant sign than tongues: "The great sign we want in connection with this Baptism

---

8. See AGSFT, 8; cf. IPHC, "Articles of Faith," 11; and Church of God, "Declaration of Faith," 9. The Pentecostal Assemblies of Canada have recently removed the expression "initial evidence": compare the "Statement of Fundamental and Essential Truths (2014)," 6.3 with "Spirit Baptism," in PAOCSET (2022), which more modestly states that "the sign of speaking in tongues indicates that believers have been baptized with the Holy Spirit." The initial physical evidence doctrine is also common in countries where Pentecostal churches have been established by North American missionaries.
9. Douglas A. Oss, "A Pentecostal/Charismatic View," in *Are Miraculous Gifts for Today? Four Views*, ed. Wayne Grudem (Leicester, IVP: 1996), 260.
10. Alexander Boddy, "The Place of Tongues in the Pentecostal Movement," *Confidence* 4, no. 8 (August 1911): 176.
11. Mary Boddy, "The Real Baptism of the Holy Ghost," *Confidence* 2, no. 11 (November 1909): 260–61 (emphasis added).

in the Holy Ghost is love."[12] In other words, even if people think of tongues as the sign of the baptism, it should not be the focus: "In Amsterdam we don't say much about speaking in tongues. More and more we are seeking to glorify Jesus, and when we speak of Tongues we are only seeking His glory, and for the edification and the building up of the Church of God, that she may glorify more and more our blessed Jesus, our Saviour. In Amsterdam it is generally believed that the Tongues is the evidence of the Pentecostal Baptism, but we are seeking only the Baptism in the Holy Spirit. We have not to seek for Tongues; Tongues are rather seeking us."[13]

Tongues are seeking us. In other words, tongues are merely a sign that flows out from the baptism in the Spirit; they are not something to be sought in themselves.

The most significant figure in the beginnings of German Pentecostalism, Jonathan Paul, strongly opposed the initial physical evidence teaching. "I don't like to say that everyone who will be baptised [in the Spirit] must speak in tongues. . . . It would be very helpful if we could [instead] say, 'I recognise the Baptism of the Holy Ghost where I see the fruits of the Spirit and the manifestations of the Spirit.'"[14] European Pentecostals eventually agreed to a statement on the baptism of the Holy Spirit that did not include tongues as the initial physical evidence: "The Baptism of the Holy Ghost and Fire is the coming upon and within of the Holy Spirit to indwell the believer in His fulness, and is always borne witness to by the fruit of the Spirit and the outward manifestation, so that we may receive the same gift as the disciples on the Day of Pentecost."[15] This declaration mentions an unspecified outward sign (not limited to tongues) *alongside* the evidence of the fruit of the Spirit.

Still today, many European Pentecostal denominations do not hold to the doctrine of initial physical evidence. Two of the three British Pentecostal denominations that emerged from the early revival, the Apostolic Church UK and the Elim Pentecostal Church, believe that the baptism in the Holy Spirit will be accompanied by "signs following." Neither specifies tongues as necessary evidence.[16] Thus, a significant proportion of Pentecostals around the

12. Gerrit Polman, "The Place of Tongues in the Pentecostal Movement," *Confidence* 4, no. 8 (August 1911): 176.
13. Polman, "Place of Tongues," 177.
14. Jonathan Paul, "The Place of Tongues in the Pentecostal Movement," *Confidence* 4, no. 8 (August 1911): 182.
15. International Pentecostal Council, "Declaration on the Baptism of the Holy Ghost and Fire" (May 31, 1912), *Confidence* 5, no. 6 (June 1912): 133.
16. Apostolic Church, "Tenets," 5; Elim SFT, 4. This does not mean that no members of those denominations believe in initial physical evidence, but that no member is obliged to believe in initial physical evidence. See Timothy A. C. Bush, "The development of the perception of the Baptism in the Holy Spirit within the Pentecostal Movement in Great Britain," *EPTA Bulletin* 11 (1992): 29. The third British denomination, the Assemblies of God, like other sister Assemblies of God movements around the world (including Europe) does

world do not hold to the absolute necessity of speaking in tongues as evidence of the baptism in the Holy Spirit.

However, many other Pentecostals see the doctrine of initial physical evidence as both taught in Scripture and a necessary component of Pentecostal identity, without reducing the baptism in the Spirit to simply speaking in tongues. French Arrington writes: "The experience of speaking in tongues does not comprise the baptism in the Holy Spirit, but it is the initial evidence that one has been filled with the Spirit. The Spirit manifests the reality of His fullness through inspired speech, showing the relationship between the spiritual experience and practical service."[17] The British Assemblies of God theologian David Petts is concerned that a less clearly defined understanding of the signs that follow the baptism in the Spirit would lead to the acceptance of unbiblical phenomena: "Tongues is the only consistently recurring phenomenon connected with Spirit-baptism in Acts. Once we stray beyond Scripture to some other form of evidence, where does it end? There would be no limit to the strange phenomena that people would claim as evidence of the Baptism! . . . Precious though the experience of other Christians, past or present, may be, we must never use their experience as a basis for our doctrine."[18]

The biggest obstacle to the initial physical evidence teaching is Paul's question in 1 Corinthians 12:30, "Do all speak with tongues?" The context makes clear that the intended answer is no, they do not. However, Petts argues that Paul is referring here to the "bringing of a public utterance in tongues," for Paul immediately goes on to ask, "Do all interpret?" (1 Cor. 12:30). Further, the overall context is public worship. Thus Petts argues that Paul's question, "when taken correctly in its context, merely implies that not all Christians will speak in tongues publicly. It in no way indicates that they may not do so privately."[19] After all, a little later in the letter Paul is happy to write, "Now I want you all to speak in tongues" (1 Cor. 14:5).[20]

---

hold to the doctrine of initial physical evidence. Outside the UK (and beyond the global reach of the Apostolic Church and Elim), the "signs following" position is also explicit in the Verbond van Vlaamse Pinkstergemeenten, "Statement of Faith," 5.1; Schweizerische Pfingstmission, "Glaubensbekenntnis," 10; Pentecostal Movement in Norway, "Basis of Faith," 5; BFP, "Glaubensbekenntnis," 4; Pentecostal Church of Finland, "The Main Articles of Faith of the Pentecostal Church of Finland," 5. No mention is made of specific evidence or signs of the baptism in the Holy Spirit in the creed of the Pentecostal Movement in Iceland; see Pentecostal Movement in Iceland, "The Creed of the Pentecostal Movement in Iceland," 8.

17. Arrington, *Christian Doctrine*, 3:65.
18. Petts, *Holy Spirit*, 78.
19. Petts, *Holy Spirit*, 76–77.
20. For a careful Pentecostal discussion of this statement, see William W. Menzies and Robert P. Menzies, *Spirit and Power: Foundations of Pentecostal Experience* (Grand Rapids: Zondervan, 2000), 139–42.

Summary

There is certainly a pattern in Acts of people being baptized in the Spirit and then speaking in tongues. The great question is whether the Scripture intends to teach us that speaking in tongues is the essential mark of the baptism in the Spirit, or a regular but not absolutely essential feature of the experience. Herein lies the difference between the two Pentecostal positions of initial evidence and signs following.

REFLECTION QUESTIONS

1. Do you see a strong connection between speaking in tongues and the baptism in the Holy Spirit in the Acts accounts?

2. How does speaking in tongues differ from the tongues of fire and the sound of a rushing wind on the day of Pentecost?

3. How do you understand Paul's rhetorical question in 1 Corinthians 12:20 ("Do all speak with tongues?") along with his statement in 14:5 ("I want you all to speak in tongues")?

4. How do the initial physical evidence and signs following positions differ? Which do you think is the stronger position?

5. Why were many early British and European Pentecostal leaders concerned about overemphasizing speaking in tongues as initial evidence? What other evidence did they seek?

PART 4

Questions About the Gifts of the Holy Spirit

SECTION A

Questions About the Gifts in General

QUESTION 21

Do the Extraordinary Gifts Continue Today?

One of the defining features of Pentecostalism is the belief that the Holy Spirit still distributes his supernatural gifts in the church today. It is not just that Pentecostals believe in spiritual gifts in general, but they believe specifically that the nine gifts mentioned in 1 Corinthians 12:8–10—the word of wisdom, the word of knowledge, faith, gifts of healings, the working of miracles, prophecy, discerning of spirits, different kinds of tongues, and the interpretation of tongues—should continue to be features of the life of the church. These gifts were "given by the risen and exalted Lord . . . to his church as a permanent and abiding provision" and will continue "until the *parousia* or second coming of Jesus."[1] We will look more at the nature of these gifts in the next chapters, but first let's consider why Pentecostals believe these gifts continue among God's people today.

The Scriptural Expectation

The New Testament shows us a church where the gifts of the Holy Spirit were in operation. Throughout the book of Acts, we see examples of healings, prophecies, and speaking in tongues. In the epistles we read instructions to regulate the use of these gifts (1 Cor. 14), as well as descriptions of Christ's giving of gifts to his church (Eph. 4:11). We also see New Testament believers being encouraged to earnestly desire spiritual gifts (1 Cor. 12:31; 14:1, 39). The New Testament church was a charismatic church, and Pentecostals see no reason to believe that the church should have changed. Jack Deere represents the view of Pentecostals when he writes, "No one ever just picked up the Bible,

1. James D. Hernando, "Continuationism—A Redemptive Historical Perspective," in *The Kingdom Case Against Cessationism: Embracing the Power of the Kingdom*, ed. Robert W. Graves (Canton, GA: Foundation for Pentecostal Scholarship, 2022), 104.

started reading, and then came to the conclusion that God was not doing signs and wonders anymore and that the gifts of the Holy Spirit had passed away. The doctrine of cessationism did not originate from a careful study of the Scriptures. The doctrine of cessationism originated in *experience*."[2]

Cessationism is "the belief that certain spiritual gifts in the New Testament—namely the more miraculous gifts—have ceased."[3] Yet, this is not an obvious teaching in Scripture. Therefore, to a certain extent, the burden of proof rests with cessationists: Why should something so significant have changed in the life of the church?

Scriptures Specifically Indicating Continuation

Joel 2:28–32; Acts 2:17–21

Apart from the instructions, descriptions, and encouragements concerning the use of the gifts of the Spirit in the life of the church, there are also a number of passages of Scripture that appear to indicate that the gifts will not cease until the return of Christ. The prophecy of Joel taken up by Peter on the day of Pentecost (Joel 2:28–32; Acts 2:17–21) speaks of a time when the Lord will pour out his Spirit on all flesh, resulting in prophesies, visions, and dreams. Joel simply states that this "shall come to pass afterward" (Joel 2:28), whereas Peter, speaking by the Holy Spirit, calls this time "the last days" (Acts 2:17). This is significant, for Peter gives no indication that this period will be succeeded by another in which prophecy, visions, and dreams will be absent. Rather, he indicates that the period characterized by these gifts of the Spirit will be the last days of the present age: the last days that began with the cross, resurrection, and ascension of Christ, and his subsequent outpouring of the Spirit at Pentecost, and that will continue until his return. These last days will not come to an end until "the day of the Lord comes" (Acts 2:20). As Douglas Oss points out, "There is not a scrap of biblical evidence that the last days are subdivided, postponed, or changed prior to the day of the Lord."[4] Craig Keener argues, "The idea that such empowerment or its prophetic expressions . . . was scheduled to cease before the Lord's return, is one that could not have occurred to Luke. For Luke, such activity characterizes the eschatological era in which the church lives; Luke would hardly emphasize that this era was inaugurated on Pentecost and then expect us to infer, without clear evidence, that the era would be phased out before its consummation at Christ's return. God would hardly pour out his Spirit, then pour it back again!"[5] Therefore, we

---

2. Jack Deere, *Surprised by the Power of the Spirit* (Grand Rapids: Zondervan, 1993), 99.
3. Thomas R. Schreiner, *Spiritual Gifts: What They Are and Why They Matter* (Nashville: Broadman & Holman, 2018), 1. Schreiner is a cessationist.
4. Douglas Oss, "A Pentecostal/Charismatic View," in *Are Miraculous Gifts for Today? Four Views*, ed. Wayne Grudem (Leicester: InterVarsity Press, 1996), 267.
5. Craig S. Keener, *Acts: An Exegetical Commentary* (Grand Rapids: Baker, 2012), 1:882.

have no reason to expect the prophecies, visions, and dreams by which Joel and Peter characterize this period to come to an end before Christ's return.

1 Corinthians 1:4–8

At the beginning of 1 Corinthians, Paul draws a connection between the presence of *charismata* in the church and the church's waiting "for the revealing of our Lord Jesus Christ" (1 Cor. 1:7). We will look at the meaning of charismata in the next chapter, but for now we must simply note that it is a word that can be used of the supernatural gifts of the Holy Spirit, but can also be used for other gracious gifts. Only the context can determine which type of gift is meant. Here, however, we have good reason to read this as a reference to the supernatural gifts of the Spirit. The charismata are here connected with being "enriched in him in all speech and all knowledge" (1 Cor. 1:5), which (as we can see clearly later in this epistle) includes prophetic speech and divinely given knowledge.[6] Furthermore, they "are not lacking in any gift" (v. 7), which would not allow for a limitation of charismata here to only the non-supernatural gifts. Paul is telling them that every spiritual gift will characterize this age of awaiting the Lord's coming. Therefore, Scripture teaches here that *all the spiritual gifts* will continue in the church until Christ's return.[7]

1 Corinthians 13:8–12

Later in the same letter we find what has undoubtedly become the focal passage in this debate:

> Love never ends. As for prophecies, they will pass away; as for tongues, they will cease; as for knowledge, it will pass away. For we know in part and we prophesy in part, but when the perfect comes, the partial will pass away. When I was a child, I spoke like a child, I thought like a child, I reasoned like a child. When I became a man, I gave up childish ways. For now we see in a mirror dimly, but then face to face. Now I know in part; then I shall know fully, even as I have been fully known. (1 Cor. 13:8–12)

Here Paul does write of a time when prophecies, tongues, and words of knowledge will cease. When will this be? "When the perfect comes." The question, then, is what does Paul mean by "the perfect"? While some have attempted to argue that "the perfect" refers to the completion of the biblical canon, even

6. See, for example, Jon Ruthven, *On the Cessation of the Charismata: The Protestant Polemic on Postbiblical Miracles*, Journal of Pentecostal Theology Supplement Series 3 (Sheffield: Sheffield Academic Press, 1993), 127.
7. For a more technical version of this argument, see Ruthven, *On the Cessation*, 126–31.

serious cessationists reject such spurious readings. Thomas Schreiner, for example, maintains that "arguments for cessationism from 1 Corinthians 13:8–10 aren't exegetically convincing." He argues, "It is almost impossible that Paul could have meant by 'the perfect' the New Testament canon" and "even more unlikely that the Corinthians would have understood the word *perfect* this way."[8] Rather, the only viable understanding of the coming of the perfect is "the second coming of Christ."[9] Yes, Paul is telling us here that spiritual gifts are temporary, but by temporary he means, as Pentecostal theologian Jon Mark Ruthven argues, that they are "characteristic of the present age, ceasing only at its end, when the full revelation of God will occur."[10] In other words, this Scripture explicitly states that the gifts of the Spirit will continue to be given until Christ returns. In light of this, Paul's instruction to "earnestly desire to prophesy, and do not forbid speaking in tongues" (1 Cor. 14:39) apply until Christ returns.

Ephesians 4:11–13

Another explicit statement of the continuation of extraordinary gifts is found in Ephesians. There Paul writes that Christ gives apostles, prophets, evangelists, pastors, and teachers "until we all attain to the unity of the faith and of the knowledge of the Son of God, to mature manhood, to the measure of the stature of the fullness of Christ" (Eph. 4:11–13). The gifts given by Christ here include prophets, which indicates prophecy will continue for this duration as well. There is no distinction made between the duration of apostles and prophets and that of evangelists, pastors, and teachers. Thus, Paul indicates that apostles and prophets (and hence prophecy) will continue in the church for as long as pastors. Ruthven concludes, "Exegetically, the gifts continue or cease as a single group."[11]

Therefore, the giving of each of these gifts will continue until the goal of attaining "to the unity of the faith and of the knowledge of the Son of God, to mature manhood, to the measure of the stature of the fullness of Christ" (v. 13) has been achieved. This standard is "essentially perfection: all of the church (no possibility for laggards or the immature) are to attain" to all of this.[12] In fact, Paul makes clear in writing this that even he has not reached this level of maturity, for he includes himself (writing of "we" rather than "you").[13] In Ephesians 4 we learn that the extraordinary gifts will continue until the ultimate spiritual maturity of the whole church. This will only take

8. Schreiner, *Spiritual Gifts*, 149–50.
9. Schreiner, *Spiritual Gifts*, 153. Schreiner admits, "If 1 Corinthians 13:8–12 were the only relevant text on the matter, then I would agree that all the gifts continue until Jesus returns," *Spiritual Gifts*, 155.
10. Ruthven, *On the Cessation*, 132.
11. Ruthven, *On the Cessation*, 156.
12. Ruthven, *On the Cessation*, 157.
13. See also Philippians 3:11–16.

place at the return of Jesus Christ, for then "we shall be like him, because we shall see him as he is" (1 John 3:2). Thus, once again, we see that the gifts will continue until Christ's return.

Summary

The most technical, scholarly cessationist arguments have received detailed, technical, Pentecostal replies (and at any rate, are rarely encountered in the church).[14] In question 34 we will consider the related question of whether apostleship continues in the church today; as Thomas Schreiner argues, "The basis for cessationism is the claim that the church was 'built on the foundation of the apostles and prophets' (Eph. 2:20)."[15] In this chapter, however, I have mainly looked at the positive biblical case for the continuation of the supernatural gifts. The Pentecostal position is not rooted in a refutation of cessationist claims, but in a positive, biblical account of the continuation of the gifts of the Holy Spirit until the end of this age when Christ returns.

REFLECTION QUESTIONS

1. What do you think of Jack Deere's claim, "No one ever just picked up the Bible, started reading, and then came to the conclusion that God was not doing signs and wonders anymore and that the gifts of the Holy Spirit had passed away"?

2. What is cessationism? Can you see any strong biblical arguments for this position?

3. How does what Peter says about "the last days" (Acts 2:17) help us think about whether or not the gifts of the Spirit continue to be given today?

4. How do you understand the teaching of 1 Corinthians 13:8–12 in relation to the question of the duration of the gifts of the Holy Spirit?

5. What does Ephesians 4:11–13 suggest in relation to gifts like prophecy?

---

14. For a response to the arguments of B. B. Warfield, see Ruthven, *On the Cessation*. For a response to the arguments of Richard Gaffin, see Oss, "A Pentecostal/Charismatic View."
15. Schreiner, *Spiritual Gifts*, 157. For more technical versions of this argument see Richard B. Gaffin, Jr., *Perspectives on Pentecost: New Testament Teaching on the Gifts of the Holy Spirit* (Phillipsburg, NJ: Presbyterian & Reformed, 1979), 89–116; Richard B. Gaffin, "A Cessationist View," in *Are Miraculous Gifts for Today? Four Views*, ed. Wayne Grudem (Leicester: InterVarsity Press, 1996), 41–60.

QUESTION 22

What Are the Gifts of the Spirit? (Part 1)

Pentecostals not only believe that the extraordinary gifts of the Holy Spirit have not ceased but also expect the Lord to work among his people by these gifts today. Pentecostals are not surprised when a message in tongues with interpretation or a prophecy is given as part of the worship service on a Sunday morning. In fact, they pray for these extraordinary gifts, believing that Scripture commands us to "desire spiritual gifts" (1 Cor. 14:1; see also 12:31). But what are these gifts for which they pray? Several terms are used in the New Testament to describe them, so looking at these terms will help us to better understand just what a spiritual gift is.

Charismata: Gifts of Grace

Since the rise of the charismatic movement, perhaps the most familiar biblical word for the gifts is *charismata*, a word that emphasizes the grace of God in the gifts. Yet, the focus of this word is so much upon God's grace that it is not a word that is in any way limited to these particular gifts of the Spirit. The same word is used for justification (Rom. 5:15–16), eternal life (Rom. 6:23), marriage and celibacy (1 Cor. 7:7), and for being saved from death (2 Cor. 1:10–11). So, the Bible does not in any way reserve charismata for charismatic gifts. All gifts of God's grace are charismata.

That this word can be used for the gifts of the Holy Spirit (1 Cor. 12:4) highlights that the origin of these gifts is not in us. We do not receive spiritual gifts because of our merits, but only through God's grace, flowing from the merit of Christ. The gifts of the Holy Spirit are gifts of God's grace and therefore depend entirely on the saving work of Jesus. Therefore, the gifts of the Spirit flow from the cross.

Pneumatika: Spiritual Things

Although we commonly use the expression "spiritual gifts" in English, this is not precisely the expression the New Testament uses. The term usually translated into English as "spiritual gifts" (*pneumatika*) simply means "spiritual things." The word "gifts" is added in English translations of 1 Corinthians 12:1 and 14:1 to clarify the type of spiritual things Paul is writing about. So the emphasis here is on the fact that these gifts are spiritual, rather than that they are gifts.

What does it mean for the gifts to be spiritual? From Paul's first letter to the Corinthians, it is clear that they are not necessarily evidence of spiritual maturity. Although the assembly at Corinth was "not lacking in any gift" (1 Cor. 1:7), it was a church divided by partisanship (1 Cor. 1:10–13; 3:1–4), where serious sexual immorality was both committed and tolerated (1 Cor. 5:1–5), where Christians were taking one another to court (1 Cor. 6:1–8), and people were getting drunk at the Lord's Supper (1 Cor. 11:21). This church, blessed with all the gifts of the Spirit, was still not a model of spiritual maturity. The Lord Jesus himself warns, "On that day many will say to me, 'Lord, Lord, did we not prophesy in your name, and cast out demons in your name, and do many mighty works in your name?' And then will I declare to them, 'I never knew you; depart from me, you workers of lawlessness'" (Matt. 7:22–23). The apostle Peter also made clear in his preaching that healing does not come from the piety of the one God uses to heal (Acts 3:12). Thus, the exercise of spiritual gifts should not be mistaken for proof of the spiritual maturity of the person exercising them.[1]

Rather, the gifts are spiritual in that God is at work through them by the Holy Spirit. In Hebrews 2:3–4 we read that God bears witness to the message of his great salvation in Christ "by gifts of the Holy Spirit distributed according to his will." So, the gifts are here seen to be spiritual in three ways: (1) they come from the Holy Spirit; (2) God uses them in pointing people to the gospel, as the Holy Spirit works to call people to faith and repentance; (3) and they are one of the ways in which the Holy Spirit glorifies Jesus (John 16:14).

That the source of these gifts is the Holy Spirit (rather than the person being used in the gifts) is also an indication of the supernatural nature of these gifts. Harold Horton, in his classic Pentecostal explanation of the gifts of the Spirit, points to the nine gifts of 1 Corinthians 12 as "the authentic supernatural manifestations of the Spirit of God," stressing "the hundred-percent *supernatural* character of each and all the Gifts."[2] In this emphasis he was

1. The declaration of faith of the Brazilian Assemblies of God reads, "[These spiritual gifts] are not personal attestations of holiness that lead people to believe that they are holier or more spiritual than others; neither do they make people super-spiritual, nor make them better or superior to other believers; they are not for display or private superiority within the Church, but are for the glory of God . . . the merit will always be the Lord's"; see Brazil DdF, 20.1.
2. Harold Horton, *The Gifts of the Spirit*, 3rd ed. (Luton: AoG, 1949), 8, 28 (emphasis original).

not alone. Donald Gee concluded, "There is only one way to consistently deal with the whole subject of these spiritual gifts, and that is to regard them as each and all involving some measure of a supernatural operation of the Holy Spirit. No other view meets the plain requirement of the context."[3] More recent Pentecostal writers on the nine gifts concur.[4]

Charismatic theologians have often disagreed with Pentecostals over the supernatural nature of the gifts of the Holy Spirit. Wayne Grudem, for example, argues against "making a supernatural/natural distinction in our minds whereby we think that some gifts are supernatural and some gifts are simply natural."[5] In this, Grudem is grouping together the nine gifts of 1 Corinthians 12 with a wider list of "gifts" found in Romans 12, which includes "serving, teaching, encouraging, contributing, and doing acts of mercy."[6] Paul does not use the word *pneumatika* for the gifts in Romans 12, however. He uses the word *charismata*. Gathering together these gift lists, Grudem argues that while some of the gifts might strike us as more supernatural and some as more natural, "the Bible makes no such distinction, and the danger of doing this is that we may tend to think that some gifts (which we think to be more supernatural) are more important or more clearly from the Lord, and we may tend to devalue or deemphasize the gifts which we think to be natural."[7] Taking this argument to its logical conclusion, Grudem cautions against seeing some of the nine gifts of 1 Corinthians 12 as supernatural. He deems it "preferable to understand [the word of knowledge and the word of wisdom] in a 'nonmiraculous' way, simply as the ability to speak with wisdom or with knowledge in various situations."[8]

However, Grudem's arguments rely on grouping together a number of New Testament gift lists, without giving sufficient attention to the differences between these lists. This elimination of distinctions relies more upon an English-language concept of "spiritual gifts" than the Greek text of the New Testament. The three major gift lists that are often grouped together are 1 Corinthians 12:7–10, Romans 12:6–8, and Ephesians 4:11. Yet, each of these lists are quite different. The Ephesians list refers to people as gifts (e.g., prophets rather than prophecy, teachers rather than teaching) and associates these gifts with the ascended Christ, rather than the manifestation of the Holy Spirit. Romans 12 speaks of "gifts" in rather general terms and does not

---

3. Donald Gee, *Concerning Spiritual Gifts*, rev. ed. (Springfield: MO: Gospel Publishing House, 1980), 34.
4. See David Petts, *The Holy Spirit: An Introduction* (Mattersey: Mattersey Hall, 1998), 91–92; Romanian CF, 17; and Brazil DdF, 20.
5. Wayne Grudem, *Systematic Theology: An Introduction to Biblical Doctrine*, 2nd ed. (London: InterVarsity Press, 2020), 1267.
6. Grudem, *Systematic Theology*, 1267.
7. Grudem, *Systematic Theology*, 1267.
8. Grudem, *Systematic Theology*, 1334.

appropriate the giving of these gifts to a particular person of the Trinity. As we have seen, *charismata* is a much more general word, with application far beyond the gifts of the Holy Spirit. The emphasis here is on the gifts which Christians possess through God's grace, rather than on God's giving of gifts. This, of course, does not mean that these gifts are not given by God—for we have nothing that we have not received from him and he is the only source of grace—but it is rather a different emphasis from the other gift lists.

The only gift included in the Romans 12 list that is also included in 1 Corinthians 12 is prophecy. And yet prophecy stands apart from the other gifts listed in Romans 12 in that, while the other gifts are listed with an encouragement in how we are to use them, prophecy is explicitly tied back to faith. Thus, Romans 12:6 points those whom God uses in the gift of prophecy away from themselves toward God, the source of prophecy, in faith. While the cheerfulness that accompanies acts of mercy and the generosity with which we are to give do indeed flow from faith in Christ, the person used in prophecy is pointed not to an effect of faith but to faith in Christ alone. There is an indication here of something different about the gift of prophecy.

There is indeed a wider grouping of "gifts" that includes gifts like prophecy and also gifts quite different from it, but the list in 1 Corinthians 12 is a more specific list of a particular type of spiritual gifts, which have more in common with the gift of prophecy. Thus, when Pentecostals speak of their belief in the nine gifts of the Holy Spirit or of these nine gifts from 1 Corinthians 12 as supernatural gifts, they are not ignoring or denying other types of gifts, but rather distinguishing that there is something different about these nine. After all, no one denies that teaching, acts of mercy, and giving continue in the church today; but some Christians do deny that the nine gifts in 1 Corinthians 12 continue. In this, even non-Pentecostals recognize something unique about these nine.

British Assemblies of God theologian David Petts advances two arguments from 1 Corinthians 12 for the supernatural nature of the nine gifts: an argument from (1) the contents of the list, and (2) the context of the list.[9] First, the list of nine gifts in 1 Corinthians 12 is made up mostly of gifts that are undoubtedly supernatural:

> Tongues, interpretation, and prophecy are clearly supernatural, as also are healings and the working of miracles. The gift of faith is almost certainly the faith that can move mountains of which Paul speaks in the next chapter (1 Corinthians 13:2). And although . . . there is some disagreement over the precise nature of "the ability to distinguish between spirits," however one understands this gift there is clearly a supernatural

9. David Petts, *Body Builders: Gifts to Make God's People Grow* (Mattersey: Mattersey Hall, 2002), 105.

> dimension to it. That leaves the "message of wisdom" and the "message of knowledge." Of course, the fact that seven out of the nine gifts mentioned here are supernatural by no means proves that the other two are! But since the Bible nowhere clearly defines these two gifts, it seems reasonable to me to assume that they are also miraculous gifts unless it can be proven otherwise by the immediate context.[10]

The only gifts on the list that are not clearly supernatural are the two that are most obscure, and so with nothing in the immediate context to indicate that they differ from the other gifts on the list in this regard, the most reasonable assumption is that they too should be understood in a supernatural way.

Second, Petts sees three significant indications from the context of the list in 1 Corinthians 12 that point us to a supernatural understanding of these nine gifts. One is the use of the word *pneumatika*: "All God's gifts to us are *charismata*, but only *these* gifts are described as pneumatika. It is at least possible that Paul reserves the term pneumatika for those gifts which are supernatural in character."[11] Another indication is the reference to idol worship in verse 2. In 1 Corinthians 10:19–20, Paul links idol worship to the demonic. Now, in the context of spiritual gifts, he warns against being misled to mute idols: "The list of gifts we are considering follows immediately after Paul's teaching on how to distinguish between manifestations which come from demons and those that come from the Holy Spirit."[12] This again suggests that he is writing of supernatural gifts. Finally, Petts argues that verse 13 refers to the baptism in the Holy Spirit, "which in Acts was accompanied by supernatural phenomena" and therefore "it seems reasonable to assume that the gifts of which Paul has just been speaking are also miraculous in character."[13] Thus, Petts concludes that both the list itself and its context point us to a supernatural understanding of each of the nine gifts. The declaration of faith of the Brazilian Assemblies of God sums up what Pentecostals believe: "These gifts are special, supernatural capabilities bestowed by the Spirit of God upon the believer for special service in carrying out the divine purposes through the church. . . . They are supernatural resources of the Holy Spirit operating through human beings."[14]

Summary

Scripture emphasizes that the gifts of the Holy Spirit are given only by the grace of God. They are not distributed according to human merit or talent

10. Petts, *Body Builders*, 105.
11. Petts, *Body Builders*, 107.
12. Petts, *Body Builders*, 108.
13. Petts, *Body Builders*, 109.
14. Brazil DdF, 20.

but instead flow from the great grace of God in Christ by the Spirit. Therefore, any use of the gifts of the Spirit must only be in humble dependence upon our gracious God. Pentecostals understand the nine gifts of the Holy Spirit listed in 1 Corinthians 12 to be supernatural spiritual gifts. These gifts are spiritual in that (1) they come from the Holy Spirit, (2) the Holy Spirit uses them in pointing people to the gospel, and (3) through them the Holy Spirit glorifies Jesus (John 16:14).

REFLECTION QUESTIONS

1. What does the word *charismata* emphasize?

2. What other charismata are found in the New Testament, in addition to the gifts of the Holy Spirit?

3. What does the gracious and spiritual nature of these gifts tell us about the people who are used in the gifts (and how the gifts should be used)?

4. Why do Pentecostals understand the nine gifts of 1 Corinthians 12 to be supernatural gifts?

5. What does the spiritual nature of the gifts suggest about their purpose?

QUESTION 23

What Are the Gifts of the Spirit? (Part 2)

Although *charismata* and "spiritual gifts" are the most familiar expressions for these gifts, they are not the only ways in which Scripture describes them. In this chapter we will examine two more expressions used for the gifts of the Spirit in 1 Corinthians 12 and the contribution these make to our understanding of spiritual gifts.

Phanerosis: The Manifestation of the Holy Spirit

In 1 Corinthians 12:7, Paul describes each of these gifts as a manifestation (*phanerosis*) of the Holy Spirit. In other words, the gifts of the Spirit are not simply things that the Holy Spirit makes possible at a distance, but rather the Holy Spirit is himself at work by these gifts in the church, and thus manifesting himself by their operation in the assembly. Through the gifts, the Holy Spirit makes his presence known. As French Arrington puts it, the nine gifts are "actions of the Spirit, demonstrating the Spirit's presence and activity. Through the gifts the work of the Spirit becomes visible and open."[1]

Charles W. Conn, former general overseer of the Church of God, argues that "the meaning of this seems to be that the spiritual gifts are resident in God, set in the church, and manifested through individuals . . . as it pleases Him."[2] Thus, "there is never any justification for an individual to claim that *he* possesses any particular gift."[3] Even when a particular member of the church is "repeatedly used for a particular manifestation . . . that it seems as though that gift belongs to him . . . the person himself must never be carried

1. French Arrington, *Christian Doctrine: A Pentecostal Perspective* (Cleveland, TN: Pathway Press, 1994), 3:116.
2. Charles W. Conn, *A Balanced Church* (Cleveland, TN: Pathway Press, 1975), 105.
3. Conn, *A Balanced Church*, 105.

away with false notions of personal possession. He must bear in mind that the gift is in God's hand and God is merely manifesting it through him."[4] Therefore, understanding spiritual gifts as manifestations of the Spirit should lead Pentecostals to greater humility.

The manifestation of the Spirit in the gifts is a further piece of evidence for the supernatural nature of these nine. Arrington argues that this designation shows that "it is a mistake to think of spiritual gifts as hidden talents or abilities. Rather, they are actions of the Holy Spirit through individual Christians" that are "evidence of the Spirit's power," which extends "beyond natural ability and the faithful use of innate talents." Thus, they are "God-given abilities manifested through the believer by the Holy Spirit."[5] This is why, traditionally, classical Pentecostals reject the idea of spiritual gift tests: Christians cannot discover a manifestation of the Holy Spirit by looking within themselves.

That the gifts are manifestations of the Holy Spirit is also connected to the classical Pentecostal understanding of the baptism in the Holy Spirit as the gateway to the gifts of the Spirit. This is expressed in the Romanian Pentecostal confession of faith: "This baptism [of the Holy Spirit] can be followed by receiving other gifts. . . . According to the Holy Scriptures, it is necessary that those called by God to proclaim the full Gospel first persevere, so that they are filled with power from above, so that signs, wonders and gifts of the Holy Spirit can accompany them."[6] Harold Horton simply explains that "the gifts of the Spirit are the outward evidence of the indwelling Spirit in those who are baptized in the Spirit."[7] However, this raises questions, for all believers are indwelt by the Holy Spirit, whether or not they have received a Pentecostal baptism in the Spirit.[8] Another British Pentecostal writer, D. T. Rennie, goes beyond Horton's suggestion to reach toward a fuller explanation. For Rennie, the manifestation of the gifts of the Holy Spirit is "consequent upon, because inseparably linked with, and indeed integral to the baptism in the Spirit," yet this is rooted deeply in union with Christ, in the distinctive purpose of the baptism of the Holy Spirit, and in the cultivation of the fruit of the Spirit.[9] He writes, "The overflowing fullness of the Holy Spirit, within and out from the believer, provides the suitable soil in which the fruits of the Spirit take root and grow to maturity of character. And this is the sphere of Christian

---

4. Conn, *A Balanced Church*, 107.
5. Arrington, *Christian Doctrine*, 3:116.
6. Romanian CF, 16.
7. Harold Horton, *The Gifts of the Spirit*, rev. ed. (Luton: Assemblies of God, 1949), 30.
8. This is very clearly expressed in the confession of faith of the Apostolic Church UK: "The Holy Spirit lives in all believers, for it is the Holy Spirit who convicts us of our sin, draws us to Christ for salvation, regenerates and unites us to Christ through faith" (ACVG, 5).
9. D. T. Rennie, *The Gifts of the Holy Spirit* (Bradford: Puritan Press, 1967), 23–24.

experience, the heavenlies in Christ Jesus, wherein the Holy Spirit freely bestows His gifts, and personal faith co-operates in their exercise."[10]

David Petts puts forward two biblical arguments for viewing the baptism of the Spirit as the gateway to the gifts. In typical Pentecostal fashion, Petts warns that "we must decide what to believe on the basis of what we understand the Bible teaches, not on the basis of our experience. Once we have done that, we may evaluate our experience in the light of Scripture, rather than trying to read our experience into God's word."[11] He then goes on to set out two lines of biblical evidence: one from the sequence of events in Acts, and the other from 1 Corinthians 12:13.

First, Petts argues that "it is significant that in Acts the baptism or infilling of the Spirit always came *before* the manifestation of spiritual gifts."[12] Although he admits that "the fact that people were usually baptised in the Spirit on the day they were saved suggests that the manifestation of spiritual gifts before being baptised in the Spirit would have been unlikely," he nevertheless sees the pattern as an important indication of God's plan.[13]

Second, Petts turns to 1 Corinthians 12:13, from which he draws a stronger case.[14] When we read in this verse that "in one Spirit we were all baptized into one body," Petts argues that Paul is not here referring to regeneration and incorporation into the body of Christ, but rather to the purpose for which believers are baptized in the Spirit.[15] The preposition *eis* would better be translated "for" here, Petts argues, rather than "into." Therefore, he translates the verse: "For we have all been baptised in one Spirit for (i.e., for the purpose or benefit of) the one body."[16] This translation, he argues, is not only justified grammatically (and in parallel to other New Testament texts), but also better fits the surrounding context.[17]

If this translation of 1 Corinthians 12:13 is accepted, then it would suggest that there is something in the very purpose of the baptism in the Spirit that is directed toward the benefit of the other members of the body of Christ, which is also the purpose of the gifts of the Spirit. So, the gifts flowing out from the baptism in the Spirit would fit with the purpose of both. Petts argues that Paul is telling the Corinthians that they "have been baptised in the Spirit for the

10. Rennie, *Gifts of the Holy Spirit*, 23.
11. Petts, *Body Builders*, 110.
12. Petts, *Body Builders*, 110.
13. Petts, *Body Builders*, 111.
14. It should be noted that not all Pentecostals interpret 1 Corinthians 12:13 in the same way as Petts.
15. For the details of Petts's exegetical argument (and his critique of the non-Pentecostal interpretation of this verse), see David Petts, *The Holy Spirit: An Introduction* (Mattersey: Mattersey Hall, 1998), 68–70.
16. Petts, *The Holy Spirit*, 69.
17. Petts, *The Holy Spirit*, 70.

good of the whole church," and thus "the spiritual gifts which result from that baptism" are to edify not merely oneself, but "the whole body of believers."[18] This then should encourage those who have been baptized in the Spirit "to press on to the gifts by eagerly desiring them and praying for them."[19] Petts's arguments are not conclusive; there is not a Scripture that explicitly states one cannot be used in a gift of the Spirit without being baptized in the Spirit (and Petts admits that God in his mercy may at times work outside this pattern), but it does suggest a normative pattern.

A simpler argument is put forward by Anthony D. Palma. The supernatural experience of the baptism of the Holy Spirit involves a willing submission "to something suprarational," and in this way "the baptism in the Spirit opens up the receivers to the full range of spiritual gifts."[20] A supernatural experiential encounter paves the way for further supernatural experiences of various kinds through the gifts. W. A. C. Rowe makes a similar argument from Luke 24:49 and Acts 1:8 where the baptism of the Spirit is described as an enduement of power. "The Baptism is a preparation of power for further supernatural visitations. It prepares the ground, for instance, for the impartation of the Gifts of the Spirit."[21] This preparation involves not only an openness to supernatural experience, but also the creation of a deep longing for the gifts of the Spirit. Furthermore, the sign of speaking in tongues "can be the forerunner of the Voice Gifts—the Gifts of Tongues, Interpretation and Prophecy."[22]

Diakonia: Ways of Service

In 1 Corinthians 12:5 Paul uses the word *diakonia* for the gifts of the Spirit. There are, he tells us, "varieties of service, but the same Lord" (1 Cor. 12:5). Describing the gifts as ways of service points us to their purpose. The Holy Spirit does not distribute his gifts for the benefit of the one through whom the gift is manifest, but rather he distributes the gift for the benefit of others, so that through the gift others may be served. As Paul puts it a few verses later, "To each is given the manifestation of the Spirit for the common good" (1 Cor. 12:7). The gifts of the Spirit are not given for individualized personal experience; they are given to serve one another for the benefit of the church. We are responsible to wisely steward God's gifts—both the supernatural gifts of the spirit and other gifts of God's grace—and use them to serve others. Peter teaches this plainly: "As each has received a gift, use it to serve one another, as good stewards of God's varied grace: whoever speaks, as one

---

18. David Petts, *Body Builders: Gifts to Make God's People Grow* (Mattersey: Mattersey Hall, 2002), 111.
19. Petts, *Body Builders*, 112.
20. Anthony D. Palma, *The Holy Spirit: A Pentecostal Perspective* (Springfield, MO: Gospel Publishing House, 2001), 169.
21. W. A. C. Rowe, *One Lord, One Faith* (Bradford: Puritan Press, n.d.), 138.
22. Rowe, *One Lord, One Faith*, 138.

who speaks oracles of God; whoever serves, as one who serves by the strength that God supplies—in order that in everything God may be glorified through Jesus Christ" (1 Peter 4:10–11). By serving one another with the gifts God supplies, the Lord is glorified among us. As one British Pentecostal theologian put it, "The endowment is bestowed for Divine glory and human benefit . . . the gifted member is responsible to the Lord and His Church."[23]

Understanding that the Lord gives these gifts in order to serve others for his glory is essential to the correct use of the gifts in the life of the church. Arrington writes: "The proper exercise of spiritual gifts ministers to the body of Christ and to its needs. The gifts are manifested through individuals; but they are given to strengthen, help, and build up the church. They promote the welfare of the community of believers rather than exalt those through whom they are manifested."[24] The gifts are neither markers of an individual's spirituality, nor are they merely demonstrations of the Lord's presence among his people. The gifts are given for a purpose, and that purpose is the building up of the church to the glory of the triune God.

Paul specifically writes of this purpose in relation to the gift of prophecy: "The one who prophesies speaks to people for their upbuilding and encouragement and consolation" (1 Cor. 14:3). In the context, a contrast is being demonstrated between prophecy (which the hearers can understand) and tongues without an interpretation. Unintelligible tongues do not build up, encourage, or console, but intelligible prophecy does. Therefore, the contrast here is between gifts of the Spirit used rightly and those that are misused. If the gifts are misused (like tongues without an interpretation) they will not build up; when the gifts are rightly used, they will. That this does not only apply to prophecy is seen as the chapter continues. All that is done when the church gathers is to be done for building one another up in Christ. "What then, brothers? When you come together, each one has a hymn, a lesson, a revelation, a tongue, or an interpretation. Let all things be done for building up" (1 Cor. 14:26). Here Paul includes both natural and supernatural elements of Christian worship; both the ordinary means of the grace and the supernatural gifts of the Holy Spirit should be used for building up the church in faith, hope, and love.

The Lord also uses the gifts of the Spirit to witness to, and open doors for, the proclamation of the gospel. The healing of the lame man in Acts 3 at the gate of the temple "called Beautiful" (v. 2) drew a crowd that was "filled with wonder and amazement at what had happened to him" (v. 10), and as a result the door was opened for Peter to preach the good news of Jesus to them (vv. 12–26) and then to the High Priest and Sanhedrin as well (4:1–12). Here a gift of healing opened the way for proclaiming Jesus.

---

23. Rennie, *Gifts of the Holy Spirit*, 31.
24. Arrington, *Christian Doctrine*, 3:118.

In Hebrews, we read, "God also bore witness [to the message of such a great salvation] by signs and wonders and various miracles and by gifts of the Holy Spirit distributed according to his will" (Heb. 2:3–4). The gifts of the Spirit, then, do not only lead to the opening of doors for the gospel to be proclaimed, but they are also one of the ways in which the Lord himself testifies to the truth of the gospel message. Thomas Schreiner writes, "The miracles given accredited the revelation, demonstrating that it was genuinely given by God."[25] We see this happening in practice after the ascension, when "they went out and preached everywhere, while the Lord worked with them and confirmed the message by accompanying signs" (Mark 16:20).[26]

That God bears witness to the gospel message through gifts of the Spirit does not mean that any message accompanied by signs and wonders will always be true; after all, Paul warns the Corinthians against accepting "another Jesus . . . a different spirit . . . a different gospel," reminding his readers that "even Satan disguises himself as an angel of light" (2 Cor. 11:4, 14). He warns the Galatians that "even if we or an angel from heaven should preach to you a gospel contrary to the one we preached to you, let him be accursed" (Gal. 1:8). We must be on guard against "false signs and wonders" (2 Thess. 2:9). Therefore, all claims to gifts of the Spirit, signs or wonders should be tested (1 Thess. 5:21).[27]

Summary

As manifestations of the Spirit, the gifts of the Spirit are one of the ways in which the Lord makes his presence known among his people by the Holy Spirit. Therefore, the exercise of the gifts always depends on the Holy Spirit who is at work. Hence Pentecostals have generally seen a connection between the baptism and gifts of the Holy Spirit. As means of service, the gifts of the Holy Spirit are given for the benefit of others. The gifts are given in order to build up Christ's church, to the glory of God.

REFLECTION QUESTIONS

1. In what way are the gifts of 1 Corinthians 12 manifestations of the presence of the Holy Spirit?

---

25. Thomas R. Schreiner, *Hebrews*, Evangelical Biblical Theology Commentary (Bellingham, WA: Lexham, 2020), 83.
26. Pentecostals have generally been happy to make use of the longer ending of Mark's gospel. For arguments in favor of the canonicity of these verses, see David Alan Black, "Mark 16:9–20 as Markan Supplement," in *Perspectives on the Ending of Mark*, 103–23; and Maurice A. Robinson, "The Long Ending of Mark as Canonical Verity," in *Perspectives on the Ending of Mark: 4 Views*, ed. David Alan Black (Nashville: Broadman & Holman, 2008), 40–79.
27. We will consider this testing particularly in relation to prophecy in question 29.

2. Why do Pentecostals tend to think of the baptism in the Holy Spirit as the gateway to the gifts? What do you think of this argument?
3. Does the idea of discovering your spiritual gifts by means of a spiritual gifts test fit with what we learn about the nine gifts of the Holy Spirit in 1 Corinthians 12?
4. What is the purpose of the gifts of the Holy Spirit?
5. In what ways do the gifts contribute to the building up of the church?

SECTION B

Questions About Specific Gifts

QUESTION 24

What Are the Word of Wisdom and the Word of Knowledge?

The first two gifts listed by Paul in 1 Corinthians 12:8, the word of wisdom and the word of knowledge, are the most mysterious. Nowhere does the Bible give a clear definition of either of these gifts, nor do we find any clearly labeled examples of these gifts in action. Therefore, we need to give careful attention to Scripture here and be careful not to assume meanings. Since the beginning of the Pentecostal movement, various definitions have been offered for these gifts from Pentecostal and later charismatic writers. Each has sought to present a scriptural definition and support it with biblical examples. Thus, each has pointed to *something* biblical; the question is whether the biblical thing to which they point is indeed one of the gifts that Paul lists in 1 Corinthians 12:8.

Before examining these positions, however, we should clarify what these gifts are not. The word of wisdom and the word of knowledge are not the same as the wisdom and knowledge that are needed by and promised to every believer in Christ (1 Cor. 1:30; 2 Cor. 4:6; Col. 3:10; 1 Tim. 2:4; James 1:5). David Rennie, a British Pentecostal leader, explains: "Wisdom, however, albeit given by God is not synonymous with the gift of the word of wisdom. In each case the wisdom is divinely bestowed, but in the former it is assimilated into the personality, forming mature Christian character. The latter, however, is a miraculous expression, a specially selected particularized extraction from the divine treasure-store of wisdom by the Holy Spirit in order to supply a particular need. The speaker becomes the channel through whom the Spirit imparts this fragment of inspired and inspiring revelation."[1]

As 1 Corinthians 12:8 highlights, these gifts are distributed among the church to some believers: "to one is given the word of wisdom through the

1. David T. Rennie, *The Gifts of the Holy Spirit* (Bradford: Puritan Press, 1967), 43–44.

Spirit, to another the word of knowledge through the same Spirit" (NKJV). This selective distribution shows that these cannot be the same as the wisdom and knowledge that accompany the salvation and sanctification of each and every one of Christ's people.

Supernatural Flashes of Revelation?

One of the most influential early Pentecostal writers on the gifts of the Spirit was the Englishman Harold Horton (1881–1969), whose book on the subject was published not only in the United Kingdom but also in the United States, and translated into several other languages.[2] For Horton, both the word of wisdom and the word of knowledge are to be understood as supernatural gifts of revelation. Each is "a miracle with no admixture of the natural."[3] They are not vocal gifts and do not need to be expressed vocally at all. Instead, they "may be received as a silent revelation on one's knees."[4] The Greek word *logos* (translated "word" in the name of each of these gifts), Horton argues, "is more than an uttered sound" but is rather the reality or revelation behind the sound. Therefore, he writes, "A word of knowledge is a revelation of knowledge, or a fragment of knowledge. It is not necessarily an utterance."[5]

Thus, Horton defines the word of knowledge as "the supernatural revelation by the Holy Spirit of certain facts in the mind of God . . . the revelation, perhaps, of the existence, condition or whereabouts of some person or object or place, of the location or occasion of some event."[6] This is not a divine "amplification of human knowledge," nor is it "acquired by study." Rather, "it is a divinely granted flash of revelation concerning things which were hopelessly hidden from the senses, the mind or the faculties of men." Therefore, the word of knowledge is "a divinely given fragment of divine knowledge."[7] In the same manner, the word of wisdom is "the supernatural revelation, by the Spirit, of Divine Purpose; the supernatural declaration of the Mind and Will of God; the supernatural unfolding of His Plans and Purposes concerning things, places, people: individuals, communities, nations."[8] Both gifts are fragmentary revelations and neither need be expressed in words. One of the ways in which Horton sees a nonvocal understanding of these gifts as helpful is that they can be "a mighty aid to effectual prayer either for God's servants in distress or for those in need of spiritual help."[9]

---

2. Harold Horton, *The Gifts of the Spirit*, rev. ed. (Luton: Assemblies of God, 1949).
3. Horton, *Gifts*, 49.
4. Horton, *Gifts*, 49.
5. Horton, *Gifts*, 50.
6. Horton, *Gifts*, 48.
7. Horton, *Gifts*, 49.
8. Horton, *Gifts*, 63.
9. Horton, *Gifts*, 57.

Supernatural Spoken Expressions of Wisdom and Knowledge?

One of the most critiqued aspects of Horton's understanding of these gifts is his argument that they need not be expressed in words. Many other Pentecostals have insisted that the fact that these are not called the gifts of wisdom and knowledge, but rather the gifts of the word of wisdom and the word of knowledge, means that they must be expressed in words. They are not simply flashes of revelation, as Horton would have it, but rather "wisdom expressed in words" and "knowledge expressed in words."[10] W. G. Hathaway of Elim argues that "God-given wisdom will always advertise its own presence in its spoken word."[11]

This understanding is more in keeping with Paul's use of the word *logos* in 1 Corinthians. Of the seventeen times this word is used in 1 Corinthians, apart from the two instances in 12:8 which we are trying to understand, and 15:54, which refers to the written Word of Scripture, every other instance refers to a spoken word, whether in preaching or some other form of speaking. As from the context it is evident that the word of wisdom and word of knowledge are not written words of Scripture, the most reasonable interpretation would be that Paul is using *logos* in the same way here as all the other instances in the letter (except 15:54) to refer to spoken words. David Petts notes that "there is no clear evidence that Paul ever uses it" to refer to "an unspoken revelation."[12] Therefore, Horton would appear to be wrong in arguing that these gifts need not involve speaking.

Hathaway, in fact, goes so far as to put the emphasis on the transmission of the knowledge or wisdom to others in speaking, rather than on the revelation of the knowledge or wisdom in the first place.[13] "It is not so much in the understanding of knowledge, but in the imparting of knowledge that the inspiration lies. . . . Evidently this knowledge is gained or gathered by the aid of the Spirit, and the word of knowledge is the ability by the Spirit to impart that knowledge to others. . . . This may be either knowledge of God, or of the ways of God."[14] In terms of the word of wisdom, Hathaway points to three areas where this spoken wisdom is of particular importance and help: "(1) In reasoning with and convincing disputers . . . (2) In the councils of the Church . . . (3) In wise guidance given in times of great difficulty."[15] In each of

---

10. "Fundamental Truths," in *The Apostolic Church: Its Principles and Practices*, amended ed. (Bradford: Puritan Press, 1961), 120–21.
11. W. G. Hathaway, *Spiritual Gifts in the Church* (London: Elim, 1933), 29.
12. David Petts, *Body Builders: Gifts to Make God's People Grow* (Mattersey: Mattersey Hall, 2002), 238.
13. D. A. Carson similarly points out that "the emphasis is not exactly on wisdom but on the messages . . . that issue from wisdom and knowledge." See Carson, *Showing the Spirit: A Theological Exposition of 1 Corinthians 12–14* (Milton Keynes: Authentic, 2010), 28.
14. Hathaway, *Spiritual Gifts*, 30.
15. Hathaway, *Spiritual Gifts*, 26–29. The Italian Apostolic Michele Strazzeri similarly argues that the word of wisdom is especially helpful "when it is necessary to solve a problem in a situation, to react or to hush an opponent" and as "the right word at the right time

these cases, it is necessary that the wisdom be expressed in words. Thus, the word of wisdom and word of knowledge should be seen not only as flashes of revelation, but as "the ability by the Spirit to impart that knowledge [or wisdom] by word to others. . . . We might rightly describe this gift as the imparting of understanding to others by the Spirit."[16]

Gifts for Preaching and Teaching?

Like Harold Horton, Donald Gee wrote a very influential book on the gifts of the Spirit, which was published on both sides of the Atlantic, translated into several other languages, and is still in print. Both were teachers from the British Assemblies of God, and both taught at the Assemblies of God Bible College, of which Gee was to become principal. The major divergence between Horton and Gee when it came to the gifts of the Spirit, however, was in their understandings of the words of wisdom and knowledge.

Gee saw that these gifts needed to be spoken. However, he took this argument further, connecting these two gifts with the ministries of preaching and teaching. Looking at how the word "wisdom" is used particularly in the first three chapters of 1 Corinthians, Gee concludes that it is connected with "the preaching of Christ and the Cross and those things that God has prepared for them that love Him."[17] Therefore, he concludes that the gift of the word of wisdom, in order to be consistent with Paul's use of language in the letter, must have the same focus. Therefore, Gee sees this gift as especially concerned with preaching.

> Only those who have sought to preach on these great and fundamental themes know how helpless they are unaided by human powers to deal with them adequately. It may be objected that it is the normal function of all Christian preaching and teaching to center on these subjects, and this we do not dispute. But in ministry of a truly Pentecostal order there ofttimes comes shining forth a revelation in words that make our hearts burn within us. Many of us have experienced the holy awe and the thrilling exaltation of spirit that accompanies a ministry of the spiritual gift of the word of wisdom on these lines.[18]

Although the preaching of Christ is its chief focus, Gee also sees a place for the gift in the government and guidance of the church. "Also of supreme value

---

or during an emergency case." See *The Gifts of the Holy Spirit*, trans. Giuseppe Guarino (Catania, Italy: Guarino, 2018), 23.

16. Hathaway, *Spiritual Gifts*, 30–31.
17. Donald Gee, *Concerning Spiritual Gifts*, rev. ed. (Springfield, MO: Gospel Publishing House, 1980), 35.
18. Gee, *Concerning Spiritual Gifts*, 35–36.

and importance to the church, is the manifestation of this gift in counsel and government."[19] This combination of preaching and governing spheres for the gift means that "the gift of the word of wisdom can most usually be looked for in those set by God in positions of government and leadership in the assemblies, such as apostles and presbyters."[20] However, the Lord does not limit his gifts only to ministers, and so "there are occasions when any believer may expect a gracious personal manifestation of any one of them in order to meet an urgent need and respond to an opportunity."[21]

The word of knowledge is, for Gee, similarly linked to another particular form of ministry. While the word of wisdom is connected with preaching, the word of knowledge is "a teaching gift in the church."[22] That this gift is connected to teaching does not mean that it is in any way less supernatural. "It seems strangely inconsistent," Gee warns, "not to expect a supernatural manifestation of the Spirit to occur in such an important ministry as that of teaching."[23] Rather, in a supernatural way in the ministry of teaching, the Lord can speak by the gifts of the Spirit. Indeed, Gee writes, through this gift he "still expounds the Scriptures on the sweetest of all themes—Himself."[24] The word of knowledge is not the whole of the teaching ministry; it must be joined together with "meditation and instruction."[25] And the church has need of a permanent "humanly trained ministry of systematic teaching that is to be transmitted from generation to generation." However, this humanly trained systematic teaching ministry can, Gee argues, "find its crowning glory whenever it becomes inspired by a more directly Pentecostal gift." For then, Gee writes, "Although the truths will be the same, and indeed the speaker may be the same, there will be something burning and shining that is nothing less than the word of knowledge manifesting afresh the anointing of the Comforter."[26] Thus, for Gee, the word of wisdom and word of knowledge not only must be spoken, but are especially tied to the ministries of preaching and teaching.

A Charismatic Alternative: Non-supernatural Gifts from God?

More recently, the charismatic theologian Wayne Grudem has had a significant impact on the understanding of the gifts of the Spirit among some

---

19. Gee, *Concerning Spiritual Gifts*, 36.
20. Gee, *Concerning Spiritual Gifts*, 38.
21. Gee, *Concerning Spiritual Gifts*, 38.
22. Gee, *Concerning Spiritual Gifts*, 134.
23. Gee, *Concerning Spiritual Gifts*, 46.
24. Gee, *Concerning Spiritual Gifts*, 47.
25. Gee, *Concerning Spiritual Gifts*, 135.
26. Gee, *Concerning Spiritual Gifts*, 137. Gee particularly sees this as connected to the ministry of the teacher and points out that teaching in the church should not be restricted to those called to the ministry of the teacher.

Pentecostals.[27] Grudem, however, argues that the words of wisdom and knowledge are not supernatural gifts at all, seeing them instead as the nonmiraculous "ability to speak with wisdom or with knowledge in various situations."[28] For this understanding he advances two arguments. First, "word," "wisdom," and "knowledge" are "not specialized or technical terms" but rather "extremely common words in the Greek New Testament" and "are not ordinarily used to denote miraculous events."[29] Second, the Bible "already has a term to describe the action of receiving a special revelation from the Holy Spirit and reporting it to the congregation"—namely, prophecy.[30] Grudem is of the opinion that "everything that modern Pentecostal and charismatic Christians call 'words of knowledge' and 'words of wisdom' would . . . fit well under the umbrella of prophecy."[31]

However, as we have seen in question 22, we have good reasons to believe that all nine gifts listed in 1 Corinthians 12:8–10 are supernatural. While Grudem may be correct in arguing that many examples of what are commonly called words of wisdom or knowledge in some charismatic circles are actually types of prophecy, these common examples are quite different from the definitions of these gifts advocated by careful Pentecostal thinkers like Horton, Hathaway, and Gee. A misunderstanding of the nature of a supernatural gift does not mean that the gift is not supposed to be supernatural. Furthermore, Grudem's argument that the terms used for these gifts ("word," "wisdom," and "knowledge") do not normally refer to supernatural events is of little help. It is not from the terms Paul chooses that we see the supernatural character of the gifts but rather from the surrounding context.

The Corinthian Context: The Wisdom of the Cross and the Knowledge of Christ

The context of 1 Corinthians 12:8 points to a supernatural understanding of these two gifts. Yet the context of the whole letter points us to a better understanding of the content of these two gifts. Gee is correct in his observation that wisdom and knowledge are above all connected with Christ and his cross in 1 Corinthians. As Gordon Fee points out, Paul is writing this letter to demonstrate to the Corinthians that "the message of Christ crucified is God's

---

27. Some Pentecostal academics do not like the fact that Grudem's *Systematic Theology* is so widely used by Pentecostals; they argue that a Pentecostal systematic theology is neither desirable nor possible. The fact that Grudem's book (despite its significant departures from classical Pentecostal doctrine) has been so widely adopted would suggest that such a Pentecostal systematic theology is, in fact, desirable.
28. Wayne Grudem, *Systematic Theology: An Introduction to Biblical Doctrine,* 2nd ed. (London: InterVarsity Press, 2020), 1334.
29. Grudem, *Systematic Theology*, 1333.
30. Grudem, *Systematic Theology*, 1334.
31. Grudem, *Systematic Theology*, 1334.

true wisdom" and "only the Spirit . . . whom we have received, understands the mind of God and reveals what he accomplished in Christ."[32] Therefore, the word of wisdom is "an utterance that proclaims Christ crucified."[33]

Paul uses "knowledge" in a similar way in his letters (1 Cor. 8:6–8; 2 Cor. 2:14–15; 4:6; Eph. 1:17). The knowledge of which he writes is not a secret known only to a select few; rather, it is always the knowledge of God in Christ, which has been openly declared to the world in Scripture and through the proclamation of the gospel.

Therefore, both these gifts direct our attention to Christ and his gospel. As such, although they are supernatural, their supernatural nature might not always be obvious to those who hear words of knowledge and wisdom. For these gifts are not astonishing revelations of mysteries but rather, like all faithful proclamation in the church, they point us to "the wisdom of Christ and His Cross, and the knowledge of God in Christ."[34] Yet, the difference between these gifts and our ordinary, faithful speaking of Christ and his cross is that "these are gifts of revelation by which we speak in situations where, otherwise, we would not have the gospel-focused knowledge and wisdom needed for that moment."[35] This is not limited to preaching and teaching but can be in all sorts of contexts—in evangelism, in discussions wherein elders need to grapple with difficult issues, in discipleship, and in pastoral care.

Summary

Pentecostals understand the word of wisdom and the word of knowledge in various ways. Some put the emphasis on the knowledge and wisdom, arguing that these gifts are flashes of revelation. Others maintain that these gifts must be expressed in words and emphasize the transmission of the wisdom and knowledge. The context of 1 Corinthians points us to Christ and the gospel as the content of wisdom of knowledge, suggesting that these gifts should be understood in that light.

REFLECTION QUESTIONS

1. Why are these gifts called the word of wisdom and word of knowledge? What is significant about them being called "words"?

---

32. Gordon D. Fee, *God's Empowering Presence: The Holy Spirit in the Letters of Paul* (Peabody, MA: Hendrickson, 1994), 166–67.
33. Fee, *God's Empowering Presence*, 167.
34. Jonathan Black, *Apostolic Theology: A Trinitarian, Evangelical, Pentecostal Introduction to Christian Doctrine* (Luton: Apostolic Church, 2016), 489.
35. Black, *Apostolic Theology*, 489.

2. Is it important for these gifts to be expressed in speech in order to fulfil the purposes of the gifts of the Holy Spirit?
3. Why does Donald Gee connect these gifts with preaching and teaching? Does he have a strong point?
4. What do you think of Wayne Grudem's argument against seeing these gifts as supernatural?
5. What does the wider context of 1 Corinthians and Paul's other writings contribute to our understanding of the content of these gifts?

QUESTION 25

What Are the Gift of Faith, Working of Miracles, and Discerning of Spirits?

In this chapter we will consider three of the gifts from 1 Corinthians 12 that are perhaps less well known: the gift of faith, the working of miracles, and the discerning of spirits.

The Gift of Faith

All Christians have faith; it is impossible to be saved without faith, and that faith is a gift of God (Eph. 2:8; Phil. 1:29–30). Yet, the faith by which all believers are saved and united to Christ is not the same as this spiritual gift of faith listed in 1 Corinthians 12:9. As the Apostolic Church explains, "This is apart from the common faith which all the children of God possess. It is a Gift which is given by the Spirit to some in the Church, and operates generally: but particularly in the hour of conflict and doubt, when it grips God for victory and holds back the power of the Enemy. It also claims the promises of God for the Church in the hour of adversity."[1]

Not all Christians possess this gift of faith, but rather, like the other gifts of the Holy Spirit, it is distributed when and to whom the Spirit wills (1 Cor. 12:11). This special gift of faith "depends entirely on God."[2] André Thomas-Brès sees this gift as "given to believers who face humanly insurmountable obstacles. It gives assurance of deliverance when everything seems lost."[3] In other words, it is a special faith that, as the non-Pentecostal scholar D. A. Carson explains, "enables a believer to trust God to bring about certain things

1. "Fundamental Truths," *The Apostolic Church: Its Principles and Practices*, amended ed. (Bradford: Puritan Press, 1961), 121.
2. French L. Arrington, *Christian Doctrine: A Pentecostal Perspective* (Cleveland, TN: Pathway, 1994), 3:136.
3. André Thomas-Brès, *La Foi Donée Aux Saints Une Fois Pour Toutes* (Grézieu la Varenne: Viens et Vois, 2016), 229.

for which he or she cannot claim some divine promise recorded in Scripture."[4] Italian Apostolic pastor Michele Strazzeri defines it as "that gift of the Holy Spirit through which God moves a person to pray or act with certainty."[5]

Paul would appear to be referring to this gift when he writes of faith "so as to remove mountains" in 1 Corinthians 13:2, for in the context he explicitly mentions the spiritual gifts of tongues and prophecy.[6] The Foursquare theologians Guy Duffield and Nathaniel Van Cleave interpret the removal of mountains as symbolic of "any apparently impossible obstacle to the mission of the church."[7]

An example of this kind of special faith in action can be seen when Peter and Paul went up to the temple and met "a man lame from birth" at the gate of the temple called "Beautiful." When the man "asked to receive alms," Peter "directed his gaze at him" and said "I have no silver and gold, but what I do have I give to you. In the name of Jesus Christ of Nazareth, rise up and walk!" Then "he took him by the right hand and raised him up, and immediately his feet and ankles were made strong" (Acts 3:2–7). Peter had no specific promise of Scripture that God would heal this particular man on this specific day, yet somehow by the Holy Spirit the Lord granted him specific faith for this healing, causing him to act upon it by both telling the man to "rise up and walk" and taking him by the hand to raise him up. (For another possible example, see Acts 27:23–26.)

This faith does not differ in *nature* from saving faith, only in *degree*. French Arrington, an American Church of God theologian, argues that in this gift "the basic faith relationship the Christian has with God is intensified so that an individual may believe God for the humanly impossible. This gift is the elevation of faith by the Holy Spirit—a strong surge of confidence that God will grant healings, miracles, and other mighty works."[8] Yet Arrington also cautions that "genuine faith gives no place to presumption or to any effort to coerce God to intervene."[9] The early British Elim theologian W. G. Hathaway, for example, warns, "This gift may not always be active in the person so that

---

4. D. A. Carson, *Showing the Spirit: A Theological Exposition of 1 Corinthians 12–14* (Milton Keynes: Authentic, 2010), 29–30.
5. Michele Strazzeri, *The Gifts of the Holy Spirit*, trans. Giuseppe Guarino (Catania, Italy: Guarino, 2018), 117.
6. This identification is generally accepted by Pentecostals; see David Petts, *Body Builders: Gifts to Make God's People Grow* (Mattersey: Mattersey Hall, 2002), 191; and William A. Simmons, *The Holy Spirit in the New Testament: A Pentecostal Guide* (Downers Grove, IL: InterVarsity Press, 2021), 93.
7. Guy P. Duffield and Nathaniel M. Van Cleave, *Foundations of Pentecostal Theology* (Los Angeles: Foursquare Media, 2008), 337.
8. Arrington, *Christian* Doctrine, 3:135.
9. Arrington, *Christian Doctrine*, 3:137.

they can use it when and where they choose; rather it will spring up from the indwelling Holy Ghost upon each occasion when He sees fit to manifest it."[10]

The Working of Miracles

The working of miracles is "a sign of the presence and the power of God."[11] The word translated "miracles" in English is, in fact, the Greek word for "power."[12] Max Turner helps us to understand the biblical concept of a miracle by summarizing four essential aspects: "(1) it is an extraordinary or startling observable event, (2) it cannot reasonably be explained in terms of human abilities or other known forces in the world, (3) it is perceived as a direct act of God, and (4) it is usually understood to have symbolic or sign value (e.g. pointing to God as redeemer, judge, and Saviour)."[13] While, in one sense, all of the nine gifts of the Holy Spirit are miraculous in that they are all supernatural works of God, these four characteristics—especially the last one—help us distinguish this particular gift. Therefore, the gift of the working of miracles is "a gift which manifests supernatural power at the same time as it reveals the good purposes of God and glorifies Him."[14] Biblical miracles are "signs," pointing back to the Lord himself, as well as "wonders," which cause people to marvel and glorify God (Acts 3:12; 4:21). Through miracles "obstacles are removed or opportunities created, so evidently that the effects are a clear demonstration of the personal intervention of God."[15]

Therefore, miracles are not merely raw displays of power. Rather, as Arrington explains, miracles "bring glory to God and minister to human needs. Miracles are not to magnify those seeking to demonstrate their own greatness. . . . Like their Lord, the early Christians were moved by compassion to minister to human needs but not to dazzle the crowds."[16] On those lines, the American Assemblies of God theologian Anthony Palma argues, "Exorcism in particular would be one function of this gift."[17]

Examples of this gift in the book of Acts may include Peter's raising of Dorcas (Tabitha), for she was dead, and thus this was not a healing but a resurrection miracle (Acts 9:36–41). Likewise, Paul's raising of Eutychus was a miracle rather than a healing (Acts 20:9–12). In Acts 19:11–12, the exorcisms

---

10. W. G. Hathaway, *Spiritual Gifts in the Church* (London: Elim, 1933), 36.
11. Strazzeri, *Gifts*, 117.
12. Gordon Fee, *God's Empowering Presence: The Holy Spirit in the Letters of Paul* (Peabody, MA: Hendrickson, 1994), 169.
13. Max Turner, *The Holy Spirit and Spiritual Gifts: Then and Now* (Carlisle: Paternoster, 1996), 272.
14. "Fundamental Truths," *The Apostolic Church: Its Principles and Practices* (Penygroes: Apostolic Church, 1937), 205.
15. Strazzeri, *Gifts*, 117.
16. Arrington, *Christian Doctrine*, 3:140.
17. Anthony D. Palma, *The Holy Spirit: A Pentecostal Perspective* (Springfield, MO: Logion, 2001), 221; cf. Carson, *Showing the Spirit*, 31.

and healings at a distance through "handkerchiefs or aprons that had touched [Paul's] skin" are called "extraordinary miracles." Philip, likewise, performed "signs" in Samaria, which included casting out unclean spirits and healing the paralyzed and lame (Acts 8:6–7). Paul's shaking off of the snake on Malta without suffering any harm from the deadly snakebite was also a miracle (Acts 28:5). A different type of miracle is seen in Acts 13:11, where Paul pronounces a judgment upon Elymas the sorcerer, causing blindness. Although this was a judgment on Elymas, this miracle was both to glorify God (whose power is far beyond that of a sorcerer) and to minister to human needs, for Elymas was trying "to oppose the evangelistic activity of Paul" and thus to keep others away from salvation.[18] The result of this miracle was that "the proconsul believed, when he saw what had occurred, for he was astonished at the teaching of the Lord" (Acts 13:12).

The Discerning of Spirits

Pentecostals believe in the reality of angels and demons. The devil is real and so are the forces of darkness. Yet we have no need to fear, for all things are under Christ's feet (Eph. 1:22) and "the God of peace will soon crush Satan under [our] feet" (Rom. 16:20). Christ has triumphed over the powers of darkness, and he defends his people.

While we need not fear the powers of darkness, we are to recognize their reality and their power, to be on our guard, and to entrust ourselves at all times to the victory of Jesus. The Bible warns us that "Satan disguises himself as an angel of light" and "his servants, also, disguise themselves as servants of righteousness" (2 Cor. 11:14–15). It is for this reason, David Rennie argues, that we have such need of the gift of the discerning of spirits.

> The enemy is subtle in his approach. He well knows that if he openly reveals himself as he is and his intentions as they really are, he would immediately be refused audience and repelled. So he adopts subterfuge, disguise, camouflage, telling a half truth and even using Scripture to suit his fell purpose. Satan is a liar; he is bad—all bad; there is no good in him. But cunningly he masquerades, intruding into our holiest moments and most spiritual experiences. . . . So the use of this gift is essential in the sanctuary in relation to other gifts of the Spirit and their infernal imitations which can be so like the real that only the Holy Spirit can unmask the deceiver and reveal his deception.[19]

18. Daniel O. Walker, "Baptism, Gifts and Fruit of the Spirit," in *Tenets of the Church of Pentecost*, ed. Opoku Onyinah (Accra, Ghana: Church of Pentecost, 2019), 264.
19. David T. Rennie, *The Gifts of the Holy Spirit* (Bradford: Puritan Press, 1967), 99.

W. G. Hathaway defines the discerning of spirits as "the power given by the Holy Ghost to discern the spirit or spirits prompting an act or utterance. It is not just natural intuition, but a definite insight into these things given by the Holy Ghost."[20] Ghanaian Pentecostal theologian Daniel Walker cautions against confusing this gift with "mind reading, telepathy, clairvoyance, psychological insight [or] fault-finding."[21]

There are three possible sources for the spirit prompting an act: the Holy Spirit, an evil spirit, or the human spirit. French Arrington warns that "it is easy for the gifts of the Spirit such as prophecy and tongues to be counterfeited by Satan or by the human spirit."[22] Therefore, discernment is essential, for accepting what claims to be an inspired message without discernment "can have dire consequences."[23] Yet, this need for discernment should not lead us to fearfulness but rather confidence in the Lord and his provision. As Donald Gee reminds us, "Happy is the believer, and happy is the assembly, that meets these enlarged spiritual sensibilities in an attitude of watchfulness, but also of a supreme faith that God will always guard the Church purchased by His own blood, and finally defeat even the subtlest attacks of the great enemy."[24]

We see this gift in action when Peter asks Ananias "why has Satan filled your heart to lie to the Holy Spirit . . . ?" (Acts 5:3). Peter not only knew that Ananias had lied, but discerned the work of Satan in this lie.[25] When Paul pronounced God's judgment on Elymas the sorcerer this may also have involved the discerning of spirits, for he called Elymas, "You son of the devil, you enemy of all righteousness, full of all deceit and villainy" (Acts 13:10). A much clearer example is seen in Acts 16, when a slave girl was following Paul and Silas around, crying out, "These men are servants of the Most High God, who proclaim to you the way of salvation" (Acts 16:17). Although her words were true, Paul responded by casting an evil spirit out of the girl (Acts 16:18). Therefore, Paul clearly discerned that the source of the girl's words was not the Holy Spirit but rather an evil spirit.

In Acts 14 we see an opposite example, where Paul discerns the work of the Holy Spirit (rather than the work of an evil spirit). Looking intently at a man crippled from birth who was listening to him speak, Paul saw "that he had faith to be made well" (Acts 14:9). Thus, the discerning of spirits does not

---

20. Hathaway, *Spiritual Gifts,* 38.
21. Walker, "Baptism, Gifts and Fruit of the Spirit," 258.
22. Arrington, *Christian Doctrine*, 3:150.
23. Arrington, *Christian Doctrine*, 3:150.
24. Donald Gee, *Concerning Spiritual Gifts*, rev. ed. (Springfield, MO: Gospel Publishing House, 1980), 71.
25. For a Pentecostal interpretation of the work of Satan in the lie of Ananias and Sapphira, see Stanley M. Horton, *Acts: A Logion Press Commentary* (Springfield, MO: Logion, 2001), 117–18.

only involve the recognition of what comes from evil spirits or the human spirit, but also when the Spirit of God is at work.

Summary

The gift of faith is included among these gifts that the Holy Spirit distributes to various members of the body of Christ. Therefore, it cannot be the same as saving faith, which all Christ's people possess. Rather, this is a special intensification of faith in a particular circumstance. The working of miracles involves supernatural signs that point to the Lord and make his presence, power, and compassion known. The gift of the discerning of spirits is an insight given by the Holy Spirit into whether he is the source of particular words or actions, or whether they find their source instead in another spirit.

REFLECTION QUESTIONS

1. How does the gift of faith differ from saving faith?

2. How might the gift of faith benefit the church?

3. In what ways are miracles signs? What do these signs point to?

4. Why does the church need the gift of discerning spirits?

5. Why do believers not need to fear evil spirits?

QUESTION 26

What Is Speaking in Tongues?

In the early years of the movement, Pentecostals were often castigated by other Christians and disfellowshipped because they spoke in tongues. Yet today this is a widespread Christian practice far beyond classical Pentecostalism; even the Archbishop of Canterbury can publicly state, "I pray in tongues every day."[1] In this chapter we will give our attention to the nature and purpose of speaking in tongues, and its place (along with interpretation) among the gifts of the Holy Spirit.

The Nature of Speaking in Tongues

The word "tongues" is not a particularly helpful one, yet it has become fossilized in many English translations of the Bible. Literally, it is simply the gift of "languages."[2] We can see this quite clearly on the day of Pentecost in Acts 2: the disciples spoke in *tongues* and the crowds heard them in their own *languages* (Acts 2:4–6). The crowds were "amazed and astonished" (v. 7) because the Galileans they heard speaking should not have been able to speak these languages. The point, of course, is that they could not; they were speaking "in other tongues as the Spirit gave them utterance" (v. 4). This is supernatural speech enabled by the Holy Spirit. Thus, speaking in tongues means speaking a language, which one has never studied or learned, by the Holy Spirit's enablement.[3] As David Petts puts it: "Tongues are *natural*

1. "Archbishop Justin Welby Prays 'in Tongues' Every Day," BBC News, January 21, 2019, https://www.bbc.co.uk/news/uk-46945022.
2. "Tongue" is simply an older English word for "language." (French, for example, uses the word *langue* for both tongue and language.)
3. Through the years Pentecostals have recounted many testimonies of occasions where a speaker of the language spoken in tongues happened to be present and could not only identify the tongue, but confirm the interpretation. For a collection of documented accounts, see Ralph W. Harris, *Spoken by the Spirit: Documented Accounts of "Other Tongues" From Arabic to Zulu* (Springfield, MO: Gospel Publishing House, 1973).

languages *supernaturally* spoken."[4] The gift of tongues is one of the supernatural gifts of the Holy Spirit.

Scripture does not indicate that speaking in tongues involves any sort of ecstatic state. Those who speak in tongues are expected to have a sufficient degree of control over themselves while they are speaking in tongues. Paul, for example, gives instructions concerning how many people can speak in tongues in the same meeting (1 Cor. 14:27) and indicates times when someone should remain silent and refrain from speaking in tongues (1 Cor. 14:28).

The Purpose of Speaking in Tongues

The Bible shows us at least three purposes for speaking in tongues: two for tongues by themselves, and one for tongues accompanied by interpretation.[5]

Prayer

Paul writes to the Corinthians that "one who speaks in a tongue speaks not to men but to God; for no one understands him" (1 Cor. 14:2; cf. v. 28). Speaking to God is prayer; therefore, tongues that are not understood by anyone else (in other words, tongues without an interpretation) are a form of prayer. Paul explicitly calls this prayer later in the chapter: "For if I pray in a tongue, my spirit prays but my mind is unfruitful. What am I to do? I will pray with my spirit, but I will pray with my mind also; I will sing praise with my spirit, but I will sing with my mind also" (1 Cor. 14:14–15). Paul does not forbid this form of prayer that is beyond the mind; rather, he encourages both this prayer "in a tongue . . . with my spirit" and prayer "with my mind." Both are valid types of prayer. Both were types of prayer practiced by the apostle Paul himself (as is further confirmed by v. 18). Both are ways of speaking to God. And just as prayer with the understanding should never be forbidden, Paul warns the Corinthians that they must "not forbid speaking in tongues" (1 Cor. 14:39).

Pentecostals have often drawn a connection between praying in tongues and Paul's teaching on the intercession of the Holy Spirit—citing his words to the Romans: "Likewise the Spirit helps us in our weakness. For we do not know what to pray for as we ought, but the Spirit himself intercedes for us with groanings too deep for words. And he who searches hearts knows what is the mind of the Spirit, because the Spirit intercedes for the saints according to the will of God" (Rom. 8:26–27). The early British Pentecostal leader D. P. Williams saw this as an aspect of Christ's heavenly ministry of intercession. Our ascended Great High Priest has poured out his Spirit in the hearts of his

---

4. David Petts, *Body Builders: Gifts to Make God's People Grow* (Mattersey: Mattersey Hall, 2002), 118.
5. A fourth purpose could be added, of tongues as a sign for unbelievers (1 Cor. 14:22). However, space prevents a detailed consideration of this theme.

people so that the Holy Spirit will intercede within them, joining in Christ's heavenly work of interceding. "He [God] hears the Son interceding for us, so He always hears the Spirit in us, because His intercession is according to the will of God. The Holy Spirit's intercession is always effectual. . . . The deep secret and purpose of the intercession of the Holy Ghost in the sanctuary of the believer's heart is so wonderful that it failed the Apostle to express it in words, but that the groanings could not be uttered. And that in the tongues He speaketh secret truths unto God."[6]

The groanings too deep for words of Romans 8:26 and the mysteries uttered in the Spirit by whoever speaks to God in tongues in 1 Corinthians 14:2 are brought together here in Williams's teaching as a deep intercession that finds its origin in the Holy Spirit's work in our hearts. It cannot be expressed with our understanding. Therefore, Paul's contrast between prayer "in a tongue . . . with my spirit" and prayer "with my mind" is not a contrast between a light emotionalism and deep, serious prayer. Rather, prayer "in a tongue . . . with my spirit" can in reality be deep and serious intercession—too deep and serious to be expressed in words we understand.

This prayer in tongues can also be a form of intimate communion with God.[7] Communion with God flows out into edification, and so prayer in tongues is also a way of edifying oneself in the Lord. As Paul writes, "The one who speaks in a tongue builds up himself" (1 Cor. 14:4).

Praise

When Christians speak to God in tongues, they utter "mysteries in the Spirit" (1 Cor. 14:2). While these mysteries may include deep groanings of intercession too mysterious for comprehensible words, they also include giving thanks (1 Cor. 14:16–17), declaring "the mighty works of God (Acts 2:11), and "extolling God" (Acts 10:46). Thus, through prayer in tongues, the Lord is glorified and praised. Tongues, then, can be a form of worship and adoration.

Such adoring praise in tongues is a form of intimate fellowship with the Lord. Believers are not simply proclaiming God's glory from afar. Rather, they must draw near; for it is the Holy Spirit who is at work in speaking in tongues, and it is only "in the Spirit" that these "mysteries" are spoken. Therefore, this adoring prayer in tongues cannot take place apart from communion with God. D. P. Williams taught that the fullness of the Holy Spirit enabled believers to recognize "and esteem the greatness, the authority and holiness of God, that they were exalting" through prayer in tongues, "thus causing humility and reverence, and in having such fellowship they were edified and nourished in

6. D. P. Williams, *The Gift of Tongues* (Penygroes: Apostolic Church, 1917), 6–7.
7. For some examples of this from early Pentecostal writers, see Randal H. Ackland, *Toward a Pentecostal Theology of Glossolalia* (Cleveland, TN: CPT, 2020), 166, 203, 232–33, 257–58, 318–19.

their spirits, giving them gracious affections."[8] Through this close fellowship with the Lord by the Spirit, expressed and experienced in prayer of worship in tongues, believers are humbled before their God, grow in humility, and are thus built up and nourished in the Lord. We edify ourselves as we pray in tongues—not because it is an activity focused on us, but because the focus is upon our glorious God, whom in mystery we extol.

Proclamation: The Gift of Tongues for Interpretation

Yet in tongues, the wonderful works of God are not only proclaimed in a mystery to God in praise but also to other human beings (Acts 2:11). While on the day of Pentecost this took place in a unique way through the presence of speakers of multiple languages in the city for the feast, the normal way this takes place is through the twin gifts of tongues and interpretation.

The Need for Interpretation and Biblical Regulation

The gift of the interpretation of tongues is "the power given to an individual by the Holy Spirit to translate into the current language spoken in the church, the words or the general meaning of whatever has been spoken aloud in the congregation through the gift of tongues."[9] Tongues *must* be interpreted in the church. This is a strict biblical rule, because everything that is done in the church must "be done for building up" (1 Cor. 14:26). Uninterpreted tongues are not intelligible and so they cannot build anyone else up (1 Cor. 14:6).[10] Daniel Walker, a Ghanaian Pentecostal theologian, writes, "The gift of tongues is unfruitful if not interpreted. It is the interpretation that comes to reveal the mind of God and edifies the church."[11] Without interpretation, public speaking in tongues brings confusion instead of building up (1 Cor. 14:23). Therefore, tongues must not be spoken out loud publicly unless accompanied by an interpretation (1 Cor. 14:27–28). Even with interpretation, speaking in tongues is to be limited to two or three people, and they must not speak at the same time but each in turn. "If any speak in a tongue, let there be only two or at most three, and each in turn, and let someone interpret" (1 Cor. 14:27).

However, there are occasions in Scripture where groups of people speak in tongues at the same time in public and without any interpretation (Acts 2:4, 11; 10:46; 19:6). Yet, each of these instances is associated with a group of people being baptized in the Holy Spirit. None of these is a description of

---

8. Williams, *Tongues*, 5.
9. Michele Strazzeri, *The Gifts of the Holy Spirit*, trans. Giuseppe Guarino (Catania, Italy: Guarino, 2018), 74.
10. However, as noted above, private uninterpreted tongues can build up the speaker (1 Cor. 14:4).
11. Daniel O. Walker, "Baptism, Gifts and Fruit of the Spirit," in *Tenets of the Church of Pentecost*, ed. Opoku Onyinah (Accra, Ghana: Church of Pentecost, 2019), 270.

the regular worship of the church. The Lord can and will fill groups of people with the Spirit all at the same time, accompanied by the sign of speaking in tongues. However, in regular public worship we have a responsibility to follow Scripture's clear instructions for the use of the gifts of the Holy Spirit to ensure that everything is "done decently and in order" (1 Cor. 14:40). The use of these gifts in church must be strictly in accordance with the rules laid down in Scripture.[12] "There are times when it is not proper to use the gift, because everything has to take place in order."[13]

Are Tongues and Interpretation the Equivalent of Prophecy?

Pentecostals commonly regard tongues accompanied by interpretation as the equivalent of prophecy.[14] However, some charismatic writers have argued that this is not the case, for tongues (and thus the interpretation of tongues) should always be directed to God rather than to human beings. Sam Storms contends that the content of tongues is always "prayer, praise, and thanksgiving." Therefore, "what we are hearing when someone speaks in tongues in a public setting is either their intercessory prayers or their worship of God."[15] Any interpretation of tongues should likewise be directed toward God as prayer or worship. If such were the case, any interpretation directed toward human beings has "not been properly interpreted."[16] Rather, the interpretation "will come forth in the form of prayers, praise, and expression of gratitude to God. The interpretation will be a *God-ward* utterance, no less than the tongues utterance on which it is based."[17] While Storms is not quite willing to argue that it is impossible for a true interpretation to be directed as a message toward people, he does maintain that "if it happens, it does so without explicit biblical sanction."[18]

Storms raises an important point. Certainly, 1 Corinthians 14:2 tells us that the "one who speaks in a tongue speaks not to men but to God." However,

---

12. For strong emphasis on this point from Pentecostals, see Strazzeri, *Gifts*, 78; Walker, "Baptism, Gifts and Fruit," 270; French L. Arrington, *Christian Doctrine: A Pentecostal Perspective* (Cleveland, TN: Pathway, 1994), 3:154; Guy P. Duffield and Nathaniel M. Van Cleave, *Foundations of Pentecostal Theology* (Los Angeles: Foursquare Media, 2008), 346; W. G. Hathaway, *Spiritual Gifts in the Church* (London: Elim, 1933), 84–88; and David T. Rennie, *The Gifts of the Holy Spirit* (Bradford: Puritan Press, 1967), 110–11, 116–17; *Introducing the Apostolic Church: A Manual of Belief, Practice & History* (Penygroes: Apostolic Church, 1988), 159.
13. Strazzeri, *Gifts*, 79.
14. Myer Pearlman, *Knowing the Doctrines of the Bible* (Springfield, MO: Gospel Publishing House, 1937), 327; Walker, "Baptism, Gifts and Fruit," 270; Strazzeri, *Gifts*, 71.
15. Sam Storms, *The Language of Heaven: Crucial Questions About Speaking in Tongues* (Lake Mary, FL: Charisma House, 2019), 95.
16. Storms, *Language of Heaven*, 96.
17. Sam Storms, *Understanding Spiritual Gifts: A Comprehensive Guide* (Grand Rapids: Zondervan, 2020), 238.
18. Storms, *Language of Heaven*, 96.

the context here is not the content of tongues speech but the fact that human beings cannot understand what is said in tongues unless it is interpreted. The verse continues by specifying that the reason the "one who speaks in a tongue speaks not to men but to God" is that "no one understands him." First Corinthians 14:2, then, is insufficient as a basis for determining whether tongues *with interpretation* are directed to God or to the congregation. First Corinthians 14:16 does demonstrate that tongues can be a form of thanksgiving but it does not limit tongues to thanksgiving or another form of prayer directed toward God.

Where 1 Corinthians 14:2 refers to the content of tongues, it says that the one who speaks in tongues "utters mysteries in the Spirit." While again this could be a reference to the unintelligibility of uninterpreted tongues, the use of the term "mystery" could also indicate that tongues have a proclamatory function. French Arrington looks to the biblical usage of the term "mystery" to suggest that these "hidden truths spoken in tongues may have to do with God's redemptive plan and blessings and involve a fresh application of these truths in the form of exhortation and comfort."[19]

Cornelius and his household were heard "speaking in tongues and extolling God" (Acts 10:46). This may suggest tongues directed toward God in praise, or it may suggest that they were both speaking in tongues and extolling God. Either way, this event does not provide a conclusive case to limit tongues to speech directed toward God. In Acts 2:11 the newly Spirit-baptized believers on the day of Pentecost were "telling in . . . tongues the mighty works of God." We are not told whether this "telling" was directed to the crowds or directed to God and heard by the crowds. The descriptions of tongues in Acts and 1 Corinthians simply do not tell us enough to be able to say that tongues are always directed toward God and never directed to human beings. Some of the examples, particularly on the day of Pentecost, may be examples of tongues directed toward human beings.

Furthermore, Robert Menzies argues that Paul's instructions concerning the interpretation of tongues in 1 Corinthians 14 point to a parallel between interpreted tongues and prophecy. Both interpreted tongues and prophecy are given for "mutual edification."[20] As a counterbalance to the view of 1 Corinthians 14:2, which would limit tongues to speech to God, Menzies points to 1 Corinthians 14:28, where we read, "If there is no one to interpret, let each of them keep silent in church and speak to himself and to God." Menzies argues, "Paul's intent here is not to define the content of the message in tongues," for the content could not be both God-ward and human-ward. Rather, this verse makes clear that Paul's purpose in 1 Corinthians 14:2 is

19. Arrington, *Christian Doctrine*, 3:159.
20. Robert Menzies, *Speaking in Tongues: Jesus and the Apostolic Church as Models for the Church Today* (Cleveland, TN: CPT, 2016), 147.

likewise "to highlight the unintelligibility of tongues (and hence the need for interpretation) rather than its content."[21]

Menzies also argues that Acts 2:11 is more clearly directed toward humans than we might first have thought. The expression "the mighty works of God" is typically used in the LXX (the Greek translation of the Old Testament used by the early church) in connection "with verbs of proclamation and, as such, is addressed to people."[22] Menzies also turns to Acts 19:6 for support, where "tongues are paired with prophecy."[23] Finally, Menzies argues that the "spiritual songs" of Colossians 3:16 are a form of singing in tongues, and thus tongues and interpretation are a way of "teaching and admonishing one another in all wisdom."[24]

The Bible does clearly give us examples of tongues directed toward God. However, we have enough evidence in Scripture to "suggest that we should not be too quick to assume that all forms of tongues speech must be addressed to God."[25] Thus, the classical Pentecostal position that tongues, when accompanied by interpretation, can function similarly to prophecy would appear to have sufficient biblical support. As Menzies puts it, "Paul declares that speaking in tongues, when exercised in concert with the gift of interpretation, can be the vehicle through which the Holy Spirit speaks to the larger church body."[26] Therefore, most classical Pentecostals are content to see two different kinds of interpretation of tongues: either an interpretation in the form of prayer or an interpretation in the form of "a message from God to the church."[27]

Summary

In Scripture, we see speaking in tongues as a way in which the Lord enables believers to pray and praise him when they are alone, and through which they can build themselves up in him (1 Cor. 14:4). Yet we also see a public role for tongues—a gift of praise and proclamation—when accompanied by the gift of interpretation. The Bible gives very clear instructions about how these gifts are to be used, which must always be followed.

REFLECTION QUESTIONS

1. Does speaking in tongues involve an ecstatic state or loss of control?

---

21. Menzies, *Speaking in Tongues*, 149.
22. Menzies, *Speaking in Tongues*, 149.
23. Menzies, *Speaking in Tongues*, 150.
24. Menzies, *Speaking in Tongues*, 150.
25. Menzies, *Speaking in Tongues*, 150.
26. Menzies, *Speaking in Tongues*, 146.
27. Strazzeri, *Gifts*, 74.

2. In what ways can a believer build himself up through speaking in tongues (1 Cor. 14:4)?

3. Is praying in tongues a less serious type of prayer?

4. What instructions does the Bible give for how the gifts of tongues and interpretation of tongues should be used?

5. Should tongues and interpretation always be addressed toward God, or can a message in tongues and interpretation be directed to the congregation?

QUESTION 27

What Is Prophecy? (Part 1)

Prophecy is a very familiar concept for Christians because there is a great deal of prophecy in the Bible. But how does the gift of prophecy relate to biblical prophecy? Is the gift of prophecy the same thing as Old Testament prophecy? Pentecostals neither argue for an exact correspondence nor a complete difference. There are very significant differences between the gift of prophecy and Old Testament prophecy and also some very significant continuities.

The major difference is that the gift of prophecy is not to be equated with Scripture. The prophecies of the Old Testament prophetic books are Scripture, and therefore they are authoritative for us all for all time. When a person exercises the gift of prophecy, however, what is said is not to be understood as Scripture. A prophecy given in a local church on a Sunday morning is not added to the Bible. Rather, prophetic words given by those with the gift of prophecy must come under the authority of Scripture—that is, they must be tested by Scripture. The declaration of faith of the Brazilian Assemblies of God explains this significant difference:

> The gift of prophecy is different from the prophecy announced by the Old Testament prophets. Canonical revelation is now closed, but God continues to speak through the Bible. The Lord has provided other resources through which to communicate with human beings, among them the gift of prophecy, as a momentary manifestation of the Holy Spirit in the life of any believer baptized with the Holy Spirit. Its objective is "edification, exhortation, and comfort" (1 Cor. 14:3). Through this gift, the Lord continues to communicate with his servants individually, but the prophecy resulting from this gift does not serve as a source of authority like that of the biblical prophets and apostles, because it is possible

> for someone to amplify the message without authorization of the Spirit, even being subject to judgment: "Let two or three prophets speak, and the others judge" (1 Cor. 14:29).[1]

The canon of Scripture is closed and Scripture alone is our supreme authority. Prophecy, unlike Scripture, must be tested, judged, and only accepted if it is in accord with Scripture. (We will look at testing prophecy in question 29.)

However, if the gift of prophecy is different from Old Testament prophecy in this way, does that mean that it is a totally new phenomenon? Let's turn to the teaching on prophecy in 1 Corinthians 14 and the examples of New Testament prophecy in the book of Acts to examine the nature of the gift.

Prophecy in 1 Corinthians 14

Paul gives detailed instructions for the use of the gift of prophecy in the church in 1 Corinthians 14, a passage from which we can learn much about the nature of the gift. The first thing Paul here draws our attention to is that prophecy is a gift that should be eagerly desired: "Pursue love, and earnestly desire the spiritual gifts, especially that you may prophesy" (1 Cor. 14:1). Likewise, the chapter concludes with a reminder that we are to "earnestly desire to prophesy" (1 Cor. 14:39). Not only are Christians encouraged to desire the gifts of the Holy Spirit, but prophecy is specifically singled out as a gift that we should especially desire. But the fact that we are encouraged to desire this gift reminds us that it is a gift; believers cannot prophesy from their own ability. It is not a natural talent or a skill that we can develop but a gracious gift of the Lord to his church by his Spirit. Therefore, we can desire and pray for this gift, but we cannot learn to prophesy as if it were a natural ability. This points us once again to the supernatural nature of the gift.

The purpose of this gift is also clearly revealed. Prophecy is not a private spiritual experience; it is not for building up oneself but for building up others. Unlike speaking in tongues, which can at times be used for personal spiritual edification, prophecy is always for others "so that the church may be built up" (1 Cor. 14:5). This also means that prophecy is to have an ongoing effect. It is not simply an experience of the Holy Spirit's presence in the moment, but rather through prophecy the Holy Spirit is at work in a transformative way so that "the one who prophesies speaks to people for their upbuilding and encouragement and consolation" (1 Cor. 14:3).

In order to bring upbuilding, encouragement, and consolation to others, the person who prophesies must speak (1 Cor. 14:3). Prophecy cannot consist merely of receiving a revelation from God, for if it is kept to oneself others will not be built up, encouraged, and edified, and thus the purpose of prophecy will not be fulfilled. Therefore, prophecy necessarily involves

---

1. Brazil DdF, 20.5.

communication. Yet this speaking that builds up, encourages, and consoles others does not come from our own ability or knowledge; rather, those who prophesy speak things that they do not (or even cannot) know by human knowledge. First Corinthians 14:25 tells us that prophecy can disclose the secrets of someone's heart, causing people to recognize the presence of God. So prophecy can speak to situations that have not been shared, situations about which only the all-knowing God knows and the person prophesying could never know anything about. That is because the source of this knowledge is God himself. Paul describes this aspect of prophecy as "a revelation" (1 Cor. 14:30). In prophecy the Lord, by the Holy Spirit, reveals some knowledge to someone who speaks it out for the edification, exhortation, and comfort of the church.

Finally, prophecy is not an uncontrolled, ecstatic behavior. The person who prophesies knows what they are doing and is in control of their actions. They can stop speaking if someone else has a prophecy (1 Cor. 14:30), for "the spirits of prophets are subject to prophets" (1 Cor. 14:32).

Prophecy in Acts

In the book of Acts, we see examples of gifts involving revelation in the life of the early church. Some of these are called prophecy or said to be spoken by a prophet. Others are not, and yet among them we can see examples that display the features of prophecy we find in 1 Corinthians 14. We will not look at every example of prophecy (or other revelatory gifts) in Acts here but focus on a few examples.

One example of this is seen when the Lord sends Ananias to speak to Saul after his encounter with Christ on the road to Damascus. We can see the features of prophecy in this event, particularly in Acts 9:10–18 and 22:12–16. First, the Lord speaks to Ananias, telling him where Saul is and directing him to go to him and lay hands on him for the restoration of his sight (Acts 9:11–12). The Lord then says to Ananias that Saul is "a chosen instrument of mine to carry my name before the Gentiles and kings and the children of Israel. For I will show him how much he must suffer for the sake of my name" (Acts 9:15–16). Then, when Ananias gets to the house where Saul is staying, he speaks to Saul on behalf of the Lord: "Brother Saul, the Lord Jesus who appeared to you on the road by which you came has sent me so that you may regain your sight and be filled with the Holy Spirit" (Acts 9:17). Further, in Paul's recollection of the event, Ananias's prophecy continues: "The God of our fathers appointed you to know his will, to see the Righteous One and to hear a voice from his mouth; for you will be a witness for him to everyone of what you have seen and heard. And now why do you wait? Rise and be baptized and wash away your sins, calling on his name" (Acts 22:14–16). What is very clear in this account is that there are two parts to what happens: first, the Lord reveals where Saul is and his purpose for Saul to Ananias, then Ananias speaks out of this revelation to Saul on the Lord's behalf. Both parts were necessary.

Although the Bible does not explicitly use the word "prophecy" here, these two parts (revelation and speech) correspond to what we learn about prophecy in 1 Corinthians 14. This account also makes explicit something that is not clear in 1 Corinthians: that the revelation and the speaking do not always need to happen at the same time. In 1 Corinthians 14:30 we see that prophetic revelation and speech can occur spontaneously in a church service so that revelation and speech occur together. Yet, the example of Ananias shows us that, like Old Testament prophecy, this simultaneity need not always be the case. Prophecy can either be spoken spontaneously as it is revealed, or it can be revealed in advance to be spoken later. (This is often spoken of by Pentecostals as "carrying a prophecy.") Thomas Turnbull, a Pentecostal prophet from the first generation, wrote of times when "the revelation is made to the prophet beforehand [who] is then charged with the responsibility of delivering his message at the appropriate time and place. God gives the message and directs the prophet as to where and when it must be delivered. The prophet is in the hands of God to speak words as God desires."[2] Turnbull points to the examples of Jeremiah (20:9) and Jonah, where "a prophet carried the word of the Lord for many days before it was uttered."[3] Ananias is a New Testament example of this.

Another significant prophetic figure in the book of Acts is the prophet Agabus. We first encounter him in Acts 11, when he comes down from Jerusalem to Antioch with some other prophets and prophesies a great famine that would take place during the reign of the Emperor Claudius (Acts 11:28). Three things are particularly noteworthy here. First, Agabus is specifically called a "prophet," yet the actual words of his prophecy are not included in the Bible. This makes very clear that prophecy, and even the prophecy of a prophet, is not to be equated to Scripture. The words of another prophecy by Agabus are recorded in Acts 21:11; however, even there they are included as an historical account of what the prophet said, rather than directly as Scripture themselves. In other words, they are Scripture insomuch as they have been included in the historical narrative of Acts, but the prophet Agabus did not write them down as Scripture. The prophecies of Agabus were not collected into an additional New Testament book.

Second, the believers in Antioch determine what they are going to do in response to what Agabus has prophesied (Acts 11:29–30). The prophecy did

2. T. N. Turnbull, *Prophecy in the Church Age* (Bradford: Puritan Press, 1971), 45.
3. Turnbull, *Prophecy*, 45. Thomas Schreiner, although a cessationist, agrees that this is true of prophecy in the Bible. "The prophet may not communicate immediately what God has revealed, but the revelation itself is spontaneous." See Schreiner, *Spiritual Gifts: What They Are and Why They Matter* (Nashville: B&H, 2018), 97.

not remove the need for godly wisdom and scriptural reasoning. Third, this is an example of the ministry of a prophet rather than the gift of prophecy. Therefore, although it is still prophecy (and so involves both revelation and Spirit-enabled speech), its scope is wider than upbuilding, encouragement, and consolation. Thus, although Agabus foretells a future famine, we should not assume that the gift of prophecy is for foretelling future events.[4] When we encounter Agabus again in Acts 21:10–11, some of his prophetic words are recorded. Here we see that he delivers his prophecy in the first person (much like Old Testament prophets). Paul, however, was free to decide what to do on the basis of the prophecy brought by Agabus (Acts 21:12–13).

Summary

In prophecy, the Lord speaks through a believer for the edification, exhortation, and comfort of the church. However, we must not confuse prophecy with Scripture. In Scripture, God has spoken to all people everywhere for all time. In prophecy, he speaks to specific people for a specific moment.

REFLECTION QUESTIONS

1. In what ways is the gift of prophecy different from Old Testament prophecy, and in what ways is it the same?
2. What is the purpose of the gift of prophecy?
3. Is prophecy an ecstatic experience?
4. What can we learn about prophecy from the example of Ananias?
5. What can we learn about prophecy from the example of Agabus?

---

4. For Pentecostal distinctions between the gift of prophecy and the ministry of the prophet, see David Petts, *Body Builders: Gifts to Make God's People Grow* (Mattersey: Mattersey Hall, 2002), 46–47; and D. P. Williams, *The Prophetical Ministry in the Church* (Penygroes: Apostolic Church, 1931), 23. For Pentecostal warnings against conflating prophecy with foretelling of future events, see Petts, *Body Builders*, 137–39.

QUESTION 28

What Is Prophecy? (Part 2)

Now that we have examined prophecy in 1 Corinthians and Acts, let's consider how classical Pentecostals have understood this gift. We will also look at a recent challenge to the traditional Pentecostal understanding.

Classical Pentecostals and Prophecy

Classical Pentecostals emphasize the supernatural nature of prophecy on both sides: the revelation given by the Holy Spirit and the speaking out of that revelation enabled by the Holy Spirit. Early Pentecostals were quite consistent in their definitions of prophecy. D. P. Williams of the Apostolic Church defined prophecy as "a Divinely generated utterance through human lips by the indwelling Spirit of God."[1] More recent classical Pentecostals have continued to understand the gift in the same way. French Arrington defines it as "an inspired utterance given by the Holy Spirit."[2] It is "a word of revelation from God . . . a Spirit-inspired word for a situation or an occasion."[3] British Assemblies of God theologian David Petts defines prophecy as "speaking to people on behalf of God by the inspiration of the Holy Spirit for the strengthening, encouragement, comfort and edification of the church."[4]

Both the revelation and the speech are the work of the Holy Spirit, and therefore prophecy is an "inspired word, a revelation given to be delivered in the words in which it has been received. . . . The believer through whom

---

1. D. P. Williams, *The Prophetical Ministry in the Church* (Penygroes: Apostolic Church, 1931), 7; cf. W. G. Hathaway, *Spiritual Gifts in the Church* (London: Elim, 1933), 54; and Harold Horton, *The Gifts of the Spirit*, 3rd ed. (Luton: Assemblies of God, 1949), 174.
2. French L. Arrington, *Christian Doctrine: A Pentecostal Perspective* (Cleveland, TN: Pathway Press, 1994), 3:142.
3. Arrington, *Christian Doctrine*, 3:142.
4. David Petts, *Body Builders: Gifts to Make God's People Grow* (Mattersey: Mattersey Hall, 2002), 137.

this gift works speaks forth words given by the Holy Spirit."[5] The words used in prophecy are not just a human attempt to report the revelation, but are themselves part of the prophecy. Ralph Riggs, former general superintendent of the American Assemblies of God, drew on 1 Peter 4:11 to argue that those who prophesy "speak the very words of God, serve as an expression of the very mind of God."[6]

Often, the revelation and the speaking out of the words occur together spontaneously, as we see in 1 Corinthians 14:30. Thus the speaking of the words often is itself the means of the revelation in prophecy. "Spontaneous prophecy," Thomas Turnbull writes, "is given as it is being revealed. This is generally the case with those who have the gift of prophecy, and it is often so with the prophets."[7]

If the words of prophecy themselves are part of the Holy Spirit's work in prophecy, then the question arises whether prophecy should be spoken in the first person or accompanied by "thus says the Lord"? Some early Pentecostals, like Harold Horton, are rather cautious about this. Horton worries that this was "flinging back responsibility upon the Lord which He has already placed upon the prophet." He goes on to appeal, "Let the prophet take responsibility in the scriptural way for his own utterances, and let him frame them—not as speaking *in the place* of the Lord, but as speaking *about* the Lord."[8] A significant concern here is that some people might not properly test prophecies if they hear them in this way.

Yet, many other Pentecostals take the opposite view: that prophecy *should* be spoken in the first person. Thomas Turnbull, an ordained prophet in the Apostolic Church, writes, "Every time the prophet speaks as such he must be able to preface his message with the words, 'Thus saith the Lord.'"[9] This is not about the style of words, but the theological nature of what prophecy actually is, for if the words are not what the Lord is saying, the speaker should be making no claim to prophecy. Prophecy does not have to use the words "thus says the Lord," but if it cannot it is in danger of taking the name of the Lord in vain.[10]

Myer Pearlman, in his internationally influential book of Pentecostal doctrine, suggests that both first-person (i.e., "Thus says the Lord. . . ") and

---

5. Arrington, *Christian Doctrine*, 3:142.
6. Ralph M. Riggs, *The Spirit Himself* (Springfield, MO: Gospel Publishing House, 1949), 152–53. Riggs is careful to distinguish between Scripture and prophecy (pp. 157–60).
7. T. N. Turnbull, *Prophecy in the Church Age* (Bradford: Puritan Press, 1971), 44–45.
8. Horton, *Gifts*, 190.
9. Turnbull, *Prophecy*, 44.
10. This isn't to argue for a proliferation of first-person prophecy, but for much more care and attention. Turnbull would not at all be in favor of expressions such as "I just feel as if the Lord might be saying." Either the Lord is speaking or he is not, and if he is not, it is a very serious and dangerous thing to suggest that he might be. The gift of prophecy is not to be taken lightly. Yet no matter how it is worded, it must always still be tested.

third-person (i.e., speaking about the Lord) prophecies should be found in the church, depending on the way the Holy Spirit works to inspire the believer to speak. Therefore, sometimes prophecy may come in the form of "I, the Lord, say to you," and at other times in the form of "The Lord would have his people know."[11] Both have scriptural precedent (Acts 9:17; 21:11). Both also meet Turnbull's test.

Charismatic Redefinitions of Prophecy: Wayne Grudem and Sam Storms

The classical Pentecostal understanding of prophecy has been eclipsed in the wider Christian world today by the popularity of a new understanding among many charismatics, taught in very popular books by authors such as Wayne Grudem and Sam Storms. Storms defines prophecy as "the human report of a divine revelation."[12] Grudem specifies that prophecy is "speaking merely human words to report something God brings to mind."[13]

To reach this definition, Grudem argues that there is much more difference between Old Testament prophecy and New Testament prophecy. "Old Testament prophets had an amazing responsibility—they were able to speak and write words that had absolute divine authority."[14] However, Grudem argues, in the New Testament it is the apostles, not the prophets, who have this ability. Therefore, he writes, "The apostles are the New Testament counterpart to the Old Testament prophets," and so "prophet" must have a different meaning in the New Testament.[15] Hence he insists, "It generally did not have the sense 'one who speaks God's very words' but rather 'one who speaks on the basis of some external influence,'" and so "the terms prophet and prophecy did not imply divine authority for their speech or writing."[16] Instead, Grudem argues, these terms apply to "ordinary Christians who spoke not with absolute divine authority but simply to report something that God had laid on their hearts or brought to their minds."[17] Therefore, "prophecies in the church today should be considered merely human words, not God's words."[18] Grudem still has room for the revelation aspect of prophecy, but for him the Holy Spirit's work is only in the revelation, which is never verbal. The Spirit does not give

---

11. Myer Pearlman, *Knowing the Doctrines of the Bible* (Springfield, MO: Gospel Publishing House, 1937), 325–26.
12. Sam Storms, *Understanding Spiritual Gifts: A Comprehensive Guide* (Grand Rapids: Zondervan, 2020), 162.
13. Wayne Grudem, *The Gift of Prophecy in the New Testament and Today*, 3rd ed. (Eastbourne: Kingsway, 2000), 51, 71.
14. Wayne Grudem, *Systematic Theology: An Introduction to Biblical Doctrine*, 2nd ed. (London: InterVarsity Press, 2020), 1294.
15. Grudem, *Systematic Theology*, 1294.
16. Grudem, *Systematic Theology*, 1294–95.
17. Grudem, *Systematic Theology*, 1296.
18. Grudem, *Systematic Theology*, 1303.

words to speak, and so the prophecy may be misinterpreted or misreported by the one who receives it.

As a result, Grudem argues that prophecy can never be given in the first-person or accompanied by "thus says the Lord" because in his understanding it consists merely of human words. Instead, he suggests saying, "I think the Lord is putting on my mind that. . ." or, "It seems to me that the Lord is showing us. . . ."[19] There can be no confident proclamation of the prophetic word with Grudem's definitions.

Grudem's understanding of prophecy is very influential among charismatics; however, it is incompatible with the classical Pentecostal understanding of the nine gifts of 1 Corinthians 12 as entirely supernatural. Although early Pentecostals were not all in complete agreement with regard to the style in which a prophecy should be delivered, they agreed that the speaking, just as much as the revelation, was a supernatural work of the Holy Spirit.

But is Grudem's position more biblical than the classical Pentecostal position? Grudem puts forward three main scriptural arguments for his understanding. First, in Acts 21:4 we read that various believers "through the Spirit . . . were telling Paul not to go on to Jerusalem." Yet Paul did go on to Jerusalem. Grudem argues that Paul disobeyed this, and "he never would have done this if this prophecy contained God's very words."[20] However, we do not know the actual words of these prophecies for they are not recorded in Scripture. Thus, we may well have here something similar to what happens a few verses later, where Agabus prophesies and then the other believers make a (wrong) inference on the basis of the prophecy (Acts 21:11–12). If that is so, then the other believers were not prophesying, but they were responding to the Spirit's work in the prophecy. Thus, they were speaking as a result of the Spirit's speaking—speaking flowing from the Spirit's activity, even though they were not prophesying and were wrong in their interpretation of the prophetic word. In that sense, they were indeed speaking *dia tou pneumatos* ("through the Spirit") yet not speaking prophecy under the Spirit's inspiration.[21] As Thomas Schreiner argues, "The prophecy that Paul would face suffering in Jerusalem was accurate and Spirit-inspired; the conclusion that people drew from the prophecy—that Paul should not travel to Jerusalem—was mistaken."[22] Craig Keener likewise concludes that "most scholars recognize that 'through the Spirit,' while suggesting that prophetic speech is involved, is ambiguous in attributing the advice itself to the Spirit. The warning not to go is the Tyrian disciples' application

19. Grudem, *Systematic Theology*, 1304.
20. Grudem, *Systematic Theology*, 1296.
21. Note the footnote to this verse in the New American Standard Version: "i.e., because of impressions made by the Spirit." While I would say "because of prophecies" rather than "impressions," my point is the same.
22. Thomas Schreiner, *Spiritual Gifts: What They Are and Why They Matter* (Nashville: B&H, 2018), 117.

rather than the Spirit's self-contradiction."[23] Rather, this prophecy should be read in light of the fuller pattern revealed later in the chapter with the prophet Agabus. "The Tyrian disciples' warning to Paul not to go is based on the Spirit's revelation of what he will suffer (cf. 20:23; 21:11); it is not the offering of a direct prophecy not to go. The Spirit's message is the occasion for, rather than the substance of, their warning."[24] Thus, although this is probably Grudem's strongest argument, there is a strong case against it.[25]

Second, Grudem turns to Acts 21:10–11, where he argues Agabus's prophecy "had inaccuracies in detail which would have called into question the validity of any Old Testament prophet."[26] Agabus prophesies, "Thus says the Holy Spirit, 'This is how the Jews at Jerusalem will bind the man who owns this belt and deliver him into the hands of the Gentiles'" (Acts 21:11). However, it is the Romans who actually bind Paul (Acts 21:33). Grudem suggests this supports his view of prophecy as being merely human words: "This text could be perfectly well explained by supposing that Agabus had a vision of Paul as a prisoner of the Romans in Jerusalem, surrounded by an angry mob of Jews," which he then related in his own, slightly mistaken, human words.[27] Grudem cedes that Paul does himself later say, "I was delivered as a prisoner from Jerusalem into the hands of the Romans" (Acts 28:17), yet argues that this does not demonstrate that Agabus's prophecy was accurately fulfilled.[28] However, Paul uses the same word for "deliver" here as Agabus used in the prophecy, which seems to suggest that he viewed Agabus's prophecy as having been fulfilled—and that he viewed the actual words of prophecy themselves, rather than merely the general idea, to be of significance.

Craig Keener argues that Grudem's charge against the accuracy of Agabus's prophecy here "likely presses Agabus's words with a pedantic literalism that no biblical prophet's (or historian's) words could long survive."[29] Old Testament prophets "exercised considerable poetic license; many of their details were imagery meant to drive home a larger point (e.g., Isa 37:29; 40:31; Jer 4:5, 8, 19–21; Mic 1:10)."[30] Likewise, Thomas Schreiner contends that "those who think that Agabus erred define error too narrowly and rigidly."[31] He continues:

23. Craig Keener, *Acts: An Exegetical Commentary* (Grand Rapids: Baker, 2014), 3:3083.
24. Keener, *Acts* 3:3083.
25. It is not only Pentecostals who reject Grudem's argument here but also cessationists such as Schreiner, *Spiritual Gifts*, 116–17. Therefore, this is not a case of Pentecostal special pleading.
26. Grudem, *Systematic Theology*, 1296.
27. Grudem, *Systematic Theology*, 1296.
28. Grudem, *Systematic Theology*, 1296–97.
29. Keener, *Acts*, 3:3106.
30. Keener, *Acts*, 3:3106.
31. Schreiner, *Spiritual Gifts*, 115.

> Agabus uses prophetic symbolism (Acts 21:11) like the Old Testament prophets in taking Paul's belt and tying his hands and feet. We are reminded of Isaiah who walked about naked, symbolizing the judgment coming on Egypt and Cush (Isa. 20:1–6). Or, we think of Jeremiah wearing a linen undergarment, which symbolized how Judah and Jerusalem should cling to the Lord (Jer. 13:1–11). Instead, the garment was hidden at the Euphrates, which ruined the garment, indicating Israel's distance from the Lord. Similarly, Ezekiel built miniature siege works against Jerusalem, which symbolized Babylon's siege of Jerusalem (Ezek. 4). The symbolism used by Agabus shows that he is in line with Old Testament prophets, that his prophecy is as truthful as theirs. The way Luke frames the prophecies of Agabus shows that Luke considered him to be in line with Old Testament prophets.[32]

That Agabus begins his prophecy by saying, "Thus says the Holy Spirit" (Acts 21:11) is a further argument against Grudem's position here. Grudem suggests that such language should not be used because prophecy uses merely human words. And yet the New Testament prophet Agabus uses these words to introduce his prophecy without any qualms. These words correspond to the words so frequently used by the Old Testament prophets to introduce prophetic oracles.[33] Agabus gets up to speak in the same way as an Old Testament prophet. Therefore, there seems to be much more continuity as to the nature of prophecy between the Old Testament and the New Testament than Grudem allows.

Third, Grudem points to the necessity of testing prophecies. He argues that 1 Thessalonians 5:20–21—"Do not despise prophecies, but test everything; hold fast what is good"—suggests that "prophecies contain some things that are good and some things that are not good."[34] Yet, Paul says nothing here that indicates a dividing up of individual prophecies into good parts and parts that are not good. In fact, John warns that it is the source of prophecy that we need to test. We must "not believe every spirit, but test the spirits to see whether they are from God, for many false prophets have gone out into the world" (1 John 4:1). For John, the weighing of prophecies and the testing of the prophet would seem to go together, just as it did in the Old Testament (Deut. 18:21–22).

Grudem claims that "if prophecy had absolute divine authority, it would be a sin" to weigh what is said (though we are commanded to do so in 1 Corinthians 14:29).[35] Nonetheless, this is a circular argument, for we do not

32. Schreiner, *Spiritual Gifts*, 115–16.
33. Keener, *Acts*, 3:3105.
34. Grudem, *Systematic Theology*, 1298.
35. Grudem, *Systematic Theology*, 1299.

know if it is a true prophecy until we have weighed what is said. Furthermore, "absolute divine authority" is an unhelpful expression here. Prophecy must always sit under the authority of Scripture, and so that in itself demands that it be tested by Scripture. In fact, throughout Scripture the Lord encourages his people to test prophecy. This is not something new in the New Testament. There is already a test of prophecy set out in the Old Testament (Deut. 18:21–22), and it was certainly not a sin to employ it.

Summary

In prophecy, a Christian "through experienced revelations, receives a message that he or she is directed to hand on to the church for its edification as part of a firm design in God's will to save, guide, and bless his people."[36] Contrary to Grudem's claims, prophecy is not "speaking merely human words to report something God brings to mind."[37] Here both Pentecostals and cessationists agree: we should not change our understanding of prophecy. Rather, prophecy must necessarily involve speaking, and that speech is the work of the Holy Spirit. "Prophecy . . . is a supernatural communication designed primarily to help believers in their Christian walk."[38] It is "a supernatural utterance by the Holy Spirit conveying edification, exhortation, comfort."[39]

REFLECTION QUESTIONS

1. How have classical Pentecostals understood the nature of the gift of prophecy?

2. Have you ever heard a prophecy? Was it spoken in the first person (e.g., "I, the Lord, say to you") or the third person (e.g., "The Lord would have you know")?

3. Does it matter whether prophecies are delivered in the first person or the third person?

4. Why do Wayne Grudem and Sam Storms argue for a different understanding of prophecy?

5. What are the practical implications of the differences between the classical Pentecostal view and the view of Grudem and Storms?

---

36. Niels Christian Hvidt, *Christian Prophecy: The Post-Biblical Tradition* (Oxford: Oxford University Press, 2007), 58.
37. Grudem, *Gift of Prophecy,* 51, 71.
38. Anthony D. Palma, *The Holy Spirit: A Pentecostal Perspective* (Springfield, MO: Gospel Publishing House, 2001), 211.
39. David T. Rennie, *The Gifts of the Holy Spirit* (Bradford: Puritan Press, 1967), 94.

QUESTION 29

Does Belief in Prophecy Undermine *Sola Scriptura*?

As we saw in question 6, Pentecostals are Bible people. They always have been and, if they are to remain faithful, always will be. Therefore, their belief in the gift of prophecy in the church today is not and cannot be in competition with their trust in the authority and sufficiency of Scripture. This has been true since the earliest days of the movement. Here is an example from 1915: "Pastor Kerr brought us good, solid teaching on the Word of God. 'Back to Books,' he emphasized; not to books written by men, but to the sixty-six books written by the finger of God. The burden the Lord put upon him, and running through all his discourses was that we might test every doctrine and every revelation; try every spirit and every 'new' thing that is brought forth, by the Word of God. Whatever will not stand the test of the Word must be set aside."[1]

Everything was to be tested by Scripture. Pentecostals have not changed their minds. Visions, miracles, and revelations must all "be examined, regulated and reformed according to Scriptures."[2] Yet sometimes the compatibility of belief in prophetic revelation and belief in the principle of *sola scriptura* has been called into question by those from outside the movement. Let's look at how the continuing gift of prophecy fits together with the Protestant understanding of *sola scriptura*.

Prophecy and the Authority of Scripture

Classical Pentecostals have always insisted that "the continuing voice of the Spirit in the church does not undermine . . . the authority of biblical revelation," for it is Scripture alone that "continues to be the only authoritative, infallible

1. "Fifteen Days with God: Seasons of Refreshing at the Stone Church Convention, May 16th–31st," *Latter Rain Evangel* (June 1915): 13.
2. AdDDF, 2.

rule for faith and practice." Therefore, prophetic "utterances are not equivalent to Scripture but rather are judged by Scripture."[3] As William Seymour insisted at Azusa Street, "when we find things wrong, contrary to Scripture, I care not how dear it is, it must be removed."[4] The American Assemblies of God leader Ralph Riggs taught that "the prophecy of the Scriptures is infallible and there is neither flaw nor imperfection therein . . . but the operation of the gift of prophecy among the members of the Corinthian church and in the churches today must be 'judged.'"[5] Riggs clarifies further, writing, "It is a false reverence which accepts everything which purports to be a divine message as if it were from God directly and without possible human admixture."[6]

For classical Pentecostals, "The Scriptures will always take precedence over any spiritual gift."[7] We should not "exalt the prophetic word to the level of the Written Word of God" in any way. Thus, we should not turn to a prophetic message "instead of being guided by the Scriptures."[8] Prophecy "can never be on equality with Scripture; indeed it must ever conform to the truth and example of the Written Word and be judged by its light and standard."[9] Between prophecy and Scripture "there is a fundamental difference," for "what is revealed in Scripture is to be received as the basis of our faith," but "what is revealed today [in prophecy] must be judged."[10] This should be reflected in the place we give to both Scripture and prophecy in the life of the church: "The primary authority of Scripture must mean that in our meetings greater attention is given to Scripture—both its reading and exposition—than to prophecy. . . . People must be steered away from the tendency to respond more to the immediacy of a prophetic utterance than to the preaching of the Word. As Pentecostals we have always been known for our commitment to the Bible."[11]

Despite the strong Pentecostal insistence on the final authority of Scripture and the need for any prophecy to be subordinated to Scripture's authority, cessationists like John MacArthur object that any present-day gift of prophecy would "undermine the uniqueness and authority of the Bible."[12] By accepting the continuation of revelatory gifts like prophecy, MacArthur insists, "We will have no way of distinguishing God's voice from man's. Eventually, anyone

3. Douglas A. Oss, "A Pentecostal/Charismatic View," in *Are Miraculous Gifts for Today? Four Views*, ed. Wayne Grudem (Leicester: InterVarsity Press, 1996), 279.
4. William J. Seymour, "Christ's Messages to the Churches," *Apostolic Faith* 1, no. 11 (October–January 1908): 3.
5. Ralph M. Riggs, *The Spirit Himself* (Springfield, MO: Gospel Publishing House, 1949), 158.
6. Riggs, *Spirit Himself*, 159–60.
7. W. G. Hathaway, *Spiritual Gifts in the Church* (London: Elim, 1933), 118.
8. Hathaway, *Spiritual Gifts*, 72.
9. David T. Rennie, *The Gifts of the Holy Spirit* (Bradford: Puritan Press, 1967), 97–98.
10. Malcolm R. Hathaway, "The Sufficiency of Scripture," in *Elim Pentecostal Church: Papers Presented to a Theological Conference* (Cheltenham: Elim, 1991), 31.
11. Hathaway, "Sufficiency of Scripture," 31.
12. John F. MacArthur, *Charismatic Chaos* (Grand Rapids: Zondervan, 1993), 75.

could say anything and claim it is God's Word, and no one would have the right to deny it."[13] Yet, this does not take into account the need to test prophecies, a practice both Scripture and Pentecostals insist upon. Nor does it acknowledge that if this argument were sufficient to rule out Pentecostal prophecy today, it would also have been sufficient to rule out the gift of prophecy in the church of the New Testament. For MacArthur, if God still speaks through prophecy today, that would mean that the canon of Scripture was not closed, and that "we should be earnestly seeking to compile and study these most recent revelations along with Scripture—and maybe even more diligently, since they speak expressly to our time and culture."[14] However, this argument makes the faulty assumption that all revelation is intended to be canonical.

On the contrary, it is clear in Scripture that God gave prophecies (in both the Old and New Testaments) that were not included within the canon of Scripture. The words of Elijah and Elisha's prophecies, for example, are not—for the most part—recorded in Scripture. Although Miriam was a prophetess (Exod. 15:20), we have only one verse of prophecy from her recorded in Scripture (Exod. 15:21). Micaiah was known to be a prophet by whom one could inquire of the Lord well before he makes an appearance in the Bible (1 Kings 22:8)—for the king knew enough of his noncanonical prophecies to be aware that he never prophesied anything good about him. Huldah was already known as a prophetess before we encounter her in Scripture (2 Kings 22:14; 2 Chron. 34:22). Not a single word of the prophetess Anna is recorded in the canon (Luke 2:36–38). Likewise, we know that Philip had four daughters who prophesied, yet we do not know what they prophesied (Acts 21:9). Although there were several prophets in the church at Antioch, only a single sentence of prophecy is included in Scripture (Acts 13:1–2). These are just some examples, but they make clear that noncanonical prophecy is a biblical thing.[15]

Not every prophecy given while the canon was open was intended to be included in Scripture for all people at all times. From surveying such biblical evidence, Don Codling concludes, "The Bible makes clear that in biblical times there was special revelation which was not canonical."[16] Thus, Scripture has no problem with the concept of a form of prophecy that is not equal to Scripture in authority. This is exactly what Pentecostals claim for prophecy today.[17]

---

13. MacArthur, *Charismatic Chaos*, 76.
14. MacArthur, *Charismatic Chaos*, 63.
15. For more examples of noncanonical prophecy mentioned in Scripture, see Don Codling, *Sola Scriptura and the Revelatory Gifts: How Should Christians Deal With Present Day Prophecy?* (Rice, WA: Sentinel Press, 2005), 63–66.
16. Codling, *Sola Scriptura and the Revelatory Gifts*, 66.
17. In this, Pentecostals stand in continuity with many of the early Scottish Presbyterians in the century and a half following the Reformation, who recognized continuing "non-apostolic, non-canonical" prophecy as a form of "extraordinary revelation resulting either in

Testing Prophecy

One of the great pioneers of Pentecostalism in Europe, Thomas Ball Barratt, turned to John Chrysostom for a definition of the gift of prophecy: "He that prophesieth, speaks all things from the Spirit."[18] Barratt was not naïve and would not unquestionably accept everything that claimed to be a prophetic word as such. Instead, he called for discernment: "Whatever may be said or done by the prophets, outside of the direct influence of the Holy Spirit, however acceptable it may be from a human standpoint, it has not the intrinsic value of the work done by the Holy Spirit through them."[19] Barratt warns further, "Where the gift is not developed to its full perfection," those who prophesy may at times "allow thoughts from their own minds to be mixed with the prophetic messages given by the Holy Spirit. That is evidently the reason why prophecies must be proved (1 Thess. 5:20, 21)."[20]

This "proving" or testing of prophecies is a scriptural command found not only in 1 Thessalonian 5:20–21, but also in 1 Corinthians 14:29 and 1 John 4:1. Therefore, every prophecy must be tested. It is not scriptural to accept prophecy without testing it. But how do we test prophecies?

The ultimate test of prophecy is Christ himself, "For the testimony of Jesus is the spirit of prophecy" (Rev. 19:10). "[N]o one speaking in the Spirit of God ever says 'Jesus is accursed!' and no one can say 'Jesus is Lord' except in the Holy Spirit" (1 Cor. 12:3). Believers are not to believe every spirit, but to test them to see if they are from God, with the test being that "every spirit that confesses that Jesus Christ has come in the flesh is from God, and every spirit that does not confess Jesus is not from God" (1 John 4:2–3). We must be on our guard not to accept "a different spirit" that proclaims "another Jesus" (2 Cor. 11:4). Therefore, we must pay attention to the doctrine of Christ proclaimed in the prophecy.

If prophecy testifies to Christ, that means that Christ himself, the head of the church, who is with us as we gather in his name, is the true judge of prophecy. Christ's judgment will always be according to his word (John 12:48). Therefore the Bible, as the written Word of God, must be the authority by which all prophecy is judged. As one prophet of the first generation of the Pentecostal movement put it, if "any prophecy deviates in any manner from the principles laid down in the Word of God, it must not be accepted."[21] More recently, William Kay has succinctly warned, "If the prophecy conflicts

---

predictions of future events or special insight into immediate circumstances" that they did not see as in any way compromising the authority or sufficiency of Scripture. See Dean R. Smith, "The Scottish Presbyterians and Covenanters: A Continuationist Experience in a Cessationist Theology," *Westminster Theological Journal* 63 (2001): 41.

18. T. B. Barratt, *In the Days of the Latter Rain*, rev. ed. (London: Elim, 1928), 107.
19. Barratt, *In the Days of the Latter Rain*, 107.
20. Barratt, *In the Days of the Latter Rain*, 108.
21. T. N. Turnbull, *Prophecy in the Church Age* (Bradford: Puritan Press, 1971), 65.

with Scripture, it is the prophecy which is wrong."[22] Kay summarizes the Pentecostal position: "Prophecy is judged by its conformity to Scripture, by its fulfilment of the functions described in 1 Cor 14:3, by the prophet's doctrinal beliefs about Jesus Christ and by the prophet's moral character."[23]

Prophecy and the Sufficiency of Scripture

Pentecostals teach that "everything which is needed by the individual or by the church, for guidance, discipline, and government, can be found within the covers of the written Word of God."[24] Although they believe in, earnestly desire, and give thanks for the gift of prophecy, they hold strongly to the doctrine of the sufficiency of Scripture. Prophecy is good and a great blessing from the Lord to his church, but Scripture is essential. Without present-day prophecy, we would still have everything we need for salvation and godliness in God's written word of Scripture. Malcolm Hathaway reminds Pentecostals, "What [the Lord] says today [in prophecy] will not contradict what he has said in the Scripture. Nor will it add to what the Scripture reveals about God or the life and work of Christ or the nature and needs of mankind. Otherwise we would have an open canon and an insufficient Bible. . . . So when God speaks today, it will be to guide and direct the Church, to apply truth from his revealed Word to the present need of the Church; to encourage, to edify, to strengthen and motivate his people."[25]

Our expectations of the role of prophecy should be in line with our trust in the sufficiency of Scripture. Prophecy today does not reveal new doctrinal or moral truths in addition to the revealed truth of Scripture. Rather, prophecy may "interpret, explain and amplify the truths already revealed."[26] This is a repetition or reminder for a specific group of people at a specific moment, drawing attention to truths already revealed in Scripture. This in no way compromises the sufficiency of Scripture, but rather points back to the sufficiency and supreme authority of what has already been revealed in the written word.

Yet, if the Scriptures are sufficient, why then should we desire prophecy in the church today? We must be careful not to confuse concepts here: "The sufficiency of Scripture does not entail the conclusion that there is no purpose left for revelatory gifts. . . . The argument that God provides only what is sufficient implies a very limited vision of the graciousness of God."[27] Codling makes a comparison with the sacraments: "The church which has the Bible, studies it diligently and applies it, but does not celebrate the sacraments, is an

22. William K. Kay, *Prophecy* (Nottingham: Lifestream, 1991), 66.
23. Kay, *Prophecy*, 67.
24. Hathaway, *Spiritual Gifts*, 67.
25. Hathaway, "Sufficiency of Scripture," 31.
26. Turnbull, *Prophecy in the Church Age*, 54.
27. Codling, *Sola Scriptura and the Revelatory Gifts*, 71–72.

impoverished church [even though] it has the sufficient Scriptures." It is the sufficient Scriptures that show us the need for the sacraments, and so, "while the Bible is sufficient, that church's application of the Bible is not sufficient."[28] This is the same for the gift of prophecy: the sufficient Scriptures teach us to earnestly desire this gift and regulate its use in the church. In the gift of prophecy, the Lord graciously speaks in ways beyond what it is necessary. Scripture is necessary; prophecy is a gracious gift that points to the necessary truth contained in the sufficient Scriptures, for prophecy "must always be in harmony with the words of the inspired page."[29]

Summary

Pentecostals firmly believe in the authority and sufficiency of Scripture and see no conflict between this and their belief in present-day prophecy. The Scriptures themselves demonstrate that God has frequently spoken through noncanonical prophecy, and therefore contemporary prophecy need not in any way signify an addition to the canon of Scripture. While God speaks by the Scriptures to all people, everywhere, prophecy is given for specific people in a specific situation. Every prophecy must be tested, and in this testing we see that prophecy is subject to the authority of Scripture. The Scriptures by themselves are sufficient for salvation and godliness. Yet, in his abundance of grace, the Lord goes beyond what is strictly necessary by speaking through prophecy. The sufficient Scriptures command us to desire this gift.

REFLECTION QUESTIONS

1. How does the ultimate authority of Scripture relate to the continued availability of the gift of prophecy?
2. What is the biblical evidence for the concept of noncanonical prophecy? How does this relate to prophecy today?
3. How should prophecy be tested?
4. Is it ever acceptable not to test a prophecy?
5. How does present-day prophecy relate to the sufficiency of Scripture?

---

28. Codling, *Sola Scriptura and the Revelatory Gifts*, 74.
29. Turnbull, *Prophecy in the Church Age*, 65.

SECTION C

Questions About Healing and Suffering

QUESTION 30

What Do Pentecostals Believe About Healing?

Pentecostals believe in healing, but they aren't necessarily agreed about *what* they believe about healing. Some Pentecostal denominations give a great deal of emphasis to healing in their confessional statements, while others make no explicit mention of healing at all (although all mention the gifts of the Spirit, which would include the gift of healing).

Yet, the questions and contentions surrounding this topic are not inconsequential. In 1939 the Apostolic Church in Nigeria divided over the matter of divine healing. When they realized that some British missionaries were taking quinine to prevent malaria, some of the Nigerian pastors saw this as a lack of faith in divine healing and left the Apostolic Church, founding what would eventually come to be known as Christ Apostolic Church. To this day the Apostolic Church and Christ Apostolic Church are two separate denominations, sharing theology and even their "Tenets," with the exception of two additions on the part of Christ Apostolic Church—one on divine healing and one on material provision. The Christ Apostolic tenet is strongly worded: "Divine healing through obedience to the command of our Lord Jesus Christ and faith in His name and merit of His blood for all sicknesses, diseases, and infirmities (Isa. 53:5, Mark 16:18, James 5:14–18)."[1]

In the eyes of Christ Apostolic Church, it was a matter of obedience to a divine command to take "all sicknesses, diseases and infirmities" to Jesus rather than the doctor.[2] Polish Pentecostals, on the other hand, are explicit in

1. CAC, "Tenets," 12.
2. CAC has had a "change of position from 'faith only' to 'faith and medicine,'" with its university now also operating a medical center with qualified medical staff. See Timothy Opeyemi Omole, "Divine Healing among the Pentecostal Churches in the 21st Century, with Reference to Christ Apostolic Church in South Western Nigeria," 10. However, a large percentage of members still believe that the church teaches that it is sinful to use medicine.

their confession that God, in his grace, makes use of medical science to heal. "The physical body of man will be redeemed only through the resurrection of the dead and the transformation of the living at the glorious second coming of Jesus Christ. . . . Yet, God also shows the grace of healing during this mortal life through the prayer of faith in the saving work of Jesus Christ, through the gifts of healing, and through medical science."[3] But this is not simply a cultural difference between African Pentecostals and European Pentecostals. The Church of Pentecost, a Ghanaian denomination that, like Christ Apostolic Church, broke away from the Apostolic Church in the mid-twentieth century, takes a similar approach to the Polish Pentecostals in their tenets: "We believe that the healing of sicknesses and diseases is provided for God's people in the atonement. However, the Church is not opposed to medication by qualified medical practitioners."[4] These different attitudes to medical science reflect differing theologies of healing. This is no minor difference; lives hang in the balance over this question.

Medicine as a Good Gift of God

Those who reject medical healing point to a small number of biblical passages that, they argue, cast medical intervention in a negative light. King Asa turned to medical treatment in an illness late in his reign. "In the thirty-ninth year of his reign Asa was diseased in his feet, and his disease became severe. Yet even in his disease he did not seek the LORD, but sought help from physicians" (2 Chron. 16:12). Sometimes this verse is used to set up an opposition between medical treatment and trust in the Lord for healing. However, this verse is preceded by a description of Asa, who had been a faithful king for most of his reign, putting his trust elsewhere late in his life. The Lord sends the prophet Hanani to Asa to warn him about his lack of reliance on the Lord: "Because you relied on the king of Syria, and did not rely on the LORD your God, the army of the king of Syria has escaped you" (2 Chron. 16:7). Asa refuses to heed the prophet and instead "put him in the stocks in prison, for he was in a rage with him because of this. And Asa inflicted cruelties upon some of the people at the same time" (1 Chron. 16:10). Although the Lord sent a prophet to warn him about his shifting faith, Asa hardened his heart and rejected the word of the Lord. Thus, when we get to his reliance on physicians rather than the Lord in verse 12, we have already seen that this is someone who has been placing his trust elsewhere for some time and hardening his heart to the Lord. This is not a matter of a believer who trusts

---

See George O. Folarin, "The Theology and Practice of Christ Apostolic Church on Divine Healing in the Context of Pentecostal Theology," *Ilorin Journal of Religious Studies* 7, no. 1 (2017): 27.

3. Pentecostal Church in Poland, "Confession of Faith," 8.
4. CoP, "Tenets," 8.

the Lord and also takes medicine; this is the rejection of the Lord and trusting only in human means (whether the King of Syria or the physicians). As David Petts explains: "Asa's fault was not that he sought help from the physicians, but that he sought help from them alone and did not seek help from the Lord. Presumably he knew that to get help from the Lord he would need to repent and ask for forgiveness, and this he was unwilling to do."[5]

On the contrary, the Bible gives us sufficient evidence to commend the use of medicine and the work of physicians as good gifts of God to humanity. Jesus compares himself to a physician when he says, "Those who are well have no need of a physician, but those who are sick. I came not to call the righteous, but sinners" (Mark 2:17; cf. Matt. 9:12; Luke 5:31). Although Jesus is not speaking directly about doctors and medical treatment here, the parallel he draws only makes sense if the work of the physician is understood as a good thing. Thus, Jesus here clearly demonstrates his approval of medical treatment. Similarly, Jesus casts medical remedies in a positive light in the parable of the Good Samaritan (Luke 10:29–37). The Samaritan treats the wounded man's injuries with oil and wine (Luke 10:34). In the context, the use of oil and wine is clearly medicinal, and this fits with what we know of ancient medical practice. While again Jesus is not directly addressing a question about medical treatment, the fact that he portrays the hero of his parable (who is in fact representing Christ himself) as someone who uses medical treatments clearly paints medicine in a positive light. Later, Christ tells John to write to and instruct the church at Laodicea, to buy "salve to anoint your eyes, so that you may see" (Rev. 3:18). Once again, this reference to medicine is metaphorical, yet the fact that Jesus repeatedly uses metaphorical references to medical means to illustrate positive spiritual truths demonstrates the goodness of the use of medical means.

A large portion of the New Testament was also written by a physician. The two-volume work of Luke and Acts comprises 27.5 percent of the New Testament, and its writer is "Luke the beloved physician" (Col. 4:14). Luke is not a former physician or a repentant physician but a beloved physician. Paul (and the Holy Spirit speaking through him in the inspiration of the book of Colossians) sees Luke's medical profession as fully compatible with his Christian faith. Furthermore, Paul instructs Timothy to make use of medicinal means for an illness. Paul specifically tells Timothy that it is "for the sake of [his] stomach and [his] frequent ailments" that he is to "use a little wine" (1 Tim. 5:23). The apostle here counsels a medicinal remedy for Timothy's stomach problems and shows no hint of any idea that this would be counter to his belief in God's healing power.

---

5. David Petts, *Just a Taste of Heaven: A Biblical and Balanced Approach to God's Healing Power* (Mattersey: Mattersey Hall, 2006), 37.

The cumulative testimony of the New Testament is that medical means are to be looked on positively. The use of medicine is approved by Christ and encouraged by his apostle. Medical means are aspects of the goodness of God's creation and his providential care for humanity. Therefore, medicine and medical treatment should be considered a good gift of God. Christians can both pray for healing and receive medical treatment. The Lord can and does use both means to heal. A blanket rejection of all medicine and medical treatment is a rejection of this good gift from God.[6] Instead, we should "recognise medical therapy as a gift of God alongside supernatural healing."[7]

Ultimate Healing: Resurrection and Glorification

In Romans 8:23 Paul writes, "we ourselves, who have the firstfruits of the Spirit, groan inwardly as we wait eagerly for adoption as sons, the redemption of our bodies." Thus, the full and complete healing of our bodies is still to come on that final day. This fullness of the restoration of humanity "will not be manifest until the return of Jesus Christ."[8] On that day we will see the fullness of healing, for "the physical body of man will be redeemed only through the resurrection of the dead and the transformation of the living at the glorious second coming of Jesus Christ."[9] Full, permanent, ultimate healing takes place only at the resurrection.

Even when we are healed in this lifetime it can never be full (i.e., ultimate) healing, for one day we will die. A particular illness may be permanently and completely healed by Jesus, but one day our bodies will fail. "No matter what we do for this body, no matter how many times we are healed, unless the rapture of the Church intervenes we shall die."[10] In the meantime, we groan and wait. And yet, the Lord breaks into our groaning and waiting with gracious gifts of healing as "a proleptic expression of the complete redemption of the human body" still to come.[11] Our ultimate healing will only take place in the resurrection, when we will be raised with imperishable, incorruptible bodies (1 Cor. 15:42, 50).

When Jesus comes and the dead are raised, the bodies of believers (both the living and the dead) will be changed (1 Cor. 15:51–52). At that moment "this perishable body must put on the imperishable, and this mortal body must put on immortality" (1 Cor. 15:53). At the resurrection of the dead, our

6. This does not mean that everything that anyone might consider to be "medicine" or a "medical treatment" is automatically good. God's creation can be misused. There may be some medical interventions that Christians should refuse on moral-theological grounds.
7. Keith Warrington, *Healing and Suffering: Biblical and Pastoral Reflections* (Carlisle: Paternoster, 2005), 148.
8. *L'Église Apostolique Suisse Romande*, "Confession de Foi," 7.
9. Pentecostal Church in Poland, "Confession of Faith," 8.
10. AG, "Divine Healing," August 2010, 6.
11. AG, "Divine Healing," 6.

perishable bodies will be raised "imperishable" (1 Cor. 15:42). What "is sown in dishonor" will be "raised in glory." What "is sown in weakness" will be "raised in power" (1 Cor. 15:43). This transformation that does away with perishability, mortality, dishonor, and weakness is the ultimate healing of our bodies, for in the life of the resurrection, "death shall be no more, neither shall there be mourning, nor crying, nor pain anymore, for the former things have passed away" (Rev. 21:4).

This message of the ultimate healing that will take place at Christ's return when he raises us in glory is a great comfort to believers now, and especially to those who do not receive healing in this life. As David Petts puts it, "The knowledge that, if I am not healed now, I will be when Jesus returns is a source of great strength and comfort."[12]

Foretastes of the Healing to Come: Healings Today

Yet Jesus does heal today, giving a foretaste of the future fullness of healing in the life of the resurrection. Even now, in this life, Jesus conveys something of that resurrection life to people through healing (even though complete healing will only be known "when Jesus returns").[13] So, our experience of healing now is "a foretaste of our future, complete restoration."[14]

Believers have received the Holy Spirit now as the "firstfruits" of the ultimate "redemption of our bodies" in the resurrection (Rom. 8:23). In the Old Testament, the firstfruits were part of the coming harvest and served as a pledge and guarantee that there was much more to come (Lev. 23:9–22). So, as the *firstfruits* of our physical redemption, the Holy Spirit gives us a foretaste of what is to come while also pointing us forward to the much greater fullness in the resurrection. Healings today are a little glimpse of the future fullness of bodily redemption at the return of Christ and point us to our blessed hope.

Christ the Healer Today

Jesus is the healer. It is Christ who pours out the Spirit on his church as the firstfruits of the coming fullness of physical redemption. Therefore, it is not a human being who heals, but only the Lord himself who heals, even when he uses human beings in gifts of healing. Nor is it ever our faith that heals, but rather it is Christ the healer in whom we believe. Pentecostals have been clear about this right from the beginning.

The first-generation English Apostolic leader Frank Hodges was emphatic on this point: "It is not our faith that heals us, though we are linked on to Him by faith, but it is Christ that heals."[15] Hodges drew on the image of the woman

---

12. Petts, *Just a Taste*, 221. Cf. PAOC, "Miracles and Healings," 14.
13. Basis of Faith of the Pentecostal Movement in Norway, God's Kingdom.
14. PAOCSET, "Salvation."
15. Frank Hodges, *Divine Healing* (Penygroes: Apostolic Church, 1926), 13.

who touched the hem of Christ's garment to describe how we today lay hold of Christ the healer in faith. "He has gone up to Heaven, but He has sent His garments down here [by] the Holy Spirit; and we can touch Him in faith. This nearness to the Person of Christ is eminently possible at the Breaking of Bread Service, when faith appropriates of health to spirit, soul and body."[16] Although Christ has ascended to the Father's right hand, we can still touch the hem of his garment in faith through the Holy Spirit and also as we encounter the living Savior in the Lord's Supper.[17]

Anointing with Oil and the Laying on of Hands

Pentecostals believe in anointing the sick with oil for healing.[18] The Bible teaches this in James 5:14–16: "Is anyone among you sick? Let him call for the elders of the church, and let them pray over him, anointing him with oil in the name of the Lord. And the prayer of faith will save the one who is sick, and the Lord will raise him up. And if he has committed sins, he will be forgiven. Therefore, confess your sins to one another and pray for one another, that you may be healed. The prayer of a righteous person has great power as it is working."

These instructions are for any believer who is sick. In fact, as David Petts observes, this is "the main way taught in the New Testament for Christians to receive healing from God."[19] But these instructions are not only directed to sick Christians; they are also directed to elders in Christ's church. Believers are not to send for one elder who happens to be known for the gift of healing—they are to "call for the elders of the church" as a group (v. 14). Therefore, "*all* elders are expected to pray the prayer of faith that the sick might be healed in the name of the Lord."[20]

In addition to praying, the elders are to anoint the sick person with oil. In the Old Testament oil carried important symbolic value, many aspects of which would speak directly to the situation of sickness and prayer for healing. Oil was a sign of the Holy Spirit (1 Sam. 16:13) and of the Lord's strengthening power (Ps. 89:20–25). Anointing with oil was also associated with the restoration and cleansing of someone who had been healed

16. Hodges, *Divine Healing*, 20.
17. We will return to the subject of healing at the Lord's Table in question 38.
18. Indian Pentecostal Church of God, "Statement of Faith," 10; Verbond van Vlaamse Pinkstergemeenten, "Wat Wij Geloven," 4.3; Assemblee di Dio in Italia, "Articoli di Fede," 8; Elim New Zealand, "Statement of Faith," 14; *Introducing the Apostolic Church: A Manual of Belief, Practice and History* (Penygroes: The Apostolic Church, 1988), 184; CoGiC, "Divine Healing," in "What We Believe."
19. David Petts, *Body Builders: Gifts to Make God's People Grow* (Mattersey: Mattersey Hall, 2002), 153.
20. Petts, *Body Builders*, 153. Cf. Warrington, *Healing and Suffering*, 166–68.

of leprosy (Lev. 14:2, 15–18). Furthermore, oil was a sign of joy (Ps. 45:7).[21] Thus it is not the oil itself which brings healing through any properties of its own; rather, the use of oil points to the Lord who pours out his Spirit to heal, strengthen, restore, and gladden. The anointing with oil by the elders in faith is an outward sign and seal of the accompanying gracious working of God.[22]

The promise here is that the Lord will raise up the one who is sick. The idea of the sick being raised up makes sense, as those who are sick are often lying down. However, the same word is also used frequently in the New Testament to speak of the resurrection. We can be certain that the Lord will hear the prayer of faith as the elders anoint with oil in the name of the Lord. He may answer that prayer immediately or gradually, with a foretaste of the ultimate healing, or he may answer it through the resurrection.[23] Therefore, "the prayer of faith is not a prayer that insists that healing must be immediate but a prayer that commits the sick one to God knowing that his will is best and that he can be trusted to 'raise up' the sick whether it be immediately by a miracle of healing or ultimately at the return of the Lord. . . . Although the passage indicates that the sick may expect to be healed, there is no guarantee that the healing will be immediate."[24]

Summary

Pentecostals believe that Jesus is still the healer today, and that he distributes gifts of healing by the Holy Spirit. In his good providence, God has also given the gift of medical means of healing. Ultimate healing will only take place when our bodies are glorified at the resurrection of the dead, but until that day the Holy Spirit gives a foretaste of that future full healing by gifts of healing here and now. The main way in which believers are to seek God's healing is by calling for the elders of the church to pray in faith and anoint with oil.

---

21. For more on biblical use of oil and its symbolism, see Warrington, *Healing and Suffering*, 177–78.
22. Elim New Zealand lists this anointing with oil alongside baptism and the Lord's Supper, as well as the laying on of hands, under the heading "The Ordinances" (as was formerly the case in Elim UK as well). See Elim New Zealand, "The Ordinances," in Statement of Faith, 14. Older British Elim publications were happy to use the words "ordinance" and "sacrament" interchangeably and freely referred to each of these acts as a sacrament. While some other Pentecostals might prefer not to use the word "sacrament" at all or to reserve it for only baptism and the Lord's Supper, God is understood to work through the laying on of hands and anointing with oil as a means of grace (and so this could be described as a sacrament).
23. See Petts, *Body Builders*, 156; Petts, *Just A Taste of Heaven*, 106–8.
24. Petts, *Just A Taste of Heaven*, 107.

REFLECTION QUESTIONS

1. Does belief in Christ's ongoing healing power mean we must reject or ignore medical treatments?

2. Why does it matter that we have a proper biblical understanding of medicine?

3. How is healing today related to the resurrection of the dead?

4. Why is the resurrection a comfort and strength to those who do not experience healing now?

5. What is the normal way the Bible teaches Christians to seek healing?

QUESTION 31

Is Healing in the Atonement?

The World Assemblies of God Fellowship includes in its statement of faith the expression that "deliverance from sickness is provided for in the atonement and is the privilege of all believers."[1] Likewise, the Church of God believes, "Divine healing is provided for all in the atonement."[2] These are strong statements. But what do they mean? As we shall see presently, there are differing understandings of the idea of healing in the atonement. However, before examining these, let's look at the scriptural basis of the concept.

Does Scripture Teach Healing in the Atonement?

This teaching of healing in the atonement essentially comes from two major proof texts: Matthew 8:16–17 and 1 Peter 2:24. In the former, Matthew states that Jesus's casting out evil spirits and healing the sick "was to fulfill what was spoken by the prophet Isaiah: 'He took our illnesses and bore our diseases'" (Matt. 8:17). The quotation is from Isaiah 53:4, in the suffering servant prophecy of the cross. Therefore, some Pentecostals have read Matthew's text in light of the full prophecy in Isaiah. French Arrington, an American Church of God theologian, argues, "Matthew placed Isaiah 53:4 in the context of the healing of Peter's mother-in-law and others (vv. 14–16), making it obvious that he had a profound grasp of the connection between the healing ministry of Jesus and the Cross. The physical healings done by Jesus fulfilled what was spoken by Isaiah. The fact that Christ 'took our infirmities [*astheneias: sicknesses*] and bore our sicknesses [*nosous: diseases*]' clearly teaches that there is healing in the Atonement. . . . Healing should not be severed from the death of Christ."[3]

1. WAGSF, 5.
2. Church of God, "Declaration of Faith," 11.
3. French Arrington, *Christian Doctrine: A Pentecostal Perspective* (Cleveland, TN: Pathway, 1993), 2:258–59. The insertion of the Greek terms and alternate translations are Arrington's.

However, Matthew is describing events that took place about three years before Christ's death, and nowhere in the context does he mention the cross. Instead, Matthew writes that this prophecy was fulfilled in the healing ministry of Jesus throughout his life. As the mid-twentieth century British Assemblies of God writer L. W. F. Woodford puts it, "Matthew was not referring to our Lord's coming passion when he drew upon this quotation, but he was referring to the actual events he was then describing."[4] David Petts, a British Assemblies of God theologian, concludes, "Since Matthew does not apply this Scripture to Jesus's death on the cross but to his healing the sick in Galilee, there is really no basis for saying that he is teaching us that Jesus died for our sicknesses as well as our sins."[5] Yet, the American Assemblies of God New Testament scholar Robert Menzies counters this argument from the immediate context with one drawn from the wider context: "If we place Matthew 8:17 in the larger context of Matthew's Gospel, we can see its full significance. It is more than simply a description of Jesus' earthly ministry in terms of healing; rather, it is Matthew's summary of the significance of Jesus' messianic mission, which culminates on the cross. . . . The salvation the Messiah-King brings includes physical wholeness; and healing now, as during the ministry of Jesus, is a testimony to this fact."[6] The question then is, in which context should we read Matthew's quotation of Isaiah? Does the second text (1 Peter 2:24) help answer this question?

Arrington thinks it does. He sees 1 Peter 2:24 as providing enough evidence to make the connection between healing and the cross, and thus between Matthew's quote of Isaiah and healing in the atonement. Here Peter writes, "He himself bore our sins in his body on the tree, that we might die to sin and live to righteousness. By his wounds you have been healed" (1 Peter 2:24). According to Arrington the first half of the verse refers to "our spiritual deliverance," while the second half ties "physical healing to the death of Christ."[7] In the Gospels and Acts, Arrington writes that often "this word *heal* (*iaomai*) has the meaning of physical healing, but it is also used in a spiritual sense (Matt. 13:15). So it is clear in the New Testament that the salvation brought by Jesus includes healing for the body."[8] Yet, the fact that a word can have such a meaning elsewhere does not mean that this is how Peter is using the word in context here.

Peter does not mention sickness or healing anywhere else in this letter. So, if this half verse is about divine healing, it is a sudden interruption in a

---

4. L. W. F. Woodford, *Divine Healing and the Atonement: A Restatement* (London: Victoria Institute, 1956), 58; cf. Keith Warrington, *Healing and Suffering: Biblical and Pastoral Reflections* (Carlisle: Paternoster, 2005), 60.
5. David Petts, *Just a Taste of Heaven: A Biblical and Balanced Approach to God's Healing Power* (Mattersey: Mattersey Hall, 2006), 127.
6. William W. Menzies and Robert P. Menzies, *Spirit and Power: Foundations of Pentecostal Experience* (Grand Rapids: Zondervan, 2000), 167.
7. Arrington, *Christian Doctrine*, 2:259.
8. Arrington, *Christian Doctrine*, 2:259.

context where that is not an issue under discussion. In fact, Peter's theme in this letter is that believers will face suffering in this life. Peter is encouraging his readers to persevere through suffering; a sudden interruption to promise healing would go against the whole tenor of the letter. However, if the "healing" is the spiritual healing of salvation (which, as Arrington admits, is a New Testament use of the word), then this makes complete sense in context. There is nothing in the context to suggest that Peter is changing subjects to write about physical healing, which is otherwise entirely absent from his letter. Therefore, there is no sufficient reason to read this verse as teaching healing in the atonement. "The passage is, in fact," as Petts puts it, "an encouragement to Christians to endure suffering, not a means of escape from it."[9]

Thus, 1 Peter 2:24 does not teach healing in the atonement. While that does not rule out the possibility of such a reading of Matthew 8:17, a single disputed proof text does not seem to give much support for a doctrine.

Is There a Wider Biblical/Theological Basis for Teaching Healing in the Atonement?

However, there is potentially a wider theological basis in Scripture. Pavel Hejzlar argues, "The healing in the atonement doctrine . . . is not without merit. Its theological strength consists in giving the highest credit to Christ's sacrifice by viewing it as the ultimate answer to all human ills. Where else should a Christian look for any aspect of salvation than to Calvary? The question is, however, when the benefits of the atonement can be expected in their fullness, whether in this life or the next."[10] Likewise, William and Robert Menzies argue that "if we are to do justice to the full breadth of the biblical witness, we must broaden our view and ask: What is the full significance of Christ's death on the cross?"[11]

Ultimately, all the benefits of salvation flow from the cross of Christ. As Jeremy Treat argues, "The establishment of [Christ's] kingdom is dependent on the defeat of evil, forgiveness of sin, and a new exodus," each of which "is accomplished primarily through Christ's death on the cross."[12] Christ's atoning death on the cross is "central, in that it is the climactic turning point from 'the present evil age' to 'the age to come.'"[13] Thus, the powers of the age to come flow to us only through the cross of Christ. As we have seen in the last chapter, healing in this present age is a foretaste of the ultimate healing in the age to come. Therefore, just as we depend wholly on Jesus and his atoning death for us in order to receive the final redemption of our bodies on the last

---

9. Petts, *Just a Taste*, 133.
10. Pavel Hejzlar, *Two Paradigms for Divine Healing: Fred F. Bosworth, Kenneth E. Hagin, Agnes Sandford, and Francis MacNutt in Dialogue* (Leiden: Brill, 2010), 81.
11. Menzies and Menzies, *Spirit and Power*, 162.
12. Jeremy R. Treat, *The Crucified King: Atonement and Kingdom in Biblical and Systematic Theology* (Grand Rapids: Zondervan, 2014), 130.
13. Treat, *Crucified King*, 137.

day when he will raise us incorruptible, so too the foretastes of that healing that we may receive now must depend entirely upon Jesus and his atoning work. As Menzies and Menzies put it, "Physical healing, like all the benefits of salvation, flows from the cross."[14] Therefore, "healing, as every good gift from God, is mediated to us by virtue of Christ's work on the cross."[15]

Healing as a Foretaste of the Fullness of Redemption to Come

This bigger, theological basis for an understanding of the connection between healing and the atonement provides us with a much more helpful way of speaking than a doctrine that relies on Matthew 8:16–17 and 1 Peter 2:24 as proof texts. It is not simply that this gives us a firmer footing for the link between healing and the atonement (although it does), but also that it helps protect against sometimes dangerous distortions of the teaching.

When viewed in light of the cross at the turning point between this age and the age to come, we are thinking of sickness as part of a bigger picture. Thus, we must ask where sickness came from and how it fits into this bigger picture. God's original creation was "very good" (Gen. 1:31). Before Adam sinned, there was neither sickness nor death (Gen. 2:17; Rom. 5:12–21; 1 Cor. 15:21–22). Yet Adam's sin led to God's judgment, which included not only human beings and the serpent but also a curse upon the earth. Thus, the whole of creation was affected by Adam's sin. The whole of "the creation was subjected to futility" and waits in "bondage to corruption" until that final day of redemption in Christ (Rom. 8:20–21). The whole world is under the curse as part of God's judgment on Adam's sin. Sickness and death are part of this curse.[16]

This is significant for how we think about sickness—for if sickness is part of the curse upon the created world, that means that sickness is not (in general terms) personal. Although we do see some occasions in Scripture where God uses an illness to bring judgment on an individual, this is not the general way that sickness works.[17] It is generally a result of living in a fallen world under the curse for sin rather than a direct personal punishment for specific personal sin. Jesus's answer to his disciples when they asked him concerning the man born blind, "Rabbi, who sinned, this man or his parents, that he was born blind?" (John 9:2), makes clear that we should never assume that someone's illness or disability is the result of their sin: "It was not that this man sinned, or his parents, but that the works of God might be displayed in him" (John 9:3). Furthermore, at times some illnesses can be caused by the devil or evil spirits (Matt. 12:22; Mark

14. Menzies and Menzies, *Spirit and Power*, 162.
15. Menzies and Menzies, *Spirit and Power*, 167.
16. Petts, *Body Builders*, 161.
17. For examples of personal sickness as a result of personal sin in the Bible, see Petts, *Body Builders*, 162–63. As Petts notes, sickness can also at times be the result of irresponsible behavior rather than a judgment on sin. For example, unhealthy eating habits can result in sickness.

9:17, 25; Acts 10:38). So, while sickness can at times be the result of our own personal sin, our own irresponsible behavior, or even the attacks of the enemy, very often sickness "may simply come because we live in a fallen world."[18]

Therefore, the ultimate remedy for sin is the undoing of the curse. This is exactly what Jesus has accomplished through his death on the cross, an accomplishment that will be fully manifest in the resurrection of the new heavens and the new earth. Ultimately, as a result of the redemptive work of Christ, "the creation itself will be set free from its bondage to corruption and obtain the freedom of the glory of the children of God" (Rom. 8:21). This bondage is the curse upon the created world, which includes sickness and death. Yet Christ has triumphed over death, trampling it down by his death on the cross and his victorious resurrection on the third day. On that final day, we will see the fullness of that victory in a world free from the curse. But in the meantime, the triumphant Lord gives glimpses and foretastes of that future day through gifts of healing here and now. This is the sense in which we can rightly speak of healing in the atonement, for through his atoning work Christ undoes the curse and defeats death, which includes the ultimate healing of the day of resurrection and thus every foretaste of that in healings today. Every healing is a glimpse of Christ's victory won at the cross. In this sense, healing may be understood to be in the atonement, but as David Petts warns, "that does not mean that Jesus died for our sicknesses just as he died for our sins."[19]

Jesus Did Not Die for Our Sicknesses in the Same Way He Died for Our Sins

One way some people have understood the idea of healing in the atonement is that if healing is in the atonement, then it must be available to all who believe, in the same way as salvation. David Petts has defined this as "the view that Christians may claim healing from sickness on the grounds that Christ has already carried that sickness for them *just as* he has carried their sins."[20] As Petts explains, this would mean that "all you have to do is claim your healing by faith and you will be healed."[21] Another British Pentecostal scholar, Keith Warrington, sums up this view as meaning "healing is available to believers today in the same way that forgiveness of sins can be received."[22]

Healing is a benefit of Christ's atoning work, but not in the same way as justification. Rather, healing will not be complete until the resurrection of the dead. Yet, now God graciously gives foretastes of that ultimate healing won for us at Calvary in gifts of healings and answers to prayer. Warrington sums this

18. Petts, *Body Builders*, 165.
19. Petts, *Just a Taste of Heaven*, 134.
20. Petts, *Just a Taste of Heaven*, 124.
21. Petts, *Just a Taste of Heaven*, 124.
22. Warrington, *Healing and Suffering*, 59.

up as the view that "because of the death of Jesus, healing is available to believers today though it may not necessarily be actualized until after death."[23] This is the position taken by the American Assemblies of God: "Provision for the healing of our bodies is part of the redemption spoken of in Romans 8:23. We receive forgiveness of sins now in connection with the redemption of our souls. We shall receive the redemption of our bodies when we are caught up to meet the Lord and our changed into His likeness. . . . Divine healing now is a foretaste of this, and, like all the blessings of the gospel, flows from the Atonement."[24]

Summary

Healing now by God's grace is a glimpse of the glory to come in the resurrection. However, that does not mean that this healing is detached from Christ's finished atoning work. The Danish Pentecostal declaration of faith has perhaps found a more helpful way to express this: "We believe that the death and resurrection of Christ opened a way to receive divine healing."[25] This statement does not give the impression of a guarantee of healing, nor does it in any way suggest that Jesus has died for our sicknesses in exactly the same way as he died for our sins. Rather, this Danish statement makes clear that the fullness of Jesus's saving work (his resurrection from the dead, as well as his death on the cross) has made healing possible. We are free to ask the Lord to heal, but we do not presume upon him. And so we can pray with great confidence in his redemptive provision, while still "with submission to His divine and sovereign will."[26]

REFLECTION QUESTIONS

1. In which passages of Scripture has the teaching of healing in the atonement traditionally been rooted? Is that the best interpretation of these verses?

2. Is there another way to understand the role of the atonement in the gift of healing?

3. How should we understand sin in relation to sickness?

4. Did Jesus die for our sicknesses in the same way that he died for our sins? Why does this question matter?

5. How does healing in the atonement relate to the age to come?

---

23. Warrington, *Healing and Suffering*, 59.
24. AG, "Divine Healing," 4.
25. Mosaik (Danish Pentecostal Movement), "Declaration of Faith," 8.
26. FDF, 14.

QUESTION 32

How Do Pentecostals Deal with Suffering?

In 1909 a Pentecostal paper published an imagined dialogue between the devil and his fallen angels, in which they discuss the creation of a counterfeit church. At the pinnacle of the delusion is that this "new church will teach that there is no such thing as sin, suffering or sickness."[1] By contrast, in the true church, there will be suffering; any claim that states otherwise is nothing but a devilish delusion.

Jesus himself warned his people that "in the world you will have tribulation" (John 16:33). Paul warns us that "through many tribulations we must enter the kingdom of God" (Acts 14:22). Pentecostals have been very clear: the Lord permits affliction and suffering among his people.[2] He even uses it. Yet when Christ's people suffer, they do not suffer alone. The Lord is with us (Ps. 23:4), and we can know Christ in "the fellowship of his sufferings."[3]

Suffering is not merely an unfortunate reality. Rather, early Pentecostals taught that the Lord works through suffering and that his "riches are only found in the depth of suffering." It is as we enter into the fellowship of Christ's sufferings and "really understand how to suffer" that we will "also understand how to love." Therefore, it is impossible "to have a glorious way without suffering," for only those who "really enter into [Christ's] steps" truly follow in his way.[4] Suffering does not earn God's favor; we are justified by grace alone,

1. Saint Clements, "The Masterpiece of Satan: An Exposure of a Great Delusion," *Latter Rain Evangel* (March 1909): 15. The article was written as a warning against the Church of Christ Scientist and was reprinted from a Christian and Missionary Alliance publication, but shows that early Pentecostals understood any claim that the children of God need not suffer to be a satanic delusion.
2. Frank Hodges, *Divine Healing* (Penygroes: Apostolic Church, 1926), 7.
3. "The Fellowship of His Sufferings," *Confidence* 4, no. 7 (July 1911): 157; cf. Philippians 3:10.
4. "The Fellowship of His Sufferings," 157.

through faith alone, in Christ alone (see question 11). Yet those who have been saved through faith in Jesus are shaped to be more and more like Jesus, and part of that shaping takes place through suffering.

Suffering Instead of Healing

Perhaps the biggest questions surrounding suffering in Pentecostal circles arise in those times when people pray for healing and yet are not healed. However, the fact that not everyone is healed is neither a surprise nor a disappointment: "It is obvious, both from Scripture and from present-day experience, that God does not choose in this dispensation to deliver every child of His from every sickness. God's purpose is primarily to call out a people for Himself, and to prepare them to spend eternity with Him. Healing will always be subordinate to this main purpose."[5] Pentecostals recognize that sometimes healing will contribute to this main purpose, and sometimes it will not. God is all wise, and heals (or withholds healing) according to his wise purpose.

Early Pentecostals recognized—and warned against—what has become a recurring danger flowing from misunderstandings of God's purpose in healing: the danger of assuming that suffering is a spiritual problem. Donald Gee cautions, "Part of the unfortunate manner in which faith in Divine healing sometimes has been sincerely promulgated by strong-minded personalities is this continual suggestion that failure to get healed is rooted in some deep spiritual failure in the one who is sick. This attitude has added mental suffering to physical suffering, and in extreme cases turned belief in Divine healing into a scourge rather than a privilege, and a burden rather than a belief."[6]

Though sickness and suffering are results of Adam's sin and the resultant fallenness of this world, we must understand that affliction is "not always due to personal sin. . . . Therefore we must not judge one another when we are attacked with sickness of any kind, and we are not to attribute evil to the person attacked."[7] The hasty attribution of "personal sickness to personal sin was the precise folly of Job's three friends that drew upon them the anger of the Almighty."[8] Therefore, there must be no place in Christ's body for "unkind criticism and judging" of those who suffer. Rather, believers should have hearts "filled with such compassion that we could take the suffering one's case as if it were our own, and care enough to spend perhaps hours or nights in pleading the prayer of faith for those who are too weary and weak and assaulted to do it for themselves."[9] The sufferings of others should draw out our

5. Aubrey Hathaway, "Editorial Comment: This Matter of Healing," *Elim Evangel* 44, no. 13 (March 30, 1963): 194.
6. Donald Gee, *Trophimus I Left Sick: Our Problems of Divine Healing* (London: Elim, 1952), 12.
7. Hodges, *Divine Healing*, 7.
8. Gee, *Trophimus I Left Sick*, 23–24.
9. "The Fight of Faith in Divine Healing," *Confidence* 4, no. 8 (August 1911): 181.

hearts in love and intercession; it should not lead us to criticism or attempts to diagnose spiritual problems. "Any doctrine of Divine healing that professes to leave no place for pain in the present order of things is palpably too shallow to be true."[10]

Suffering and Sanctification

We should not assume that suffering is a sign of God's disfavor, for very often the Lord uses suffering in our sanctification. Frank Hodges, the early English Apostolic leader, pointed to the example of Job whose "sufferings were allowed of God for the perfecting of his character, the trial of his faith, and to demonstrate the power of God to sustain and carry through trials of the fiercest nature, and to heal and restore abundantly more than he lost."[11] Mary Boddy pointed to the example of Christ himself recorded in Hebrews 5:8: "Yes, though we are [God's] children, we too must learn true obedience; it is often a difficult lesson to learn, especially when it is through suffering—even unto death sometimes. We are so anxious to be out working and winning souls. We see the fields whitening unto harvest; the sick, the needy all around us. We long to be out witnessing for Christ, and lo, we are called aside to suffer—to be, as it were, helpless."[12] Yet, this is God's work and God's teaching. "The earthly instruments God uses for this are many and varied. . . . Our Father makes no mistakes. He knows the way He wishes us to go."[13] In our suffering, we are called to trust in his fatherly care, "standing firmly on His Word, knowing that Christ is our life, that we are in Him, and therefore, as each trial comes, a more difficult lesson given, we can cheerfully submit to it in perfect faith."[14]

On the other side of the ocean, Aimee Semple McPherson wrote of suffering as God's crucible, in which he is refining his people as pure gold to reflect the image of his Son. Yet in the midst of the sufferings of God's crucible, we can know his peace, as Christ is formed more and more within us: "It has become a place of rest, in the very hand of God. . . . The Master sees His face and form reflected there." So, McPherson teaches her Pentecostal readers to pray: "Burn on! Burn on, O fire of God—work out Thy will, Thy pattern, and Thyself in me—Thy sufferings and Thy triumphs! Heed not the murmurs of the flesh, but have Thy way—*Thy* way in me."[15] As another early Pentecostal woman, Kate Knight, put it, through suffering the Holy Spirit "working as fire . . . wars against the flesh, and brings us victory over it and the world."[16]

---

10. Gee, *Trophimus I Left Sick*, 26.
11. Hodges, *Divine Healing*, 8.
12. Mary Boddy, "Obedience," *Confidence* 8, no. 6 (June 1915): 111.
13. Boddy, "Obedience," 111.
14. Boddy, "Obedience," 111–12.
15. Aimee Semple McPherson, "The Crucible of God," *The Bridal Call* 4, no. 1 (June 1920): 3.
16. Kate Knight, "The Baptism of Fire," *Confidence* 8, no. 12 (December 1915): 234.

The Lord uses sufferings to further our sanctification, yet that does not mean we should seek out suffering. Knight continues, "We do not need to seek suffering, for it will come."[17]

Suffering and God's Fatherly Chastening

Suffering in this life may also at times flow out from God's fatherly discipline of the children whom he loves. Hebrews tells us, "For the moment all discipline seems painful rather than pleasant, but later it yields the peaceful fruit of righteousness to those who have been trained by it" (Heb. 12:11). God's discipline of his children, although it may be painful to endure, has a good purpose in the fruit of holiness in our lives. When we come under the Lord's discipline, we are to remember that "God is treating [us] as sons. For what son is there whom his father does not discipline?" (Heb. 12:7). It is in his fatherly love that the Lord disciplines us, in order to turn us from our sin to him (cf. 1 Cor. 11:32). As Donald Gee wrote, "Sometimes Divine love and wisdom permit a measure of suffering as a result of sin, in order to teach us to sin no more, and make us love righteousness and hate iniquity."[18]

Suffering and the Baptism of the Holy Spirit

The baptism of the Holy Spirit equips Christ's people for suffering. As one early Pentecostal hymn put it, in being filled with the Spirit, we are "filled for service, *suffering*, sowing."[19] For the early Welsh Pentecostal leader D. P. Williams, true Pentecostal power is always "power with Blood on it"—it is always cross-shaped power.[20] Therefore the baptism in the Holy Spirit "will always lead to suffering."[21] As we are filled with the Spirit, we should come to know "mutual fellowship in suffering with Christ, and with every member of the Body; the ministry of compassion and weeping."[22] It is in the context of writing of the weakness and suffering of this life that Paul writes of the baptism of the Holy Spirit as both a guarantee of the eternal weight of glory that God has prepared for us (2 Cor. 4:16–5:5) and the outpouring of the love of God in our hearts (Rom. 5:2–5). Thus, the baptism in the Holy Spirit is not an escape from sufferings, but rather through it the Lord Jesus equips and strengthens us in the midst of our sufferings.

In fact, some Pentecostals see suffering and the baptism of the Holy Spirit as even more tightly linked. "It is a two-fold baptism . . . in the Holy Ghost and *fire*," and by fire, Jesus "evidently meant suffering" (cf. Matt. 3:11;

---

17. Knight, "The Baptism of Fire," 234.
18. Gee, *Trophimus I Left Sick*, 22.
19. M. W., "Filled With God," *Confidence* 4, no. 8 (August 1911): 171 (emphasis added).
20. D. P. Williams, "Exposition," *Riches of Grace* 11, no. 1 (September 1935): 42.
21. D. P. Williams, "Exposition," *Riches of Grace* 1, no. 9 (1920): 5.
22. D. P. Williams, 'Exposition," *Riches of Grace* 3, no. 1 (March 1927): 45.

Luke 3:16).[23] When Ananias was sent to pray for Saul to be filled with the Spirit, the Lord spoke to him concerning both the future apostle's evangelistic mission and his sufferings (Acts 9:15–17). Paul's "baptism in fire . . . was fully filled in the almost unparalleled sufferings of his life."[24] As one early Pentecostal put it, the "trials of life, as well as severe pain and sickness, heart anguish and bitter affliction, are all part of the baptism of fire God has planned we shall pass through" to keep "melting us all through our lives, and by thus keeping us melted [to] stamp the clear image of Jesus in the melted wax."[25] This "suffering will bring a strength of faith otherwise impossible" and make us "able to help others."[26] Suffering is not a sign of the absence of God; rather, the Lord often works very powerfully in and through our sufferings.

Summary

The Bible tells us that believers will face suffering in this life. The Bible also promises us the Lord's faithful presence with us in our sufferings and encourages us to see that he is at work even in the most difficult situations for our good and for his glory. We should not seek to flee from all suffering, as if it were the opposite of God's grace. Rather we should pray, like the early Pentecostals, for faithfulness and godliness in the midst of suffering.

> O Lord, grant unto me Love that I may enjoy sorrows and be thankful for trials, and rejoice in tribulation, and magnify Thy Name in the midst of the storms of life, and that I may say that every day of my life is full of Thy goodness and mercy towards me, O God, whatever may come to meet me, and that also the things that seem contrary to me, are in Thy hand, O God, the means of transforming me to the likeness of Thy Son, and that I may embrace Thee, O my Father, when I am chastened of Thee, and that I may have a full realisation of Thy presence in every charge of Thine, that I may be perfected. Amen.[27]

---

23. Knight, "The Baptism of Fire," 231.
24. Knight, "The Baptism of Fire," 231.
25. Knight, "The Baptism of Fire," 231.
26. Knight, "The Baptism of Fire," 232–33.
27. D. P. Williams, *Prayer: Love Remaineth*. This prayer was printed, originally in either Welsh or English, in every Apostolic Church publication throughout the earliest years of Pentecostalism, to be prayed regularly by all the members.

REFLECTION QUESTIONS

1. Does the Bible promise Christians a life free from suffering?

2. What problems arise with regard to suffering if we assume that God always guarantees healing here and now to those who have faith?

3. Can suffering play a role in sanctification?

4. Have you ever considered the connection between the baptism of the Holy Spirit and suffering? How does the outpouring of the Spirit help us in our sufferings?

5. Have you ever prayed a prayer like the one at the end of the chapter? Is this a normal part of your prayer life?

PART 5

Questions About the Church and the Second Coming

SECTION A

Questions About the Church

QUESTION 33

How Do Pentecostals Understand the Church?

Early Pentecostals gave a great deal of attention to ecclesiology (the doctrine of the church). The church is not merely a helpful gathering to encourage Christians in mission and life. Rather, it is "an essential part of God's plan" and "the especial object of the love of Christ."[1] As D. P. Williams, the early Welsh Apostolic leader, wrote: "There is nothing higher nor nearer the heart of our glorified Lord than His Church."[2]

The Body of Christ

For Pentecostals, the body of Christ is not merely a metaphor but the very definition of the reality of the church: the church "is the Body of Christ."[3] This is "a living organism, a living body composed of all true believers" and "a divine structure in which the life of Christ indwells."[4] The first statement of fundamental truths of the American Assemblies of God defined the church as "a living organism; a living body; yea the body of Christ; a habitation of God through the Spirit."[5] Likewise, in their confession of faith, Hungarian

1. Freie Christengemeinde—Pfingstgemeinde Österreich, "Glaubensbekenntnis," 8a; Gilbert T. Fletcher, "God's Picture of His Church," *Elim Evangel* 7, no. 23/24 (December 6, 1926): 290.
2. D. P. Williams, foreword to Thomas Rees, *The Divine Masterpiece* (Bradford: Puritan Press, n.d.), 2.
3. Apostolic Church, "Tenets," 6; Indian Pentecostal Church of God, "Statement of Faith," 11; Hungarian Pentecostal Confession, 10.
4. Elim Pentecostal Church, "Statement of Fundamental Truths" (1922 edition), 6; D. P. Williams, "The Ministry of the Word," in *The Enduring Word* (Penygroes: Apostolic Publications, 1944), 174.
5. AG, "A Statement of Fundamental Truths Approved by the General Council of the Assemblies of God," in *Minutes of the General Council of the Assemblies of God* (St. Louis: General Council of the Assemblies of God, October 2–7, 1916), no. 8, 11.

Pentecostals declare, "We believe that the church is the body of Christ, a living, developing organization (organism), animated by the Holy Spirit, and whose Head is Jesus himself."[6]

As the body of Christ, the church belongs to Christ. "The Head of the Church is our Lord Jesus Christ, and it forms His body."[7] This means that the church can only exist in relation to Christ. The church that Christ builds is the one which he calls "*my* church" (Matt. 16:18, emphasis mine). Therefore, the church cannot have an independent, human existence apart from Christ the head; the church must live continually in dependence upon Christ and in submission to him.

This body of Christ is a single body (Rom. 12:4–5). There is one head and one body; "one flock, one shepherd" (John 10:16). Therefore the church is a unity. In the words of the Nicene Creed, there is "*one*, holy, catholic and apostolic church." One church does not exist to compete with another church, but rather each local assembly is "the visible expression of the universal church which is the Body of Christ, which is not delimited by denominations."[8] Every believer is part of this one body of Christ. Therefore, "the Christian life is not solitary; for no member lives apart from the body."[9]

However, it is not merely that there is a single church and that this church belongs to Christ. Rather, as the body of Christ, this one church is a living organism. The church is not simply a group of people united by their common belief in Jesus, their common desire for spiritual growth, or their common mission to make Christ known to the world. Rather, the church is a living body, filled with the life of Christ the Head. "The Church is the body of Christ, the habitation of God through the Spirit."[10] Christ fills his body with his fullness (Eph. 1:23) and with the Holy Spirit (Eph. 2:20–22). Therefore, the triune God dwells in the church, unites the church, and gives the church life and being. The church lives not with an independent life of its own but with life in the Trinity.[11] The life of the church, then, is life in communion with the triune God, which is God's eternal purpose for his church: "It is God's eternal plan to live in communion with man during his earthly life and after that in eternity."[12]

As a living body, the church is an organism. But as a body, this organism is organized. The body of Christ is "a living, developing organization

6. Hungarian Pentecostal Confession, 10.
7. Romanian CF, 20.
8. AdDDF, 7.
9. Brazil DdF, 11.2.
10. Indian Pentecostal Church of God, "Statement of Faith," 11.
11. Jonathan Black, *Apostolic Theology: A Trinitarian, Evangelical, Pentecostal Introduction to Christian Doctrine* (Luton: Apostolic Church, 2016), 552–53.
12. Hungarian Apostolic Confession, 7b.

(organism)."[13] It is "a divine structure in which the life of Christ indwells."[14] Life and structure, organism and organization, are not opposed to one another in the body of Christ; rather, both are necessary to healthy church life. This is what we see in Paul's description of the body in 1 Corinthians 12:12–31.

The Temple of the Holy Spirit

The body of Christ is filled with the life of God by the Holy Spirit. Therefore, Pentecostals emphasize that the church is "the Temple of God, a dwelling place of God through the Spirit and the body of Christ."[15] Paul challenges the believers in Corinth, "Do you not know that you are God's temple and that God's Spirit dwells in you?" (1 Cor. 3:16). He is writing to the Corinthians corporately together as the church here ("you" is plural in the Greek). It is not simply that individual believers are indwelt by the Holy Spirit, but that the Holy Spirit dwells in the church corporately. By the Holy Spirit, believers are joined to one another as well as to Christ their head and built up in Christ "into a holy temple in the Lord . . . a dwelling place for God by the Spirit" (Eph. 2:21–22).

This temple is made up of living stones, for it is the priests of God themselves (that is, all believers) who form the temple (Heb. 3:6; 1 Peter 2:5). This is not a static image but a dynamic and living reality. God by his Spirit dwells in the people of Christ, corporately together, forming them into a living temple. Their bodies are temples of the Holy Spirit because he lives in them (1 Cor. 6:19–20). But more than that, together they are one temple of God by the Spirit because they are the body of Christ, and Christ is himself the true temple and dwelling place of God (John 2:18–22; Col. 2:9).

Christ himself, the head of the church, forms this temple which is his body. In Ephesians 2 we see that it is through "the blood of Christ" that we "have been brought near" (v. 13), so that both Jews and Gentiles are "reconcile[d] . . . to God in one body through the cross" (v. 16) and together, through Christ, we "have access in one Spirit to the Father" (v. 18). Thus, it is through the cross of Christ and the Spirit who has been poured out by Christ that we are built into this "holy temple in the Lord" (v. 21). Christ, by his shed blood and poured out Spirit, joins those who trust in him together into the one body of which he is head, and in which God dwells as his temple. The body of Christ is the temple of God by the Spirit.

The Bride of Christ

At Azusa Street, William Seymour taught that "the Holy Spirit today is seeking a bride for the Lord Jesus, God's only begotten Son. . . . We that are

13. Hungarian Pentecostal Confession, 10.
14. Williams, "The Ministry of the Word," 174.
15. Romanian CF, 20.

Christ's bride must forsake all and cleave to Christ."[16] Alongside the definition of the church as the body of Christ, right from the earliest days of the Pentecostal revival, Pentecostals have loved to emphasize that the church is also Christ's bride.[17] In Revelation, the church (as the New Jerusalem) is described as "the Bride, the wife of the Lamb" (Rev. 21:9) and the church on earth now is destined for "the marriage supper of the Lamb" (Rev. 19:9). In Ephesians, we see that human marriage on earth points us to the great "mystery" of "Christ and the church" (Eph. 5:30), for "Christ loved the church and gave himself up for her" (Eph. 5:25).

This powerful image of the lovingkindness of Christ for his church drew Pentecostals to speak, preach, and sing a great deal about Christ as the Bridegroom and the church as his bride. As the Brazilian Assemblies of God confesses, "The intimacy, love, beauty, joy and reciprocity that marriage provides make it the symbol of the union and relationship between Christ and his Church."[18] Or, in the words of the Romanian Pentecostal confession, "The church is the Bride of Christ. Between her and Christ, the highest unifying force is love."[19] Thomas Rees, an early Welsh Pentecostal preacher, emphasized the unbreakable nature of this love of Christ: "The Bridegroom King and His chosen Bride [are] joined together in an indissoluble union of love."[20] Another Welsh Pentecostal, D. P. Williams, emphasized the experiential nature of this love, for the church is Christ's "Bride in the sense that Christ, the Bridegroom, holds affectionate relationship with the redeemed as the object of His love."[21] The love of Christ for his church is not only to be known in the age to come; already now, in this age, Pentecostals long to experience the great love of Christ by the Holy Spirit.

Yet, the church as the bride of Christ also points our attention to the future and the marriage supper of the lamb at Christ's return (Rev. 19:9). The constant call of the first generation of Pentecostals was "The Bridegroom is coming."[22] Early Pentecostals sang:

> Then be ready, brother, sister
> Ever watching unto prayer,

16. William J. Seymour, "Rebecca: Type of the Bride of Christ," *Apostolic Faith* 1, no. 6 (February–March 1907): 2.
17. Romanian CF, 20; Hungarian Pentecostal Confession, 10; Brazil DdF, 11.1.
18. Brazil DdF, 11.1.
19. Hungarian Pentecostal Confession, 10.
20. Rees, *The Divine Masterpiece*, 54.
21. D. P. Williams, *Minutes of the International Council of Apostles and Prophets of the Apostolic Church March 1928* (Penygroes: Apostolic Church, 1928), 153.
22. E.g., W. H. Cossum, "Mountain Peaks of Prophecy and Sacred History," *Latter Rain Evangel* (November 1910): 16; cf. Aimee Semple McPherson, "The Bridal Call," *The Bridal Call* 1, no. 1 (1917): 1.

For the Lord is coming quickly
To receive His Bride so fair.[23]

In the meantime, "the very absence of the Lord at the present time for those who are longing for His return is bringing to a head, to maturity, the love of the bride for the Bridegroom, which otherwise never could be brought to such maturity."[24] Thus, emphasis on the church as the bride of Christ brings together a focus on Christ's love for the church, the church's love for Christ, and her longing for his return. For Pentecostals, this longing for Christ's return also involves missions and evangelism, so that others too are ready for the coming of the Savior. Therefore, the bride of Christ must be a missionary church.

Recognizing the Visible Church

So far, we have been thinking about what the church *is*. Yet much of this is not necessarily visible externally. Furthermore, the definitions we have considered are true not only of the church presently on earth but of the whole church. The church currently on earth is not the whole of Christ's church; rather, as the Polish Pentecostals confess, the church is composed of "believers born again of the Holy Spirit . . . both those who live on earth and those who have fallen asleep in Christ." The dead in Christ "constitute the Triumphant Church, and those who are still alive on earth, the Pilgrim Church."[25]

How, therefore, can we recognize this visible pilgrim church on earth? A gathering of Christians is not enough to make a church; Christians can gather in all sorts of ways and for all sorts of reasons, and Pentecostals recognize this. Therefore, what constitutes a group of believers as a church? Pentecostals recognize several marks of a true church.

First and foremost, Christ and his gospel must be at the center of any true church. The Brazilian Assemblies of God declaration of faith declares, "We deny that there is a church if Christ is not glorified in it and if the Gospel is not proclaimed, believed and obeyed."[26] The church is Christ's body and bride; it cannot exist apart from him and in all ways he must have preeminence in his church (Col. 1:18).

Further, Paul warns the Corinthians against receiving "another Jesus than the one we proclaimed, or . . . a different spirit from the one you received, or . . . a different gospel from the one you accepted" (2 Cor. 11:4). Therefore, the church must ensure that it is the true Christ and his true gospel which is proclaimed, received, and believed. The true Christ and true gospel are the

23. "Christ is Coming," *The Bridegroom's Messenger* 3 (May 1910): 1.
24. "Love Links," *Weekly Evangel* 214 (November 10, 1917): 4.
25. Polish Pentecostal Confession of Faith (Wyznanie Wiary Kościoła Zielonoświątkowego), 9.
26. Brazil DdF, 11.2 (p. 69).

Christ and gospel revealed in the Scriptures. Thus, the Bible must be central to the life of the true church. As the Assemblies of God in France confesses, "We believe that the local church is the visible expression of the universal church which is the Body of Christ. . . . By its assemblies gathered around the Holy Scriptures, it builds and outworks its unity of faith, life of piety, and missionary vocation."[27] A true church is an assembly gathered around the Holy Scriptures, and the true life of the church (flowing from Christ the Head) will be built, fostered, and sustained by the Word of God.

The true life of the church is also sustained by the Lord Jesus as his people meet with him at his Table in the Breaking of Bread. A Bible study group is not a church; the sacraments of baptism and the Lord's Supper are essential elements of the life of a true church, without which it cannot be a church. The British Assemblies of God made clear in their inaugural magazine issue that it was "gathering round . . . the Lord's Table" that constituted gatherings of believers into a church.[28]

A British Pentecostal catechism drew on the Pentecostal love of the Bible in its answer to the question "How is the Church on earth known?" to set out a Pentecostal vision of the marks of a true church "as the body of people who continued steadfastly in the apostles' doctrine, and fellowship, and in breaking of bread, and in prayers (Acts 2:42)."[29] The proclamation and teaching of Scripture and the Lord's Supper are both essential, alongside the called ministry (for the church must remain in the apostles' fellowship) and prayer, the chief expression of faith in the living God.

A fuller description is found in Aimee Semple McPherson's declaration of faith for the Foursquare Church, which defines "the visible church of Christ upon the earth" as "a congregation of believers who have associated themselves together in Christian fellowship and in the unity of the Spirit, observing the ordinances of Christ, worshipping Him in the beauty of holiness, speaking to each other in psalms, and hymns and spiritual songs, reading and proclaiming His Word, laboring for the salvation of souls, giving their temporal means to carry on His work, edifying, encouraging, establishing one another in the most holy faith, and working harmoniously together as dear children who are many members but one body of which Christ is head."[30]

McPherson gives a particularly Pentecostal emphasis to evangelism, body ministry, and worship as marks of the church, while still maintaining the necessity of word and sacrament ministry—for example, when she insists on "observing the ordinances of Christ," while "edifying, encouraging,

---

27. AdDDF, 7.
28. J. Nelson Parr, "Editorial," *Redemption Tidings* 1, no. 1 (July 1924): 8.
29. J. B. Clyne, *Asked and Answered: A Catechism of Apostolic Principles* (Bradford: Puritan Press, 1953), 24.
30. FDF, 16.

[and] establishing one another in the most holy faith"—for authentic church life. There can be no church without the true proclamation of the Word and sharing together in the sacraments. There can be no ongoing church without building one another up in the most holy faith and proclaiming the good news of Jesus to others who do not yet know him, so that they too might meet him in his saving power and be added by him to his body, the church.

Summary

The church is not merely a gathering together of believers. Rather, it is a body united by the Holy Spirit to Christ the head who fills it with his life and fullness. As such it is a temple in which God dwells by his Spirit. As the special object of Christ's great love, the church is his bride and longs for the return of her heavenly Bridegroom. In the meantime, the church is visible on earth and found where believers gather to Christ and his gospel, under his word and around his Table, worshipping the triune God, building one another up in the most holy faith, praying in the Spirit, and reaching out to the lost with the good news of Christ.

REFLECTION QUESTIONS

1. What does it mean for the church to be the body of Christ?

2. In what way is the church a temple of the Holy Spirit, and what implication does that have for believers?

3. What is the significance of the church's identity as the bride of Christ?

4. Is the church only made up of believers who are currently alive on earth?

5. How do we recognize a true church? How might we distinguish a true church from a false church?

QUESTION 34

Could There Be Biblical Apostleship Today?

In 1913, something almost unprecedented in the history of the Christian church took place. Pastor William Oliver Hutchinson of Bournemouth (England) was ordained as an apostle in the body of Christ. The next year, Pastor Daniel Powell Williams of Penygroes (Wales) and Pastor Andrew Murdoch of Kilsyth (Scotland) were also both ordained to the apostleship.[1] Perhaps of all Pentecostal beliefs, it is the belief in apostleship in the church today that is most controversial. Cessationists maintain "the temporary nature of the apostolate,"[2] with some going so far as to insist that "it is contrary to Scripture for Christians to use 'apostle' for an office or spiritual gift in the church today," and that "to claim that there are apostles today leads to doctrinal confusion and ecclesiastical tyranny."[3] Yet, Pentecostals reject these cessationist claims and instead "recognize and encourage the operation of the manifold gifts given to Christ's church, including the apostolic ministry gift."[4]

Apostles in the New Testament

When we think of apostles, our attention turns, naturally enough, to the Twelve whom Jesus chose during his earthly ministry and "whom he named apostles" (Luke 6:13). Although it is common to refer to the Twelve as "the

1. It was not entirely unprecedented, as twelve apostles had been "separated" in London in 1835 in the Catholic Apostolic Church. In fact, the last apostle of the Catholic Apostolic Church had only died in 1901; thus Britain had only been without a ministry of apostleship for twelve years when Hutchinson was ordained.
2. Richard B. Gaffin, Jr., *Perspectives on Pentecost: New Testament Teaching on the Gifts of the Holy Spirit* (Phillipsburg, NJ: P&R, 1979), 89.
3. Joel R. Beeke and Paul M. Smalley, *Reformed Systematic Theology: Volume 1, Revelation and God* (Wheaton, IL: Crossway, 2019), 424, 426.
4. PAOC, "Contemporary Apostles," 1.

twelve apostles," this expression is only found twice in Scripture: once when their names are listed for the first time (Matt. 10:2–4); and once in John's vision of the New Jerusalem, where it is actually part of the longer expression "the twelve apostles of the Lamb" (Rev. 21:14). The Bible more commonly refers to them simply as "the twelve."[5] Thus, although the Twelve were indeed apostles, apostleship is not numerically linked to the Twelve. This is particularly evident when Paul is called to be an apostle.[6] Paul does not replace Judas, for Matthias has already been chosen to take Judas's place (Acts 1:23–26). Therefore, with the apostleship of Paul, the number of apostles in the New Testament rises to at least thirteen. Yet, Paul's apostolic ministry is not inferior to that of the other apostles (Gal. 2:8–9; see also 2 Cor. 11:5; 12:11).

However, when Paul's apostleship is introduced in the book of Acts, it is alongside the apostle Barnabas. Both are set apart together in Antioch through the prophetic word (Acts 13:1–3) and then, when identified as apostles for the first time in the next chapter, they are listed as "the apostles Barnabas and Paul" (Acts 14:14), with no indication of a distinction between their ministries. The sharing of Paul and Barnabas in the same ministry of apostleship is also indicated in that they both received the right hand of fellowship from the pillars of the church in Galatians 2:9, in recognition of the similarity of Paul's and Barnabas's apostolic ministry to that of Peter (Gal. 2:7–9). J. B. Lightfoot was adamant that "the apostleship of Barnabas is beyond question. St Luke records his consecration to the office as taking place at the same time and in the same manner as St Paul's."[7]

The prophetic word through which Barnabas and Paul were called to this ministry gives a further indication that they were each called to the same ministry. The Lord tells the prophets and teachers in Antioch to set the two apart "for the work to which I have called them" (Acts 13:2). The word "work" is singular, indicating that the two have been called to the same work—which, we discover in the next chapter, is the work of apostleship. Barnabas, it is worth noting, is listed first. Furthermore, in his first letter to the Corinthians, Paul writes of himself and Barnabas sharing in the same privileges of apostleship (1 Cor. 9:1–6).

The "pillars" in Galatians 2:9 who gave recognition to the apostolic ministry being exercised by Paul and Barnabas included Peter himself, along with John. But the first name on the list is that of James (the Lord's brother), who

---

5. This is common throughout the four Gospels, and the same designation is also found in Acts 6:2 and 1 Corinthians 15:5.
6. See Acts 14:4, 14; Romans 1:1; 11:13; 1 Corinthians 1:1; 4:9; 9:1, 5; 15:9; 2 Corinthians 1:1; 12:12; Galatians 1:1; Ephesians 1:1; Colossians 1:1; 1 Timothy 1:1; 2:7; 2 Timothy 1:1, 11; Titus 1:1.
7. J. B. Lightfoot, *The Epistle of Saint Paul to the Galatians* (Grand Rapids: Zondervan, 1957), 96.

was not one of the Twelve, and yet is here placed on par with Peter and John.[8] In Galatians 1:19, Paul writes that he "saw none of the other apostles except James the Lord's brother," thus explicitly designating James an apostle. This clarifies the prominence of James's role in the recognition of the ministry of Paul and Barnabas, and also at the Jerusalem Council of Acts 15. James, as one of a group of apostles in Galatians 2, recognizes the ministry of another group of apostles; as one of the group of apostles in Acts 15, he leads the discernment process among the apostles and elders. French Pentecostal teacher Jacques Gloaguen notes that this apostolic "authority is seen in the way in which James uncontestedly presided over the difficult debate on the matter of the observance of the Mosaic law by Gentile converts."[9]

In 1 Thessalonians 2:6, Paul writes that "we could have made demands as apostles of Christ." Here he uses the plural "we," suggesting that he is referring to more than one apostle. While some suggestions have been made that this could be a plural of majesty, referring to Paul alone, this view "is only a slight exegetical possibility."[10] A more plausible explanation is that Paul is including his two cowriters, Silvanus (Silas) and Timothy (2 Thess. 1:1) as apostles. A similar use of the plural by Paul in 1 Corinthians 1:19 explicitly includes Silvanus and Timothy. It might be objected that Silas is specifically designated a prophet in Acts 15:32. However, Paul too held another ministry—that of teacher—in addition to being set apart as an apostle (1 Tim. 2:7; 2 Tim. 1:11).

There are several other figures who are potentially named apostles in the New Testament; however, more debate surrounds these claims. For our present purpose it will suffice to see that, in addition to the Twelve and Paul, at least Barnabas, James, Silas, and Timothy are also designated apostles. This means both that (a) New Testament apostleship was not limited to the Twelve (or the Twelve plus Paul), and that (b) there were apostles in the New Testament who were not among Christ's disciples during his earthly ministry. As such, could it be possible for apostleship to continue in the church today?

Arguments Against Apostleship Today

Wayne Grudem argues that the qualifications for apostleship in the New Testament rule out the possibility of apostleship in the church today. He sees two qualifications: one must have (1) "seen Jesus after his resurrection with one's own eyes" and (2) "been specifically commissioned by Christ as an

8. James, the brother of John, had already been executed by this time (Acts 12:2).
9. Jacques Gloaguen, *Apôtres d'hier et d'aujourd'hui* (Lillebonne: Editions Foi et Victoire, 2021), 54. For a similar assessment of the apostleship of James from a cessationist scholar, see Thomas R. Schreiner, *Spiritual Gifts: What They Are and Why They Matter* (Nashville: Broadman and Holman, 2018), 26.
10. R. Schnackenburg, "Apostles Before and During Paul's Time," in *Apostolic History and the Gospel: Essays Presented to F. F. Bruce*, eds. W. Ward Gasque and Ralph P. Martin (Grand Rapids: Eerdmans, 1970), 294.

apostle."[11] Grudem roots the first qualification in Acts 1:22, where the new apostle chosen to replace Judas among the Twelve is to be "a witness to his resurrection," and then goes on to focus on how Paul meets this qualification. However, the qualifications for this final place among the Twelve not only included being an eyewitness to the resurrection, but also accompanying Jesus and the other apostles "during all the time that the Lord Jesus went in and out among us, beginning from the baptism of John until the day when he was taken up from us" (Acts 1:21–22)—a qualification which Paul did not meet. Grudem makes an arbitrary distinction among the qualifications that Peter sets out for Judas's replacement in order to make space for Paul but exclude all others. Either all apostles must fulfil the whole of Peter's criteria in Acts 1:21–22 (which Paul did not) or else these criteria should not be read as a general set of qualifications for apostles but more literally as the qualifications of the Twelve alone. In either case, Scripture does not support Grudem's selective claim here.

Grudem's second qualification is also weak in scriptural support. He does not explain what it means to be "specifically commissioned by Christ as an apostle," and groups together language of Christ's choosing of apostles, sending of apostles, and Paul's commissioning by Christ.[12] Yet the Scriptures he groups together here describe a wide variety of phenomena, ranging from Jesus calling and sending out the Twelve during his earthly ministry (Matt. 10:1–7), to the apostles casting lots to choose Matthias (Acts 1:24–26), and Christ appearing to Paul (Saul) on the road to Damascus (Acts 26:14–18). There is a rather significant difference between the Lord revealing his choice through the casting of lots and his appearing on the Damascus road, and Grudem does not further clarify what he means by a specific commission from Christ. While we might not think it in accordance with Scripture to expect a Damascus-road style of appearance by the risen Christ to commission apostles today (1 Cor. 15:8), there is nothing that specifically rules out commissioning that looks more like the casting of lots. Thus neither of Grudem's claimed qualifications of apostleship, on which he bases his argument that there can be no apostles in the church today, stand up to scrutiny.

A stronger theological argument is put forward by Richard Gaffin, who argues that the foundational nature of apostleship (Eph. 2:20) means that it had to be a temporary ministry, limited to the first generation of the church: "The foundation here is absolute and historical in character. It does not describe particular situations which the gospel reaches for the first time, regardless of time and place. Rather, it is part of a single, comprehensive redemptive-historical image (house-building) which pictures, in the case of the apostles

11. Wayne Grudem, *Systematic Theology: An Introduction to Biblical Doctrine*, 2nd ed. (London: InterVarsity Press, 2020), 1117.
12. Grudem, *Systematic Theology*, 1117–18.

as well as Christ, what is done once, at the beginning of the church's history, and does not bear repeating."[13] Yet, Gaffin's reading of "the foundation of the apostles and prophets" in Ephesians 2:20 is not the only way to understand a foundation. Opoku Onyinah, a Ghanaian Pentecostal theologian, as well as an apostle and former chairman of the Church of Pentecost, makes much of the foundational nature of apostleship in his argument *for* present-day apostleship. For Onyinah, the foundational nature of apostleship is something ongoing that the church always needs, in that apostles "begin a work and build on it."[14] This foundation-laying is seen in "the ability to lay sound foundation in doctrines," as well as beginning new churches and growing new churches to maturity through teaching the Word of God and appointing elders.[15] As such, the foundational role of the apostles will constantly be needed throughout the history of the church rather than limited to the first generation.

Jon Ruthven has put forward an alternative view of "the foundation of apostles and prophets" in Ephesians 2:20, arguing that it "represents the recurring apostolic and prophetically-inspired 'foundational *confession*' . . . which is *revealed* to and *confessed* by *all* Christians at *all* times."[16] He points to a "fatal dilemma" in the cessationist reading of this passage: Jesus is himself the cornerstone of this foundation in Ephesians 2:20; therefore if the foundation is limited to the first generation, then Christ's own foundational work would be over and done with in the past. "On the other hand, if Christ is alive and active in His ministry in the Holy Spirit, then the 'foundation' must be stretched to include the present time."[17] Yet, the next verses go on to make clear that Christ is the cornerstone of this foundation "in whom the whole structure, being joined together, grows into a holy temple in the Lord" (Eph. 2:21). "If Christ is limited to the first-century 'foundation,'" Ruthven asks, "then how can subsequent generations of Christians, indeed the whole Church, be so emphatically 'in Christ'?"[18]

The cessationist argument for a single generation of foundational apostles relies strongly on a particular idea of apostles "as *essentially* serving as repositories of yet-to-be-written Scripture."[19] Yet, as Ruthven points out, this idea is no more than a caricature. "The connection between these gifts and the New

13. Gaffin, *Perspectives on Pentecost*, 92.
14. Opoku Onyinah, *Apostles and Prophets: The Ministry of Apostles and Prophets Throughout the Generations* (Eugene, OR: Wipf and Stock, 2022), 181.
15. Onyinah, *Apostles and Prophets*, 181–87.
16. Jon Ruthven, "The 'Foundational Gifts' of Ephesians 2:20," *Journal of Pentecostal Theology* 10, no. 2 (2002): 34.
17. Ruthven, "Foundational Gifts," 38.
18. Ruthven, "Foundational Gifts," 39.
19. Ruthven, "Foundational Gifts," 41; cf. Schreiner, *Spiritual Gifts*, 158.

Testament canon is simply not as explicit in Scripture itself as the cessationists would have us believe."[20]

Ephesians 4 and Apostleship After the Ascension

The key Scripture for Pentecostal teaching on apostleship in the church today is found in Ephesians 4, where we find not only the purpose of the ministry gifts, but also significant information regarding the timing and duration in which they are given. First, the Scripture makes no distinction here between the five ministry gifts of apostles, prophets, evangelists, pastors, and teachers: they are all listed in the same way in verse 11 and treated as a whole in verses 12–16. Thus, there is no indication in the text for the cessationist claim that some of these gifts (pastors, and possibly teachers and evangelists) will continue throughout the history of the church, while others (especially apostles and prophets) would cease after the first generation. As John Ruthven puts it, "Exegetically, the gifts continue or cease as a single group."[21] Even John Calvin, who distinguished between the temporary "extraordinary" offices of apostles and prophets and the permanent ministry of pastors and teachers, could not make this a complete divide among the ministries of Ephesians 4, admitting that "I do not deny that the Lord has sometimes at a later period raised up apostles, or at least evangelists in their place, as has happened in our own day."[22]

Second, we read here that Christ gave these gifts of ministers *after* his ascension (Eph. 4:8–11). Thus, Jesus did not stop giving apostles to the church after the Twelve (whom he gave *before* his ascension). When Matthias was chosen to replace Judas among the Twelve, one of the qualifications was that he must be "one of the men who have accompanied us during all the time that the Lord Jesus went in and out among us, beginning from the baptism of John until the day when he was taken up from us" (Acts 1:21–22). Therefore, Matthias had to already have been qualified for this ministry (and thus given, even though not yet recognized) *before* the ascension. Yet in Ephesians 4, apostles are given *after* the ascension. Thus, this qualification that Matthias had to fulfil was not a basic qualification of apostleship, but rather a qualification of the Twelve as witnesses to Christ's resurrection (Acts 1:22). Hence, Barnabas and Timothy could later be called as apostles, even though neither had been disciples of Jesus from the Jordan to the cross to the empty tomb to the Mount of Olives. Neither Barnabas nor Timothy (nor even the apostle

---

20. Ruthven, "Foundational Gifts," 41.
21. Jon Ruthven, *On the Cessation of the Charismata: The Protestant Polemic on Postbiblical Miracles* (Sheffield: Sheffield Academic Press, 1993), 156.
22. John Calvin, *Institutes of the Christian Religion*, trans. Ford Lewis Battles, ed. John T. McNeill (Louisville: Westminster Press, 1960), 4.3.4 (p. 1057). McNeill notes here that Calvin elsewhere called Luther "a distinguished apostle of Christ by whose ministry the light of the gospel has shone."

Paul) fulfilled the criteria of Acts 1:21–22; they did, however, fulfil the criteria of post-ascension apostleship in Ephesians 4.

Third, Ephesians 4:13 states that these ministry gifts (including apostles) are given by Christ to his church "until we all attain to the unity of the faith and of the knowledge of the Son of God, to mature manhood, to the measure of the stature of the fullness of Christ." The end point here is the perfect maturity of the church in its faith and knowledge of Christ. Such a level of spiritual development has not yet been reached by the church, nor will it be until the return of Christ. This is the eschatological goal for the church, not a point in the history of the early church. Therefore, the fivefold ministry must continue until Jesus comes.

Summary

Although the label of "apostle" has not been widely used in the history of the church, Scripture does not limit it only to the Twelve. Rather we have scriptural evidence for a larger number of individuals who are specifically called apostles in the New Testament. Ephesians 4 also specifically refers to apostles given *after* Christ's ascension, with the implication that the head of the church will continue to give such apostles until the church comes to full maturity at Christ's return.

REFLECTION QUESTIONS

1. What evidence can you see that the word "apostle" was not only used for the Twelve in the New Testament?

2. What are Wayne Grudem's arguments against apostleship today? Do you think he makes a strong case?

3. How does Ephesians 2:20 relate to the question of whether or not apostles continue in the church today?

4. What is the relationship between the ascension of Christ and apostleship?

5. What is the purpose of Christ's giving of the ministry gifts? Has that purpose been fulfilled yet?

QUESTION 35

What Is Apostleship?

In the last question, we looked at the biblical case for the continuation of the apostolic ministry in the church today. In this question, we will give our attention to the nature of contemporary apostleship and consider how Pentecostals understand the nature of that ministry, as well as how a more recent concept of apostleship differs from classical Pentecostal positions.

Apostles of the Lamb and Apostles of the Church

Although the New Testament exhibits more than twelve apostles, it does testify to something unique about the ministry of the Twelve. Apart from Matthias, the Twelve were all called by Jesus during his earthly ministry (Luke 6:13). Yet, even Matthias was called before the outpouring of the Holy Spirit on the day of Pentecost and had been with the Lord Jesus and the rest of the Twelve "all the time that the Lord Jesus went in and out among us, beginning from the baptism of John until the day when he was taken up from us" (Acts 1:21–22). Thus, the Twelve are to some degree distinct from those apostles given after the ascension of Christ (Eph. 4:8–11). They are also distinguished as a group in the book of Revelation, where they are called "the twelve apostles of the Lamb" whose names are inscribed on the foundations of the New Jerusalem (Rev. 21:14).

Yet, as we have seen in the last chapter, the New Testament tells us of other apostles beyond these twelve apostles of the Lamb. There is clearly a distinction to be made. Yet there is also some sense of continuity or overlap in their ministry, for the apostle Paul insisted that he was in no way inferior to other apostles (2 Cor. 11:5; 12:11) and compared his apostolic ministry to that of Peter (Gal. 2:8). James is also included alongside Peter and John as a pillar of the church (Gal. 2:9) and appears to take the lead in the Jerusalem Council (Acts 15:13–21). In these cases, no distinction seems to be made between the apostles of the Lamb and other apostles outside of the Twelve such as Paul and James.

Thus, rather than two exclusively defined ministries, the New Testament seems to point to two subgroups within the apostleship: the Twelve (or apostles of the Lamb), and apostles of the church (or post-ascension apostles). This helps us to understand why Paul or Barnabas did not need to fulfil the same criteria as Matthias to be an apostle, for the criteria that Matthias fulfilled were criteria only for the apostles of the Lamb. Jacques Gloaguen explains that the twelve apostles of the Lamb "form a very particular group, for they occupy a unique position, historically and prophetically."[1]

Christ Our Apostle

The book of Hebrews tells us that Jesus Christ is himself "the apostle and high priest of our confession" (Heb. 3:1). In John's gospel, the verb *apostellō* is used seventeen times to describe the Father sending his Son into the world.[2] When praying for his apostles in John 17:18, Jesus uses this verb for "send," speaking both of the Father sending him into the world and of his sending of his apostles: "As you sent me into the world, so I have sent them into the world." Christ is *the* apostle, uniquely. He is "the perfect apostle, the embodiment of the apostolic office."[3]

Yet, as his prayer demonstrates, there is a connection between his apostleship and that of the apostles he sends. Apostleship, then, should always direct our focus to Christ, the true apostle, as its source. The church can only have apostles as they "partake of His anointed office."[4] Authentic apostleship is "the Apostle-Christ in action" through the apostles he has given to his church.[5] If Christ is the true apostle, there is need for plurality and collegiality among the apostles of the church, for no one human being could take on the fullness of Christ's ministry of apostleship. This is not only true of apostles but of all ministers in Christ's church, for "as the Head and Giver of grace and gifts, it is Christ who is the true source of all ministry. Therefore, it is really Christ who ministers through the ministers."[6]

The Ministry of Apostleship

In Acts 6:4, we see that "prayer and . . . the ministry of the word" are essential to the ministry of apostles. The first deacons were appointed so that essential tasks in the life of the church could be carried out, without taking the

1. Jacques Gloaguen, *Apôtres d'Hier et d'Aujourd'hui* (Lillebonne: Editions Foi et Victoire, 2021), 11.
2. David Petts, *Body Builders: Gifts to Make God's People Grow* (Mattersey: Mattersey Hall, 2002), 24.
3. Everett Ferguson, *The Church of Christ: A Biblical Ecclesiology for Today* (Grand Rapids: Eerdmans, 1996), 302.
4. B. J. Noot, "Apostles and Prophets," in Hugh Dawson, B. J. Noot, and Thomas Napier Turnbull, *Church Government by Apostles, Prophets, Evangelists, Pastors, Teachers, Elders, and Deacons* (Bradford: Puritan Press, n.d.), 13.
5. W. A. C. Rowe, *One Lord, One Faith* (Bradford: Puritan Press, n.d.), 247.
6. Jonathan Black, *Apostolic Theology: A Trinitarian, Evangelical, Pentecostal Introduction to Christian Doctrine* (Luton: Apostolic Church, 2016), 663.

apostles away from their central ministry of prayer and the word. The early church "devoted themselves to the apostles' teaching" (Acts 2:42). Thus, the ministry of apostleship cannot be separated from prayer and the proclamation of the Word, including gospel preaching and teaching.

Through the proclamation of the gospel, new churches are established. We can see this church planting especially clearly in the ministry of Paul and his companion apostles. However, even apostles who did not found new churches were involved in building churches up and establishing them in the truth of God's Word. Not all apostles are church planters, and not all church planters are apostles.

The apostles also set the newly established churches in order. Paul and Barnabas "appointed elders for them in every church, [and] with prayer and fasting committed them to the Lord" (Acts 14:23). Paul likewise left Titus in Crete to "put what remained into order, and appoint elders in every town" (Titus 1:5), and provided Timothy and Titus with guidelines for the qualifications for those they were to ordain as elders (1 Tim. 3:1–7; Titus 1:5–9). The seven in Acts 6:6 were also ordained by the apostles, through prayer and the laying on of hands.[7] The ordination of elders and ministers is an aspect of the apostles' care for all the churches (2 Cor. 11:28). This general oversight also includes care for the doctrine of the churches (Acts 15) and the exercise of church discipline (1 Cor. 5:1–5; 2 Cor. 2:5–11; 1 Tim. 1:20; 3 John 10).

One influential early Pentecostal apostle, D. P. Williams, defined the apostolic ministry:"The apostleship is invested with power and authority to carry forth the revelation committed unto them: in prayer, intercession, the ministry of the Word; to preach, teach and heal; to toil, labour and suffer; to ordain elders, impart spiritual gifts (confirmed of God with signs and wonders); to rule and govern with demonstration of Divine wisdom, knowledge and discernment."[8] Williams paints a picture of apostleship as an ongoing and vital ministry in the contemporary church. This is the common understanding of apostleship among Apostolic Pentecostals. To a large extent, Pentecostals recognize "a close resemblance" between the apostolic ministry and the role of bishops in the history of much of the church.[9]

---

7. There are differences among Pentecostals with regard to ordination. Some do not ordain; some do not insist on ordination by apostles; others (generally the Apostolic Pentecostals) require ordination by the laying on of hands by apostles. "The Lord sets apart His choice to the ministry in ordination through prayer and the laying on of the apostles' hands for the impartation of grace," see ACVG, 9.
8. D. P. Williams, "Apostleship," *Riches of Grace* (June 1924): 17.
9. IPHC, "Apostolic Biblical Statement and Practical Guidelines," 1. See also p. 16: "It is also a well-established fact of church history that the terminology of bishop superseded the terminology of apostle in the post-apostolic church."

It is important to note that Pentecostals do not see apostles as Scripture writers.[10] While some New Testament apostles did write Scripture, that inspiration and authority was not inherent in the office of apostle itself. Apostles today stand in continuity with the ministry of the majority of New Testament apostles who did not write any portion of Scripture. The authority of the apostleship, like all ministerial authority, is derived *from* Scripture. Apostles must always "appeal to the Gospel and the Written Word."[11]

Three Pentecostal Perspectives on Contemporary Apostleship

Today, more than twenty-eight million Pentecostals around the world are part of Apostolic Pentecostal denominations.[12] The term *Apostolic* needs some clarification, particularly in North America, where several non-Trinitarian groups use the label. While in the United States the term may, to some readers, carry connotations of Oneness, the Apostolic Pentecostals considered here are solidly Trinitarian. Instead, the term *Apostolic* refers to their understanding of the ordained ministry and church government. Apostolic Pentecostals believe that the ascended Christ continues to give gifts of apostles, prophets, evangelists, pastors, and teachers to his church, and so they ordain to each of these ministries. Many other Pentecostals recognize apostles in some way. The presiding bishop of the Church of God in Christ, for example, is also its chief apostle.[13]

Other Pentecostals, such as the Elim Pentecostal Church and the British Assemblies of God, believe in Christ's continued gift of apostles to the church today without seeing the need to ordain particular ministers to the apostleship.[14] These Pentecostals recognize that "it is reasonable to believe the ministry gift of the apostle has always existed in the Lord's church and continues to this day" while maintaining a separation between the ministry gifts and the governing offices of the church.[15]

A third group of Pentecostals, including both the American Assemblies of God and the Pentecostal Assemblies of Canada, take a more reticent approach. While considering apostleship as part of "the historical and contemporary

---

10. PAOC, "Contemporary Apostles and the Pentecostal Assemblies of Canada," November 2002, 10.
11. AC, Minutes of the Convocation of Apostles and Prophets of the Apostolic Church (1928), 36.
12. The three major Apostolic Pentecostal denominations are the Apostolic Church, with twenty million members; Christ Apostolic Church, with five million members; and the Church of Pentecost, with 3.3 million members.
13. The office of chief apostle is unique to the Church of God in Christ. This title is not used by other Pentecostal denominations that recognize apostles; other denominations instead emphasize the collegiality of apostolic ministry.
14. Elim SFT, 8; Assemblies of God (AoG), "Statement of Faith," 9; Donald Gee, *The Ministry Gifts of Christ* (Nottingham: Assemblies of God Publishing House, 1930), 35–37.
15. International Pentecostal Holiness Church, "Apostolic Biblical Statement and Practical Guidelines," 8.

heritage of the church,"[16] they are reluctant to allow the identification of specific ministers as apostles. Rather, they warn "that applying the word apostle for these individuals has led to confusion, even division, at times in church history,"[17] and argue that "such contemporary offices are not essential to the health and growth of the church, nor its apostolic nature."[18]

The New Idea of Apostleship (NAR)

More recently, a new focus on apostleship, along with a new understanding of the ministry of an apostle, has emerged in some parts of the charismatic world. Influenced by the Latter Rain movement in the middle of the twentieth century, the "Toronto Blessing" of the 1990s, and the teachings of Peter Wagner, various networks of ministries emerged that Wagner began to label a "New Apostolic Reformation" (NAR).[19] Adherents of the movement see contemporary apostles as "the key to discipling nations . . . the key to fulfilling the Great Commission."[20] These are very strong claims, and not claims that classical Pentecostals had ever made about apostleship. As Douglas Geivett and Holly Pivec are careful to point out, "NAR teachings do not represent the views of most charismatics or classical Pentecostals, but are, rather, entirely different."[21]

The difference in claims for apostleship goes hand in hand with a very different definition of apostleship within the NAR. Ché Ahn defines an apostle as "a Christlike ambassador with extraordinary authority called and sent out by Jesus Christ with a specific assignment to align the Church to bring Heaven's culture to earth and fulfil the mandate to disciple nations."[22] Ahn argues that because "God has appointed in the church first apostles" (1 Cor. 12:28), this means that God "has given extraordinary authority to apostles."[23] This includes the authority to bring revival, to wage spiritual warfare through making apostolic decrees, and to "govern on all seven mountains of culture, whether it's in the church, government, education, business, media, arts, and entertainment, or family."[24]

16. AG, "Apostles and Prophets," August 2001, 9; PAOC, "Contemporary Apostles," 1.
17. PAOC, "Contemporary Apostles," 9.
18. AG, "Apostles and Prophets," 8.
19. Ché Ahn, *Modern-Day Apostles: Operating in Your Apostolic Office and Anointing* (Shippensburg, PA: Destiny Image, 2019), 29–33; R. Douglas Geivett and Holly Pivec, *A New Apostolic Reformation? A Biblical Response to a Worldwide Movement* (Wooster, OH: Weaver, 2014), 1–8 ; C. Peter Wagner, *Apostles Today: Biblical Government for Biblical Power* (Ventura, CA: Regal, 2006), 9.
20. Ahn, *Modern-Day Apostles*, 33.
21. R. Douglas Geivett and Holly Pivec, *God's Super Apostles: Encountering the Worldwide Prophets and Apostles Movement* (Wooster, OH: Weaver, 2014), xiv.
22. Ahn, *Modern-Day* Apostles, 39.
23. Ahn, *Modern-Day Apostles*, 70.
24. Ahn, *Modern-Day Apostles*, 70–78, 124. This concept of governing on seven mountains is a NAR teaching called the "seven mountain mandate," which sees the church called to

Pentecostals do not accept this concept of a special, extraordinary authority given to apostles alone or the idea of apostolic governance beyond the church. Christ gives authority to his ministers by his word to govern in his church, under the ultimate authority of Christ the Head, expressed in the Scriptures. Their authority is not extraordinary but ministerial. True apostolic authority should also always be exercised collegially, not by an individual apostle. As the confession of the Apostolic Church puts it, Christ's servants (including his apostles) "are not called independently, as mere individuals, but in union with Christ and reliance upon Him, and collegially with one another. True collegiality in the ministry of Christ's Church means that her ministers must sit at one another's feet and hear the word of Christ in humility and love. Christ exercises His power of binding and loosing through His ministers both in the proclamation of the Gospel and in church discipline."[25]

In classical Pentecostal understandings of apostleship, there is not a special, mysterious type of authoritative revelation reserved for apostles alone. Rather, apostolic revelation "comes in the same way as all revelation from God," which is "why the main priorities of the apostles in Scripture are the Word and prayer (Acts 6:4)."[26] Such apostleship must not "assert dominance and control," nor should it "usurp an authority not granted by scripture."[27]

Summary

Apostles today are not Scripture writers, but minister only under the authority of the sufficient Scriptures. Nor do they possess an extraordinary authority over the church and beyond. Rather, apostles are servants sent by Christ, through whom Christ ministers to his people from his Word. At the heart of apostolic ministry is prayer and the Word, and it is through this ministry that apostles establish, build up, and care for churches and ministers. Where apostles have a role in governing the church (like in the Apostolic Pentecostal denominations), they are to govern together collegially and in full dependence on the Lord for his wisdom, knowledge, and discernment.

REFLECTION QUESTIONS

1. What is the relationship between the apostles of the Lamb and the apostles of the church?

---

advance the kingdom of God by taking control of these seven areas of culture. See Geivett and Pivec, *New Apostolic Reformation*, 161–64.

25. ACVG, 9.
26. Black, *Apostolic Theology*, 674.
27. PAOC, "Contemporary Apostles," 10.

2. How is the ministry of Christ as our apostle connected to the ministry of apostles in the church?
3. What are the three Pentecostal views of the place of apostleship in the church today? Which, if any, do you think is the most scriptural?
4. How does the Pentecostal understanding of apostleship differ from that of the New Apostolic Reformation?
5. To what role in a non-Pentecostal tradition could apostleship be compared?

SECTION B

Questions About Worship

QUESTION 36

What Is Pentecostal Worship?

Looking back over the first seven decades of the Pentecostal movement, William Menzies was struck by what he called the "reality" of Pentecostal worship. One could not look back "without being keenly aware of the sense of God's presence the people felt. Their services were 'holy ground.' Theirs were worshipping communities . . . their lives were bathed in prayer."[1] In their worship, "there was a sense of the manifest presence of God," for there they met with "the intensely real and very much alive" risen Lord Jesus.[2] From the earliest days, Pentecostals have seen worship as "the highest function of human life."[3] As the contemporary American Pentecostal scholar Lee Roy Martin puts it, "Worship is the highest occupation of the Church and . . . fulfils the ultimate purpose for which the people of God are redeemed."[4] For Pentecostals, worship matters a great deal. In practice, "worship burst forth spontaneously wherever the Spirit-filled congregated."[5]

Yet Pentecostal worship is often misunderstood. Frequently, those outside the Pentecostal movement confuse it for a particular style, with a particular emphasis on music and emotion. However, Pentecostals around the world (and throughout the last 120 years) have worshipped in vastly varying styles and made use of an incredible diversity of musical genres. The first British Pentecostal hymnbook included both the *Te Deum* (an ancient hymn of the

1. William W. Menzies, "Giving Thanks for Our Heritage," *Pentecostal Evangel* (November 24, 1974): 5. He adds: "Only later was the sense of the holy cheapened in some places by raucous music and whipped-up enthusiasm."
2. Menzies, "Giving Thanks," 5.
3. George Holmes, *O Come Let Us Adore Him: Studies in Worship* (Luton: Assemblies of God Publishing House, n.d.), 8.
4. Lee Roy Martin, "Introduction to Pentecostal Worship," in *Toward a Pentecostal Theology of Worship*, ed. Lee Roy Martin (Cleveland, TN: CPT, 2016), 1.
5. Edith Blumhofer, *Restoring the Faith: The Assemblies of God, Pentecostalism, and American Culture* (Urbana: University of Illinois Press, 1993), 91.

church, traditionally sung at morning prayer) and the *Benedictus* (Zechariah's song from Luke 1:68–79, also traditionally sung at morning prayer), both pointed (i.e., set out) for chanting, which is not a style many people would immediately associate with Pentecostal worship.[6] The hymns of Wesley and Watts, simple four-line choruses, nineteenth-century gospel songs, singing the Psalms and other songs taken word-for-word from the Bible, contemporary hymns, the latest worship songs, and reworkings of the traditional liturgical music of the historic church can all be found in different Pentecostal churches. (And, quite often, all in the same Pentecostal church as well!)[7]

There is not a single Pentecostal musical style. While many Pentecostal churches now accompany their singing with a band of electric guitars, keyboards, and drums, in many others you will find an organ or piano, and in some parts of the world Pentecostals do not use any musical instruments at all. In fact, no musical instruments were used to accompany worship in Azusa Street.[8]

Gathering in the Presence of the Lord

Pentecostals expect "a personal, experiential encounter of the Spirit of God."[9] We do not only accept by faith that the Lord is present among us as we gather to worship, but we expect to experience something of the reality of God's presence. Pentecostals have always recognized that "if they made room for God, he would come into their midst to bless, to heal, to convict, to save."[10] This is a key element in understanding Pentecostal worship. Pentecostals do not expect only to hear about God in the preaching of the Word, but to encounter the Lord in his grace and power in the Word. They expect "the manifestation of the Spirit" (1 Cor. 12:7) in their worship services in gifts like prophecy, or tongues and interpretation. Pentecostals do not simply sing *about* the Lord and his wondrous works; they sing *to* the Lord, as they stand (or sit, or kneel) in his presence. They fervently believe that "where two or three are gathered in [Christ's] name, there [he

6. *Apostolic Faith Church Hymnal*, ed. W. O. Hutchinson (Bournemouth: Apostolic Faith Church, n.d.), nos. 83, 14.
7. For examples of Pentecostal reworkings of liturgical music see the Jesus Church album *It is Finished*, and the song "Lamb of God" on *Breath of Heaven* from NCU Worship Live. Jesus Church is a Norwegian Pentecostal church, and the entire album is a setting of the Eucharist, including one of the few contemporary settings of the Nicene Creed. NCU Worship Live is a ministry of North Central University, an Assemblies of God institution in Minneapolis, Minnesota; the song "Lamb of God" is a contemporary setting of the *Agnus Dei* in both English and Latin. The same album contains a setting of Psalm 6.
8. Frank Bartleman, *Azusa Street: An Eyewitness Account* (Gainesville, FL: Bridge-Logos, 1980), 64.
9. Keith Warrington, *Pentecostal Theology: A Theology of Encounter* (London: T&T Clark, 2008), 20.
10. Menzies, "Giving Thanks," 5.

is] among them" (Matt. 18:20),[11] and that the church is the temple of God in which he dwells by his Spirit (Eph. 2:22). Therefore, they expect to encounter the presence of the Lord as they gather to worship. Ralph Riggs described Pentecostal worship as "a consciousness of the presence of God and a response to that consciousness, and a love for God which proceeds from the heart as the expression of the deepest soul."[12]

Over the last few decades, a new understanding of worship has crept into many Western (and Western-influenced) Pentecostal churches. However, this new teaching is quite different from the older, classical Pentecostal theology of worship. The newer concept of worship looks to Psalm 22:3 that, in the King James Version, speaks of the Lord who "inhabitest the praises of Israel," to see singing or music itself as mediating God's presence. Lester Ruth and Lim Swee Hong have traced this history of this interpretation back to a small town in British Columbia in 1946, where Reg Layzell developed a new theology of worship just as the Latter Rain movement was about to emerge.[13] According to Layzell's new teaching, "we produce or release the presence" of the Lord when we engage in corporate praise.[14] This "praise and worship" teaching ties "a biblical promise of God's presence . . . to specific practices, especially praise."[15]

The classical Pentecostal understanding of worship, however, does not look at God's presence as something we can "produce" or "release" by anything we do. The Lord *is* present among his people as they worship. We do not enable his presence; everything we do in a worship service depends on the fact that he is already there. Yet we do pray and ask him "to manifest His presence among His people."[16] Pentecostals trust in the promise of God's presence with his worshipping people and pray for him to make his presence known. "Pentecostals testify of a present experience, not of a vague emotional thrill

---

11. The context of this verse is not the worship of the church, but church discipline. However, Pentecostals do not see a problem applying the truth it conveys to any situation in which we gather in Christ's name, with no situation being more of a gathering in Christ's name than when the church gathers to worship.
12. R. M. Riggs, *The Spirit-Filled Pastor's Guide* (Springfield, MO: Gospel Publishing House, 1948), 206.
13. Ruth and Hong note that Aimee Semple McPherson did refer to this verse in describing a worship service and that Jack Hayford has described Pentecostal preachers exhorting people with this verse while he was growing up. However, Hayford was only twelve years old when Layzell developed his new worship teaching. Lester Ruth and Lim Swee Hong, *A History of Contemporary Praise and Worship: Understanding the Ideas That Reshaped the Protestant Church* (Grand Rapids: Baker, 2021), 9–10.
14. Reg Layzell, *Pastor's Pen: Early Revival Writings of Pastor Reg Layzell* (Vancouver: Glad Tidings, 1965), 95; quoted in Ruth and Hong, *History of Contemporary Worship*, 22.
15. Ruth and Hong, *History of Contemporary Worship*, 309.
16. D. Kongo Jones, "The Apostolic Form of Christian Worship," *Riches of Grace* 3, no. 1 (March 1927): 48.

but of a vital encounter with God's transforming and uplifting presence in vivid foretaste of joyful abiding eternally in God's presence."[17]

South African Pentecostal theologian Mathew Clark warns that the "newer [worship] practices . . . seem to domesticate the presence of God into 'praise and worship' techniques" and so challenge the Pentecostal understanding of the church.[18] "The recent emphasis on the crucial priestly and prophetic role of music," he points out, does not stem from classical Pentecostalism but rather the pragmatic adoption of Latter Rain thinking. Clark bemoans that "few contemporary practitioners seem to either know or care about this."[19] In this pragmatic, "performance-centered" model that has now entered many Western (and Western-influenced) Pentecostal churches, "'Worship' teams and leaders . . . fulfil the priestly mediatory function of mechanistically leading the congregation into the presence of God. . . . The musicians effectively bring about the presence of God in the gathering."[20] Clark wisely observes that this brings about a "performer-observer divide, and makes singers and musicians indispensable to the communal encounter with God."[21] This newer approach is "not a case of a different form of Pentecostal worship and singing emerging . . . but of a radically alternative form being imported" in which "the lyrics and melody often play a role so secondary as to be irrelevant. . . . The lyrics rarely centre on the great redemptive acts of God but on the works of God in nature, and on the subjective process and experience of 'worship' itself."[22]

Classical Pentecostal worship, however, was firmly rooted in the redemptive work of God for us in Christ Jesus. "All worship is established on Christ's redemptive work and empowered by the Holy Spirit."[23] Therefore, the words we sing are to reflect this. As one British Pentecostal leader put it, "The peak of devotion is not attained until we worship Jesus Christ as the Redeemer of men," for "the Holy Spirit witnesses to the redeeming Blood."[24] Indeed, "Christ brings the Father into focus [and] the Holy Spirit magnifies Christ."[25]

In early Pentecostal writing about worship, music was barely mentioned. Yes, Pentecostals love to sing. But singing is not the heart of Pentecostal worship. As one early Pentecostal leader bluntly put it, "Worship is not all singing."[26] Where, however, they did mention singing, it was generally to warn

---

17. Tony Richie, *Essentials of Pentecostal Theology: An Eternal and Unchanging Lord Powerfully Present and Active by the Holy Spirit* (Eugene, OR: Resource, 2020), 85.
18. Mathew Clark, *Pentecostals Doing Church: An Eclectic and Global Approach* (Newcastle: Cambridge Scholars Publishing, 2019), 22–23.
19. Clark, *Pentecostals Doing Church*, 47.
20. Clark, *Pentecostals Doing Church*, 160.
21. Clark, *Pentecostals Doing Church*, 160.
22. Clark, *Pentecostals Doing Church*, 180.
23. Richie, *Essentials of Pentecostal Theology*, 94.
24. Holmes, *Come Let Us Adore*, 26.
25. Holmes, *Come Let Us Adore*, 26.
26. Jones, "Apostolic Form of Christian Worship," 49.

against problems that could arise. Singing was to involve the whole congregation lifting their voices together, and any music should contribute to that. "As a church grows lukewarm and apostate," the American Assemblies of God leader Ralph Riggs warned, "the ministry of singing is taken over by the choir and the congregation largely is silent. . . . Let no human talent be displayed for human admiration, but let all singing rather be sincere and humble and only for the glory of the Lord."[27] Choirs and instruments are not to drown out the voice of the congregation; the lips of the priesthood of all believers are not to be silenced by the sound of a worship group.

New Testament Worship: A Regulative Principle

Although the term "regulative principle" is not often associated with Pentecostal worship, it is a helpful way to understand the traditional classical Pentecostal approach to worship. Tony Richie explains the Pentecostal regulative approach: "Pentecostal worship endeavours to restore or bring back Christian worship to its former position or condition. On the one hand, this improvement may require removing the impairments of later accretions. On the other hand, and, perhaps most importantly, it requires reclaiming the original worship practices of the NT."[28]

Pentecostals might refer to it as the restoration of New Testament worship, worship according to the biblical pattern, the Apostolic form of worship, or by some other expression, but what they mean is a desire to return to the way the New Testament church worshipped, and thus to regulate their worship by Scripture. Like many Pentecostals around the world, Kongo Jones insists, "The Apostolic form [i.e., the New Testament pattern] of Christian worship is the only true form for every age."[29] As the declaration of faith of the Brazilian Assemblies of God expresses it, "Our liturgy is simple and Pentecostal, following the model of the New Testament."[30]

For this New Testament model, Pentecostals look particularly to 1 Corinthians 14, and especially verse 26. Here "we have a glimpse of the Apostolic form of Christian worship. The New Testament writers know nothing at all of an individualistic conception of Christianity. . . . Every member on the same floor, worshipping the same God, and serving the same King."[31] In addition to the Lord's Supper, the elements of this New Testament form of worship consist of "prayer, praise, Bible reading, exposition of the Holy Scriptures or witness and financial contributions, that is offerings and tithes."[32] We cannot add our own elements, for the order has been given to

27. Riggs, *Spirit-Filled Pastor's Guide*, 202, 204.
28. Richie, *Essentials of Pentecostal Theology*, 95.
29. Jones, "Apostolic Form of Christian Worship," 50.
30. Brazil DdF, 15.3.
31. Jones, "Apostolic Form of Christian Worship," 48.
32. Brazil DdF, 15.3.

us by the Lord who teaches us how to worship him in beauty and holiness. "Liberty without order is not true freedom, but licence. There is an order of worship for baptized believers, and it is the order of the Holy Spirit."[33]

The Power of the Word: Preaching, Scripture Reading, and Scripture Songs

For Pentecostals, God's word does not return to him void but will always accomplish his purpose (Isa. 55:11). Thus, it is by his word that the Lord is present among his worshipping people. "The goal of Pentecostal preaching is that God himself will come down in the midst of the congregation . . . that the hearers may be transformed by the Holy Spirit."[34] Yet, it is not only in the preaching of the Word that the Lord makes himself powerfully known, but also as the Scriptures are read. Traditionally, classical Pentecostal worship has made much space for the reading of the Word, for "the reading of God's Word . . . does produce wholesome spiritual benefit among the people."[35] The Lord speaks and makes his presence known and his authority felt through his own words read from the Bible in the midst of his church. The long-standing Pentecostal practice of singing choruses made up of short portions of Scripture means that the Lord also addresses us while we sing, for as we sing these Scripture songs, we are immersing ourselves in God's Word and meditating upon it.[36]

The fact that the singing, reading, and preaching of God's Word are central to Pentecostal worship means that Pentecostal worship is a dialogue in which we hear the Lord speak by his Word and then respond with our prayer and praise. The Brazilian Assemblies of God declaration of faith expresses this "dialogical principle": "We understand that public worship is an encounter with God for dialogue: we converse with Him through our prayers, songs and offerings, and God speaks to us through His Word (preaching and teaching) and the manifestations of spiritual gifts."[37] Both halves of this dialogue—both the hearing and the response—constitute our worship, for "the flame of praise is fed by the Word of God" and "to worship is to feed the heart and mind with the truth of God."[38]

---

33. Jones, "Apostolic Form of Christian Worship," 50.
34. Lee Roy Martin, "The Uniqueness of Spirit-Filled Preaching," in *Spirit-Filled Preaching in the 21st Century*, eds. Mark L. Williams and Lee Roy Martin (Cleveland, TN: Pathway, 2013), 200–201.
35. Riggs, *Spirit-Filled Pastor's Guide*, 210.
36. Simon Chan, *Spiritual Theology: A Systematic Study of the Christian Life* (Downers Grove, IL: InterVarsity Press, 1998), 166, cf. 146.
37. Brazil DdF, 15.1.
38. Holmes, *Come Let Us Adore*, 10.

Gazing at the Glory: The Contemplative Nature of Pentecostal Worship

Pentecostal worship involves "contemplating the glory and greatness of God and the excellency of the glorified Christ."[39] As we worship the Lord, "the Spirit proceeds to carry the worshipper onward and upward till the whole being and spiritual vision is filled with the glorified Christ" and we delight in "the mysteries of the atonement and the marvels of communion."[40] It is this glorious vision of the Savior that transforms our affections as we worship, for "gazing with rapture upon the glorified Lord and constantly seeing fresh gleams and glimpses, the glory becomes reflected into the worshipper's soul, filling him with ecstasy and yet with a deep awareness of the dignity and Lordship of the One he adores."[41] In worship, the Holy Spirit lifts our gaze by the Word to contemplate the glory of Christ.[42]

Christ-centered Worship: The Table at the Center

Just as the Pentecostal faith is centered on Christ, so too Pentecostal worship is centered on him. This is seen above all in "public worship . . . centered around the Lord's Table on the Lord's Day."[43] Donald Gee, after his extensive travels around the world, lamented the lack of the weekly Breaking of Bread services in the United States. "Monthly communion services take its place, but seem a poor substitute."[44] While American Pentecostals had the "altar call" as the culmination of their service and a place to meet with Jesus, in the UK and many other countries the high point of worship and the place to meet with the Lord was at his Table.[45] And with the Table at the center, there could be no bypassing the cross. "At a breaking-of-bread service, we feel we cannot beg. We must just praise Him for all that He has done for us, and rejoice in His presence."[46] But whether around the Table on one side of the ocean or at the altar on the other, for Pentecostals "the test of the value or power of a meeting may be the degree in which Jesus is exalted, becomes present to the spiritual senses, and in which His name is really above every name."[47]

---

39. Holmes, *Come Let Us Adore*, 9.
40. Holmes, *Come Let Us Adore*, 14–15.
41. Holmes, *Come Let Us Adore*, 14.
42. Holmes, *Come Let Us Adore*, 26.
43. Holmes, *Come Let Us Adore*, 39–40.
44. Donald Gee, *The Pentecostal Movement: A Short History and an Interpretation for British Readers* (Luton: Redemption Tidings, 1941), 190.
45. Gee, *Pentecostal Movement*, 189.
46. William Barton, "A Thanksgiving Service," *Elim Evangel* (December 13, 1929): 523.
47. Arthur Booth-Clibborn, "Salvation Conferences," *Confidence* 3, no. 6 (June 1910): 142.

Summary

In worship, Pentecostals draw near into the presence of the Lord and respond to the reality of the glorified Lord in their midst, with love, praise, thanksgiving, and adoration. Pentecostal worship is rooted in the redemptive work of God in Christ and regulated according to Scripture. It is dialogical worship, for the Lord addresses us in his Word (in preaching, Bible readings, and the gifts of the Spirit), and we respond in prayer and praise. The contemplative and Christ-centered nature of Pentecostal worship is highlighted by the centrality of the Lord's Supper.

REFLECTION QUESTIONS

1. How does the older classical Pentecostal understanding of worship differ from the newer, Latter Rain–influenced understanding of praise and worship?

2. How does Scripture regulate worship?

3. What is the role of the Word in Pentecostal worship? Do you see this happening in your church services?

4. In what way is worship a dialogue?

5. In what ways is Christ at the center of Pentecostal worship?

QUESTION 37

How Do Pentecostals Understand Water Baptism?

A few years ago, I was helping to look after a Nigerian Pentecostal church in a big British city. They didn't have a pastor at the time and needed one to administer the sacraments. So, their presbytery asked me, which meant that I had the joy and privilege of baptizing their new believers, serving them at the Lord's Table, and learning some lessons from them about the sacraments along the way. At one baptismal service, a lady who was about to be baptized came to me and the elders just before we began to ask for prayer for healing. Immediately, one of the Nigerian elders responded, saying: "But you are about the meet with Jesus in the waters of baptism, and he is the Healer." "Amen! Hallelujah!" said the woman, and went joyfully to the healer in the sacrament instead.

That day the faith of these Nigerian believers challenged me, as I saw just how high a regard they had for baptism as a means of grace. For Pentecostals worldwide, baptism is "beautiful and wonderful. It pictures the death, burial, and resurrection of Christ, and of the believer in fellowship with Him."[1]

Pentecostals and Believers' Baptism by Immersion

From the earliest days of the Pentecostal revival, there has been a remarkable degree of unity among orthodox Pentecostals in their practice of believers' baptism by immersion.[2] From Azusa Street, Pentecostals could proclaim, "We believe in water baptism because Jesus commanded it after His Resurrection. . . . It sets forth the believer with Christ in death, burial, and resurrection. . . . Baptism is not a saving ordinance, but it is essential because

1. P. C. Nelson, *Bible Doctrines*, rev. ed. (Springfield, MO: Gospel Publishing House, 1981), 43.
2. Although in North America there was a baptismal controversy over "the New Issue," this was due to the rise of Oneness teaching and so was not a dispute among the orthodox and did not register to a significant degree beyond North America. See question 9.

it is a command of our Lord. . . . It is obedience to the command of Christ, following saving faith. We believe every true believer will practice it."[3] And this summary from Azusa Street still sums up the Pentecostal consensus today.

As the more recent confession of the Apostolic Church in Italy puts it, Pentecostals believe in "baptism by immersion in water of those who, being capable of understanding and willing, believe in Jesus Christ as Lord and Savior. This Baptism is in the name of the Father, of the Son and of the Holy Spirit, and symbolically expresses the participation of the believer in the death and burial of Jesus, dying to sin and the old life (immersion), and then rising with Jesus to a new life (emergence)."[4] The tenets of the Church of Pentecost express the position of nearly all Pentecostals: "Infants and children are not baptised but are dedicated to the Lord."[5]

This rejection of infant baptism in favor of believers' baptism, along with the practice of baptism by immersion rather than aspersion (sprinkling) or affusion (pouring), is almost universal within the Pentecostal movement. However, there is one major exception. Chilean Pentecostalism emerged directly from Chilean Methodism and carried across the Methodist practice of infant baptism. The Methodist Pentecostal Church of Chile continues to practice "sprinkling baptism for repentance; the baptism of children for consecration."[6] The Evangelical Pentecostal Church in Chile believes that "baptism is not only a sign of profession and a distinctive mark by which Christians are separated from the unbaptized, but also a sign of regeneration to rebirth [and] infant baptism should be kept in the church."[7] In this, Chilean Pentecostals are exceptional among the worldwide Pentecostal movement.

Most other early Pentecostals were unaware of the situation in Chile. Instead, they saw believers' baptism by immersion as a hallmark of the movement. Thomas Ball Barratt was a Norwegian Methodist minister who spread the Pentecostal message to many countries in Europe. Although he was baptized in the Spirit while still a Methodist and only later left the Methodist Church and received believers' baptism, he quickly came to view believers' baptism as an essential Pentecostal distinctive. Describing the beliefs of Pentecostalism as a whole, he wrote: "We believe that the Lord's decree concerning water-baptism, for all who believe, has never been recalled. The apostles and first Christians clearly practised believers' baptism, for old or young—the age is not stated, merely the necessity of faith. . . . If we would be in harmony with apostolic practice, then we must be obedient to the Lord's command also in this respect."[8] Barratt's wide travels allowed him to see that

3. "The Ordinances Taught by Our Lord," *Apostolic Faith* 1, no. 10 (September 1907): 2.
4. Chiesa Apostolica in Italia, "Articoli di Fede," 5.
5. CoP, "Tenets," 6.
6. Iglesia Metodista Pentecostal de Chile, "Declaración de Fe," 4.
7. Iglesia Evangélica Pentecostal, "Artículos de Fe," 17.
8. Thomas Ball Barratt, *In the Days of the Latter Rain*, rev. ed. (London: Elim, 1928), 217.

this was a view shared by Pentecostals internationally.[9] As one Pentecostal confession of faith put it, "There is nothing in the Ordinance for the unregenerate and unbelieving."[10]

Believers' baptism is, for Pentecostals, necessary but not salvific.[11] As Donald Gee sums it up, "Baptism in water follows saving faith, arises out of it, and confirms it; but it must never be confused with it."[12] Salvation comes only through "faith in Christ upon repentance from sin. Without that faith the merely physical act of baptism becomes sheer mockery."[13] Yet, he continues, "Refusal to be baptized is extremely serious . . . not because the ordinance itself possesses saving power, but because such an attitude of wilful neglect and rebellion reveals a condition of heart towards the revealed will of God that may make us justly doubt the possession of that grace, which, through repentance and faith, can alone bring us salvation."[14] For Pentecostals, baptism in water is not optional. It is an essential beginning to Christian life and discipleship for all those who trust in Christ.

The way in which people are baptized is also a major Pentecostal concern. Apart from the Chilean exception, sprinkling is unacceptable, and Pentecostals are at pains to stress this point. "The mode is important. It is imperative that we keep exactly to the Master's methods."[15] Pentecostals see this as a matter of obedience to Christ and faithfulness to Scripture. "Fidelity to Christ demands that we do exactly what His Word teaches, and that we do not substitute some other 'mode.' In loyalty to the Lord we must keep the ordinances as they were delivered to us by the apostles."[16]

Yet there is also a theological reason for the insistence on immersion as the only mode of baptism. "As Pentecostals, we practice immersion in preference to sprinkling because immersion corresponds more closely to death, burial, and resurrection of our Lord."[17] This correspondence is very important

---

9. Many early Pentecostal leaders received the baptism in the Holy Spirit while members or ministers in paedo-baptist denominations. Some, like Thomas Ball Barratt and D. P. Williams, received believers' baptism and went on to be major figures in the first generation of classical Pentecostal churches. Others, such as Alexander Boddy and Cecil Polhill, did not and faded out of Pentecostal life as Pentecostal churches began to emerge.
10. *The Apostolic Church: Things Most Surely Believed* (Penygroes: The Apostolic Church, n.d.), article 7b.
11. See CoGiC, "Water Baptism," in "What We Believe"; cf. Michael M. Kopah, "The Ordinances of Baptism and the Lord's Supper or Communion," in *Tenets of the Church of Pentecost*, ed. Opoku Onyinah (Accra, Ghana: Church of Pentecost, 2019), 204.
12. Donald Gee, "Baptism and Salvation," in *Water Baptism and the Trinity* (Springfield, MO: Gospel Publishing House, n.d.), 9.
13. Gee, "Baptism and Salvation," 8.
14. Gee, "Baptism and Salvation," 13.
15. W. A. C. Rowe, *One Lord, One Faith* (Bradford: Puritan Press, n.d.), 196.
16. Nelson, *Bible Doctrines*, 45.
17. CoGiC, "Water Baptism," in "What We Believe."

for the Pentecostal's personal understanding of what is happening as they pass through the waters of baptism: "When the candidate goes down into the water and is covered by it, he is proclaiming: 'I recognize that I am guilty sinner condemned by God's righteousness. His judgment is just. I merit this death.' But, when he comes up out of the water, he is affirming with certitude that: 'Christ has forgiven my sins and taken away my condemnation. I have become a new creation.'"[18] And this correspondence in form to death, burial, and resurrection is also significant to the Pentecostal understanding of the power of the sacrament of baptism.

Pentecostals and the Power of Baptism

In 1919, Miss Davies was baptized in the Skewen assembly of the Apostolic Church (in South Wales). Before passing through the waters of the sacrament, she said, "I am glad that I know Jesus and I want to be created a new person in Jesus Christ. I want to rise up from this water in newness of life tonight."[19]

As we've already seen, Pentecostals do not hold to baptismal regeneration. It's also clear that's not what Miss Davies meant, for she already knew Jesus. She had already received new life in Christ, yet somehow in the sacrament of baptism she expected to rise up in newness of life. She had already been made a new creation in Christ Jesus in salvation, yet somehow she could still express a desire to see this new creation in her life and connect it with her baptism. Baptism might not justify or regenerate, but baptism is powerful. It is not an empty symbol.

Pentecostals do use words like "symbolic" to describe baptism, and it can be easy to misunderstand what they mean. As the Ghanaian Pentecostal theologian Michael Kopah points out, "In the New Testament, symbols and reality are shown to be closely associated."[20] Thus, early Pentecostal writers did not understand symbols to be empty of content; rather, they saw the Lord at work through symbols to administer the reality seen in the symbol.[21]

Such an understanding means that Pentecostals could see baptism as a powerful means of grace by which the Lord is at work through the conjunction of the outward human act and the inward divine act. "If the outward rite is accompanied by an inward work of grace, you will walk with Christ in newness of life in the Christian community."[22] Therefore, baptism is not an empty

18. André Thomas-Brès, *La Foi Donnée aux Saints Une Fois pour Toutes*, reédition (Grézieu la Varenne: Viens et Vois, 2016), 280.
19. The Apostolic Church, Welsh Presbytery Minutes for 1919, "Yr Ordinhad o Fedydd," 73.
20. Kopah, "Ordinances," 204.
21. For a discussion of this in early Pentecostal theology, see Jonathan Black, *The Theosis of the Body of Christ: From the Early British Apostolics to a Pentecostal Trinitarian Ecclesiology* (Leiden: Brill, 2020), 124–25.
22. T. N. Turnbull, *The Full Gospel* (Manchester: Puritan Press, n.d.), 16. The "inward work of grace" to which Turnbull refers is union with Christ for salvation by faith, not an additional work of grace.

ceremony, but rather in baptism "we identify ourselves with Christ: as He was buried and rose again, even so we are spiritually to be buried and rise, and live on the resurrection side of the grave."[23] In other words, in the sacrament we lay hold of the grace that we have already received in Christ. Through faith, we have been united to Christ in his death and resurrection. And in baptism, trusting in what Christ has done for us, we can expect to see the power of that union expressed in our lives. That's what Miss Davies was talking about at her baptism in 1919.

Therefore, for Pentecostals, there is a connection between baptism and sanctification and growth in grace. As the former president of the Foursquare Church Jack Hayford put it, "A solid grasp of water baptism is an essential part of cultivating the inner life."[24] Hayford emphasizes that baptism is not only a momentary act. Rather, it is the beginning of the baptized life. Believers are to "accept the discipline of baptism—both by being baptized and living as one baptized."[25] And living as one baptized will involve seeing the ongoing effects of baptism in the Christian life. "To live the baptized life," Hayford explains, "is to live in an abiding recollection of my baptism."[26] "In [baptism] I obey the Lordship of Jesus. In it I welcome the Holy Spirit. In it I bury my past. In it my heart is circumcised so new life power and God's fullest promise for my life might be realized. In it every bondage and every yoke is broken, and my future is opened to fullest freedom in Christ that I may arise and walk in the life-giving power of my living Savior."[27]

Therefore, living in an abiding recollection of baptism points to these graces as ongoing realities. The power of baptism is not momentary, for the power of baptism lies not in the waters but in Christ, to whom we are united in his death, burial, and resurrection. The baptized life is a life of looking to Christ, to whom we are united, to work by "the life-giving Spirit of God to resurrect you on a daily basis, *lifting* you above the dead habits of the past and into newness of life for today and tomorrow."[28] For the sacrament "is the outward and visible sign of an inward and spiritual experience 'reckoning yourselves to be dead indeed unto sin, but alive unto God through Jesus Christ our Lord.'"[29] Baptism flows out into a life of mortifying sin and living "unto righteousness. We not only rid ourselves of the 'old man,' we put on a 'new

23. Turnbull, *Full Gospel*, 15.
24. Jack Hayford, *Living the Spirit-Formed Life: Growing in the Ten Principles of Spirit-Filled Discipleship*, rev. ed. (Minneapolis: Chosen, 2017), 56.
25. Hayford, *Living the Spirit-Formed Life*, 69.
26. Hayford, *Living the Spirit-Formed Life*, 61–62.
27. Hayford, *Living the Spirit-Formed Life*, 67.
28. Hayford, *Living the Spirit-Formed Life*, 64.
29. "Fundamental Truths," *The Apostolic Church: Its Principles and Practices* (Penygroes: Apostolic Publications, 1937), 214–15.

man.' If we do not do so, our baptism has been a false profession and has been in vain."[30]

Thus, for Pentecostals, even if they don't always use the language, baptism is "a means of grace and a source of great joy."[31] For "God has ordained, that by means of the ordinance, He would communicate a rich impartation."[32] Yet, this grace and impartation can never be independent of Christ and his cross and empty tomb. One way Pentecostals have expressed this is that "the Lord through the waters of baptism . . . seems to gather up all that has been known about Calvary and the Risen Life in the moment of the portrayal of the ordinance and carries it forward in deeper realization. This, of course, depends upon the measure of faith."[33] We can see this expressed in Donald Gee's testimony of his baptism:

> I shall never forget the joy that flooded my soul the night after I had been baptized when, at three o'clock in the morning, I read Rom. 6:4 once again, and found myself able personally to appropriate in all its glorious significance the typical truth contained therein. . . . My joy over my baptism consisted in the fact that at last I was able personally to appreciate and appropriate the rich typical meaning of the verse because I had been literally and actually "buried" through baptism by immersion. I knew now what those words of Paul meant in a new way.[34]

Gee had a fresh, joyful realization of being "in Christ—buried, risen, and walking in newness of life."[35] Yet that is not the only way Pentecostal believers have experienced the reality and power of union with Christ at baptism. While passing through the baptismal waters, "some have received the Baptism of the Holy Ghost with signs following. Others have been instantaneously healed of physical maladies."[36] Hayford testifies to this: "To live the baptized life is to be open to the fullness of the Holy Spirit. . . . Hardly a week goes by at The Church On The Way when we don't witness people who, *as they come up from the waters of baptism*, are at the same time filled—right there—with the Holy Spirit. They begin to worship the Lord supernaturally by the power of the

30. Turnbull, *Full Gospel*, 16.
31. John Lancaster, "The Ordinances," in *Pentecostal Doctrine*, ed. P. S. Brewster (Cheltenham: Elim, 1976), 85.
32. Rowe, *One Lord, One Faith*, 198.
33. Rowe, *One Lord, One Faith*, 198.
34. Gee, "Baptism and Salvation," 11.
35. Gee, "Baptism and Salvation," 11.
36. Rowe, *One Lord, One Faith*, 198.

Holy Spirit!"[37] But baptism, Hayford also writes, is "*intended to be a moment of deliverance.* . . . Things to which we have been enslaved, the snares in which we have been entangled through the actions of our adversary—when deliverance is needed from hellish oppression, *all are broken.* Water baptism is . . . a miracle moment!"[38]

Summary

Pentecostal baptismal services might not involve elaborate ritual. But they are far from minor moments. Baptism is not an empty sign but a powerful means of grace, and Pentecostals rejoice in "the richness of its spiritual significance."[39]

REFLECTION QUESTIONS

1. Why do Pentecostals practice the baptism of believers by total immersion?
2. How is baptism related to salvation?
3. Is baptism necessary? Why?
4. In what way is baptism powerful?
5. What does it mean to live the baptized life?

---

37. Hayford, *Living the Spirit-Formed Life*, 62. The Church on the Way is the church Hayford pastored in California.
38. Hayford, *Living the Spirit-Formed Life*, 66–67.
39. Gee, "Baptism and Salvation," 6.

QUESTION 38

Why Is the Breaking of Bread So Significant for Pentecostals?

"At the Table of the Lord . . . we are face to face with the holiest mystery of the universe."[1] These are not words from another tradition; they are very Pentecostal words. (In fact, they were penned by Harry William Greenway, the General Superintendent of the Elim Pentecostal Church in the UK.) In the Breaking of Bread, the incarnation and atonement are set forth,[2] as we "feast on the Lord Jesus, in all His glorious reality."[3] In the Lord's Supper, "we are having fellowship with the Son of God Himself."[4] As another Elim leader put it, "Pentecostals love the communion service beyond all occasions [for] it is then . . . that the Lord draws the closest."[5] D. P. Williams of the Apostolic Church expressed this delight at the Lord's Table in a Welsh Communion hymn:

> The earth's best glories
> And the world's highest esteem,
> Fade away into nothingness,
> In enjoying your countenance;
> Your smiles are the sun of the heavens,
> Eternal summer is Your face,

1. H. W. Greenway, *This Emotionalism* (London: Victory Press, 1954), 151.
2. Myer Pearlman, "The Christian and the Lord's Supper," *Pentecostal Evangel* (December 8, 1934): 9.
3. W. F. P. Burton, *What Mean Ye By These Stones? Bible Talks on the Lord's Table* (London: Victory Press, 1947), 53.
4. Myer Pearlman, "The Bread and Blood Covenant," *Pentecostal Evangel* (September 12, 1942): 3.
5. George Canty, *In My Father's House: Pentecostal Explorations of the Major Christian Truths* (London: Marshall, Morgan & Scott, 1969), 58.

And delight for endless ages
In enjoying your Feast of Love.[6]

Pentecostals delight in this sacramental feast, for, as Donald Gee put it, in the Breaking of Bread "he whose presence makes heaven itself what it is, [is present] in our very midst."[7]

The Centrality of the Supper

That is why, in many parts of the world, Pentecostals have historically gathered *every* Lord's Day around the Lord's Table for the Breaking of Bread as their primary act of worship.[8] In fact, in many countries, the main weekly worship service is generally simply called "the Breaking of Bread" to reflect the centrality of the Supper. As Greenway put it, "A church without the sacrament is lacking the fundamental basis of all true worship."[9] The sacrament of the Supper is central not only to the Sunday service; it is central to the life of Pentecostal churches. Another notable past Pentecostal denominational leader, John Bond of the Assemblies of God in South Africa, argued, "Far from being peripheral, the Breaking of Bread emphasises every central fact of Christian belief. . . . It places Jesus Christ at the centre of faith and practice."[10] Therefore, "the Breaking of Bread should be celebrated when the whole congregation is gathered together . . . once a week on Sunday."[11] To celebrate the Supper less frequently than weekly reflects, Bond argues, a lack of understanding "of its meaning as the staple of Christian life."[12] The Lord instituted the Breaking of Bread as the "setting for the whole life of Christ's Church, as permanent as the Church itself," and as the "focus around which the life and worship of the whole church should take form."[13] As such, the Breaking of Bread should not be reduced to "a hasty appendage to some or other preaching service or celebration of chorus singing," nor should the meaning of the service be distracted by "man-centered actions, right at the time of all times when manward things should be forgotten in the light of Godward

6. D. P. Williams, "Mae rhyw ddyheadau cryfion," in *Molwch Dduw* (Penygroes: Apostolic Church, 1952), no. 315.
7. Donald Gee, "A Visit to Elim," *Elim Evangel* (May 1923): 81.
8. This has been the historic, classical Pentecostal form of worship in the UK, Ireland, Australia, New Zealand, and South Africa, and anywhere where Pentecostalism was introduced by missionaries from these countries. It is also the standard pattern in the Pentecostal churches with which I am familiar in Belgium and France.
9. Greenway, *This Emotionalism*, 151.
10. John Bond, *A Study on the Breaking of Bread Service* (Cape Town: AoG, n.d.), i.
11. Bond, *A Study on the Breaking of Bread Service*, 16. Bond insists that "the practice in some circles of relegating the Breaking of Bread to house meetings is unbiblical and would not occur were the true meaning understood" (p. 1).
12. Bond, *A Study on the Breaking of Bread Service*, 4.
13. Bond, *A Study on the Breaking of Bread Service*, 1–2.

worship."[14] For Pentecostals, the Breaking of Bread takes such a central place because at this Table the Lord's death is proclaimed and we encounter the crucified and living Savior. The Breaking of Bread is a vital *means of grace*.[15]

One Bread, One Body

The Breaking of Bread is central not only to the worship of the church but to the being of the church. Through our sharing in the Supper, the Lord Jesus bakes believers together so that "we who are many are one body, for we all partake of the one bread" (1 Cor. 10:17). This is reflected in Pentecostal confessions around the world: one Romanian Pentecostal confession states that the Lord's Supper "is foundational in the life of the Church," while Hungarian Pentecostals confess that "in the Lord's Supper, we live."[16] Another Pentecostal leader expressed it this way: "In the Breaking of Bread He constitutes the assembled believers into one body by the sharing of the one loaf. It is in this shared meal that the membership in the body is truly represented much more than in some church register or record of members. By the eating and drinking together of the bread and wine an existential bond is formed which in the truest sense establishes church membership."[17] Christ himself, on whom we feed in the Supper, is the bond that binds us together. As we each eat and drink of the same Christ, we are bound together by him as one in the body of Christ.

Commemoration and Proclamation

The Breaking of Bread is the feast of Christ's cross, and so Pentecostals place a great deal of emphasis on this memorial proclamation of Calvary in the Supper. As the Main Articles of Faith of the Finnish Pentecostal Church confesses, "The Communion proclaims the reconciliatory work of Jesus and is a participation in His Death and Resurrection."[18] The Foursquare declaration calls "the blessed sacrament" a "commemoration" and "a blessed type which should ever remind the participant of the shed blood of the Savior."[19]

When the Lord Jesus instituted the Supper, he said, "Do this in remembrance of me" (1 Cor. 11:24–25). However, in Scripture, a remembrance is not simply a memory aid. The Old Testament Passover had been given as a remembrance (or memorial). Yet, the Passover was not merely an object

---

14. Bond, *A Study on the Breaking of Bread Service*, 4.
15. See ACVG, 7; Daniel L. Black, "We Believe in the Lord's Supper," *Church of God Evangel* (Sept. 2007): 7; Pearlman, "Bread and Blood Covenant," 2; and D. P. Williams, "Editorial Note: The Lord's Table," *Riches of Grace* 3, no. 7 (May 1928): 276.
16. Pentecostal Theological Institute Bucharest, "Confession of Faith," 9; Hungarian Pentecostal Confession, 8.
17. Bond, *A Study on the Breaking of Bread Service*, 7.
18. Pentecostal Church of Finland, "Main Articles of Faith," 8.
19. FDF, 9.

lesson to remind people of a long-past historical event. Rather, it was a powerful proclamation of the present reality of the Lord's great deliverance of his people. Likewise, "the Breaking of Bread is more than a mere remembrance of past events. It *relives* the act of redemption. It goes back to the supper room and Calvary."[20]

The sacrifices in the tabernacle were also given as memorials, but these memorials were sent up to the Lord (Lev. 2:2, 9, 16; 5:12; 6:15). They were memorials before God rather than memorials before human beings. The Lord, however, can never forget. Therefore, this shows us that the biblical concept of memorial is something much more powerful than a reminder. Jesus did not say, "Do this so you will remember," but simply, "Do this *in* remembrance." The Breaking of Bread is not only our remembrance of Christ's sacrifice, but God's remembrance of all that he has done for us in Christ.[21] As Myer Pearlman, one of the most influential teachers of Pentecostal doctrine of the twentieth century, explained, in the sacrament of the Supper, the bread and wine are "*presented to God the Father* in memorial of Christ's inexhaustible sacrifice."[22]

This remembrance is the powerful proclamation of "the Lord's death until he comes" (1 Cor. 11:26). Christ's words—"This is my body, which is given for you" (Luke 22:19), and "this is my blood of the covenant, which is poured out for many for the forgiveness of sins" (Matt. 26:28)—are spoken at his Table, proclaiming the good news of Christ's death for us on the cross. In the broken bread and poured-out wine we have a visible word proclaiming the Lord's death. Both audibly and visibly, the gospel is proclaimed in the Breaking of Bread.

Anticipation

The Breaking of Bread is not only connected back to Christ's death for us on the cross but also forward to his return. We keep this feast only "until he comes" (1 Cor. 11:26). As the Foursquare declaration puts it, the Lord's Supper is "a glorious rainbow that spans the gulf of years between Calvary and the coming of the Lord, when in the Father's kingdom, He will partake anew with His children."[23] Romanian Pentecostals confess that the Supper is "a prophecy of His second coming."[24] As we meet with Christ in bread and wine at his Table, we long for the day when he will return and we will feast with him at the marriage supper of the Lamb (Rev. 19:6–9). In the meantime, the "present consciousness of the living Christ at His table is a foretaste of

20. Bond, *A Study on the Breaking of Bread Service*, 6 (emphasis original).
21. Jonathan Black, *The Lord's Supper: Our Promised Place of Intimacy and Transformation with Jesus* (Minneapolis: Chosen, 2023), 56–57.
22. Pearlman, "The Christian and the Lord's Supper," 9 (emphasis added).
23. FDF, 9.
24. Romanian CF, 14.

the richer coming fellowship in His Kingdom."[25] Therefore, every Breaking of Bread is an anticipation of the return of the Savior and of the eternal communion we will enjoy with him in the resurrection.

Participation

Paul puts a rhetorical question to the Corinthians concerning the Lord's Supper: "The cup of blessing that we bless, is it not a participation in the blood of Christ? The bread that we break, is it not a participation in the body of Christ?" (1 Cor. 10:16). The clearly intended answer is: yes, the Breaking of Bread is a participation in the body and blood of Christ. Therefore, Pentecostals generally come to the Lord's Table expecting this communion; they expect to meet with the Savior. They do not all agree as to *how* they will meet with Christ in the Supper (other than to reject the Roman Catholic concept of transubstantiation), but for the most part they agree that "the Breaking of Bread is more than a mere remembrance of past events."[26] By partaking of the Lord's Supper, Indonesian Pentecostals confess, we "strengthen our fellowship with God and one with another."[27] Or, as Norwegian Pentecostals put it, "We celebrate Communion to have communion with Jesus and each other."[28] Austrian Pentecostals confess that, in the Supper, believers "meet their exalted Lord."[29] In Romania, Pentecostals believe that "through participation in the Lord's Supper believers enter into fellowship with their divine Lord, Jesus Christ."[30] Likewise, the Church of God in Christ (the largest Pentecostal denomination in the United States) confesses that "the communicant by faith enters into a special spiritual union of soul with the glorified Christ."[31]

British Pentecostal leaders D. P. Williams and Donald Gee warned against the possibility of overreacting to transubstantiation by losing sight of Christ's presence. "In rightly rejecting this theory [i.e., transubstantiation] Protestants need to watch that they do not go too far away from some real truth."[32] Both insist that we must not fail to grasp the true communion we have with Christ in the Supper, in the "mystical union of eating his flesh and drinking his blood . . . [being] made partakers of the Living Christ."[33] Rather, in partaking of the Breaking of Bread, believers should have "a strong apprehension of the spiritual presence of Christ" and truly partake "of the life of Christ in the act

25. Bond, *A Study on the Breaking of Bread Service*, 6.
26. Bond, *A Study on the Breaking of Bread Service*, 6.
27. Gereja Bethel Indonesia, "Confession of Faith," 11.
28. Pentecostal Movement in Norway, "Holy Communion," in "Basis of Faith."
29. Austrian Free Pentecostal Church, "Doctrinal Principles," 9.
30. Pentecostal Theological Institute Bucharest, "Confession of Faith," 9.
31. CoGiC, "The Lord's Supper (Holy Communion)," in "What We Believe."
32. Donald Gee, *Keeping in Touch* (London: Elim, 1951), 75; see also D. P. Williams, "The Path to Maturity 8," *Herald of Grace* 6, no. 3 (March 1946): 67.
33. Williams, "Path to Maturity 8," 68.

of Communion."[34] In the Supper, "we partake substantially . . . of his body and his blood, to be sustenance for the spiritual life."[35] As such, many Pentecostals are very happy to speak of "*the real presence* in the Breaking of Bread."[36]

When explanations of Christ's real presence have been offered, many Pentecostals have put forward a Reformed understanding—that through partaking of the elements of bread and wine, the Holy Spirit lifts us up to feed upon Christ's body and blood in the heavenlies; others have taken a more Lutheran approach—that we receive the body and blood of Christ along with the bread and wine. A Canadian Pentecostal catechism, for example, teaches that "the Body and Blood of Christ [are partaken of by] true believers only . . . spiritually in the Lord's Supper."[37] This is for "the strengthening and refreshing of our souls by the body and blood received in the Lord's Supper."[38] The catechism goes on to explain that "the Body and Blood of Christ [are] received in the Lord's Supper . . . after a heavenly and spiritual manner only, and not in a material sense."[39] Polish Pentecostals make a similar declaration: "Christ's presence in the Supper is real, but spiritual, not material."[40] There are also some Pentecostals who are uncomfortable with either concept of the real presence by bread and wine, and instead prefer a concept of Jesus's powerful presence as host of the feast in the midst of his people as they eat and drink.[41] Pentecostals have not had any significant divisions over this question, as it is the presence of Jesus (rather than the way in which his presence is explained) that they see as most important. Pentecostals who take each of these differing approaches to understanding Christ's presence can all agree that in the Supper the Holy Spirit "causes Jesus Christ to be present to us, and . . . ushers us into the presence of the Father . . . Christ is really present. The past Calvary is really transported into the personal present. We are really fed and comforted by the presence of Jesus."[42]

Healing at the Table

The Lord "receive[s] us at His table with forgiveness, love and blessing."[43] In the sacrament, "by sensible signs the grace of God in Christ, and the benefits

34. Gee, *Keeping in Touch*, 75.
35. D. P. Williams, *Athrawiaethau Sylfeinol* (Penygroes: Apostolic Church, 1914), 10.
36. Bond, *A Study on the Breaking of Bread Service*, 7.
37. *Concerning the Faith*, (Toronto: Full Gospel Publishing House, 1951), 72, q. 444.
38. *Concerning the Faith*, 72, q. 446.
39. *Concerning the Faith*, 72, q. 445.
40. Pentecostal Church in Poland, "Komentarz do Wyznania Wiary," 7.
41. For more on these Pentecostal views, see Jonathan Black, *Apostolic Theology : A Trinitarian, Evangelical, Pentecostal Introduction to Christian Doctrine* (Luton: Apostolic Church, 2016), 603–12.
42. Bond, *A Study on the Breaking of Bread Service*, 6.
43. Bond, *A Study on the Breaking of Bread Service*, 7.

of the covenant of grace are represented, sealed, and applied to believers."[44] This includes Christ's "giving of life, strength, and joy to the soul."[45] The Jesus who is present to bless in his Supper is the healer, and therefore "there is healing at the Table" because the healer is at the Table.[46] Pentecostals have recounted many testimonies of healing at the Breaking of Bread.[47] However, the sacrament is not a mechanical means of healing. Receiving Communion does not guarantee healing, and we must guard against teachings which would appear to place the power of healing (or any other blessing) in the taking of Communion itself, rather than in the Lord whom we meet in the Supper.[48] As we come to the Table, we must discern the Lord's body (1 Cor. 11:29). It is in recognizing Christ's presence that we see the true source of healing in the Supper.[49]

Summary

Pentecostals love the Breaking of Bread because they love Jesus whom they meet there. Although in some places the Pentecostal emphasis on the presence of Christ in the Supper has in more recent years received less emphasis (or even been forgotten, often through the influence of teaching from other evangelical traditions), this has been a long-standing emphasis in much of the Pentecostal world. At the Lord's Table, we proclaim his death, rejoice in his living presence, and look forward to his return. As we partake of the Supper, the Lord Jesus binds us together into one body in him, and we can receive all the blessings that are found in him, including healing.

REFLECTION QUESTIONS

1. In what way is the Lord's Supper a remembrance?

2. Why have many Pentecostals found weekly (or more frequent) Communion so important?

---

44. CoGiC, "The Ordinances of the Church," in "What We Believe."
45. CoGiC, "The Lord's Supper (Holy Communion)," in "What We Believe."
46. W. A. C. Rowe, *One Lord, One Faith* (Bradford: Puritan Press, n.d.), 211.
47. For examples, see Black, *Lord's Supper*, 171–72.
48. Some recent neocharismatic writings on the Supper as a source of healing veer off in this direction, e.g., Beni Johnson, *The Power of Communion: Accessing Miracles Through the Body and Blood of Jesus* (Shippensburg, PA: Destiny Image, 2019). The result is a sort of quasi-magical view of Communion, which ends up treating it like some sort of fetish or charm.
49. Black, *Lord's Supper*, 165–76; Chris E. W. Green, *Toward a Pentecostal Theology of the Lord's Supper: Foretasting the Kingdom* (Cleveland, TN: CPT, 2012), 275–77.

3. How do you understand Christ's presence in the Breaking of Bread?
4. Do you believe that there is healing at the Table? Why or why not?
5. How does the Breaking of Bread help us look forward to Christ's return?

SECTION C

Questions About the Second Coming

QUESTION 39

What Do Pentecostals Believe About the Return of Christ?

"We Apostolic people are always mentioning the Second Coming," wrote Thomas Jones, a first-generation Welsh Pentecostal leader.[1] The Norwegian Pentecostal pioneer Thomas Ball Barratt pointed to this looking "forward to the second coming of Christ with expectant hearts and great joy" as one of the distinguishing marks of Pentecostals.[2] This same emphasis on the Lord's return was true across Pentecostal denominations around the world. Eschatology and Pentecostalism are so closely intertwined that "any attempt to understand Pentecostalism," argues James Glass, "necessarily entails consideration of [its] eschatological outlook."[3]

The Importance of Eschatology to Pentecostal Theology and Identity

Pentecostals believe that Jesus "is the coming King, who will personally come again to take His church to Himself to be with Him forever."[4] The second coming of Christ "is expected and longed for by all believers."[5] This is "our great hope."[6] Pentecostals place so much emphasis on the return of Christ that the Church of God in Christ places it in third position (after only the inspiration of Scripture and the doctrine of the Trinity) in its statement of faith.[7] For the Assemblies of God (in the United States), the second coming

1. Thomas Jones, "Christ the Shepherd," *Riches of Grace* 1, no. 9 (1920): 16.
2. T. B. Barratt, *In the Days of the Latter Rain*, rev. ed. (London: Elim, 1928), 222.
3. James Glass, "Eschatology: A Clear and Present Danger—A Sure and Certain Hope," in *Pentecostal Perspectives*, ed. Keith Warrington (Carlisle: Paternoster, 1998), 122.
4. Verbond van Vlaamse Pinkstergemeenten, "Wat Wij Geloven," 4.4.
5. Mosaik (The Danish Pentecostal Movement), "Declaration of Faith," 2; cf. Pentecostal Movement in Iceland, "Creed," 6.
6. Pentecostal Assemblies of Canada, "Restoration," in "Statement of Essential Truths."
7. CoGiC, "Statement of Faith," 3.

of Christ is (along with salvation, baptism in the Spirit, and divine healing) one of its "four core doctrines."[8] Many Pentecostals place a similar emphasis on Christ's return by speaking of a foursquare (or fourfold) gospel of Jesus as Savior, healer, baptizer in the Holy Spirit, and soon-coming King.[9] This Pentecostal emphasis on the Lord's return is good news, Stanley Horton reminds us, for it "draws attention to the truth that God is a personal God who has a purpose and a plan for the future as well as for the present, and He can be counted on to carry out His plan."[10]

So important was the soon return of Christ to early Pentecostals that William Faupel argues that "the second coming of Jesus was the central concern of the initial Pentecostal message."[11] However, as time went on, "gradually the focus of the message turned from announcing the coming of the kingdom to give attention to the growing demands of a fledgling church."[12] Yet, Christ's return has remained a very important theme for Pentecostals, even if it is not always a central theme of contemporary preaching. In some Pentecostal churches the second coming continues to receive a major (and sometimes even disproportional) emphasis, while in others ministers have "grown weary of pop-eschatology and [have] become little more than agnostics about anything having to do with the return of Christ . . . simply avoid[ing] the topic altogether."[13] Poor eschatological teaching (or unbalanced focus in eschatological teaching) has scared large numbers of younger Pentecostals away from giving significant attention to the topic. Thus, an urgent task for many (particularly western) Pentecostal churches in the twenty-first century is to recover healthy and Christ-exalting ways to give the Lord's return the attention it is rightly due, so that the next generations of Pentecostals—if the Lord tarries!—"will continue to love and look for the Blessed Hope, the imminent return of Jesus Christ."[14]

---

8. AG, "Four Core Doctrines," in "Beliefs."
9. E.g., The Foursquare Church and the Elim Foursquare Gospel Alliance—the legal name of the Elim Pentecostal Church—both directly reference this foursquare gospel in their denominational names. The article on Christ in the Flemish Pentecostal confession of faith is structured by this foursquare motif. See Verbond van Vlaamse Pinkstergemeenten, "Wat Wij Geloven," 4.
10. Stanley M. Horton, *Our Destiny: Biblical Teachings on the Last Things* (Springfield, MO: Gospel Publishing House, 1996), 14.
11. D. William Faupel, *The Everlasting Gospel: The Significance of Eschatology in the Development of Pentecostal Thought* (Sheffield: Sheffield Academic Press, 1996), 20.
12. Faupel, *Everlasting Gospel*, 308–9.
13. Daniel D. Isgrigg, *Imagining the Future: The Origin, Development, and Future of Assemblies of God Eschatology* (Tulsa, OK: Oral Roberts University Press, 2021), ix.
14. Isgrigg, *Imagining the Future*, 279.

Imminence: The Soon-Coming King

For Pentecostals, the return of Christ is not a distant prospect. Back in Azusa Street, William Seymour encouraged his flock: "Behold the Bridegroom cometh! O the time is very near. . . . He is coming soon."[15] And Pentecostal pastors have continued to preach the same promise of the Lord's soon return since. Jesus is not just the coming King, but the *soon-coming* King. He could return at any moment, and his people should always be ready. "The Lord warns us to be ready," wrote Seymour, "for we know not the day nor the hour."[16]

This belief in the Lord's imminent return is characteristic of Pentecostalism all over the world. Chilean Pentecostals confess: "We believe in the second coming of Christ to earth imminently, personally and premillennially."[17] The Hungarian Pentecostal confession of faith states that "this day is near, it is on the threshold, but we do not know its exact time," while the Hungarian Apostolic Church confession notes that "only the Father alone knows the time of this, but we know from the signs revealed in the Word that it is near."[18] The World Assemblies of God Fellowship sums up the faith of most Pentecostals worldwide by confessing that Christ's return will be "premillennial, imminent, and personal."[19]

For Pentecostals, this imminent return of the Savior is not simply a fact for establishing a timeline of future events. Christ's imminent return has significant implications for our lives here and now. Aimee Semple McPherson sets out this doctrine of imminence and its practical implications for the Christian life in the Foursquare Declaration of Faith:

> We believe that the second coming of Christ is personal and imminent; that He will descend from Heaven in the clouds of glory with the voice of the archangel and with the trump of God; and that at this hour, which no man knoweth beforehand, the dead in Christ shall rise, then the redeemed that are alive and remain shall be caught up together with them in the clouds, to meet the Lord in the air, and that so shall they ever be with the Lord; that also seeing that a thousand years is as a day with the Lord, and that no man knoweth the hour of His appearance, which we believe to be near at hand, each day should be lived as though He were expected to appear at even, yet that in obedience to His explicit command, "Occupy till I come," the work of spreading the gospel, the

15. William J. Seymour, "Behold the Bridegroom Cometh," *Apostolic Faith* (January 1907): 2.
16. Seymour, "Behold the Bridegroom Cometh," 2.
17. Methodist Pentecostal Church of Chile, "Statement of Faith," 7.
18. Hungarian Pentecostal Confession, 13.3; Hungarian Apostolic Confession, 4b.
19. WAGFSF, 11.

> sending forth of missionaries, and the general duties for the upbuilding of the church should be carried on as diligently, and thoroughly, as though neither ours nor the next generation should live in the flesh to see the glorious day.[20]

The imminence of Christ's return encourages faithfulness in life each and every day, as this might well be the day of his return. As the World Assemblies of God Fellowship puts it (drawing on 1 John 3:3), "Having this blessed hope and earnest expectation, we purify ourselves, even as He is pure, so that we may be ready to meet Him when He comes."[21] This expectation of the Lord's return at any moment also encourages evangelism and missions, for we want as many people as possible to hear the good news of Jesus and come to know him as Savior and Lord before it is too late. Yet, the Foursquare declaration also encourages a seriousness and careful preparation for this missionary task. We are to live for and serve the Lord as if today were the last day; yet we are to plan and prepare for his work as if his coming will not be for several generations. The imminence of Christ's return is not to be an excuse for laziness or a haphazard and ill-prepared approach to mission and ministry.

Premillennialism and Pentecostal Eschatology

Most Pentecostals not only believe that Jesus is coming soon but that He is coming to reign upon the earth. Christ's return will be "premillennial, imminent, and personal."[22] As the Dutch Pentecostals confess, "We believe in the return of Jesus to reign as King in glory."[23] This glorious reign of Christ after his return is known as his "millennial reign on earth."[24]

This belief in Christ's millennial reign upon earth after his return is rooted in Revelation 20:1–10. Most Pentecostals argue that "the simplest way to interpret these prophecies is to place the return of Christ, the resurrection of believers, and the judgment seat of Christ before the Millennium."[25] When Christ returns, He will "establish his reign by destroying satanic power."[26] Satan "will be imprisoned in the abyss for a thousand years . . . so that he will have no possibility of any activity on earth during that period."[27] Meanwhile,

20. FDF, 15.
21. WAGFSF, 11.
22. WAGFSF, 11.
23. VPE, "Geloofsbasis," 12.
24. Apostolic Church, "Tenets," 3. For a detailed and helpful Pentecostal presentation of issues surrounding the millennial reign, see Horton, *Our Destiny*, 161–214.
25. Stanley M. Horton, "The Last Things," in *Systematic Theology*, rev. ed., ed. Stanley M. Horton (Springfield, MO: Gospel Publishing House, 1995), 622.
26. André Thomas-Brès, *La Foi Donné aux Saints Une Fois Pour Toutes* (Grézieu la Varenne: Foi et Victoire, 2016), 308.
27. Horton, "The Last Things," 629.

on earth "those who participated in the resurrection of life will be priests and kings of God and of Christ" during this "thousand years of peace."[28] During this thousand-year reign, "all rule, power, and authority will be subjected to Christ (Revelation 19:15) and righteousness will prevail throughout the earth (Isaiah 2:2–4; Micah 4:4; Zechariah 9:10)."[29] Thus, the millennial kingdom is "a golden age that precedes eternity."[30]

Dispensationalism and Pentecostal Eschatology

For much of the last century, Pentecostal eschatology has been strongly influenced by dispensationalism.[31] From the beginning of the movement, the eschatology of classical Pentecostals has been "most often articulated using the dispensational teaching that there are two phases of Christ's second coming."[32] In the *Pentecostal Evangel*, William Theodore Gaston wrote of this "double aspect of the Lord's coming" in a way that would be familiar to Pentecostals through the decades and around the globe: "He is to come as a Bridegroom and He is to come as a Warrior. He is to come for the saints, and He is to come with the saints."[33] The first aspect is the rapture; the second is Christ's coming to establish his millennial kingdom on earth.

This two-stage framework is included in many (though not all) Pentecostal statements of faith. Finnish Pentecostals, for example, confess that "Jesus Christ will rapture His Church to be with Him according to His promise after which He will come to rule the whole world as King."[34] Likewise, in Indonesia, the largest Pentecostal denomination teaches that "the Lord Jesus Christ will come again to raise up all his people who have died and raise all his people who are still alive and meet Him together in the air" before then establishing "a thousand year Kingdom on this earth."[35] The Church of God declares its faith "in the premillennial second coming of Jesus. First, to resurrect the righteous dead and to catch away the living saints to Him in the air. Second, to reign on the earth a thousand years."[36] Likewise, the American Assemblies of God teaches that "the second coming of Christ includes the rapture of the

---

28. Stanley M. Horton, *Into All Truth* (Springfield, MO: Gospel Publishing House, 1955), 133.
29. French L. Arrington, *Christian Doctrine: A Pentecostal Perspective* (Cleveland, TN: Pathway Press, 1994), 3:246.
30. Kwesi Otoo, "The Second Coming of Jesus Christ and the Next Life," in *Tenets of the Church of Pentecost*, ed. Opoku Onyinah (Accra, Ghana: Church of Pentecost, 2019), 380.
31. Otoo, "The Second Coming of Jesus Christ and the Next Life," 366–68.
32. Isgrigg, *Imagining the Future*, 111.
33. W. T. Gaston, "Coming for and with His Saints," *Pentecostal Evangel* 565 (September 27, 1924): 2.
34. Pentecostal Church of Finland, "Main Articles of Faith," 10.
35. Gereja Bethel Indonesia, "Confession of Faith," 13.
36. Church of God, "Declaration of Faith," 13.

saints, which is our blessed hope, followed by the visible return of Christ with His saints to reign on the earth for one thousand years."[37]

Other Pentecostal statements of faith include further details of the dispensational scheme. The Francophone Swiss Apostolics confess their "hope . . . founded on the outworking of God's plan of salvation revealed in the Bible: the rapture of the Church, the great tribulation, the return of Christ and the establishment of his thousand-year reign, the last judgment, the establishment of a new earth and new heavens in which regenerated human beings will enjoy eternal and perfect blessedness in the immediate presence of God."[38] Both the Romanian and Brazilian Pentecostals set out a detailed eschatological sequence beginning with the "rapture of the church," followed by "the great tribulation and the appearance of the Antichrist," "the coming of the Lord Jesus in glory," "the kingdom of God on earth or the Millennium," "the universal resurrection of the last judgment," and, finally, "the new heaven and the new earth."[39] Many doctrinal handbooks or systematic theology texts published by Pentecostal denominations also give significant attention to most of these aspects of dispensational teaching about Christ's return.[40]

Eschatological Changes

In some parts of the world, Pentecostal approaches to thinking about Christ's return have been changing. In Britain, the rise and influence of the "new churches"—independent Restorationist charismatic churches and networks (such as Newfrontiers), which are otherwise theologically very similar to classical Pentecostalism—have led to new ways of thinking among many British Pentecostals. While Pentecostal eschatology is focused on Christ's return and millennial reign, Restorationists advocate an eschatological vision of "the kingdom of God as a present reality."[41] A renaissance in evangelical scholarship also has led to increasing critiques of dispensationalism.[42] Eventually, both the Elim Pentecostal Church and the Assemblies of God in Great Britain removed premillennialism from their statements of faith. Similar changes have been made in Australia and New Zealand where Acts Churches New Zealand, Acts Global (Australia), and Australian Christian Churches (the

37. AGSFT, 14.
38. L'Église Apostolique Suisse Romande, "Confession de Foi," 10.
39. Romanian CF 31a–f; cf. Brazil DdF, 22–23 (pp. 103–13). The wording here is from the Romanian confession, but there is also a paragraph on each of these aspects in the two chapters of the Brazilian confession cited.
40. Arrington, *Christian Doctrine*, 3:219–54; Guy P. Duffield and Nathaniel M. Van Cleave, *Foundations of Pentecostal Theology* (Los Angeles: Foursquare Media, 2008), 523–64; Horton, "The Last Things," 597–638. An exception that avoids any discussion of the tribulation or timing of the rapture, etc., is Jonathan Black, *Apostolic Theology: A Trinitarian, Evangelical, Pentecostal Introduction to Christian Doctrine* (Luton: Apostolic Church UK, 2016), 341–54.
41. Glass, "Eschatology," 141.
42. Glass, "Eschatology," 143–44.

Assemblies of God in Australia) have each removed their confessional belief in a premillennial return of Christ. Premillennialism is also absent from many European Pentecostal statements of faith.[43] Writing a few years after Elim made the change, James Glass, however, clarifies the implications of these changes: "It would be wrong to give the impression that Elim pastors have suddenly been converted wholesale to a- or post-millennialism. . . . The reason that premillennialism was removed from the Elim fundamental beliefs was not because Elim had suddenly been converted to some other school of prophetic thought, but rather signalled a desire not to make one school of thought a basis of fellowship."[44] No investigation has been made into whether such a conversion has taken place in the intervening quarter of a century.[45]

Summary

Pentecostalism was birthed with a longing for Christ's return and a desire to live in light of his coming, both in taking the good news to every nation and in living lives of holiness in readiness for the day of his return. In some places, Pentecostal anticipation of Christ's return has waned, sometimes due to unbalanced teachings or emphases.

REFLECTION QUESTIONS

1. Has much emphasis been placed on the return of Christ in the life of your church and in your own walk with the Lord?
2. What are some reasons some Pentecostals have changed their eschatological position or placed less emphasis on the second coming?
3. What is the doctrine of imminence, and what are its implications for our lives?
4. What is the biblical basis for premillennialism?
5. How does the Foursquare declaration help us to think about how we should live in light of Christ's return?

---

43. E.g., Poland, France, Austria, Estonia, Flanders, Denmark, The Netherlands, Iceland, Germany. In some cases, this may have been a change from a previous position.
44. Glass, "Eschatology," 145.
45. A quarter of a century later, it is evident that there is little fervent expectation of the Lord's imminent return among the student body at Elim's theological college where I teach. The removal of premillennialism from the foundational truths to make allowance for other views now appears to have led to a situation where classical Pentecostal premillennial eschatology is unfamiliar to younger members of the denomination.

QUESTION 40

Why Do Pentecostals Place So Much Emphasis on Missions?

In the very first issue of the Azusa Street revival magazine *The Apostolic Faith*, the connection between the new movement (with its emphasis on the baptism and gifts of the Holy Spirit) and world missions was prominently proclaimed: "Many are the prophesies spoken in unknown tongues and many the visions that God is giving concerning His soon coming. The heathen must first receive the gospel. One prophecy given in an unknown tongue was interpreted, 'The time is short, and I am going to send out a large number in the Spirit of God to preach the full gospel in the power of the Spirit.'"[1]

The Lord's imminent return highlighted the urgent necessity of taking the gospel to those who had never heard, all over the world. The baptism of the Spirit would provide the power for this evangelistic endeavor. The time was short and the need was great, but now the Lord was providing the power for this urgent mission. And people went. That first issue of *The Apostolic Faith* already contained reports of missionaries leaving for Jerusalem, Africa, and Arizona. All over the world, "one conspicuous result of the new Pentecostal Movement . . . was the kindling of an ardent zeal for foreign missions."[2] The combination of the exclusivity of the gospel of Jesus Christ, the baptism of the Spirit, and the imminence of Christ's return made sure that missions were at the top of the Pentecostal agenda. And they have

1. "Pentecost Has Come," *Apostolic Faith* 1, no. 1 (September 1906): 1.
2. Donald Gee, *The Pentecostal Movement: A Short History and Interpretation for British Readers* (London: Victory Press, 1941), 50.

remained there ever since. As Keith Warrington has put it, "Mission is central to Pentecostalism."[3]

The Exclusivity of Salvation in Christ and Missions

Jesus Christ is the only Savior. He is "the way, and the truth, and the life" and "no one comes to the Father except through [him]" (John 14:6). Pentecostals proclaim Christ Jesus boldly all over the world because "there is salvation in no one else, for there is no other name under heaven given among men by which we must be saved" (Acts 4:12). As Keith Warrington points out, "Pentecostals take seriously the commissions of Jesus to his disciples where he commanded them to evangelize the world (Mt. 28:19–20) and assume it applies to them."[4] Jesus is the only Savior, and he has commissioned us to tell others of the salvation found only in him.

Pentecostals have perhaps written more on missions than anything else, so in this chapter I will focus on one particular early British Pentecostal leader, D. P. Williams of the Apostolic Church, as a representative of the missionary heart of the movement. Williams reminded Pentecostals that the fact that Christ alone saves means that we have a great responsibility to make him known to the world: "Inasmuch as the Church has known her Lord and the Power of His Salvation, she has a right to declare that salvation and that Lordship; and, as He is able to save 'to the uttermost,' it is her duty to do so. The more so, since she knows that there is no other way, and no other Name but Jesus and His Cross for the Salvation of the whole world; so that the obligation acquires the added force of necessity."[5]

The exclusivity of Christ's salvation sends us out into the mission field, for though salvation is exclusive to those who trust in Jesus, it is open to all who will come to him. The exclusive claims of Christ also motivate us to pray for missions and evangelism, and encourage us to persevere in prayer. "When you are on your knees in the missionary prayer meeting," Williams wrote, "remember Jesus is in Glory, and that He is there reigning, hearkening to your petitions and ready to answer your prayers and to do the deed on earth."[6] The Pentecostal missionary (and all who pray for missions) must, as another leader of the Apostolic Church missionary movement put it, know "full well the power of the Blood of Christ to transform [lost] human beings into the image of the Son of God."[7]

---

3. Keith Warrington, *Pentecostal Theology: A Theology of Encounter* (London: T&T Clark, 2008), 246.
4. Warrington, *Pentecostal Theology*, 248–49.
5. D. P. Williams, "The Apostolic Commission," *Apostolic Church Missionary Herald* 1, no. 1 (October 1922): 14.
6. D. P. Williams, "The First Missionary Prayer Meeting," *Apostolic Church Missionary Herald* 1, no. 5 (April 1924): 138–39.
7. H. Cousen, "The Lure of the Missionary Call," *Apostolic Church Missionary Herald* 1, no. 1 (October 1922): 6.

The Baptism of the Holy Spirit and Missions

At Azusa Street, "the baptism with the Holy Spirit was understood to be inextricably related to end-times evangelistic service."[8] When Pentecostals raised the problem "of how to carry the message of Salvation to 'the uttermost parts of the earth' (Acts 1:8)," the answer was obvious to them: it would require the baptism of the Holy Spirit, "who has manifested His power amongst us in many remarkable ways."[9]

Although some very early Pentecostals (following Charles Fox Parham) assumed that speaking in tongues was to give them the ability to speak in a foreign language for missionary service (without having to study), many never accepted this view—and those who had soon realized they were mistaken. As D. P. Williams clarifies, "We do not find it recorded in Scripture that the Holy Spirit ever manifested Himself in this manner afterwards in *known* tongues."[10]

Minnie Abrams (of the Mukti revival in India) taught that the baptism of the Holy Spirit will cause "the fire of God's love [to] so burn within you that you will desire the salvation of souls . . . and realize that He to whom all power is given has imparted some of that power to you, sufficient to do all that He has called you to do."[11] Thus, the baptism of the Holy Spirit provides both the motivation and empowerment needed for missions. Pentecostals also connected this explicitly to overseas missionary service, for the baptism of the Spirit "fills our souls with the love of God for lost humanity, and makes us much more willing to leave home, friends, and all to work in His vineyard, even if it be far away among the heathen."[12]

D. P. Williams insisted that "there is no true evangelization possible, but by a special outpouring of the Holy Spirit."[13] Thus the prayerful waiting of the disciples in the upper room for the outpouring of the Spirit on the day of Pentecost (Acts 1:14) was "the first missionary prayer meeting."[14] Pentecostals today must continue such prayer, for "you cannot have a real Missionary Church, you cannot have real missionary interest without the Holy Ghost coming down and baptising each member."[15]

The baptism in the Holy Spirit empowers missions in two particular ways. First, "power is given in order to testify . . . to proclaim the Gospel at all times,

8. Edith L. Blumhofer, *Restoring the Faith: The Assemblies of God, Pentecostalism, and American Culture* (Urbana: University of Illinois Press, 1993), 60.
9. H. V. Chanter, "Editorial Note," *Apostolic Church Missionary Herald* 1, no. 1 (October 1922): 1.
10. D. P. Williams, "The Inception of the World-Wide Missionary Cause," *Apostolic Church Missionary Herald* 1, no. 7 (April 1925): 212.
11. Minnie F. Abrams, *The Baptism of the Holy Ghost and Fire*, rev. ed. (Kedgaon: Mukti Mission, 1906), 44.
12. J. Roswell Flower, "Editorial," *The Pentecost* 1, no. 1 (August 1908): 4.
13. Williams, "The Inception of the World-Wide Missionary Cause," 209.
14. Williams, "The First Missionary Prayer Meeting," 135.
15. Williams, "The First Missionary Prayer Meeting," 138.

in all places and to all nations; to win souls in wisdom, sympathy and boldness; to suffer the loss of all things."[16] Second, the Spirit gives divine compassion for others: "Compassion is the most essential quality needed by the Church. . . . May the Holy Spirit impart to the hearts of the saints more Divine compassion for the souls of their fellow-creatures; more of the pleading intercessory spirit that will bleed out, as it were, in entreaty that labourers be sent by the Lord of the harvest; that the sickle of mercy may gather in the Redeemed of the Lord into His Garner, before the sickle of judgment shall go forth over all the nations; for our Lord is at hand."[17]

The speaking in tongues on the day of Pentecost symbolizes this missionary nature of the baptism in the Holy Spirit, for on that day the tongues were understood by the crowds, demonstrating that "it was the voice of God to the nations."[18] Thus, the tongues at Pentecost point to the fact that the universal mission of the church "was going to be accomplished only through and by men [and women] filled with Divine Power, obtained by a Baptism of the Spirit sought or tarried for; heated and tempered by the same unction of heaven; fully equipped, not with the talents of human eloquence . . . but equipped with the gifts of God."[19]

The Imminence of Christ's Return and Missions

Yet, perhaps even more important to Pentecostal missions than even the baptism in the Spirit was the hope and expectation of Christ's imminent return. As Gary McGee highlights, "Pentecostal missions arose within the theological and missiological milieu of radical evangelicalism, whose proponents anticipated the restoration of the apostolic power of the early church to bring closure to the Great Commission before the imminent and premillennial return of Jesus Christ."[20] And Pentecostals held onto this expectation. D. P. Williams argues, "The whole teaching of the Apostolic ministry was based upon the personal Second Advent of the Lord. . . . This should be the motive of the Church, to go forth preaching the Gospel to every creature, so that she may be complete for the King when He shall come."[21] This blessed hope of Christ's imminent return should also motivate our prayers for missions and evangelism, as well as our giving toward world missions and other contributions to the evangelistic cause. Williams expounds on this motivation in this way: "Jesus is going to come again for the insignificant people that love Him

16. Williams, "The Apostolic Commission," 14–15.
17. Williams, "The Apostolic Commission," 16.
18. Williams, "The Inception of the World-Wide Missionary Cause," 212.
19. Williams, "The Inception of the World-Wide Missionary Cause," 213.
20. G. B. McGee, "Missions, Overseas (N. American Pentecostal)," in *New International Dictionary of Pentecostal and Charismatic Movements*, eds. Stanley M. Burgess and Eduard M. van der Maas (Grand Rapids: Zondervan, 2002), 899–900.
21. Williams, "The Apostolic Commission," 17.

and that are looking for His coming [like you and me]. When you are on your knees praying for the unsaved world, knowing that He is on the throne, remember always that He is coming. Then you will have no time to waste, you will have no money to waste, when you realise that God wants to save all that will come before Jesus will return."[22]

Where less attention has been given to Christ's return among some Pentecostals in recent years, this eschatological drive to mission has faded. Yet many Pentecostals long for a recovery, arguing like Keith Warrington that this "original impetus to evangelism motivated by eschatology needs to be rediscovered."[23]

Summary

From the outset, Pentecostalism has been a missionary movement. As long as it holds onto its distinctive beliefs, it will continue to be a missionary movement, for, at the heart of Pentecostal identity is the expectation of Christ's imminent return as our soon-coming King, the evangelistic empowering that comes from outpouring of the Holy Spirit upon the church by Jesus our Spirit-baptizer, and faith in the Lord Jesus Christ who invites all to come and receive him as the only Savior.

REFLECTION QUESTIONS

1. Does the fact that missionaries had already been sent out from Azusa Street before the first Pentecostal magazine was even produced help you to see how missions is part of the identity of the Pentecostal movement?

2. How does the Pentecostal belief that salvation is found only through faith in Jesus Christ who was crucified and rose again for us fuel missions?

3. What is the connection between the baptism in the Holy Spirit and missions?

4. What do you think about D. P. Williams's argument that compassion from the Holy Spirit is the greatest need of the church with regard to evangelism and missions?

5. Does your understanding of Christ's return encourage you to tell others about Jesus and support missions?

---

22. Williams, "The First Missionary Prayer Meeting," 140.
23. Warrington, *Pentecostal Theology*, 259.

Scripture Index

John

Acts

Romans

1 Corinthians

2 Corinthians

Galatians

PICTURE CREDITS

We have tried to contact all copyright holders, but if you feel there has been a mistaken attribution, please contact the publisher. **2** Michael Ochs Archive/Getty Images. **6** all from family albums of Agnes Taylor Lee/Diane Lee. **7** Chuck Boyd. **8** top: GAB Archive/Redferns; center ad Domenic Priore; lower ad Diane Lee. **9** top: Jan Persson/Redferns; below: Michael Ochs Archive/Getty Images. **10** top: Hank Lee; below: Michael Ochs Archive/Getty Images. **11** Jan Persson/Redferns. **12–13** Michael Ochs Archive/Getty Images. **13** Diane Lee. **14** letter Diane Lee. **14–15** main picture Peter Pakvis/Redferns. **15** Diane Lee. **16** top: Justin Fox Burks/Arthur Lee collection/Diane Lee; below: Robert Leslie Dean robertlesliedean.com. **28** family albums of Agnes Taylor Lee/Diane Lee. **60** Mark Linn. **94** GAB Archive/Redferns. **127** Michael Ochs Archive/Getty Images. **156** Michael Ochs Archive/Getty Images. **193** Arthur Lee collection/Diane Lee. **226** Arthur Lee collection/Diane Lee. **259** Robert Leslie Dean robertlesliedean.com. **288** Arthur Lee collection/Diane Lee. **318** David Fairweather.

Website: www.lovearthurlee.com

ALSO AVAILABLE FROM JAWBONE PRESS

Riot On Sunset Strip: Rock'n'roll's Last Stand In Hollywood **Domenic Priore**

Million Dollar Bash: Bob Dylan, The Band, And The Basement Tapes **Sid Griffin**

Bowie In Berlin: A New Career In A New Town **Thomas Jerome Seabrook**

To Live Is To Die: The Life And Death Of Metallica's Cliff Burton **Joel McIver**

Jack Bruce Composing Himself: The Authorised Biography **Harry Shapiro**

Return Of The King: Elvis Presley's Great Comeback **Gillian G. Gaar**

Seasons They Change: The Story Of Acid And Psychedelic Folk **Jeanette Leech**

A Wizard, A True Star: Todd Rundgren In The Studio **Paul Myers**

The Resurrection Of Johnny Cash: Hurt, Redemption, And American Recordings **Graeme Thomson**

Entertain Us: The Rise Of Nirvana **Gillian G. Gaar**

Adventures Of A Waterboy **Mike Scott**

Read & Burn: A Book About Wire **Wilson Neate**

Big Star: The Story Of Rock's Forgotten Band **Rob Jovanovic**

Recombo DNA: The Story Of Devo, or How The 60s Became The 80s **Kevin C. Smith**

What's Exactly The Matter With Me? Memoirs Of A Life In Music **P.F. Sloan and S.E. Feinberg**

My Bloody Roots: From Sepultua To Soulfly And Beyond **Max Cavalera with Joel McIver**

Throwing Frisbees At The Sun: A Book About Beck **Rob Jovanovic**

Confessions Of A Heretic: The Sacred & The Profane, Behemoth & Beyond **Adam Nergal Darski with Mark Eglinton**

Long Promised Road: Carl Wilson, Soul Of The Beach Boys **Kent Crowley**

Who Killed Mister Moonlight? Bauhaus, Black Magick, And Benediction **David J. Haskins**

Lee, Myself & I: Inside The Very Special World Of Lee Hazlewood **Wyndham Wallace**

Complicated Game: Inside The Songs Of XTC **Andy Partridge and Todd Bernhardt**

Seeing The Real You At Last: Life And Love On The Road With Bob Dylan **Britta Lee Shain**

The Monkees, Head, And The 60s **Peter Mills**

Perfect Day: An Intimate Portrait Of Life With Lou Reed **Bettye Kronstad**

Becoming Elektra: The Incredible True Story Of Jac Holzman's Visionary Record Label **Mick Houghton**

I Scare Myself: A Memoir **Dan Hicks**

Fearless: The Making Of Post-Rock **Jeanette Leech**

Earthbound: David Bowie and The Man Who Fell To Earth **Susan Compo**

The Yacht Rock Book: The Oral History Of The Soft, Smooth Sounds Of The 70s And 80s **Greg Prato**

What's Big And Purple And Lives In The Ocean? The Moby Grape Story **Cam Cobb**

Swans: Sacrifice And Transcendence: The Oral History **Nick Soulsby**

Small Victories: The True Story Of Faith No More **Adrian Harte**

AC/DC 1973–1980: The Bon Scott Years **Jeff Apter**

King's X: The Oral History **Greg Prato**

Keep Music Evil: The Brian Jonestown Massacre Story **Jesse Valencia**

Lunch With The Wild Frontiers: A History Of Britpop And Excess In 13½ Chapters **Phill Savidge**

Wilcopedia: A Comprehensive Guide To The Music Of America's Best Band **Daniel Cook Johnson**

Lydia Lunch: The War Is Never Over: A Companion To The Film By Beth B. **Nick Soulsby**

Zeppelin Over Dayton: Guided By Voices Album By Album **Jeff Gomez**

What Makes The Monkey Dance: The Life & Music Of Chuck Prophet And Green On Red **Stevie Simkin**

So Much For The 30 Year Plan: Therapy? The Authorised Biography **Simon Young**

She Bop: The Definitive History Of Women In Popular Music **Lucy O'Brien**

Relax Baby Be Cool: The Artistry And Audacity Of Serge Gainsbourg **Jeremy Allen**

Seeing Sideways: A Memoir Of Music And Motherhood **Kristin Hersh**

Two Steps Forward, One Step Back: My Life In The Music Business **Miles A. Copeland III**

It Ain't Retro: Daptone Records & The 21st-Century Soul Revolution **Jessica Lipsky**

All I Ever Wanted: A Rock 'n' Roll Memoir **Kathy Valentine**

Southern Man: Music And Mayhem In The American South **Alan Walden with S.E. Feinberg**

Renegade Snares: The Resistance & Resilience Of Drum & Bass **Ben Murphy and Carl Loben**

Frank & Co: Conversations With Frank Zappa 1977–1993 **Co de Kloet**

Here They Come With Their Make-Up On: Suede, Coming Up ... And More Adventures Beyond The Wild Frontiers **Jane Savidge**

This Band Has No Past: How Cheap Trick Became Cheap Trick **Brian J. Kramp**

Gary Moore: The Official Biography **Harry Shapiro**

Holy Ghost: The Life & Death Of Free Jazz Pioneer Albert Ayler **Richard Koloda**

Conform To Deform: The Weird & Wonderful World Of Some Bizzare **Wesley Doyle**

Happy Forever: My Musical Adventures With The Turtles, Frank Zappa, T. Rex, Flo & Eddie, And More **Mark Volman with John Cody**

Johnny Thunders: In Cold Blood—The Official Biography (Revised & Updated) **Nina Antonia**

Absolute Beginner: Memoirs Of The World's Best Least-Known Guitarist **Kevin Armstrong**

Turn It Up: My Time Making Hit Records In The Golden Age Of Rock Music **Tom Werman**

Revolutionary Spirit: A Post-Punk Exorcism **Paul Simpson**

Don't Dream It's Over: The Remarkable Life Of Neil Finn **Jeff Apter**

Chopping Wood: Thoughts & Stories Of A Legendary American Folksinger **Pete Seeger with David Bernz**

Through The Crack In The Wall: The Secret History Of Josef K **Johnnie Johnstone**

I Wouldn't Say It If It Wasn't True: A Memoir Of Life, Music, And The Dream Syndicate **Steve Wynn**

Jazz Revolutionary: The Life & Music Of Eric Dolphy **Jonathon Grasse**

Down On The Corner: Adventures In Busking & Street Music **Cary Baker**